A GENERATION OF RADICAL EDUCATIONAL CHANGE

How much have teachers and their pupils benefited from the top-down, Westminster-led control of policy held in place by a powerful national inspection regime?

A Generation of Radical Educational Change: Stories from the field is an exploration of the revolutionary impact of the greater and continuing involvement of central government in education policy making, which began in 1976 and was accelerated by the 1988 Education Act and subsequent legislation.

In the book, a dozen distinguished contributors from a wide range of sectors explain and reflect on how they worked to do their best for their schools, teachers and pupils in these years of great change. They understand the reasons, explained by Lord Baker in his early chapter, for a National Curriculum in 1988, and also the reasons for a more effective national inspection system. Yet their stories accumulate to become a powerful critique of the top-down policies of the last two decades. These policies, they say, have been too numerous, short-term, incoherent and partisan; governments have been indifferent to professional opinion and serious research, and have relied excessively on measurable outcomes and simplistic Ofsted judgments. Our current system is narrower and less democratic than it was, but evidence is hard to find that English pupils are doing any better in international comparisons.

The combined reflections in this volume are timely in these years of lively educational debate, as are the suggestions for future policy. *A Generation of Radical Educational Change* is an invaluable read for current and aspiring headteachers, policy makers and those with an interest in education policy and how it evolves.

Richard Pring is currently Professor of Education at Winchester University, UK, and was previously Director of the Department of Educational Studies, University of Oxford, UK (1989–2003).

Martin Roberts was appointed to the headship of The Cherwell School, Oxford, UK (1981–2002). At present, he is a member of the Academic Steering Committee of The Prince's Teaching Institute.

A GENERATION OF RADICAL EDUCATIONAL CHANGE

Stories from the field

Edited by
Richard Pring and
Martin Roberts

Routledge
Taylor & Francis Group

LONDON AND NEW YORK

First published 2016
by Routledge
2 Park Square, Milton Park, Abingdon, Oxon OX14 4RN

and by Routledge
711 Third Avenue, New York, NY 10017

Routledge is an imprint of the Taylor & Francis Group, an informa business

© 2016 Richard Pring and Martin Roberts

British Library Cataloguing in Publication Data
A catalogue record for this book is available from the British Library

Library of Congress Cataloging in Publication Data
Names: Pring, Richard. | Roberts, Martin, 1941–
Title: A generation of educational change: stories from the field/edited by
Richard Pring and Martin Roberts.
Description: Abingdon, Oxon; New York, NY: Routledge is an imprint of
the Taylor & Francis Group, an Informa business, [2016] | Includes
bibliographical references and index.
Identifiers: LCCN 2015019499| ISBN 9781138941892 (hardback) |
ISBN 9781138941915 (pbk.) | ISBN 9781315673417 (e-book)
Subjects: LCSH: Education and state – Great Britain – History – 20th century.
| Education and state – Great Britain – History – 21st century. | Educational
change – Great Britain – History – 20th century. | Educational change –
Great Britain – History – 21st century.
Classification: LCC LC93.G7 G46 2016 | DDC 379.41 – dc23LC record
available at http://lccn.loc.gov/2015019499

ISBN: 978-1-138-94189-2 (hbk)
ISBN: 978-1-138-94191-5 (pbk)
ISBN: 978-1-315-67341-7 (ebk)

Typeset in Bembo and Stone Sans
by Florence Production Ltd, Stoodleigh, Devon, UK
Printed and bound in Great Britain by
Ashford Colour Press Ltd, Gosport, Hampshire

CONTENTS

Conclusions 203

16 Stories from the field – summarised 205
Richard Pring and Martin Roberts

17 The way forward for the next generation 209
Richard Pring and Martin Roberts

CONTRIBUTORS

Lord Kenneth Baker had a distinguished political career as a minister in first the Thatcher and then the Major governments. From Minister for Information Technology in 1981 he was promoted first to the Environment and then from 1986 to 1989 to Education where he initiated the decisive reforms that are the main subject of this book. He then became Chair of the Conservative Party and after that Home Secretary. As a life peer, Lord Baker of Dorking, he joined the Upper House in 1997 and with the late Lord Dearing set up the Baker–Dearing Trust, which currently promotes energetically University Technical Colleges (UTCs).

Sir Tim Brighouse started teaching in schools and was a deputy head by the age of 26. He then moved into educational administration becoming CEO of Oxfordshire via posts in Monmouthshire, Buckinghamshire and the Inner London Education Authority (ILEA). After achieving great success as CEO of Birmingham he then, as Chief Commissioner, led the transformation of London's schools through the London Challenge. He was knighted for services to education in 2009.

Tony Eaude is Research Fellow at the Department of Education, Oxford University, and an independent research consultant. After working in special and primary schools he was for nine years headteacher of a multi-cultural first school in Oxford. He has written widely on primary and early years education, notably *Thinking through Pedagogy for Primary and Early Years* (2011) and *How Do Expert Primary Classteachers Really Work?* (2012).

Kenny Frederick spent her teaching career teaching in inner-city schools. She has just retired after 17 years as headteacher of George Green's school on the Isle of Dogs, Tower Hamlets. She is passionately committed to an inclusive education for all pupils whatever their needs. A former member of the Executive of the National Association of Head Teachers, she has written frequently for *The Guardian* and commented on educational issues both on television and radio.

Margaret Maden became a deputy head aged 31 at a time when men dominated senior positions in secondary schools. She soon became headteacher of Islington Green School, and later director of the Islington Green Sixth Form Centre, gaining a national reputation for her achievements. From there she moved first to Warwickshire as Chief Education Officer and then to Keele University to run the Centre of Successful Schools. She has written many articles and books. From 1999 to 2002 she was a member of the National Commission for Education.

Sir Peter Newsam started his working life as a civil servant before spending a few years teaching in Oxford. He then moved into educational administration. Chief Education Officer of the Inner London Educational Authority from 1975 to 1981, he then chaired the Commission for Racial Equality. In the early 1990s he directed the London Institute of Education, before becoming Chief Schools Adjudicator. He was knighted for his services to education and to racial equality. His papers and other publications are now held at the Institute Library and London Metropolitan Archive

Pat O'Shea, from teaching English in a Kent comprehensive school, became a lecturer at the Oxford University Department of Education, and subsequently Deputy Head of Peers School, then nationally famous for its innovative curriculum. She then became a headteacher, first of Bottisham Village College in Cambridge and second of Lord Williams' Thame in Oxfordshire. A much respected LEA adviser and SIP adviser, until recently she was an Ofsted inspector. Jointly with two former headteachers she now runs an education consultancy.

Tim Oates is Director of Assessment, Research and Development at Cambridge Assessment and was appointed in 2011 by the Coalition government to lead the National Curriculum Review Expert Panel. His career has been in educational research at the London Institute of Education, the National Council for Vocational Qualifications and the Qualifications and Curriculum Authority. His many publications have won for him an international reputation. His 'Could do better – using international comparisons to refine the National Curriculum' has been particularly influential. In recognition of his contribution to education, he was honoured with the CBE in 2015.

Richard Pring retired in 2003 as Director of Oxford University Department of Educational Studies after 14 years, having previously been Dean of the Faculty at Exeter University, lecturer in Curriculum Studies at the Institute of Education, teacher at Goldsmiths College and a London comprehensive, and Assistant Principal in the Ministry of Education. From 2003 to 2009, he led the Nuffield Review of

14–19 Education and Training for England and Wales. Richard Pring is a Fellow of Green-Templeton College Oxford, where Sir David Watson was Principal from 2010.

Martin Roberts was headteacher of The Cherwell School in Oxford for 20 years, in which time it changed from a struggling ex-secondary modern to one of the best-regarded schools in the county. He then helped to create the Prince's Teaching Institute, which is now the leading provider of subject-specific training for secondary teachers. He has written articles and books, the latest of which is in collaboration with Michael Young and others, 'Knowledge and the Future School', 2014.

Wendy Scott, OBE, is currently honorary president of TACTYC (Training, Advancement and Co-operation in Teaching Young Children). Headteacher of a nursery school, she then moved to Roehampton Institute as senior lecturer in early years' education. From district inspector first for ILEA and then for Kensington and Chelsea, she became a registered Ofsted inspector. She has also been Chair and Chief Executive of the British Association of Early Childhood Education and an adviser to the Department for Education.

Geoff Stanton worked for 20 years in FE colleges, as a teacher and subsequently as an FE teacher trainer. For eight years he was Director of the Further Education Unit (FEU), which pioneered pre-vocational courses. He was also Special Adviser to the Commission on Adult Vocational Training and Learning. He is currently a member of the Qualifications Committee of the OCR Examination Board of the Council of the City and Guilds. In the last 15 years he has been engaged in numerous research and development projects, leading to a range of publications.

Peter Wilby helped to run a university newspaper while still a student at Sussex University. He began his adult career at *The Observer* in 1968, becoming its Education Correspondent four years later. He has become one of the country's leading education journalists, writing also for the *New Statesman* and *The Sunday Times*. He has had periods of editing *The Independent on Sunday* and the *New Statesman*. Nowadays he writes as a columnist for the *New Statesman*, *The Guardian* and *The Observer*.

FOREWORD

Baroness Estelle Morris

Many people teaching today will have witnessed the present education revolution since its start; others will have joined along the way. The careers of longer serving teachers frame the years of this period of change in schools. They will have qualified before the days of the national curriculum, national testing and inspection, and will be able to remember when local authorities, not central government, were at the centre of what happened.

They are the generation who have seen the changes at first hand, but, if change is to be an ally and not a threat, all of us need to understand its context and the journey we are travelling.

The contributors to this book have played key roles at important times in different parts of the education service. Some have been champions of change, others would have preferred a different route, all have had to try to make the changes work. In this sense, these chapters set out the often conflicting views and opinions that have been the background of education policy and practice for three decades and in doing so they come together to build a narrative of the times.

Anyone looking back at this period could describe it as a time of upheaval. School and college structures, curricula, inspection frameworks, qualifications have all been introduced, amended, and often discarded before there has even been time to properly assess their impact. Sometimes the reasons for change have been badly explained; often the initiatives have seemed relentless.

Yet there have been strong strands of continuity as well. The principles of greater autonomy, a national framework offering an entitlement for all young people, the need for teachers to be held to account, the importance of school and college leadership and the impact of high quality teaching have been threads that have stood the test of time.

Education doesn't exist in isolation, and the pressures for change come as much from outside the system as within. It is no coincidence that a period of great change in education has been also a time of significant change in the wider society.

Greater demands on services, less tolerance of failure, the belief that everyone must succeed and the freedom to exercise choice, all characterise the present public attitude to key services – and these too have been some of the pressures for change.

Equally, the speed of development in communication and the opportunities offered by digital technology have transformed our understanding of how children learn, and schools must reflect this if they are to remain relevant to those they teach.

Education has at times led change – the achievement of ethnic minorities, for example – yet in other areas it has been slow to change. Schools embraced educational technology long after most other sectors and they are only just beginning to give it the importance it deserves.

These are not easy times for those who teach but, at its core, education remains the greatest route to freedom, self-respect, fulfilment and social justice. It will always attract the attention of others who share the ambition to change the world for the better and, as a result, it cannot and must not stand still.

Although change will be an ever-present force for those who work in education, we must get better at how we lead it, manage it, evaluate it and take others on the journey. This book is not only a testament to the past but a most valuable source of wisdom for the future. We should all learn from it.

Editors' note: Virtually all the text of this book was written in the months before the General Election of May 2015. We have left it unchanged since, in the few months since then, the Conservative government, which replaced the Coalition, has left the main thrust of educational policy-making unchanged, as exemplified by its drive against 'coasting schools' and its continuing pressure on schools to become academies.

BACKGROUND

The 1944 Education Act introduced secondary education for all in a 'maintained system' – that is, a system maintained by local education authorities in partnership with the voluntary bodies (mainly the churches) who owned many of the schools, along with the teaching profession and with central government (which had overall responsibility for ensuring there would be sufficient schools and teachers).

The 70 years since this major Act of Parliament have seen considerable changes:

- to greater government control in the partnership between central, local government and schools;
- in the evolving structure of 'secondary education for all' up to 16 (then education or training for all up to 18);
- in the creation of a teaching profession (through initial and continuing professional education) appropriate for these changes and higher aspirations;
- in the development of a national curriculum;
- in developing systems of testing and examining to reflect the achievements of all;
- in the increasing accountability of schools and of the system; and
- in the world of employment and higher education into which pupils are to enter.

Throughout this period, there have been considerable demographic and economic changes to which schools, colleges and the system have had to adapt, some more successfully than others.

More recently, many of the principles of the 1944 Education Act have given way to a system that:

- puts much greater power in the hands of the Secretary of State (diminishing thereby the powers of local authorities);

- has introduced voluntary, private and for-profit organisations into the control of schools; and
- made accountability much more focused on measurable targets.

The changes since 1976 are very substantial, therefore – indeed, revolutionary.

Much has been written about these developments, but in a fragmented way. What too often are lacking are concrete examples, which give life to successes and difficulties as schools, colleges, teachers, education establishments, examination boards and local authorities navigate their way through the changes.

This book, therefore, seeks to provide cases of the hopes and fears, the successes and failures over four decades in response to national policies. Then, drawing on these accounts and learning lessons from them, the book looks to the future, making a number of proposals for the way forward.

PART I

Introduction

Setting the scene

1

HISTORY AND OVERVIEW OF CHANGES 1976–2014

Martin Roberts and Richard Pring

Introduction

The last 40 years have witnessed such radical changes in the educational and training system that few who are now engaged in teaching, and few among the general public, can have much conception of where the system has emerged. But it is important that they should do so. It is important to see how and why a system has changed in order to understand it critically and to see how it might be changed yet further for the better.

This book therefore seeks to provide an account of those changes, not simply through a historical narrative (although such a narrative permeates the chapters and is explicitly provided in this introductory chapter), but also through the experiences of those who have lived and worked through the changes and who have had to adapt, often critically, to them.

In Chapter 17 we draw together some of the major themes that emerge from the following chapters and make some recommendations for the next generation.

Setting the scene

In particular, the 1944 Education Act preceded our history by several decades. But reference to it is necessary for two reasons. First, it shaped the educational system for 30 years, and the period covered in this book reflects the gradual erosion of that post-war political settlement. Second, such a reference shows starkly how matters have changed.

The 1944 Act created 'a national service locally administered'. It established a partnership between central government (which had ultimate responsibility for overall expenditure), local education authorities (which provided education to all children 'according to age, ability and aptitude'), the voluntary bodies (that is churches and non-denominational bodies that provided many of the schools now entering the national system) and the teachers. The Minister had two major responsibilities – to ensure there were enough school places for all pupils and to ensure there were enough teachers to teach them. The Minister had no control over what was taught or how it was taught – these were regarded as too important to be put in the hands of politicians. After all, a war was being fought against totalitarian governments whose government ministers controlled the schools and what was taught in them.

The Act never dictated how 'according to age, ability and aptitude' should be interpreted. That was in the hands of the local education authorities (LEAs) and the teachers. Most LEAs interpreted this for the new secondary system of education in terms of three types of school fitting (in the words of the 1943 Norwood Report) three types of adolescent, namely, grammar schools for the few capable of abstract thought and interested in ideas; technical schools for those interested in and capable of the application of ideas in technology; and secondary moderns for the majority who were more concerned with practical activities and the immediate environment. However, some authorities – London County Council, West Riding of Yorkshire and Leicestershire – decided to develop schools attended by children of all abilities and aptitudes as comprehensives.

Subsequent years saw the gradual questioning of this threefold division of adolescents and therefore of schools – a questioning that was evolving significantly during the period covered by this book. .

Hence, this chapter provides an outline of the political and social changes that impacted on educational institutions between 1976 and 2015, as these have affected the 'national system locally administered'. Our contributors illuminate many of them in the following chapters.

The political context

Labour and Conservative governments 1945–2015

In the 70 years since the Second World War, Labour formed governments for 30 years, the Conservatives, including a Tory-dominated coalition, for 40. In our chosen period since 1976, Labour governed for 16, the Conservatives for 23. The sequence was as follows: Labour 1945–1951 (Attlee), Conservatives 1951–1964 (Churchill, Eden, Macmillan, Douglas-Home), Labour 1964–1970 (Wilson), Conservatives 1970–1974 (Heath), Labour 1974–1979 (Wilson, Callaghan), Conservatives 1979–1997 (Thatcher, Major), Labour 1997–2010 (Blair, Brown), Conservative–Liberal Democrat Coalition 2010–2015 (Cameron).

The 1970s were a watershed in British politics. The quadrupling of the oil price after 1973 led to extraordinary inflation, which hit a record 25 per cent per annum in 1975. Simultaneously destructive industrial unrest caused the British economy, already weak, to lurch from crisis to crisis. In 1976, Denis Healey, Labour Chancellor of the Exchequer, had to negotiate a huge loan from the International

Monetary Fund. The implicit consensus between the two main parties began to break. The final breaking point was the 'winter of discontent' in 1979 when public sector workers, fighting the attempt of Callaghan's government to sustain a pay policy, went on strike. Rubbish piled up in the street. Schools closed. A public sense that something was badly wrong helped Mrs Thatcher to power. Conservative policy after 1979 consciously shook off the One Nation Toryism of Macmillan and Heath. Similarly Blair's New Labour, which emerged in the 1990s, distanced itself in policy as well as in name from the Labour values of Wilson, Callaghan and Attlee, further developing policies initiated by Mrs Thatcher.

The pre-1970s consensus

In 1954, *The Economist* coined the term 'Butskellism' to describe the common features of the policies of Butler, the Conservative Chancellor of the Exchequer, and Gaitskell, his Labour counterpart. They both accepted the main achievements of the Attlee government, particularly the welfare state (which meant comparatively high and redistributive taxation) and the nationalisation of the country's major industries. They believed in a mixed economy with both private and public ownership. They were Keynesian in that they believed that the state should increase public spending in times of crisis to sustain overall demand and avoid significant rises in unemployment. They accepted that trade unions mattered and believed in the effectiveness of local authorities.

The Thatcher/Blair consensus, 1979–the present

The Thatcher government rejected Keynesianism, which it considered to be the cause of serious inflation and the enemy of private enterprise. Influenced by Friedrich Hayek who argued for a diminished role for the state and by Friedman who considered inflation a greater threat than unemployment and whose monetarist doctrine stated that inflation was best reduced by the government controlling the amount of money in circulation, the Conservative government managed to bring inflation under control but at the price of high unemployment, which reached 3.2 million in 1985. Rather than a mixed economy it proved a firm believer in the superiority of private enterprise over public ownership. Major industries were privatised, for example British Gas and British Rail, and where possible market forces were given ever-greater freedom. The 'big bang' of 1986 deregulated the financial markets of the City of London and made possible, for good and ill, the rapid expansion of the City as a major player in global finance.

The Centre for Policy Studies, founded by Sir Keith Joseph in 1974 together with Margaret Thatcher and Alfred Sherman, argued the case for a Social Market economy and privatisation of such public monopolies as education and health – more deregulation and liberalisation. It considered 'educational vouchers' but thought that too big an undertaking. The philosophical thinking of Hayek and Friedman thereby entered into the management of public services in general and education in particular. It was cogently expressed by Sir Keith Joseph, later to become Secretary of State for Education, that:

> the blind, unplanned, uncoordinated wisdom of the market is overwhelmingly superior to the well-researched, rational, systematic, well-meaning, cooperative, science-based, forward looking, statistically respectable plans of government.
>
> (Joseph, 1976)

Thatcher's government kept a strict control over public expenditure, capping the funds it made available to local government, which it regarded as bloated and too close to the unions. As for public services, where she could not privatise, Mrs Thatcher centralised.

A new 'management language' was emerging in a series of Government White Papers that straddled the Thatcher/Blair years. The shift in the control and management of public services was explained in a series of Government White Papers from HM Treasury and the Cabinet Office: *Modern Public Services in Britain: Investing in Reform* (1988, Cm. 4011); *Public Services for the Future: Modernisation, Reform, Accountability* (1998, Cm. 4181); *The Government's Measures of Success: Outputs and Performance Analyses* (1999, Cm. 4200); *Modernising Government* (1999, Cm. 4310). One important consequence of these White Papers (and thus of the 'modernisation' of public services) was what was referred to as 'public service agreements'. These were agreements over funding from HM Treasury, first to Departments of State in terms of overall targets, which were then 'cascaded down' in more precise forms, to the institutions that were the responsibilities of the respective Departments. In education, this was spelt out partly in terms of the proportion of students at different schools achieving so many GCSEs at different grade levels. But that gradually emerged as a way of rewarding teachers through 'performance-related pay'.

Where possible Thatcher's government cut income tax (for example, Lawson's 1988 Budget, which reduced the tax on the rich to 40 per cent and on everyone else to 25 per cent). As for the trade unions, breaking their power was a Thatcher priority, broadly supported by public opinion. Here 1984 was the key year when Scargill, the Marxist leader of the National Union of Mineworkers, who had humiliated Heath's government a decade earlier, called an all-out strike to end pit closures. The government was well prepared with plenty of coal stocks and police effectively deployed to prevent aggressive picketing. After a year the miners went back to work, totally defeated. The government passed a series of laws that severely restricted the power of the unions.

The Conservatives were able to stay in power for 18 years, but not because their policies were particularly popular. In the general election of 1987, when Mrs Thatcher was at her strongest, she won only 42 per cent of the vote with a turnout of 75 per cent of the electorate. Labour's problem in the 1980s was that it was dominated by the Left and the trades unions, and its moderates had split away to form the Social Democratic Party, which was to merge with the Liberals. Social and economic changes had undermined Old Labour and its traditional working class support in declining industrial areas. More voters thought of themselves as middle class. If Labour was ever to gain power, Blair with his small group of allies – Brown, Mandelson and Gould – decided that the party needed to be rebranded as New Labour and to accept the main Thatcherite policies of privatisation, low taxes, friendly towards business, cool towards the unions and local government, and centralising where public services were concerned. With the UK needing to compete in an increasingly global market, Blair and Brown saw no alternative but to encourage free enterprise. Blair, though he thought Mrs Thatcher a bit dotty, had much respect for her achievements, and she came to regard him as her real successor.

Like Thatcher, Blair's popularity was less well-rooted than it seemed. The main reason for New Labour's success in 1997 was the unpopularity of the Conservatives. He won only 44 per cent of the vote, less than Attlee and Wilson, and the voter turnout was lower too, at 71 per cent. His popularity declined in 2001 to 42 per cent of the voters, with 59 per cent voting. In 2005, his share of the vote had further declined to 35 per cent, with 61 per cent of the electorate voting. Throughout these years of radical reform neither Conservatives nor Labour had the explicit support of more than one in three of the electorate. After 2001 it dropped to one in four. More and more young people did not bother to vote.

Though in many ways the New Labour government had its distinctive policies, particularly with regard to relieving child poverty and support of minorities, the main thrust of its economics was similar to that of its predecessor, so much so that Peter Riddell writing in *The Times* commented that 'an economist from Mars would conclude that the same government had been in charge throughout the second half of the 1990s'.

The implications for education of this dramatic political change post-1979

Erosion of the political consensus

What did this mean for education? Before 1976, the political consensus accepted that schools should have freedom over the curriculum and gave LEAs the funding and discretion necessary to develop systems that best met local needs. Broadly speaking, it supported the end of selection at 11 plus and the spread of comprehensive schools. In the early 1970s Mrs Thatcher, as Secretary of State for Education, oversaw an accelerating comprehensive programme. The Schools Council, an advisory council on curriculum development and examinations, dominated by teachers but abolished by the Tory Sir Keith Joseph in 1984, was set up in 1964 by the Tory Sir Edward Boyle. The universities, expanding after the Robbins Report of 1963, were independent of government controls, their funding coming mainly through the independent Universities Grants Committee (UGC). Further Education (FE) too was expanding but remained the responsibility of LEAs.

However, when Callaghan spoke at Ruskin College in October 1976 this consensus was disintegrating. Within a few years, governments reduced education spending, the powers of local government and the independence of teachers. They encouraged the market through greater parental choice and a variety of schools (for example, Grant Maintained, City Technology Colleges, Specialist Schools, Academies, Free Schools and University Technical Colleges). The main criterion of the success of the education sector was to be seen in the extent to which it contributed to the economic success of UK plc. Ofsted would ensure accountability. And that accountability was expressed and conducted increasingly in the new language of management, that is, in terms of targets and performance indicators.

The key legislation, of course, was the 1988 Education Act, which in effect replaced that of 1944. Now the government was in charge of pupils' learning, establishing a detailed National Curriculum with ten levels of assessment, and funding directly (by-passing the LEAs) the new City Technology Colleges. From a 'national system locally maintained' was evolving a 'national system nationally maintained'.

The Conservatives had a deep-seated distrust of what they tended to describe as the 'education establishment', which in 2013 the Coalition Secretary of State, Michael Gove, referred to less decorously as 'the Blob'. This distrust had in the early 1970s been reflected in the Black Papers, edited by Cox and Dyson (1967–1972) for the Centre for Policy Studies, which attacked in particular the growing attachment to comprehensive schools. They were particularly suspicious of university-based teacher training, as reflected in Sheila Lawlor's paper 'Teachers Mistaught' (Lawlor, 1990).

By the Higher and Further Education Act of 1992, both higher and further education passed under greater government control. Mrs Thatcher distrusted university teachers as much as schoolteachers. A Higher Education Funding Council (HEFC) replaced the UGC and made sure that universities directed their efforts towards national priorities as defined by the government that, again like schools, were to increase the economic competitiveness of the UK. As for further education, the polytechnics became independent of LEAs, were renamed universities and funded through the HEFC. Other FE colleges also passed out of LEA control and were funded through the Further Education Funding Council (FEFC) until the new Learning and Skills Council took on its functions in 2001. Both the Labour and Conservative parties in the twenty-first century came to believe that Higher Education (HE) and FE fees were unavoidable, though they argued about the fees' level.

New Labour accepted the main thrusts of Tory education policy, *Choice and Diversity* (the title of John Patten's White Paper in 1992) becoming a mantra. Blair thought teachers were among the forces of conservatism hampering him in his mission to modernise Britain, as set out in the White Papers referred to above. LEAs fared no better. When New Labour introduced its Academies programme in the 2002 Education Act, they would be directly answerable to the Secretary of State. In other ways New Labour was even more centralising than the Conservatives, enacting many laws and regulations and creating quangos. It was stronger too on accountability, Ofsted swelling in its size and authority after 1997. The influential teacher unions of the 1970s, particularly the National Union of Teachers (NUT), declined, especially after the protracted but fruitless strikes of 1985–1987.

Again there was considerable continuity when the Coalition took over from Labour in 2010. Michael Gove, the new Secretary of State, accelerated the Academies programme, introduced academy chains to establish many more academies run by churches, charities and for-profit companies such as Serco and Capita, and increased diversity and choice by introducing Free Schools. He continued the custom of Secretaries of State, if with unusual passion, to intervene in the curriculum and assessment.

As more women were working and keen to return to work after child-bearing, early years and nursery education gained a higher profile. One of the last Acts passed by John Major's government was the Nursery and Grant-Maintained Act of 1996, the aim of which was to encourage the expansion of nursery schools. A major and valuable initiative of New Labour was the Sure Start Programme, aimed at families living on benefits. It was intended not only to give potentially deprived children a better start in life but to help their mothers back to work. Since 2010 the Sure Start local programmes have become Sure Start Children's Centres and have the theoretical support of the main parties. Furthermore, the Labour government's 2004 Childen's Act *Every Child Matters* set out five outcomes for all children (be healthy, stay safe, enjoy and achieve, make a positive contribution to society, and enjoy economic wellbeing). However in the post-2008 austerity, many of the Centres have suffered cuts.

Examinations and examination standards

GCE O- and A-Level examinations started in 1951. In 1976 schools could choose from syllabuses offered by eight independent boards, which had started as university-run enterprises and had university teachers actively involved in the setting and evaluation of papers. They could also choose CSE syllabuses for their less academic pupils. The Certificate of Secondary Education was introduced in 1962 (first sat for in 1965) to provide a final examination goal for secondary modern students originally intended for the next 40 per cent of the ability range, after the 20 per cent who took O Level. It is worthy of note that, until this time, there were no publicly funded examinations for those not taking O-Level examinations. The CSE was conducted by many regional boards. However, as more schools went comprehensive, this dual system became increasingly clumsy and the two systems merged, with the first exams sat in 1988. GCE boards also merged and so now there are four main ones – AQA, Edexel, OCR and WJEB. Active involvement by university teachers is less. A new examination between GCSE and A Level, AS, was introduced in 2000. Much to the irritation of teachers, pupils and their parents, ministers tinkered frequently with exam details, for example, coursework and the recent proposal to decouple AS Level from A Level (see Chapter 10 for a deeper understanding of these changes).

The English and Welsh exam system has chalked up some impressive achievements. It caters for ever-increasing numbers, setting and marking to a tight timescale each year. Standards appear to be rising substantially over time. In 1976 only 23 per cent of pupils gained 5 A-C O-Level passes and 15 per cent of school leavers gained no grade at all. In 2014, 69 per cent reached the equivalent GCSE score with hardly any candidates failing to get at least one grade. At A-Level in 1976 only about 70 per cent gained at least one pass. In 2014 it was 96 per cent.

However, the question of whether or not present examinations are as difficult as their predecessors is hard to answer. Where A-Level pass rates are concerned, comparing 1976 with 2014 is impossible because in 1976 the results were norm-referenced, allowing only a fixed percentage to pass. In the 1980s the Boards introduced criterion referencing – that is, meeting specific levels achieved, not determined by formerly agreed norms. Some critics ascribe the striking improvements in grades to changes in the format of the exam papers. The syllabuses specify in greater detail how marks are allocated, and teachers have become evermore skilful in getting their pupils to concentrate on these specifications. Many of these critics would then argue that 'teaching to the test' in such a way is not obviously good educational practice. Recently teacher confidence in the reliability of the marking has lessened and the Boards have had difficulty in finding well-qualified markers. Moreover, in the attempts to bring equivalences between different sorts of examination within a single system, a National Qualifications Framework (NQF) was established in the 1990s, superseded by the Qualifications and Credit Framework (QCF) in 2007, intending to show how the myriad of vocational, prevocational, GCSE and A-Level qualifications related to each other in terms of equivalence in standard, even though they were radically different in content and purpose. By deft use of equivalences, schools' GCSE results rose dramatically, as did their place in the league tables.

In 2008 New Labour set up Ofqual to supervise the whole system.

Successive governments have used this apparent (though, as indicated above, severely questioned) improvement in exam results, especially at GCSE, to argue that their reforms are working. The jury is out on this case. Not until the late 1990s did the Education Reform Act (ERA) reforms bed down. GCSE results improved rapidly from their start in 1988. Would they not have continued to improve if schools had been left to get on with the job?

Vocational education and training

In 1851, the year of the Great Exhibition, Britain was the leading industrial power whose inventors, engineers and technical prowess were the envy of the world. Soon that status was challenged, first by the USA and Germany and latterly by Asia. Since the nineteenth century, the inadequacy of our technical and vocational education, particularly in comparison to continental Europe, has been a frequent refrain. The Royal Commission on Technical Instruction articulated it strongly in 1884, so did the Spens Committee in 1938. The 1944 solution to the problem, new technical schools, failed because the near bankruptcy of the immediate post-war years meant that only a handful were ever built. Between 1945 and 1976 the best vocational education occurred in some secondary modern schools or post-16 colleges offering examinations provided by the City and Guilds of London Institute (CGLI) and by the RSA.

An important thread of the 1976 Ruskin speech was the need for the education system to respond more directly to the needs of the world of work. The collapse of manufacturing during the 1970s and 1980s and the jump in unemployment as a result of the first Conservative budgets after 1979 made technical and vocational education a priority of every government since then. A priority it may have been but, of all the unequivocal policy failures of the last 40 years, the inability to create a thriving vocational offer for 14–19-years-olds must rank among the worst.

Therefore, to promote more vocational *education* in schools, the Department for Education established the Further Education Unit (FEU) to develop general education courses and qualifications based on occupation-related interests. The FEU published a series of papers, beginning with *A Basis for Choice* and *Vocational Preparations*. These led to a series of ever-changing qualifications – CGLI 365, succeeded by CPVE, succeeded by DoVE, succeeded by 14–19 Diplomas, succeeded by nothing yet.

The Conservative government did get off to a good start in 1982 when it announced TVEI, the Technical and Vocational Education Initiative, which tied in with these pre-vocational courses. Run not by the DfE but the Manpower Services Commission, established in 1974 so as to by-pass LEAs in the promotion and financing of employment-related activities in colleges and schools, it funded local projects where schools, colleges, LEAs and businesses developed their own schemes. The Education Reform Act (ERA) in 1988, with its emphasis on a new National Curriculum, effectively scuppered TVEI, which by 1997 had petered out. The Thatcher government also set up the National Council for Vocational Qualifications which established a system of National Vocational Qualifications (NVQs) and employer-led Training and Enterprise Councils (TECs) to take responsibility for local youth training needs. In 1995, Major's government called on Sir Ron Dearing, who had already 'slimmed down' the National Curriculum, to bring some coherence to a messy range of academic and vocational qualifications. He recommended three pathways, (i) GCSEs/A Levels, (ii) GNVQs (General NVQs) and (iii) NVQs.

New Labour set up a new quango, the Learning and Skills Council, to provide a more coherent approach to education and training. However, in its short life of nine years that coherence eluded it. There were simply too many national, regional, local organisations and business interests competing for student-led funds. Experts clamoured for a new approach that would bring 'parity of esteem' between the academic and vocational pathways. In 2004 the Tomlinson Report on the 14–19

Reform seemed to find a way forward with its plan for an overarching Diploma. However, despite its widespread professional support (and the Secretary of State, Ed Balls' claim that this would be the qualification of choice for all 14–18 year olds), Prime Minister Blair vetoed it as electorally too risky as it might seem to challenge the A-Level gold standard. A new big idea of Advanced Diplomas sank under the weight of its ambitions. The essence of the British problem with vocational education was, as Alison Wolf put it in 2002, that it was 'a great idea for other people's children'. The many attempts to design an effective vocational pathway were for the most part designed by civil servants and advisers who themselves had little experience of industry and business and had no thought of encouraging their own children to follow such a pathway. Most pupils, looking at the world around them, decided that their life chances were better if they stuck to GCSEs and A Levels.

The Coalition government abolished the Learning and Skills Council and called in Alison Wolf to review the existing state of vocational qualifications. She recommended a cull of many of the Applied GCSEs and other qualifications that had emerged over the years, endorsed BTEC as an A-Level equivalent and apprenticeships as a good way forward (Wolf, 2011). The government accepted her recommendations. Nonetheless our technical and vocational provision remains poor compared with much of the developed world.

Social contexts

Female empowerment

The first challenges to the many post-war conventions, which were to change British society irrevocably, occurred in the 1960s. These conventions included the importance of marriage, the disapproval of sex outside marriage and of divorce and only a limited number of jobs being regarded, at least by the middle classes, as suitable for women. In the 1970s, the pace of empowerment quickened. Germaine Greer's *Female Eunuch* was published in 1970 and feminist attitudes proved infectious. Also in 1970, the Labour government passed the Equal Pay Act, following the 'Made in Dagenham' strike of female machinists at the Ford plant. The contraceptive pill became available on the NHS in 1975. Women increasingly believed that the opportunities which men had always taken for granted should be also open to them and that they could organise their lives to seize them.

This new ambition was expressed particularly clearly in education. Girls had always done better than boys at 11+ but in the 1980s they did better at GCSE, continued into the sixth form and then on to university. By 1996 women applicants just about outnumbered male ones but, by 2014, when a record number of students (about 40 per cent of the cohort) entered university, women significantly outnumbered men. There remained an issue about choice of subjects, with physics and technological subjects still being male-dominated both at school and university. Nonetheless, though full equality had yet to be achieved, the transformation of

British society has been great. Britain had had a female prime minister. Whereas in the 1979 election, 11 women had been elected to Parliament, in 2010 it was 142. Many of the country's outstanding headteachers were female, and England's women's cricket, football and rugby teams often did better on the international stage than their male counterparts. For the most part, schools and universities (even the once proudly segregated Oxbridge colleges) contributed positively to this change.

Immigration and race relations

Another socially transforming trend has been immigration. Starting after the war with immigrants from the West Indies, others from the Indian sub-continent soon followed. By 1956, the new immigrant population was assessed at about 180,000 and rapidly increased during the 1960s. Governments quietly approved of immigration as its mainly cheap labour boosted the economy. However, immigration caused public disquiet, which was extravagantly though popularly expressed in 1968 by the Conservative MP Enoch Powell in his 'rivers of blood' speech. Successive governments have tried both to limit immigration by a series of Immigration Acts and to encourage racial harmony by such measures as the Race Relations Acts of 1968 and 1976. Efforts to limit numbers have failed. In 1981, the immigrant population had reached more than 2 million, about 4 per cent of the population. According to the 2011 census, the proportion of whites had fallen to 86 per cent, with ethnic minorities rising to more than 10 per cent. They tended to be concentrated in conurbations, especially London and the West and East Midlands. This increase has been due partly to legal immigration (though much unquantifiable illegal immigration has taken place) and people seeking asylum from trouble spots like Somalia, and partly to the higher fertility rates of immigrant families. In recent years, immigration from countries of Eastern Europe that are members of the EU, particularly Poland, has risen sharply. In 2013, though the Coalition government was trying to lessen it to 'tens of thousands', net migration into the UK was c.212,000.

Relationships between the races have often been difficult. Serious race riots occurred in 1981 in Brixton, Toxteth and Moss Side (mainly against the police), in 1985 in Brixton and Birmingham, and in 2001 in some northern towns. The Ouseley Report in 2003, *Community Pride, Not Prejudice*, made strong recommendations on the important role of schools. The worst riots of all in 2011, which started in London and spread to other cities, had racial elements. They were sparked by the police shooting of a black man who they suspected of gun crime, and more than half the rioters were black youths. However, many white youths attacked the police and property, making the rioting more anarchic than racist.

A low point in race relations came in 1993 when a black teenager, Stephen Lawrence, on his way home from school, was murdered by a white gang. The Metropolitan Police botched the inquiry and failed to bring the suspects to justice. The subsequent Macpherson Report accused the Met of institutional racism.

The DfE, LEAs and urban schools have responded to this immense challenge impressively. The impact of London Challenge on the performance of these schools in particular has been impressive. But, much previously, the Wilson government started Section 11 funding to help ethnic minorities. This funding continues as the Ethnic Minority Achievement Grant (EMAG). Almost without exception schools have committed themselves to an explicit anti-racist agenda.

Religious trends

English people, though most still call themselves Anglican, have largely stopped being practising Christians. Barely 10 per cent attended church regularly in the 1970s and that number has steadily fallen. Though the Church of England remains the national Established Church, it came to look increasingly anachronistic, especially because of its protracted debates about homosexuality and whether women could become priests. On the other hand, it should be noted that the 1944 Act, in order to create a national system, had to include within it 'voluntary controlled' (Anglican) and 'voluntary aided' (Catholic) schools that, at that time, provided education for the majority of pupils. The national system was, and remained until recently, a partnership between the government, the local education authorities and the churches.

Paradoxically, within education, Christian and other 'faith' schools have flourished. In 1976 the only 'faith' schools were Christian or Jewish. They proved popular and tended to show up well in the league tables that appeared in the 1990s. Their supporters argued that their religious ethos gave their schools extra cohesion and purpose; their critics, that they did better simply because their admissions procedures favoured able pupils. By 2014 not only were there more Christian schools (one of which taught the 'creationist' explanation of evolution) and Jewish ones, but in addition 18 Muslim, eight Sikh and four Hindu. Blair's New Labour government particularly encouraged new 'faith' schools though many warned that they were potentially socially divisive.

Governments still required all non-faith state schools to have a daily collective act of worship of a broadly Christian character, a requirement that most, supported by their governors and parents, ignored. When in 2014, a few schools in Birmingham with predominantly Muslim pupils, some 'faith' schools, some not, developed distinctly Islamic traits, the Coalition government quickly drew up a list of 'British' values that all schools had to be seen to foster. The list of values was unexceptional, including respect for English laws, individual freedom and the toleration of other people's beliefs. They do not include any mention of Christianity.

Minorities

Britain became a more tolerant society. As well as more accepting of different races and religions, the disabled got a better deal. The Disability Discrimination Act of

1995 aimed to ensure that disabled people were treated in a fair and equal way, especially with regard to shops, facilities and services. Wherever possible, disabled people should feel integrated. The Warnock Report of 1981 about Special Needs reflected the same philosophy. Physically disabled pupils and those with learning difficulties should attend mainstream schools. Although the subsequent Special Needs regulations have been strongly criticised by many, including Baroness Warnock, schools and colleges have fulfilled the aims of the report.

Another area of human activity to which Britons generally have become more tolerant is sexual differences. Homosexuality was decriminalised in 1967. 'Coming out' grew more common. Eventually, though the Tory Right and many religious groups opposed it, the Coalition government legislated for same sex marriages.

Inequality, poverty and class

Britain remained one of the most class-conscious nations in the world. Though the class system was more porous and more people thought of themselves as 'middle class' and lived what was seen as a middle-class life style in housing, taste and holidays, an upper or upper-middle class continued to dominate. With the decline of the trade unions, the Labour leadership became more meritocratic while the Tories retained a leadership with independent school and Oxbridge backgrounds. One clear consequence of the Thatcher revolution was increasing inequality. Comparatively high levels of unemployment left many working-class people in poverty and dependent on benefits. Wealth did not obviously trickle down from the rich to the poor, and London and the South East obviously prospered more than the North. Blair and Brown certainly tried to tackle inequality after 1997 but by and large they failed. The 2008 crash and following recession, the worst since the 1930s, made matters much worse, and the popular perception was that the austerity measures of the Coalition after 2010 hit everybody hard except the rich.

That inequality was reflected particularly in education where 7 per cent of the pupils are educated in independent schools, many of which are much more lavishly resourced than those within the state system, reinforcing the class divide.

In education, New Labour tried a number of policies of which Sure Start proved the most lasting. It set up Education Action Zones (EAZs) in 1998 as part of a New Deal for Communities. These to some extent were modelled on the Education Priority Areas that had been created in 1962 and that enabled resources and extra teachers to be directed at schools in deprived inner-city areas. Another initiative, Excellence in Cities, aimed at inner-city schools, was launched the same year as the EAZ's. The EAZ's foundered after a few years but Excellence in Cities proved more effective. Initially New Labour aimed its new Academies at poverty stricken areas. For its part, the Coalition has created a 'pupil premium' aimed at disadvantaged children in order to reduce the attainment gap between them and their peers. Though the evidence is mixed, a combination of such initiatives, of others like the London Challenge of 2003 and the success of many individual schools serving deprived areas, seem to have improved examination results, and more importantly, raised the aspirations of many of our most disadvantaged pupils.

Youth culture

Youth culture is an amorphous topic but one that obviously affects schools. Often it is defined by activities that interest the media, social problems that schools are expected to solve – drugs, alcohol abuse, knife crime, teenage pregnancies, early sexualisation, lack of respect for authority, racism and so on. Other trends may be more important since they could affect pupils' attitudes more generally: for example, excessive interest in celebrities, consumerism and interactive mobile phones and tablets, disinterest in national or international politics in local clubs and societies, or more positively a greater commitment to educational success. In his *Education in Britain 1944 to the Present* (2003) Ken Jones detected 'a new student culture emerging in which successful examination performance had a central part'. Pink Floyd's 'We don't need no education' of 1979 resonated less.

However, accounts of education usually neglect the importance of the Youth Service, which serves young people still at school. According to the National Youth Agency in 2010, 28 per cent of all 13–19-year-olds were in contact with some form of youth service, many of them from the most desperate backgrounds in terms of family breakdown and potential abuse. But youth centres suffered worst from the cuts to the education budget at the beginning of the Coalition government. In Greater London, eight of its thirteen youth centres were closed. In some other local authorities there was 100 per cent closure.

National identity

Britain joined the European Union in 1973. As the years have passed, critics of the EU have grown more vociferous and gained greater public support. Governments have granted greater devolution to Scotland, Northern Ireland and Wales. Should England and its regions have greater autonomy is a live question in 2015, so too is how healthy is British democracy? Ethnic minorities, notably Muslim communities, seem to be retaining their own cultural values. Governments have expected schools to contribute to a sense of national identity, whether it was the Conservatives requiring more British history in the National Curriculum, or New Labour introducing compulsory citizenship education, or the Coalition insisting on 'British values' being taught. Such initiatives pose difficult philosophic questions for teachers in a free society.

The digital revolution

Currently education systems are grappling with the implications of this technological revolution, which began in the late 1970s and has accelerated since then. British governments were swift to respond to it. From 1981 to 1984 the Thatcher government gave £8 million to schools through its Microelectronics Education Programme (MEP). Both primary and secondary schools purchased in large numbers the BBC Acorn computer and Research Machines (RM) products. Information and Communications Technology (ICT) became part of the National Curriculum. New Labour strongly supported greater investment in ICT. It set up the British Education Communication and Technology Agency (BECTA) in 1999 and made £230 million available to schools. ICT and Computer Science courses proliferated. However there were problems. For headteachers, investment in the best technology posed significant problems, partly because of the cost, partly, in the early years, because of reliability and partly because of the pace of innovation. Pupils too often had more sophisticated equipment at home than their schools. Teacher training lagged behind the investment in hardware and in the early twenty-first century pupils reported being bored with their ICT lessons, which focused on the introduction of comparatively undemanding computing skills. The numbers taking GCSE and A-Level courses fell. The Coalition government abolished BECTA in 2010 and in 2014 had the National Curriculum in ICT revised so pupils would gain a deeper understanding of computer technology through learning, for example, what algorithms are and how to create and debug computer programs.

In most schools digital technology is now ubiquitous, with electronic white-boards, iPads and other tablets, an array of computers in staff rooms and depart-mental offices, and linking parents to the school. As yet the impact on learning remains unclear. Most teachers agree that used well, digital technology improves motivation and is an immediate help with individual project work. It seems to be proving a real help for pupils having difficulty with basic literacy and numeracy. There are however no obvious signs yet of digital technology superseding the teacher at the heart of the learning process.

Conclusion

Consequently, there have been 40 years of radical political and economic change and of far-reaching social trends, to which schools, colleges and universities have had to respond. The central question on which the contributors to this book reflect is the extent to which the Thatcher-Blair-Cameron consensus has created an educational policy framework that has enabled our teachers to help their pupils flourish to their individual benefit and to the advantage of their country.

References

Jones, K., 2003, *Education in Britain 1944 to the present day*, Oxford: Blackwell.
Joseph, K., 1976, *Stranded on the middle ground?: reflections on circumstances and policies*, London: Centre for Policy Studies.
Lawlor, S., 1990, *Teachers Mistaught*, London: Centre of Policy Studies.
Wolf Report, 2011, *Review of Vocational Education*, London: DfE.

2

THE REVOLUTION BEGINS

Lord Kenneth Baker

Introduction

In 1976 James Callaghan, the Prime Minister, startled the educational world by making a speech that dared to question the quality of education being provided in many schools. Prime ministers were not meant to do this; they should not trample in the sacred vineyard of a school's curriculum. Callaghan's views were strongly opposed by virtually all the different bodies in education: teachers, teacher unions, schools, colleges, local education authorities and the departments of education in universities. Indeed his own Secretary of State, Shirley Williams, opposed his views and so little was achieved, but by the 1979 election he had started the ball rolling.

When Margaret Thatcher became Prime Minister in 1979 it was expected that there would be new and innovative ideas introduced on education and some were tried, like school vouchers, but after a short time they were withdrawn. The Assisted Places Scheme gave state pupils a scholarship to attend certain private schools – this was the first measure to be scrapped by the Labour government in 1997. But there were no major radical steps in the development of a national curriculum and by 1985 there was a general feeling that little had been achieved. Indeed Oliver Letwin, an adviser in No. 10 to Margaret Thatcher and who was later to become a cabinet minister under David Cameron, sent a minute to the Prime Minister in 1982 when Letwin was returning from politics to banking, which started, 'Dear Prime Minister, You have failed in education'. He could have softened his minute by saying, 'Your ministers have failed' or 'Your government has failed' but no, he attributed it to Margaret's own personal lack of interest in making significant educational changes.

The whole education scene in the mid-1980s had been dominated by a teachers' strike that had been ongoing for 18 months. In 1986 Margaret decided that she really had to make a change – Keith Joseph, her education minister whom she admired enormously and listened to a great deal, said he wanted to step down. I was lucky enough to be asked by Margaret to become the Secretary of State of Education and Science at a time when British industry was highly critical of the output of schools: many students on leaving school were barely literate or numerate and many were ill-disciplined for the world of work.

Secretary of State of Education and Science

When I went to see Margaret Thatcher on my appointment in May 1986 I expected to be given a list of things that she wanted done, but that wasn't how it happened. She said to me, 'Kenneth we have the teachers' strike and we must try and resolve it as soon as possible, but as regards policy go away and work up some ideas and come back to me in a month's time'. This was just what I wanted because I had my own ideas as to what needed to be done. She warned me about the Department for Education (DfE) and I remember her saying to Keith Joseph in 1983, 'You have an awful Department'. I set about shaping the changes with discussions, always roundtable, with senior civil servants, the other ministers, and my political adviser Tony Kerpel to agree what changes we would like to see.

There were two changes in particular that I wanted to introduce. I had come to realise that a national curriculum was necessary as the current arrangement meant that every school shaped its own curriculum, and so when you had a good headteacher you had a good curriculum; with a mediocre headteacher a mediocre curriculum; and with a poor headteacher a poor curriculum. Moreover there was tremendous inconsistency all over the country so when a family moved from, say, Northumberland to Devon their children joined a very different almost foreign system of education. I agreed very much with the phrase that Rab Butler once used, that all children should go through 'the common mill of education'. That was the really inspiring justification of the National Curriculum.

I also wanted to establish Technical Schools. Back in 1981 when I was the minister of Information Technology I had visited a college in Notting Hill that specialised in taking 16-year-olds who had left the education system with no certificate whatsoever and training them in computing. It was very interesting to see young people, particularly black students, sitting at computers, enthusiastic to learn and paying great attention. They knew among other things that to make music well they had to master a computer. In the wake of the Brixton riots in April 1981 we established a network of such colleges called Information Technology Centres (ITechs) across the country and I saw real transformation in the experience and life opportunities of their students. I had talked about the possibility of establishing such colleges with Keith Joseph on several occasions but never really got anywhere.

I compiled a list of proposals for the Prime Minister that included:

- The establishment of a national curriculum in a number of basic subjects.
- The provision of testing the achievement of students at the ages of 7, 11 and 14.

- The publication of the results of schools – league tables.
- The establishment of colleges independent of local authorities – City Technology Colleges – focusing upon computer technology, being funded partly by business.
- A system whereby schools as a result of a ballot of parents could move to become grant-maintained, independent of local education authorities.
- Polytechnics to cease being controlled by local authorities and become independent education institutions.
- Probably one of the most important changes: to devolve the management of a school's budget from the local education authority to the management of the head and the governing body. A trial in Cambridgeshire had shown secondary schools could do this and I built on this; and
- Per capita funding for schools and universities so that money would follow the student.

After many ministerial discussions this list was approved and it featured in the 1987 Conservative election manifesto, running over nine pages. It was the most systematic and thorough overhaul of education since 1945. After the election it fell to me to put flesh on the bones. I knew these proposals would be controversial, even to many Conservative local education authorities, so I was at great pains to balance the various working groups with a complete range of views and opinions from Left to Right, from top to bottom. I hoped that some curriculum groups would be free of controversy, like maths, but not at all. Feudal armies seemed to march in favour or against students being allowed to use calculators, to learn tables by heart, or to teach calculus below 16. It took some time to get agreement. I knew that history would be controversial so I took pains to get an outsider involved – Commander Michael Saunders-Watson who owned a stately home with a large educational wing attached to it and who was later to become chairman of the National Library. On English I appointed some of the people on the Right who had written the *Black Paper* series – very controversial and critical papers of the educational system – in the hope they would come up with a rigorous proposal, but I was to be disappointed – they were not concerned with basic punctuation or grammar. I set up another group, headed this time by an engineer, to produce a much more down-to-earth curriculum.

I also set about selling the idea of City Technology Colleges to groups of businesses. I went to see all the large companies like Rolls-Royce, ICI, and Shell but they were not interested at all. They wanted the basic state system to be improved, but none were clear how that might be done. Then I turned to entrepreneurs like James Hanson, Harry Djanogly, John Hall, Phil Harris, Stanley Kalms, Geoffrey Leigh and Peter Vardy, who were prepared to put £1 million towards sponsoring a school and get involved with a curriculum that aimed at improving the quality of education and life chances of its students. Eventually, long after I had left the Department, some 15 City Technology Colleges existed, the first of the academies and still some of the most successful schools in the country.

It was clear that the comprehensive system imposed by the Labour government in the 1960s was failing our children. All-ability classes were holding many back and the staying on rate at 16 was one of the lowest in the developed world. Only 12 per cent of our 18-year-olds went on to higher education. The remaining grammar schools, together with the private schools, were creating an elite of very well-educated students. What I wanted to achieve was for state-funded schools to strive to do as well and give to parents the greater choice in deciding which school was best for their children.

The Labour Party said they were opposed to virtually everything I had introduced and they promised to repeal them once in government. It was important therefore for the Conservatives to stay in office as long as possible to ensure that the reforms had bedded down. In the event there was not a general election that Labour could win until 1997 and that allowed the National Curriculum and the other reforms to be established. I am very glad to say that Tony Blair, his first Education Secretary David Blunkett, and their education adviser Andrew Adonis kept intact 90 per cent of the reforms I had introduced. In fact Tony Blair came to develop academies using the City Technology College as his model. He wanted more schools to be independent of local education authorities, and Andrew Adonis encouraged Blair to announce in 2004 that Labour wanted to see a target of 200 academies established. When Labour left office in 2010 there were in fact 273.

The changes were so radical that many Conservative authorities did not like them and sought to continue running their own schools. There was always a number of backbench MPs who tried to weaken the changes, by example setting a very high level of support in the parental elections for Grant Maintained Schools. Throughout Margaret Thatcher gave me her full support and that's what you expect from a great leader supporting one of her embattled ministers.

The overall impact of my proposals was to devolve as much power as possible to the individual schools and colleges. The metaphor I used at the time was that I wanted to move things out from the hub of the wheel to the rim, because at the rim schools could be independent and use their own inventiveness and creativity. I was often accused of concentrating too much power in the centre by creating the National Curriculum but I was quite prepared to defend it – the government was right to create the basis of core knowledge that pupils should follow, and I never attempted to tell teachers how to teach it. There was sufficient choice within the National Curriculum for schools to be as varied and creative as they wished to be.

The big regret I have from that time was that I was unable to extend the teaching day by at least one period. I did not bring in that change because in the eventual settlement of the teachers' strike I had to agree the number of hours that a teacher spent a year teaching. If it was increased by 45 minutes I would have opened up a huge new Pandora's Box of debates with the unions and I was not prepared to undertake another battle with them.

So what did I learn as an education reformer?

- First, if you want to change fundamentally the performance of traditional schools, you must create an institution that can show that it will lead to a better result for students. Parents, students and the local community must be able to see the new institution actively working. We had to get a City Technology College up and running. It was not easy as local authorities were not willing to create competition by releasing an empty school. One of the few education authorities held by the Conservatives was Solihull and they offered a failing and closing school in Kingshurst, and we were lucky to find an outstanding head, Valerie Bragg. The Kingshurst CTC soon became one of the most successful schools in the country, a position it holds to this day. This CTC became an exemplar for a further 14.

- You cannot secure reform alone. To develop CTCs I appointed Cyril Taylor, an independent education expert, who injected dynamism into the team that I had set up in the Department. Tony Kerpel, my personal and political adviser, became a key figure particularly by ensuring that my intentions were understood by the key officials in the Department.

- You do need allies. The educational establishment in the universities was hostile to any politician who wanted something fundamentally different. The teacher unions were predictably hostile, but I remembered Keith Joseph's advice to me: 'Don't make the mistake I made of attacking the teachers'. I decided to get the parents on my side. The publication of school results was key since it gave to parents essential information that could allow them to exercise choice for the education of their children. Parents were also given a vote to decide whether their school should be Grant Maintained. A new variety of schools gave parents for the first time an opportunity to choose.

In 1997 I left the House of Commons and I was pleased that Tony Blair's first government, David Blunkett his first Education Secretary, and Blair's main educational adviser Andrew Adonis decided to accept the reforms that had been implemented since the passing of the Education Reform Act in 1988. The only significant change was the abolition of Grant Maintained Schools, which had to be brought back under the control of local authorities – it was Labour's sop to the Left, but even that was partially reversed with the later introduction of Trust Schools.

University Technical Colleges

Over the years I had kept in touch with Ron Dearing whom I had first met when he was the Chairman of the Post Office and after his retirement I was the first to offer him a post in education with the Council for National Academic Awards, the body that regulated polytechnic qualifications. The position launched him in a very influential post-retirement career in education – he produced several key reports on student fees, curriculum reform, technical qualifications and foreign language in primary schools, quite apart from actively supporting new Christian academies. We met up again in 2007 and decided that the one thing that was missing in the English education system was good technical high schools.

The model Ron Dearing and I developed we called University Technical Colleges. They were for students from 14 to 18 and we both agreed that Mike Tomlinson's report to the Labour government supporting a 14–18 curriculum was absolutely the correct direction for English education. UTCs operate from 8.30 a.m. to 5 p.m. for 40 weeks of the year. This extended day and shorter holidays added a whole extra teaching year over the four years. The curriculum would devote 40 per cent of the teaching time for 14–16-year-olds to practical, technical, vocational hands-on learning, and 60 per cent to the basic GCSE subjects – English, maths, the three sciences, a foreign language and a humanities subject. The other key features were that a university would be asked to sponsor the UTC – this meant that the university would go into the UTC to help with teaching and to introduce students to the resource riches of a university. The university would also be partly responsible for shaping the specialist curriculum. In this it would be helped by local companies and employers who knew what skills were needed locally. The Baker Dearing Educational Trust (BDET) expects employers not only to help shape the specialist technical curriculum with the university, but also to provide projects for the students and then help with teaching them.

The BDET is grateful to the Edge Foundation for granting us £150,000 to get started. We used the grant to print a brochure explaining UTCs and to commission Exeter University to produce a report on how all the schemes and proposals to improve technical education since 1870 had failed.

Ron and I then went to see the Schools Minister Andrew Adonis who immediately liked the UTC idea and said that he would provide financial support for two. We were buoyed up by this generous support and decided that I should begin by approaching a university. I rang up Julia King, the Vice Chancellor of Aston University, one of our leading engineering universities, and who is herself a qualified engineer. Julia liked the UTC concept very much and committed her university to support us. We then won the support of Birmingham Council, where the education director and leader of the council, Mike Whitby, provided an empty site very close to the university. We met with several local employers – national and small – who wanted just this sort of school: the Aston University Engineering Academy is today over-subscribed.

Ron Dearing and I then had to make a big decision. Should we proceed with the two UTCs for which we had the government's support by getting them open in, say, two years and then measuring their success after a further three or four years? This would mean if the UTCs were successful we would not find out until 2014–2015. We agreed that the demand for such schools was so pressing we must get as many going as soon as possible, but we also recognised that such a policy had real risks. These were novel and unique schools blending technical and academic education, and while some would succeed there could also be failures. Undaunted we decided to go flat out to establish as many as we could. We managed to get five groups interested to establish the first five UTCs, and sure enough two ran into difficulties. But the next 12 UTCs were infinitely better – some are now outstanding – it was a reminder that the path of reform is never a faultless road.

As an election was approaching in 2010 it was necessary to win the support of the other political parties. I met David Cameron, the Leader of the Opposition, George Osborne, and Michael Gove all of whom liked the UTC idea and committed an incoming Conservative government in their manifesto to establish 12 UTCs. David Cameron picks up new ideas very quickly and saw how UTCs could certainly help with his 'Broken Society' by engaging the disengaged 13–14-year-olds who were fed up with the education they were getting in their comprehensives. I am glad to say that UTCs have gained all-party support: created under Labour and expanded under the Coalition.

The target of all UTCs is to ensure that when students leave at 16 or 18 none should join the ranks of the unemployed – no NEETs. It is a target that we meet. UTCs are major agents of social mobility: we provide opportunities for thousands of young people that they would not have had if they had remained at their previous schools.

One of the extraordinary features of the UTC movement is that it has been left to a charity, the Baker Dearing Educational Trust, to be the main promoter of UTCs and also to help them to become properly established as well as to ensure they meet the criteria of their specialist technical curriculum. This requires our charity to retain a significant team of ex-headteachers and inspectors, and to maintain a constant relationship with officials in the DfE and in some cases with local education authorities. If it had been left to the DfE to promote UTCs I do not believe that by now as many as 60 would have been approved.

PART II
Schools

3

THE EARLY YEARS

Wendy Scott

Introduction

It has been extremely interesting to reflect on the radical change in education over two generations. The trajectory of changes in early years education, as this chapter will show, though as radical as those affecting primary and secondary sectors, is different and more complicated.

I must immediately acknowledge the deep and lasting value of the Froebel training that I undertook between 1958 and 1961. Having refused to go to Cambridge and instead entering the Froebel Educational Institute (FEI) with the intention of teaching secondary maths, I was waylaid by the early years programme. It was taught socratically, and included the philosophy, psychology, sociology and history of education. During the three-year course, we also had lectures from health and social services professionals as well as artists and artisans. Molly Brearley, the FEI Principal, had a strong influence on *Children and their Primary Schools*, the Plowden Report, which was published in 1967.

Although more recent research has questioned some conclusions of the Report, Plowden's central tenet remains as true for effective education of young children in 2015 as it was in 1967: 'At the heart of the educational process lies the child'. In the early years, children have not yet learned to be pupils. They bring such varied expectations and experience with them to school, that teachers must pay attention to each individual in the context of their families and cultures. The most radical change in education policy since the 1980s is that individual children's needs and broader potential achievements have become secondary to the current standards agenda, directed by political ideology that is aligned with a simplistic economic model.

Teaching 1976–1981

In 1974, I returned to teaching after seven years at home looking after my two young children. I was appointed to open a new nursery class during the brief period of expansion of nursery provision in Education Priority Areas, introduced by

Margaret Thatcher when she was Secretary of State for Education. Given a headteacher with little awareness of or interest in the early years, and a demountable classroom across the playground from his office, I had complete autonomy on curriculum and organisation and was able to work closely with parents and also with health visitors and the probation service. This freedom continued throughout the time I was teaching, up to the mid-1980s.

Headship 1981–1986

I then became the teaching head of a demonstration nursery school on a university campus. This role involved full curricular, pastoral and management responsibilities in addition to full-time teaching. As headteacher, I had total freedom to design and implement the curriculum in collaboration with outstanding staff, and had control of the budget, apart from the costs related to the premises and staff salaries. The nursery built strong links with lecturers: I believe it was the first school in the country to introduce philosophy seminars for four-year-olds, and our ground-breaking work with the BBC B computer and the remote-controlled 'turtle' was made possible through additional expert support from the college. We welcomed many students and visitors from around the world; at this time, there was global interest in the enlightened British approach to primary and early years education.

Because of the advantages the nursery school enjoyed, we were able to specialise in the education of children with language difficulty and delay, and worked closely with other services. A speech therapist agreed to hold her clinic in an adjoining tutorial room. There she was able to observe her clients in a naturalistic environment through the one-way windows and advise on children where there were concerns. A school doctor came in regularly to undertake health checks. The publication of the Warnock report on Special Educational Needs (SEN) in 1978 provided a framework for our commitment to work on SEN.

I was fortunate in having a headship at a high point for nursery education and consider that this was the time in my career when I was able to have the most effective influence on children, their families, students and other colleagues through respectful reciprocal relationships.

Some of the main developments in nursery education and the early years curriculum

I left headship in 1986. As I moved to a variety of non-school posts, it will be useful at this stage to outline some of the main national policy shifts in both nursery education and the early years curriculum.

Nursery education

Historically, the provision of nursery education has been patchy across the UK. The *Effective Provision of Preschool Education* (EPPE) study showed that highly qualified early years staff make a crucial difference to children's achievement, at least up to the end of Key Stage 2, but although they have by far the highest proportion rated outstanding by Ofsted of any part of the education system, the number of maintained nursery schools in England since the 1990s has fallen by more than 20 per cent. They are often the preferred setting for inclusion and social care referrals for vulnerable children and their families. Sixty per cent of nursery schools in England already offer funded places for disadvantaged two-year-olds and more are in the process of setting this up. Given the difficulty of finding sufficient high-quality places for the two-year-old programme, these placements are a vital resource. Nevertheless, maintained nursery schools are facing an uncertain future as a result of reducing budgets and the drive to a Single Funding Formula across providers in each local authority (LA). Nursery school headteachers now have to manage very complex demands, especially where the school forms part of a Children's Centre. In common with primary and secondary education, the role of headteacher has changed considerably, not least because of the high levels of accountability. The particular demands of work in disadvantaged areas, where outreach to parents is a high priority, are not generally recognised, although the recent introduction of the Pupil Premium, albeit at a much lower level than for school-aged children, will go some way to addressing these problems.

In 2013, the Education Select Committee recommended that government should 'set out a strategy for ensuring the survival of those [maintained Nursery Schools] that remain'. The government response to this recommendation failed to address the issue and showed a worrying lack of understanding of the distinctive qualities of nursery schools led by specialist headteachers.

Key government initiatives from 1989

Just after the introduction of the National Curriculum for children of statutory school age, the DES published guidance on *The Education of Children Under Five*, written by HMI in 1989. It provided illustrations of a play-based curriculum expressed through nine interlinked areas of learning and experience, which offered

> a broad, balanced, differentiated and relevant curriculum which takes into account the assessment of children's progress, promotes equal opportunities irrespective of gender, ethnic grouping or socio-economic background, and responds effectively to children's special educational needs life.

The Rumbold Report (1990) provided an authoritative guide to provision for the early years, which remains pertinent to this day and informs the principles of the current Early Years Foundation Stage. These are hard to sustain given the increasingly demanding expectations of school readiness and other accountability measures.

In 1992, the government commissioned a discussion paper, *Curriculum Organisation and Classroom Practice in Primary Schools*, which recommended among other things that the teacher should be an instructor rather than a facilitator and that there should be a more direct emphasis on subject teaching. Written by Robin Alexander, Jim Rose and Chris Woodhead, it became known as 'The Three Wise Men's Report'. Tricia David, Audrey Curtis and Iram Siraj-Blatchford (three wise women), concerned by the focus on instruction and the likely negative effect of this on the early years, countered in 1993 with a well-referenced booklet *Fostering Children's Learning in Nurseries and Infant Classes*.

In 1996 the School Curriculum and Assessment Authority identified *Desirable Outcomes for Children's Learning before Compulsory School Age* (DLOs). This was the first time that outcomes had been specified in early years and there was considerable unease among practitioners who feared that teaching would be unduly influenced by expectations of outcomes rather than being seen as extending children's learning in a developmentally appropriate way.

The DLOs were replaced by the Labour government that came into power in 1997, who instead put in place Early Learning Goals as part of the Foundation Stage, introduced in 2000.

As nursery provision expanded through Sure Start (see below), which drew in younger children, *Birth to Three Matters* was published in 2002 to provide information, guidance and challenge for all those with responsibility for the care and education of children up to the age of three. It valued and celebrated babies and children, recognised their individuality, efforts and achievements, and acknowledged that all children have a need to develop learning through interaction with empathetic people and exploration of the world around them, from birth. The Framework took the child as its focus, steering away from subjects, specific areas of experience and distinct curriculum headings.

The *Birth to Three Matters* Framework, though based on a thorough analysis of the literature and welcomed across the sector, was discontinued in 2012, following the review of the Early Years Foundation Stage (EYFS) and the Early Years Profile (the assessment at the end of the Foundation Stage) undertaken by Dame Clare Tickell in 2011. This resulted in a simplification of the Profile, and combined regulatory standards and guidance for children from birth to the end of the reception year. Higher expectations were introduced for literacy and mathematics. These, combined with the downward pressure from the Year 1 phonics check, are leading to a significant increase in teacher-led instruction, making it more difficult to respond to spontaneous events and children's existing knowledge and interests.

The simplified EYFS Profile may become voluntary from 2016, although the Study of Early Education and Development (SEED) project, recently commissioned by the DfE, relies on Profile data for the 5,000 children they are following through to the end of Key Stage 1, and assessments undertaken by the health service are linking with it too. Annual entry to primary school means that a whole class is admitted in the September of the year in which children become five, although the statutory age of entry is the term after a child's fifth birthday. Many children are thus only just four on entry to school. Pre-schools and nurseries, which have proliferated in the private, voluntary and independent (PVI) sector since 1997, lose the influence and example of the older cohort of children, and the children themselves, particularly the youngest in the group, have a major adjustment to make when they enter their reception class.

PVI nurseries and pre-schools are staffed by people with generally lower levels of qualification than obtain in nursery and reception classes in primary schools; this divide between the maintained and non-maintained sectors is a continuing issue. In 2011, the Coalition government commissioned a review of early years qualifications from Professor Cathy Nutbrown. *Foundations for Quality* was published in 2012. Among other things, it recommended that a specialist qualification should be established for early years teachers, equipping them to work with children from birth to seven. The government response to this was to establish entry qualifications comparable to those for teacher training and to re-badge as Early Years Teachers the cadre of Early Years Professionals who had a graduate-level qualification, without granting them Qualified Teacher Status. This is causing considerable frustration and confusion.

The split in provision for the Foundation Stage in the UK is unusual; most other European countries have a coherent early years curriculum, offered in one setting, typically for children up to the age of six or seven, and staffed by professionals well qualified in early years pedagogy. Downward pressures for more formal approaches are increasing in England. The phonics check in Year 1 and the drive for narrowly defined school readiness as well as the raised standards in the EYFS Profile are resulting in unrealistic expectations of what children know and can do, achieved at the expense of more effective approaches to learning with understanding. Summer-born and premature children are particularly at risk of misdiagnosis of special educational needs. Proposals for on-entry baseline assessment designed to enable measurement of school effectiveness are causing concern as they will take teachers away from their first priority of settling up to 30 new children into school. Accountability is increasingly to a system, rather than to children.

LEA Inspector and Adviser 1987–1990

In 1987, I became a District Inspector for the Early Years with the Inner London Education Authority (ILEA). I had been impressed by papers on the impact of race, class and gender on achievement published by ILEA in the 1980s and was delighted to join the Authority. My role offered unequalled opportunities to learn from expert colleagues and to observe a wide range of practice across nursery schools and classes in four London Boroughs. It involved the line management of an expert group of advisory staff; the induction of up to 100 newly qualified EY teachers annually; links with specialist teachers' centres and experience of inspection as a professional and constructive way of working with schools. It offered the capacity to support new initiatives as well as to make proactive intervention where necessary. ILEA recognised that work in the early years requires specialist expertise and funded any primary teacher who converted to nursery teaching for a term's re-training. Secondary teachers were required to undertake a year-long course.

The unjustifiable abolition of ILEA resulted in the loss of considerable expertise, including specialist Teachers' Centres, among them the Centre for Language in Primary Education (CLPE), which is now an independent UK charity with a global reputation for the quality of its research into literacy and teaching. For many years CLPE pioneered approaches to formative, observation-based assessment, creating the Primary Language Record (PLR). The PLR was recommended by the Cox Committee, which developed the English National Curriculum as a model for a national system of record keeping and is now in use in widely differing systems throughout the world.

Unitary Authority Inspector/Adviser 1990–1993

In 1990, I was appointed as the primary and early years' inspector in the Royal Borough of Kensington and Chelsea (RBKC). This role demanded broader responsibility across the primary age range, working with specialist subject inspectors on the National Curriculum; supporting and moderating the introduction of Standard Assessment Tasks in Key Stage 1; a strong focus on professional development; and implementation of the Children Act 1989.

It was instructive to move from the largest Education Authority in England to RBKC, one of the smallest. Links with Social Services were close, although the Director of Education at the time turned down the innovative possibility of a combined service. Given the complexity of the role of current Directors of Children's Services, he was perhaps wise, although the implementation of the Children Act would have been more effective given joint working. The Borough was served by two health authorities that had radically different approaches to collaboration. Regrettably, professional boundaries still persist in some areas, in spite of the opportunities offered by Sure Start, and growing political awareness at local as well as national level.

It was during the three years that I worked in RBKC that Standard Assessment Tasks at the end of Key Stages 1 and 2 were introduced. The first tasks for seven-year-olds were designed around active learning, providing challenges to children to design a maths game and to have first-hand experience of scientific experiments. This required a learner-centred way of working, which was better aligned to children's interests than more formal approaches. Although complex to administer, it gave multi-layered opportunities to show what each child understood and could do and was arguably a more informative assessment than current, more limited tests. I learned a great deal in my role as moderator in this and in assessing children's progress in reading and writing.

It is a source of concern as well as regret that the role of local authority advisers and inspectors is now seriously undermined due to the introduction of academies and free schools, as well as heavy budget cuts.

Ofsted Registered Inspector and Nursery Inspector and Trainer 1993–1998

The establishment of Ofsted in 1992 meant that many local authority inspectors became redundant. I was fortunate to be offered early retirement, as having a pension released me to do voluntary work as well as to undertake Ofsted training as a Registered Inspector and also a Nursery Inspector and Trainer. My first experience as a member of an Ofsted team was the inspection of a large primary school under the guidance of an HMI who led eight of us through a five-day inspection. He insisted that the inspection team and all the staff met together before the inspection started, and explained in detail what we would be doing. His final remarks to the teachers were: 'If you don't feel you have had the best professional development for free by the end of the week, then we will have failed'. As a Registered Inspector myself, I always remembered his words and still consider that it is unprofessional and wasteful not to build constructively on the detailed observation involved in inspection. For several years, I chose to tender for inspections of maintained nursery schools in differing local authorities across the country, as I was interested to see how this non-statutory service was supported, both professionally and politically.

Since then, Ofsted has become a data-driven organisation, which is particularly unhelpful in the early years when assessment and evaluation need to be holistic and judgements must be nuanced, taking into account many aspects of children's lives. Given that inspections are now brief, usually with one unmoderated inspector, it is worrying that Ofsted is deemed to be the sole arbiter of quality across the early years. For a while, early years was not reported on separately in Section 5 school inspections. This has now been reinstated, but there are concerns about the lack of knowledge and relevant experience of some inspectors. It is to be hoped they will be guided by the definition of teaching given in Ofsted's evaluation schedule for inspections of registered early years provision:

> Teaching should not be taken to imply a 'top down' or formal way of working. It is a broad term which covers the many different ways in which adults help young children learn. It includes their interactions with children during planned and child-initiated play and activities: communicating and modelling language, showing, explaining, demonstrating, exploring ideas, encouraging, questioning, recalling, providing a narrative for what they are doing, facilitating and setting challenges. It takes account of the equipment they provide and the attention to the physical environment as well as the structure and routines of the day that establish expectations. Integral to teaching is how practitioners assess what children know, understand and can do as well as take account of their interests and dispositions to learn (characteristics of effective learning), and use this information to plan children's next steps in learning and monitor their progress.[1]

Voluntary organisation

From 1994 to 1997 I was Vice-Chair and then Chair of The British Association for Early Childhood Education (BAECE, now known as Early Education), then Chief Executive, from 1997 to 2000.

Moving to freelance working enabled me to offer voluntary support to Early Education. At that time, Cheryl Gillan, then a junior minister in the Department for Education and Employment, opened discussions on the need for childcare, and plans to introduce nursery vouchers were announced. On behalf of Early Education, I gave evidence to the Education Select Committee on the undesirability of the scheme, which would have made planning and quality control difficult.

New Labour 1997–2010

In 1994, the RSA published *Start Right*, a report written by Sir Christopher Ball, which strongly endorsed the importance of the early years, recommending that all children should have access to high-quality nursery education, which should also support parents. With the election of a Labour government in 1997, a strong policy of expansion of provision for young children was introduced that gave powerful impetus to Early Education's work. The growing recognition of the value of investing in the early years enabled the appointment of a Development Officer in each of the four countries of the UK and also a Chief Executive, thanks to grant funding.

When the research into the Effective Provision of Pre-school Education (EPPE) was announced in 1997, I was invited to join the consultative group and am very pleased that they took up my suggestion of including some maintained nursery schools in the project. These emerged consistently as offering the highest-quality provision, with a positive influence on children's later achievement at least until the end of Key Stage 2.

My involvement in the selection of Early Excellence Centres, which were introduced as models for joint working, drew on my varied experience. I also attended meetings in Westminster as a 'Friend of Sure Start', where possibilities were discussed as the Labour government shaped its thinking about early years care and education. It was an exciting time, full of possibilities for improving provision for young children and their families. Day-care mattered, but the focus was very much on children's learning and on supporting parents, in recognition of the crucial importance of the home learning environment.

1999 Chair of the Early Childhood Forum (ECF)

Dame Gillian Pugh, the first director of the Early Childhood Unit at the National Children's Bureau, saw the need to bring together different services with varying perspectives so that they could learn to understand each other and to collaborate. She instituted the Early Childhood Education Forum, now the Early Childhood

Forum (ECF) in 1993. This brought together the major national organisations concerned with the care and education of young children from the PVI and the maintained sectors. Services for children with special needs, parents, governors, inspectors and local authorities from across the UK were also represented. The over-riding purpose was to speak with a united voice in pursuit of agreed aims. The ECF grew to a total membership of nearly 40 organisations with an interest in early years; observers from the Departments of Health and Education and from Ofsted attended meetings. It was highly influential in the development of Sure Start, and I was honoured to become the first elected chair.

The ECF worked on proposals for an approach to the early years curriculum for some time and published *Quality in Diversity in Early Learning* in 1998. This is a major piece of work directed by Vicky Hurst, which involved practitioners and academics from all sectors across the country, who put together an agreed framework, influenced by New Zealand's inclusive Te Whariki curriculum, as a guide to provision for children from birth to six. This was superseded by the Curriculum Guidance for the Foundation Stage, a government-imposed framework, developed in consultation with expert advisers. In spite of this child-centred guidance, the prescriptive Literacy and Numeracy Strategies introduced into primary schools in 1998 resulted in pressure on nurseries and pre-schools to begin to do more formalised work in these areas of learning.

Since the Coalition government came into power in 2010, there has been strong ministerial control of the curriculum and assessment across all key stages. The revised Early Years Foundation Stage sets statutory standards that all early years providers, in the PVI sector as well as in maintained schools, must meet.

An EYFS Profile must be completed for each child at the end of the reception year in primary school. The main purpose is to provide a rounded and accurate assessment of individual children's levels of achievement at the end of the EYFS. The profile describes each child's attainment against 17 early learning goals, together with a short narrative about their learning characteristics. It is increasingly being used by health professionals as a measure of children's achievement, and is included in the SEED (Study of Early Education and Development) research project as a baseline measure, so current proposals that it should become voluntary are of concern, especially as this is allied to the introduction of a baseline measure for all children on entry to the reception year.

The current emphasis on progress rather than on simple measures of achievement is welcome, but is resulting in counter-productive demands on staff due to simplistic expectations of linear progression, which must be evidenced in detail for each child. Assessment now rules practice, and teachers no longer have scope to apply their professional judgement and to ensure that children have a rounded educational experience. The prime areas of learning, namely personal, social and emotional development, communication and language, and physical development are being sidelined in the push for academic achievement. This is disastrous in the early years, where the focus should be on broader intellectual growth.

Sure Start

Sure Start was one of the most radical policy initiatives undertaken in this country. Norman Glass, who was Deputy Director (micro economics) in HM Treasury between 1995 and 2001, was the person who brought it about, alongside Margaret Hodge MP, Minister for Children. I never imagined that I would attend consultations in the Treasury, let alone meet a civil servant with such sympathy with the aims of the programme and grasp of the issues. As his obituary in *The Independent* noted, Norman chaired the Comprehensive Spending Review that led to the setting up of Sure Start. He ensured the programme was based on good research evidence and underpinned by core values. He was keen that childcare not be 'captured' simply as a route towards the greater employability of parents: it should be both cost effective and socially just, to ensure that children had the best possible start in life.

Glass went on to lead the Interdepartmental Review, which resulted in the creation of a Cabinet Committee on Children and Young People and a cross-departmental Children's Unit to coordinate policy and administer the proposed Children's Fund. He chaired the official steering group to implement the Sure Start programme, which was designed to narrow the gap in achievement between more and less advantaged children, now an increasing problem.

Adviser to the Department for Education and Employment 2000–2002

I attended several meetings of the Friends of Sure Start after Labour came into power in 1997 and was appointed to the DfEE in 2000 as part of a team working with the newly established Early Years Development and Childcare Partnerships (EYDCPs) across England, helping to develop effective multi-professional collaboration and planning for growth.

The expansion of nursery classes under Thatcher had been short-lived, and provision for non-statutory early years education across the country remained patchy, depending largely on political priorities in different local authorities; indeed, the Pre-school Playgroups Association (now the Pre-school Learning Alliance) was founded in 1962 in order to fill the gaps in the availability of nursery schools and classes. Historically, independent and private providers have also been part of the mix. When the Labour government decided to expand provision, giving an entitlement to 12 hours of nursery education to all three- and four-year-olds and allowing choice as to sessions attended, it relied on PVI nurseries to fill the gaps. The push towards collaboration and multi-agency working was expressed through EYDCPs in each local authority. There was a wide range of existing provision, which was very scarce in some areas. The qualifications of staff in the PVI sector were generally lower than in maintained nursery schools and classes, although staffing ratios were better. A recent proposal to trade improved qualifications for lower ratios of adults to children was rejected by the sector.

As well as considerable professional challenge, this period gave me deep insights into the very different approaches to early years care and education across the south east of England and the influence individual politicians, local authority officers, or practitioners could have, at both micro and macro levels. I also learned a lot about the complexities of a government department.

I already knew that any proposal that took up more than a single A4 sheet of paper was unlikely to be considered and that long-term strategic thinking had little traction as each government made its own decisions. Criticism was not welcome unless accompanied by proposed solutions. I discovered that the timeframe for policy change was shorter than a parliamentary term, as it was conditioned by finances. A Comprehensive Spending Review, when the Treasury allocates funding to each Ministry, takes place every two years, so planning is tied to that. However, the Education Department sees an annual battle over spending priorities between the various divisions, for example schools, special needs, FE and so on. A new initiative such as Sure Start must show that it is effective very quickly, or lose further investment. This explains the rushed implementation, not just of Sure Start, but of other initiatives, for example the Neighbourhood Nurseries or the current push to make provision for disadvantaged two-year-olds. The Sutton Trust has recently advised that this policy should be slowed down until enough places of good enough quality are available, but it is nevertheless proceeding, with schools encouraged to take these very young children into a less than ideal situation.

I saw little evidence of corporate memory in the Department, partly because of the career structure in the Civil Service, where people tend to move on every two or three years. This churn means that continuity is compromised. Governments claim that evidence-based policy prevails and that consultations are meaningful, but my experience, endorsed by subsequent observation, suggests that decisions are largely ideologically based and the use of evidence may be selective, even when drawn from research commissioned by the government itself. I checked recently on consultation procedures, and the DfE confirmed that each submission counts as a single response, even if it comes from a large group. I was told that some are read more carefully than others. It is admirable that an analysis of responses is now put up on the DfE website, but the clear statement that a proposal will happen, although only a minority of people agree, is not very reassuring. It is disheartening that the Minister who advocates direct instruction grounded in prescribed phonics programmes has no experience of the complexity of literacy teaching and is advised by people who gain financially from the policy.

It was refreshing to spend the following year working with the Early Excellence Programme and its evaluation. Just over a hundred Centres were identified as models of good multi-professional practice. In every case, there was dynamic, determined and visionary leadership, and a sympathetic and enlightened local authority also contributed to their success. These Centres were important in addressing the underlying aim of *Every Child Matters* (ECM), introduced in 2004 with the aim of safeguarding children and giving each one the best chances in life. Now that ECM has been withdrawn and the Department for Children, Schools and

Families has become the Department for Education, one has to wonder whether every child does still matter. Recent cuts mean that Children's Centres have been closed, or are accessible for very short hours and only able to offer signposting to declining family support and other services.

Working as a consultant in China and the Maldives as well as the UK 2000–2007

A very interesting career development emerged just before I moved to work with the government in 2000. I was asked to welcome a high-level delegation of visitors from China who wanted to find out about the British approach to early years education. A professor from the Normal University in Beijing had looked around the world and decided that our approach was what was needed to enable China to broaden its provision so that children could be more expressive and creative. The British Council funded several such delegations over five years and also supported annual visits of English Early Years experts to different parts of China. I have subsequently worked for UNICEF in a post-tsunami programme developing early years provision in the Maldives, where there is a similar acknowledgement of the value of our heritage of high-quality early education. The tragedy is that we are losing our focus on quality in England, as the prime aim of support for children's learning and development is being displaced by the push for affordable childcare, and the pressure for ever-earlier formal teaching is resulting in the loss of children's confidence in themselves and of their disposition to learn.

Conclusion

The erosion of overarching educational values and ethical principles at policy level means there is no longer a proper context for constructive, reasoned debate. Unrealistic expectations and inappropriate top-down pressures are undermining the stated principles that underpin the statutory framework for the Early Years Foundation Stage (2012), which covers the education and care of all children up to the end of the reception year. Teachers of all age groups need scope to customise education to individual pupils, not only in order to accommodate cultural differences, but also to take account of the changes and chances that are part of life for us all.

In 2008, Graham Allen MP advised the government on ways of eliminating or reducing costly and damaging social problems for individuals. His report examined how this could be done by giving children and parents the right type of evidence-based programme, especially in the children's earliest years. Allen warned:

> If we continue to fail, we will only perpetuate the cycle of wasted potential, low achievement, drink and drug misuse, unintended teenage pregnancy, low work aspirations, anti-social behaviour and lifetimes on benefits, which now typifies millions of lives and is repeated through succeeding generations.[2]

The report stresses that only early intervention can break the inter-generational cycle of dysfunction and under-achievement. Socially and emotionally capable people are more-productive, better-educated, tax-paying citizens who can help our nation to compete in the global economy, and make fewer demands on public expenditure.

In 2010, Frank Field endorsed Sure Start by saying that investment in the Foundation Stage and support for families and parents are the most effective ways of ensuring that young people are able to break through economic and social barriers to achieve in later life.

All political parties appear to be committed to investment in the vital early years as a means of equalising children's life chances at a time when poverty and inequality are increasing. The current political climate and blame culture, the deliberate rejection of expert advice from specialists who have dedicated their professional lives to education, and the highly selective use of evidence are demoralising staff and harming children's life chances. Nevertheless, teachers, with support, can do much to help create a more equal society.

Advice to future policy makers:

- Implement in full the recommendations of the Nutbrown Review of early years qualifications, and provide mentoring for all working in the early years.
- Reform the accountability system, ensuring that it is primarily to children and families, and convert inspection into a positive opportunity for improvement and professional development.
- Take decisions on the curriculum away from politicians and recognise teachers and other staff as professionals.

Notes

1   Ofsted 2013 Evaluation Schedule for Inspections of Registered Early Years Provision, guidance and grade descriptors for inspecting registered early years provision p. 7, footnote 8.
2   Graham Allen MP, 2011 *Early Intervention: The Next Steps*, Independent Report to the Government, Ref: 404489/0111 Department for Work and Pensions and The Cabinet Office

Further reading

Association of Teachers and Lecturers (2002) *Inside the Foundation Stage, a report on practice in reception classes*. London: ATL.

Blakemore, S.-J. (2000) *Early Years Learning: The POST Report*. London: Parliamentary Office of Science and Technology.

David, T. *et al.* (2003) *Birth to Three Matters: A Review of the Literature*. London: DfES Publications.

Department for Education (2014) *Statutory Framework for the Early Years Foundation Stage*. London: DfE Publications.

Early Years Curriculum Group (1995) *Four-Year-Olds in School: Myths and Realities*. Oldham: Madeleine Lindley.

Gopnik, A. (2000) *The Philosophical Baby: What Children's Minds Tell Us about Truth, Love, and the Meaning of Life*. New York: Farrar, Straus and Giroux.

Goswami, U. (2015) *Children's Cognitive Development and Learning*. CPRT Research Survey 3.

Save Childhood Movement, www.savechildhood.net/ and www.toomuchtoosoon.org/.

TACTYC Occasional Papers, www.tactyc.org.uk/occasional-papers/.

WAVE Trust (2013) *Conception to Age 2 – The Age of Opportunity*. London: DfE Publications.

4

PRIMARY EDUCATION

Can we escape the legacy of elementary education?

Tony Eaude

Introduction

My career as a primary teacher started in a suburban school in 1976, a few weeks before the speech in which Prime Minister James Callaghan launched what came to be called the 'Great Debate' and about ten years after the Plowden Report (1967), which represented a vision of primary education very different from that of elementary schools before the 1944 Act, where:

- the curriculum involved a narrow emphasis on what Alexander (2010, p. 242) calls Curriculum 1 ('the basics'), with little time for Curriculum 2 ('the rest');
- teaching was mainly based on instruction and transmission of content knowledge; and
- teachers were poorly qualified.

In 1980 I moved to a large school in a new town, becoming deputy head in 1983. I was appointed as headteacher of a first school in 1989, just after the 1988 Education Reform Act, and left that post in 1998 to study for a doctorate. Since then, I have worked independently, mostly researching and writing about young children's education and working with teachers in primary schools and teacher educators. So, my professional life falls neatly into three main periods, with cut off points in 1989 and 1998.

The next three sections describe the key changes in these periods in the curriculum, pedagogy, assessment, accountability and school structures and reflect on less tangible aspects such as how these changes were perceived at the time. I then provide an overview of these four decades of change in relation to primary education. The final section suggests lessons for those concerned with policy and practice, if primary education is to escape from the enduring legacy of elementary education.

From 1976 to 1989

As a primary class teacher, in the 1970s and 1980s, I had considerable autonomy over the curriculum. Teachers were expected to hear children read regularly and do mathematics, much of it practical and working through text books. There was a strong emphasis on art, physical education and what was usually called topic work. I was able to choose a topic for a half-term or a term. The idea of 'good primary practice' was prevalent. Although never clearly defined, this often involved starting from a first-hand experience or an artefact and children writing, drawing, measuring and finding out more about it.

Teachers could, within the constraints of breaks, assemblies and hall times, structure the timetable as they wished. I adopted an integrated day with some separate lessons, especially for maths and handwriting, but most of the timetable was not divided into separate lessons or subjects. The day usually ended with me reading a story. Children were expected to organise their own time, often over a few days. For example, I recall two boys spending most of two days completing a beautiful painting of a fish. My teaching involved relatively little direct instruction and was largely what Alexander (see Eaude, 2011, pp. 14–15) calls facilitation, underpinned by a philosophy that children should be allowed to develop at their own pace and that this should involve a broad range of experiences.

The curriculum was largely a matter for the school to decide, prompted but not determined by national policy. The early 1980s saw a greater emphasis on science. Increasingly, from the middle 1980s, our school developed an approach to teaching reading based on 'real books' (as opposed to a reading scheme). Following the Swann Report (1985), which called for schools to cater more for the needs of an ethnically diverse society, my largely white school undertook a great deal of work about racism, resulting in my doing the DES 20-day course on ethnic diversity.

There was little detailed lesson planning and no expectation, except in the first year or two of teaching, that one's plans would be scrutinised. I was on my own for most of the time at my first school, teaching all subjects except music. At my second, team-teaching meant that two teachers were responsible for two classes between them. Support from learning support assistants was usually for only one or two sessions a week, with their role often washing paintbrushes or hearing individual children read. Teachers had no expectation of non-contact time.

There were no external tests. Some teachers tested times tables and spelling regularly. I did neither, though was, at my first school, encouraged to concentrate more on children learning their times tables. Nor was there regular monitoring or inspection. I recall attending a conference in around 1980 on accountability addressed by an HMI, who gave little indication of what this might involve in the future. In 1981, when HMI came to inspect the school, no one seemed worried, and teachers did not change how they worked. The inspectors did not seem to have a clear plan. For instance, I remember one asking a colleague to point him towards any science. I thought that we would be criticised for an approach to teaching reading that left many of our children – mostly from disadvantaged backgrounds – poor readers. No report was published, and no individual feedback was received, though the head said that the school had been judged to be in the top 10 per cent nationally. Nothing seemed to change as a result.

The 1981 Education Act meant that schools were required to identify, and make provision for, children with Special Educational Needs (SEN), helping to provide more consistent assessment of need and provision. The middle 1980s were characterised by industrial unrest, in which I, as the local secretary of the National Union of Teachers, was heavily involved, but there was very little direct interference from government or the Local Education Authority (LEA) affecting how I taught.

I, and my colleagues, worked hard but felt that we were largely in control. Teaching was enjoyable despite all the frustrations inherent in the task. We were fairly sure that what we were doing was on the right lines, and primary education in England was highly regarded. There was a sense of optimism that in hindsight seems more like naïveté. It now seems remarkable the extent to which teachers and schools were trusted and given autonomy, how untouched by external events most teachers were and how little most of us working in primary schools in the 1980s saw what was coming.

One should always be cautious of generalising from personal experience, but my experience illustrates a few wider trends. The research (for instance Alexander, 2010, p. 30 and Campbell and Neill, 1994, p. 177) indicates that progressivism was never as prevalent as often thought and nationally provision was very uneven, with a lack of consistency across the system and low expectations in several respects. The curriculum was largely dependent on the school's, and the headteacher's, priorities. Reading, writing and mathematics were emphasised, but the importance of a broad range of experiences, creativity and catering for 'the whole child' was recognised. There was little external pressure on schools and almost no structural change. Teachers were trusted and mostly left alone, though whether that trust was justified is arguable. It was the age of what Hargreaves (2003, pp. 125–9) calls 'permissive individualism'.

From 1989 to 1998

In 1989, I became the headteacher of a multi-cultural first school in East Oxford with some 300 children. The first two years were ones of relative calm, although the implementation of the 1988 Act was starting to change primary education. Then, on 15 June 1991, one of the two buildings was severely damaged by fire. As a result, we worked on a split-site with most of the school in temporary accommodation for two years, while the school was rebuilt. I then stayed for another five years. So the second period of my career was as a headteacher, roughly from the 1988 Act until just after the election of the Labour government in 1997.

A key principle underlying the introduction of the National Curriculum was that of entitlement, to try and ensure greater consistency of provision. The 1990s also saw a move towards inclusion, with more children with special educational needs educated in mainstream schools. My main recollection of the first National Curriculum is the huge number of ring binders containing a very detailed, subject-based set of requirements. Primary teachers struggled to understand these and find ways of integrating the contents into coherent plans and topics. Soon, it was clear that the National Curriculum and assessment procedures were absurdly top-heavy. The 1994 Dearing Review led to a slimming-down of content but the structure, based on separate subjects, remained unchanged.

Standard Assessment Tasks (SATs) were introduced in English, mathematics and science, involving a mixture of tests and Teacher Assessments, in our school only for seven-year-olds. My most vivid memory is of the chaos of trying to assess how well individual children understood the idea of 'floating' by placing oranges in buckets of water. As a school, we struggled for some while with a cumbersome method of collecting evidence for Teacher Assessment. With the governors' support, I refused to return the school's data, on the grounds that these were simplistic outcome measures which did not reflect what really mattered most, but after two years then complied.

I was not inclined to introduce significant changes in pedagogy to a school that was both popular and good, though some teachers were inevitably better than others. I wanted to retain a cross-curricular approach and trusted and tried to support teachers, recognising and accepting that they had different strengths. In 1995 or 1996, Robin Alexander challenged those attending a headteachers' conference to define good primary practice, reflecting Simon's (1981) and his own (2004) belief that teachers are extraordinarily reluctant to discuss pedagogy. My (silent) response was that of course I could, given a little time. However, increasingly, pedagogy was affected by external demands, based on raising standards of attainment in Curriculum 1.

The most significant changes came in external accountability, particularly with Ofsted inspections and published reports. As headteachers, we were ill prepared for what inspection involved and the consequences of not meeting what was expected. One nearby school, inspected early in the cycle, was unexpectedly put into special measures. As a result, other headteachers took more notice of how to satisfy the demands of inspection teams, with a strong emphasis on (often hastily prepared) written policies. In 1998, my school was inspected and received a reasonably favourable report. However, I remember feeling very resentful that an inspection team who know little of the complexity of the context could produce so definitive a report based on a three-day visit, on criteria with which I disagreed, when I had worked there for nine years and many colleagues for far longer.

The introduction of Local Management of Schools (LMS) affected me as headteacher considerably. The funding formula continued to reflect historic patterns, where primary schools were funded less generously than early years (rightly so) and secondary and tertiary education (for reasons that are less obvious). The workload implications were considerable, not least because this coincided with the time after the fire. Initially, managing the school's budget was exciting, and much of any 'spare' money was spent on employing more support staff, but the process became far more time-consuming and difficult with increasing pressure on school budgets.

The change of culture that accompanied LMS was evident, even at the time, notably with the money that accompanied a child on the basis of being on the register on one day in January. Early on, I delayed the transfer of a child for a few days to help a neighbouring school that was struggling. Once, on the day itself, I suggested that a child transferring to us should start that same afternoon. Worst of all, I remember doing a quick calculation of the financial benefit over several years if a family of four joined the school, though this had no influence on my decision whether to admit.

Structural changes, such as grant-maintained schools, outside local authority control, as part of a policy based on parental choice, affected primary schools less than secondary schools. Locally schools continued to try and preserve the role of the LEA, which had, in my own situation, been very supportive at the time of the fire and subsequently. However, it soon became clear that the LEA's role was changing, with a reduction in advisory services and advisers moving into a more inspectoral role.

As a headteacher, my energy was for most of two years taken up with the aftermath of the fire, when the emphasis was on rebuilding the school and maintaining staff morale. However, my main focus was always based on meeting the needs, as I perceived them, of a varied, ethnically diverse, school community. For instance, this led to the introduction of halal meals, which proved largely uncontroversial. However, when single-sex swimming was introduced to accommodate the wish of Muslim parents, this proved much more so. While national policies were important, local issues remained my main concern, except when inspection was imminent.

The 1990s were a time of frequent, and often exciting, exhausting and unwelcome, change – in the curriculum, in funding, in accountability – all of which had implications in terms of relationships, identity and beliefs. While I tried to remain true to my philosophy, this became increasingly difficult as external demands became more insistent in an age of greater regulation.

From 1998 to 2015

In 1998, I left headship to undertake a masters' degree and then a doctorate, looking at how teachers of young children understand spiritual development. Since 2003, I have worked independently, researching, writing and working with teachers and teacher educators, mostly in areas associated with spiritual, moral, social and cultural development and primary teachers' pedagogy and expertise. I continued to teach young children until about two years ago. The third period of my career has spanned the 13 years of Labour governments and the five years of the Conservative/Liberal Democrat Coalition, in various roles, mostly outside schools.

The most obvious change in relation to the curriculum and pedagogy has been the level of government involvement, with the explicit rationale (see Barber, 2005) that primary teachers needed to be told how to teach, as a route towards 'informed professionalism'. The National Literacy and Numeracy Strategies were introduced in 1998 and 1999, respectively, prescribing not only content but how it should be taught. For instance, the Literacy Hour was based on a model of instruction, with each lesson divided into discrete sections, with teachers expected to plan and follow a largely pre-planned script. A subtle but important change of emphasis occurred from 'pupils should . . .' in the 1988 National Curriculum to 'teachers should . . .' in the National Literacy and Numeracy Strategies. The Strategies were amalgamated in 2003 into the Primary National Strategy. While adopting the Strategies was not compulsory, only a brave minority of schools did not adopt them.

These initiatives were followed by *Excellence and Enjoyment* (DfES, 2003) and *Every Child Matters* (TSO, 2003), which led to the Children Act of 2004. The former called for learning to be more enjoyable, arguing that a dichotomy between that and standards of attainment is false. While this may, in principle, be true, the remorseless pressure for results meant that this was greeted with scepticism. The emphasis on the whole child and interagency collaboration in *Every Child Matters* was widely welcomed. The 2006 Rose Review on reading signalled the start of a greater emphasis on phonics. The number of new initiatives – and this list is far from complete – was considerable, leading to initiative fatigue.

The Coalition government has given mixed messages, continuing to intervene and exercise control, while saying that headteachers and teachers should have greater autonomy. So, for instance, the prescriptive nature of the 2013 National Curriculum in English and mathematics and the introduction of the phonics test for six-year-olds indicate how reluctant politicians are to trust professional judgement, especially in the primary sector. Teachers are required to use one particular method (systematic, synthetic phonics) of teaching reading and are increasingly exhorted to adopt methods from countries in East Asia to teach mathematics. Academies and free schools, outside local authority control, are not required to teach the National Curriculum, on the basis that this will encourage innovation. However, if so, it seems incomprehensible why this should not apply in all schools.

Since 1997, primary education has been increasingly driven by the demand to raise children's scores in English and mathematics, resulting, to some extent, from the international comparisons in PISA (Programme for International Student Assessment). The result is a focus on what Ball (2003) calls 'performativity' and is linked to accountability mechanisms where Ofsted judgements are heavily influenced by the data. Assessment of pupils has become very 'high-stakes' and when talking to headteachers and teachers the discourse is often dominated by what Ofsted have said, or will say next time they visit.

The years from 1997 to 2010 saw much more money allocated to young children's education. This was particularly evident in relation to the early years, less so for primary schools, though they are significantly better funded than before 1988. Teachers were entitled to 10 per cent of their time for planning, preparation and assessment and became used to having a second adult to provide additional support. A huge investment in computers was often wasted because teachers were unsure how best to use them to enhance learning.

My interest in recent years has been in trying to answer the question of what really constitutes good primary practice, based on research about how young children learn. In Eaude (2011, 2012), I discuss issues related to pedagogy and expertise, indicating that teaching a class of young children is much more complex than any assessment of one lesson, however 'outstanding', can capture and requires highly qualified teachers and sustained professional development.

The last 17 years have seen government, of whichever party, increasingly legislating and trying to micro-manage, not only the detail of the curriculum, but how it is taught, based on techniques, programmes and 'what works'. Yet ideas such as effectiveness and 'what works' only make sense in relation to aims and depend heavily on context. What works in one respect may have damaging consequences in another, for instance where an emphasis on decoding words may improve test scores but militate against reading for pleasure. Any suggested alternative to a remorseless emphasis on raising scores in literacy and numeracy is treated with scorn and the indication that this implies low teacher expectations. This was epitomised by the immediate dismissal by the government of the Cambridge Primary Review (Alexander, 2010) when it was published in 2009.

The language has increasingly been one of military metaphors and education as a commodity; of standards, targets and delivery, reflecting a greater emphasis on teaching than on learning, and on children as vessels to be filled rather than eager learners to be encouraged. Teachers have been subjected to greater regulation and surveillance through a prescriptive National Curriculum and data on attainment being made public. Accompanying this has been an emphasis on performativity and what the Cambridge Primary Review (Alexander, 2010) calls a culture of compliance – 'just tell us what to do and we'll do it'. Fear permeates the system.

Looking back

Reflecting on four decades of change risks the dangers of nostalgia for a golden age that never existed and of over-generalising, when the extent and impact of change, inevitably, vary between contexts. My experience is far from typical but illustrates some wider trends.

Much has not changed a great deal. Children of primary age are taught for most of the week by one teacher in a class of about 30, though there is more adult support. Most children behave well most of the time and spend a large part of the week reading, writing and doing mathematics, though the emphasis on these is now much greater. Teachers continue to try and meet the broad range of children's needs, taking account of policy, though they are much more driven by external expectations.

There have been improvements. The National Curriculum has helped to provide a level of entitlement and been welcomed by most teachers and parents/carers. Mathematics – or at least numeracy – is certainly taught better, and children with disabilities, bilingual children and looked-after children are, mostly, catered for much better, largely as a consequence of the move towards entitlement and inclusion. There is little doubt that primary teachers plan more carefully – they certainly spend much longer doing so – and collaborative planning is more common.

Much has, in my view, got worse. The focus on performativity reflects, and leads to, an over-emphasis on measurable results and content knowledge. Paradoxically, the scope of the curriculum has shrunk while its size has increased. Particularly damaging for young children has been the loss of breadth and balance, with reduced time and importance for the humanities and the arts. One may question whether such a curriculum is genuinely inclusive if many children are not engaged with what interests them. This is exacerbated by the tendency towards adopting instructional and transmissive teaching methods at an increasingly early age, to try and cover curriculum content within a set time and achieve short-term results. For many children, notably those with special educational needs and/or not attaining well, the curriculum is fragmented, with a plethora of interventions designed to 'drive up' standards. Planning is often inflexible, focused on literacy and numeracy and dominated by content, based on 'scripted instruction', leaving little space for 'disciplined improvisation', to use Sawyer's (2004) terms. The rhetoric of setting teachers free remains hollow if assessment and accountability mechanisms are so high-stakes that these determine what happens in the classroom.

For me, teaching a class of young children has always been hard work, but also enjoyable – at least most of the time. However, there is far less enjoyment, for teachers and children, with more pressure for results. The last four decades have seen a move from permissive individualism to regulated surveillance, affecting everyone from teachers to headteachers to local authorities. This is evident in the tendency of many headteachers and teachers to try and guess what will help them most in the next inspection, rather than basing their decisions on evidence or professional judgement.

The last 25 years have seen continual political interference and attempts to micro-manage, resulting from a short-term desire to achieve measurable results. Policy is based on, at best, a sketchy and partial view of evidence from research, and frequently on the political complexion of the government, or even the whim of a minister. The result has often been selective policy borrowing, despite the well-attested difficulty, and potential danger, of doing so (see Phillips and Ochs, 2003), with claims often based on data of questionable reliability and validity.

The culture of primary schools has changed profoundly but gradually, with considerable consequences for teachers as well as children. Ball (2003) argues that what he calls the terror of performativity requires teachers to organise themselves in response to targets, indicators and evaluations and to set aside personal beliefs and commitments. Initiative fatigue and a culture of compliance have altered many teachers' ideas of professionalism, moving broadly from one based on autonomy towards one based on compliance. Nias (1989) argued that the close link between primary teachers' professional and personal identity meant that they were affected particularly strongly when asked to act in ways that conflicted with their beliefs.

Two major difficulties with an approach based on prescription are that:

- the context of the primary classroom is so fluid that teachers require a wide repertoire of pedagogies and the judgement to respond appropriately; and
- prescription inhibits rather than encourages the development of expertise, especially in a context where immediate, measurable results are required.

Whereas the amount of legislation and guidance has massively increased, many structures designed to support schools have fragmented. While LEAs were often frustrating and bureaucratic, their demise has had serious consequences for primary schools, because most are too small to have the necessary specialism and advice. In other professions, from medicine to law, accounting to engineering, there is a long period after qualification akin to an apprenticeship where people are still learning. Yet, in teaching, especially in primary schools, there is too often no expectation of, or coherent structure for, sustained professional learning.

As a teacher and headteacher, I relied mainly on short courses and a very sketchy knowledge of Piaget and Vygotsky. Students – both in initial teacher education and at masters' level – engage with research far more than I did at comparable stages of my career. However, serious engagement with research findings, as opposed to responding to data, is too often absent among those teaching in schools, in part because of the pressure to meet requirements in terms of attainment. The lack of a solid research basis for pedagogy has made the profession vulnerable to political interference, affecting primary schools especially because this opens the door to simplistic, but inappropriate, models of how to teach young children.

The importance of primary education continues to be downplayed, with primary schools' role often seen as mainly to ensure that children are 'secondary-ready'. This reflects a lack of vision among policy makers and politicians of primary education being about much more measurable outcomes in literacy and numeracy and what can be measured. Although primary schools are far better resourced than in the 1980s, funding is still skewed against primary schools. And initiatives such as the Strategies, and suggestions that teachers of young children do not need to be qualified – as with what came to be called 'Mum's army' in the 1990s – reflect an ongoing belief that those who teach young children do not have, or require, a similar level though different type of qualification and expertise as those teaching older ones.

Despite many improvements, the focus on Curriculum 1 and models of teaching that rely heavily on instruction mean that primary education has not escaped the legacy of the elementary school. While education has been a greater political priority, politicians seem not to have learned that top-down imposition has huge limitations. Long-term improvement requires a partnership where politicians establish the framework and trust teachers to teach and not always to be accountable for their every action. The implications are considered in the next section.

Looking to the future

Much of this chapter may seem very remarkable to those whose experience of primary schools is only in the last 20 years. However, there must be, and is, an alternative to the narrow legacy of elementary education, neither harking back uncritically to the period before 1988 nor falling into the prescription and micro-management since.

There is a growing consensus that major policy decisions must not be dependent on political short-termism. For instance, Bell (2015), previously Her Majesty's Chief Inspector and a senior civil servant, recently argued for 'trusting the frontline' and less political interference. While he was referring to science teachers, this is no less true in primary education. As Fullan (1991, p. 117) claims, 'educational change depends on what teachers do and think. It's as simple and complex as that'. But the policy context within which teachers work affects what, and how, they teach. So, there is a strong argument for a body independent of government to provide an evidence-based and long-term view of the curriculum and assessment.

It is too easy just to blame politicians and policy makers. If the profession is to avoid being open to political interference, teachers, both as a group and individually, must articulate what constitutes good primary teaching, across the curriculum, drawing on both experience and an increasing knowledge of how young children learn and how adults can enable this.

Neuroeducational research provides some promising evidence, though one must be wary of thinking that knowledge of how the brain works is easily translated into practical applications and of neuromyths such as that everyone is either a visual, auditory or kinaesthetic learner. The Teaching and Learning Research Programme (TLRP, 2006) argued for the importance of learning relationships in all phases, and Mercer (2000) and many others have highlighted the centrality of children's talk, emphasising the social and active nature of learning. Both are especially important when working with young children. Gardner (1993) and Dweck (2000) have rightly challenged simplistic notions of intelligence and fixed ability, which underlie much of the current policy. In particular, both teachers and policy makers need to take account of the evidence (see Alexander, 2010, chapter 14) that a broad, balanced and engaging curriculum leads to higher standards of attainment in the long term. The humanities and the arts must not just be an add-on when the serious work of literacy and numeracy allows. A world of constant change requires more emphasis on qualities, attributes and dispositions – in children and teachers – such as resilience, creativity and criticality and on procedural knowledge, if young children are to learn actively through experience (see Eaude, 2011, pp. 62–5) and if schools are to be genuinely inclusive.

Teachers, and children, must recapture a sense of risk, adventure, creativity and enjoyment. Expectations must be broad as well as high. Because context is so important, more flexibility and reliance on teachers' judgement is required, if learning is to be reciprocal. For instance, technology offers many opportunities, but interactive white boards can, paradoxically, lead to a transmissive style of teaching. While subject knowledge is important, the challenge for primary class teachers is to develop pedagogical content knowledge (see Shulman, 2004, p. 203) in many subject areas and a wide repertoire of pedagogies, so that links can be made across subject boundaries. This emphasises the importance of formative assessment and of primary teachers having a deep understanding of child development, and for policy to be focused more on improving teacher quality and expertise. As Hargreaves (2003, pp. 127–9) suggests, this requires a move away from individualism and towards collaboration within professional learning communities.

If such developments are to occur, policy must enable rather than make these difficult. Politicians have to recognise that they can set the framework but not try to micro-manage what happens in classrooms, either by dictat or using indirect levers. Funding is important, but even more so is a culture of less change and interference, with:

- a reduction in the current obsession with grading of schools, teachers and children;
- a revision of accountability mechanisms, to end the culture of compliance and encourage greater trust in teachers' judgement and professionalism;
- a more coherent set of structures to support schools and teachers; and
- a greater emphasis on teacher education as a continuum, with structured opportunities, especially in the years soon after qualification.

These are necessary in all phases. But, to escape the legacy of elementary education, primary education requires a clearer articulation of its aims, recognising that the standards agenda is too limiting and that we must build on improvements made in recent years while not forgetting broader lessons from the past and from research. This will be hard and may take another 40 years. We will need to be optimistic but without being naïve, 'living without illusions without being disillusioned', as Gramsci wrote, if we are to create a system of primary education to meet the broad range of young children's needs, now and for a future of constant change.

References

Alexander, R. (ed.) (2010). *Children, their World, their Education: Final report and recommendations of the Cambridge Primary Review.* Abingdon, Routledge.

Alexander, R.J. (2004). Still no pedagogy? Principle, pragmatism and compliance in primary education. *Cambridge Journal of Education*, 34 (1), 7–33.

Ball, S.J. (2003). The teacher's soul and the terrors of performativity. *Journal of Education Policy*, 18 (2), 215–28.

Barber, M. (2005). Informed Professionalism: Realising the Potential. Presentation to a conference of the Association of Teachers and Lecturers, London.

Bell, D. (2015). Science education: Trusting the Frontline, via www.reading.ac.uk/news-and-events/releases/PR618539.aspx.

Campbell, R.J. and Neill, S.R.StJ. (1994). *Primary Teachers At Work.* London, Routledge.

DfES (Department for Education and Skills) (2003). *Excellence and Enjoyment: A Strategy for Primary Schools*. Nottingham, DfES Publications.

Dweck, C.S. (2000). *Self Theories: Their role in Motivation, Personality and Development*. Philadelphia, Psychology Press.

Eaude, T. (2011). *Thinking Through Pedagogy – Primary and Early Years*. Exeter, Learning Matters.

Eaude, T. (2012). How Do Expert Primary Classteachers Really Work? A critical guide for teachers, headteachers and teacher educators. Critical Publishing: www.criticalpublishing.com.

Fullan, M. (1991). *The New Meaning of Educational Change*. London, Cassell.

Gardner, H. (1993). *Frames of Mind: The Theory of Multiple Intelligences*. London, Fontana.

Hargreaves, A. (2003). *Teaching in the Knowledge Society: Education in the Age of Insecurity*. New York, Teachers College Press.

Mercer, N. (2000). *Words and Minds – How We Use Words to Think Together*. London, Routledge.

Nias, J. (1989). *Primary Teachers Talking: A Study of Teaching as Work*. London, Routledge.

Phillips, D. and Ochs, K. (2003). Processes of Policy Borrowing in Education: Some explanatory and analytical devices. *Comparative Education*, 39 (4), 451–61.

Plowden Report (1967). Children and their Primary Schools – A Report of the Central Advisory Council for Education (England). London, HMSO.

Sawyer, R.K. (2004). Creative Teaching: Collaborative discussion as disciplined improvisation. *Educational Researcher*, 33 (2), 12–20.

Shulman, L.S. (2004). *The Wisdom of Practice – Essays on Teaching, Learning and Learning to Teach*. San Francisco, Jossey Bass.

Simon, B. (1981). Why no pedagogy in England? pp. 124–45 of Simon, B. and Taylor, W. (eds) *Education in the Eighties: The central issues*. London, Batsford.

Swann Report (1985). Education for All – Report of the Committee of Enquiry into the Education of Children from Ethnic Minority Groups. London, HMSO.

The Stationery Office (TSO) (2003). *Every Child Matters*. London, TSO.

TLRP (Teaching and Learning Research Programme) (2006). *Improving Teaching and Learning in Schools*. London, TLRP (see www.tlrp.org).

5

SECONDARY EDUCATION 1976–2015

A shire county view

Martin Roberts

1976–1988 Bedfordshire and Oxfordshire: powerful LEAs, new comprehensives, curriculum freedom

Sandy Upper School to 1980

LEAs responded to Tony Crosland's 10/65 circular at different speeds. Bedfordshire, then Conservative controlled, did not rush to reorganise. Rather it carefully husbanded its resources and introduced a three-tier system that made best use of its existing schools in a predominantly rural county. Where there were gaps in the secondary provision it built new 13–18 upper schools. One of these new schools was in Sandy on the A1. When I was appointed in 1974 as Deputy Head I was one of 11 teachers responsible for creating a new 13–18 Upper School and Community College. We started with 130 Year 9 pupils in temporary accommodation in the grounds of the old secondary modern. By 1980 we had grown to 1300 pupils and 75 staff in buildings, that had risen around us.

It was a marvellous job. My own background was highly selective – independent schools and Oxford with my first post teaching history at Leeds Grammar School – but I had become convinced, like so many of my generation, that social justice demanded the end of selective schooling. Within the framework provided by the LEA, which in the case of Bedfordshire was relaxed, we could create the kind of school we believed in.

What was that? Such a school would enable its pupils to get the best possible jobs, lead fulfilling lives and become good citizens. A new comprehensive school would do all those things better than the old selective system. In particular it would raise the aspirations of all its pupils. What did we need to be successful? A good headteacher: that we had in John Francombe, intelligent, essentially traditional in much of his thinking, strict and fair. A good staff: getting a new school started enabled us to attract some able teachers. Good discipline: strong heads of year created an effective pastoral system alongside a strict code of behaviour held in place by detentions and sometimes the cane (corporal punishment was not abolished in English state schools until 1987). A general ethos that pupils and their parents appreciated: we had replaced a small secondary modern and with our new buildings, which were open to the community in the evenings, we had no difficulty winning local support.

An appropriate curriculum: Sally Tomlinson, in her *Education in a Post-Welfare Society* (2001) describes how the new comprehensive schools approached the construction of their curricula. Some tried to maintain the old grammar school academic offer for their more able pupils and a more vocationally directed 'secondary modern' provision for the rest. Though at Sandy Upper we were building on a secondary modern base, we constructed a common curriculum for all in the Third Form (Year 9), which was based on a range of subjects, some academic, such as French, and some more practical, such as woodwork. In Years 10 and 11 we had a core of English including literature, maths and science plus options examined either through GCE O Levels or CSEs. Initially our only clearly vocational courses were RSA Secretarial Studies and CGLI courses run by our Technical Department.

We appointed heads of department on a subject basis and then allowed them considerable freedom. For support, they could look to the local LEA. For example, we found the history adviser Cynthia Cooksey excellent. She was an enthusiast for the Schools Council History Project as were we. Staff could look to other professional support through subject associations such as the ASE for science and NATE for English.

As for accountability, we measured our performance primarily through our GCE and CSE results. John used to have an annual meeting with Heads of Department. In an era before appraisal and performance management we aimed to have a professional ethos where all staff would do their best and expect to be chased by the senior team if they did not. HMI came the term after I left and gave the school's performance a thorough, supportive analysis, confidential to the staff and governors.

Central government did not impinge upon us except through two major committees of enquiry – Bullock on Language for Life and Warnock on Special Needs. Curriculum advice came from the Schools Council.

The Cherwell School, Oxford 1981–1988

The downs and ups of being an LEA school

When I told Ernest Sabben-Clare, the kindly headmaster of Leeds Grammar School (then quasi-independent with 'direct grant' status), that I intended to join the state sector, he tried to change my mind. LEA bureaucracies, he told me, suffocate good teachers. I remembered his advice in my first years in Oxfordshire as I negotiated over the telephone about staffing levels, getting leaky roofs repaired, securing new buildings and defending our exceptional if maverick RE teacher from the RE adviser who wanted to be sure that he was following the Agreed Syllabus. My first success as a new head was to get my district officer to agree to increase the school's staffing allowance for 1981–1982 from 36.2 to 36.4!

The situation in the City of Oxford in 1981 was significantly different to that of rural Bedfordshire. Oxfordshire had reorganised piecemeal in the sixties and seventies and its Conservative-controlled council had botched the reorganisation of the city by creating, on the cheap, a three-tier system with seven small to medium-sized upper schools. This was at a time when school rolls were beginning to fall and for these upper schools to be able to run viable sixth forms, their number needed to reduce by at least two or possibly three. The LEA began a consultation about which schools were to close that was to run indecisively for the next two decades, creating harmful uncertainty for its schools during that period.

Against such a background, my priority had to be increasing our pupil numbers and strengthening the sixth form. Unlike rural Bedfordshire, in Oxford parental choice was already a reality. Cherwell, with 633 pupils, was an ex-secondary modern, in inadequate buildings with a poor local reputation. It sits in the heart of North Oxford, a suburb of the city that has the highest concentration of graduates of anywhere in England, with possibly the exception of Hampstead, and in easy reach of numerous independent schools. (It also contained two among the most deprived wards in Oxfordshire.) We needed urgently to win the confidence of this well-educated and generally prosperous neighbourhood. That determined our curriculum offer: broad and balanced, including strong art, drama and music. Once results were on an upward trend and discipline secure, our roll increased steadily, which led to more frustrating discussions with the LEA. Its statistics department continued to forecast incorrectly that our roll would fall, and so our only additional accommodation came in the form of temporary classrooms. By 1990, we had 1,000 pupils, with a sixth form of 250. A third of our accommodation was in huts. I used to teach Y9 history in one of them in a gloomy corner of the site. It was too cold in winter, too hot in summer and showed wear and tear only too quickly.

To be fair to the LEA, financial restraints in the 1980s and 1990s gave it little room to manoeuvre. After a high point in 1975, education's share of government spending fell back, only rising again under New Labour. It needed a clever deal, initiated by an architect governor, involving the sale of some surplus land for undergraduate accommodation, which enabled a substantial building programme to proceed in the early 1990s.

There were, though, many compensations working for Oxfordshire. The CEO was Tim Brighouse, at an early stage in his remarkable career (see Chapter 12). He was brilliant at strengthening an esprit de corps among Oxfordshire schools. The Oxfordshire Secondary School Head Teachers Association (OSSHTA) flourished and decamped annually to Bournemouth to confer with Tim and his LEA team. Brimming with ideas, he got most of us to sign up to a joint scheme with Leicestershire, the Oxford Certificate of Educational Achievement (OCEA).

Tim realised that academic attainment was just a part of the achievements of young people and that, if an accredited recording of personal achievements could be made, such a record would both motivate less academic pupils and encourage schools to value highly extra-curricular activities. An innovator himself, Tim encouraged us to innovate.

The LEA also had a sensible self-evaluation process that encouraged staff and governors to evaluate their own performance and then discuss the evaluation with their local councillors. With my lively governors I found this a stimulating activity.

Nationally, the takeover of education by the Thatcher government was beginning. In 1982 Sir Keith Joseph had funded and supervised, not by the DES but by the newly created Manpower Services Commission (MSC), projects that would improve areas where the government considered the existing system defective. One of these was TVEI, the Technical and Vocational Education Initiative, in which LEAs competed to win MSC money. Tim Brighouse identified Oxford City as the local area most likely to benefit from TVEI. Our 1984 bid succeeded. Led by LEA officers and involving the College of Further Education and local businesses we made considerable progress collaborating to devise new vocational courses accessible to 14-year-olds in the city. In 1986, Tim engineered a year's secondment for me to plan the 16–18 phase of TVEI which I finished in 1987. Nothing came of it. In Westminster the DES and MSC had been battling for the control of education. The DES won and in 1988 proceeded with the introduction of the National Curriculum, fatally undermining TVEI nationally. So a turf war between politicians and civil servants destroyed an important and timely vocational project.

The worst year of my headship was 1985–1986 when the teachers' strikes were at their height. The claim for better pay was in many ways justified, but the tactics of the teacher associations were uncoordinated and counterproductive. The government was in no mood to negotiate, and media and public opinion grew more hostile the longer strike action lasted. I had to deal with three associations following different kinds of action while minimising the harm to the pupils. Each day I had to decide how many classes could take place, how could adequate supervision be organised at break and lunchtime and how to keep hard-pressed parents informed about what was going on. The harm done was great and lasting. Many teachers who had worked to rule during the strikes refused to resume the extra-curricular activities that formerly they had led. For example, Drama at Cherwell, which had previously been brilliant, was not to recover for a decade. By the Teachers Pay and Conditions Act of 1987, Kenneth Baker, who had succeeded Sir Keith Joseph as Secretary of State, abolished the previous pay negotiating procedures and put in their place an advisory Pay Review Board. Teachers now had to work 1,265 hours per year at the direction of the headteacher, a ruling that led to endless discussions about what should be within 'directed time'. These strikes greatly weakened the teacher associations and strengthened the government's conviction that teachers needed policing.

Revolution, the Education Reform Act (ERA) of 1988 and its aftermath: powerful central government, weakened LEAs, more autonomy for schools

Then in 1988 came the Education Reform Act. Insofar as it affected secondary schools like Cherwell, its main elements were the National Curriculum, open enrolment giving greater parental choice of school, the opportunity to create schools independent of the LEA (Grant Maintained schools) and Local Management of School (LMS), which required LEAs to delegate a substantial part of their education funds to schools on a per capita basis, giving heads, with their governors, new powers to manage the school's budget.

Seen as a headteacher 1988–2002

Though I had a keen interest in politics and education policy in particular, I somehow missed the changing mood in Westminster. I had read the Black Papers and the headlines about William Tyndale but thought them right-wing sensationalism. I do not remember the Ruskin speech, or being upset by the abolition of the Schools Council, or realising the political novelty of TVEI. Substantial extra funding was then more than acceptable, whatever the source. So when the outlines of ERA appeared in the Conservative manifesto for the 1987 election, which Mrs Thatcher won with an increased majority, I was amazed how radical it was. It transformed my role as a headteacher. By and large I had gained promotion because of my interest in creating effective curricula. ERA took that curriculum responsibility away and instead made budget management and marketing the school my prime responsibility. The shift of funding through LMS inevitably altered the relationship between schools and the LEA, substantially weakening the latter.

In theory, I supported a National Curriculum, but, because it was implemented top-down and driven by distrust of teachers, its introduction was needlessly controversial and chaotic. The content of three 'core' subjects and seven 'foundation' subjects had to be defined as did ten levels of performance. Ringbinders of 'interim' then 'final' reports of the subject working groups piled up on my desk. Secretaries of State came and went in quick succession – Baker, Macgregor, Clarke, Patten. In 1993, teachers boycotted the new Key Stage 3 tests. The original NC plan was too detailed and had to be slimmed down considerably. During these years of chaotic change I had to keep bewildered and often angry staff teaching their existing courses well. Then once decisions were made centrally about the new courses and the timetable for their introduction I had to ensure that they were introduced smoothly.

History in the National Curriculum: a case study

Of the NC subjects, history caused the most controversy in which I became involved, as in 1988 I was Chair of the Secondary Committee of the Historical Association (HA). The right wing of the Conservative Party disliked much of the history being taught in schools. It particularly disliked the influential Schools Council History Project (SCHP), which built its course on the methodology of history including empathy (the skill of getting inside the culture and minds of people in a particular period). The Conservative Right thought SCHP too short on facts, especially on British history, and too long on skills, particularly empathy. Backed by much of the national press it declared war on trendy history teachers who spent too much time on soft skills and not enough on the great achievements of Britons over the centuries. English teachers faced a similar challenge from the Conservative Right, who wanted the canon of great English literature to be the essence of the NC English.

A dilemma we faced at the HA was that, unlike any European country other than Albania, history in England was not compulsory to 16. We regarded the subject as central to any serious understanding of the world in which young people were growing up and had as our priority safeguarding its new foundation subject status. Professor Ralph Davis, President of the HA, and I co-authored a draft core curriculum that included 50 per cent British history, which might prove helpful to those empowered to create NC history. We had underestimated how strongly many of our colleagues felt about any prescription in general and prescription by a Tory government in particular and met considerable criticism. Baker then set up a Working Group, chaired by a member of the landed gentry, Commander Saunders-Watson. In the circumstances it did a brilliant job, managing to combine enough British history with enough of the elements of the SCHP. Mrs Thatcher hated it, but after considerable debate, including in the media, it was finally agreed. Professor Davis and I then did our best to rally history teachers behind the Working Group. However, our efforts were in vain. Sir Ron Dearing, called in to sort out the emerging unworkability of the original overcrowded Baker National Curriculum, decided that history, geography, art and music should become optional at 14. Another Working Group had to rewrite the original 11–16 versions to fit the 11–14 age range.

This episode demonstrated a number of things – the lack of a coherent philosophy underpinning the National Curriculum; the dangers of partisan politicians interfering with curricular details; the malfunctioning of the Department for Education; the low esteem in which teachers were held by the Conservative administration; the role of the press unhelpfully simplifying and sensationalising complex issues, for example the teaching of varying historical interpretations; and the time, energy and money wasted by political in-fighting.

It was all to happen again 25 years later when the Secretary of State, Michael Gove, an enthusiastic amateur historian (he was an English graduate), decided to write the review of National Curriculum history in 2013. It was so idiosyncratic and unworkable that some of us thought that he and friends had put it together one evening aided by an excellent bottle of whisky. Along with 20 others I was summoned to Westminster to a meeting chaired by Gove himself and asked to come up with something workable. This a number of us did. Our version seemed acceptable to history teachers who had been outraged by the original Goveian version. Our revision was not that different to the one Professor Davis and I drafted in 1988.

Parental choice, GM schools and LMS

Parental choice was already active in Oxford, but the open enrolment clauses in ERA intensified it. By 1988 Cherwell was already over-subscribed, but that over-subscription increased. The correlation between a school's popularity and the desirability of its location became evermore obvious.

No secondary schools in Oxfordshire went GM. I think that this was largely due to the Brighouse factor, though Tim had left by then and was on his way to Birmingham. There was a sense of loyalty to Oxfordshire and the belief that local democracy was worth preserving.

I found LMS liberating if initially terrifying, the financial responsibility of the governors and myself now being measured in millions of pounds rather than thousands. The ability to appoint additional staff when needed was the crucial benefit plus being able to redecorate and make minor improvements to the premises. Once we had LMS I could see no reason to leave the LEA.

Tests, targets and league tables

By 1993, when the tumult of ERA had subsided, I had been in post for 12 years. Parents seemed happy with the way the school had progressed, and I was disinclined to allow national politicians to blow us off course. Our governors agreed. They were broadly left of centre – my Chair of Governors was a former educational journalist. We came to live with the publication of each year's exam results, which the local press immediately turned into league tables. Of 36 Oxfordshire schools we were usually sixth or seventh at GCSE and first or second at A Level. As long as we stayed close to these positions I avoided pressurising the staff to give greater emphasis to improving examination performance *per se* rather than teach in a stimulating way. Concentrating on exam grades at all costs leads to a Gradgrind, deadening, essentially anti-educational culture. I had the same attitude to externally set targets. On the whole we were slowly improving on most measures, as a consequence of internal policies that were shared by governors and most staff. When appraisal and performance management became a national requirement, I worked with staff to find a 'modus operandi' with which they were comfortable. Nowadays, Ofsted would doubtless class me as complacent and insufficiently directive.

Specialist schools

One effect of the government's many interventions in the curriculum and the assessment was to dissuade schools from innovating themselves but to get involved in government projects that had funds attached. Of the many initiatives pouring out of Whitehall the major one we took on was to become a specialist school, not because we saw any merit in the specialism concept, but funding continued so tight in the 1990s we needed the linked funds. We opted for the science specialism since it would mean the minimum alteration to our curriculum. In due course we succeeded. It was during the application that I became aware of the 'gaming' schools, which were now having to play to hit the targets set out in their application. We had an external consultant advising us. I commented that the GCSE improvement targets looked demanding. He advised me not to worry but to change from our traditional courses to the new Applied GCSEs, which were easier. When I indicated that such a change would not be in our pupils' interest, 'then you will have problems' was the gist of his comment. With the proliferation of new GCSEs and vocational courses, 'equivalences' between courses became a live issue about which Whitehall found consistency difficult. As for the specialist initiative, the Coalition government killed it in 2010. As an approach to secondary education it had won only a few adherents among teachers and parents.

Ofsted

As with the National Curriculum, I thought that the introduction of a reformed national inspection system was desirable. Taxpayers paid for state schools, which should therefore be accountable. I assumed that the previous HMI system, which took schools as it found them and was respected for its thoroughness and quality of its advice but did not inspect frequently enough, would be streamlined but visit schools more often. What emerged was very different, driven by the Conservative belief that teachers needed policing. Schools would be inspected every four years by teams of private inspectors supervised by reformed HMIs. Ofsted's Chief Inspector became a major public figure. Two, notably Chris Woodhead and Michael Wilshaw, gained reputations as scourges of weak teachers and schools. Cherwell experienced two inspections before I retired in 2002. The first in 1993 to my surprise was a team from the LEA led by an adviser I knew well. It was a tame affair but not unhelpful. The second, which came in 1999, was very different. In the intervening years Ofsted had become more number-crunching and the 1999 team arrived with some inaccurate data that indicated that the school was going rapidly downhill. Its information omitted the existence of two units in the school, one for autistic pupils and another for the visually impaired. We had not helped our cause by ignoring the NC regulation to make technology and MFL compulsory to 16. I failed to achieve any rapport with a humourless Lead Inspector and was only able to turn the inspection round by arranging a lunch half-way through the inspection for him and some of my best-informed governors. Eventually we emerged as a good school with some outstanding features, which in the circumstances was a relief. I was angered though, not only by the team coming misinformed, but by how disruptive it was. Staff had put so much into the late January inspection that it was not until March that the school was back to normal.

New Labour and 'education, education, education'

My immediate reaction to Tony Blair's election in 1997 was that a new era had dawned. Disillusion followed swiftly. What Blair meant by education was an intensely focused enterprise, directed from Whitehall, which would produce pupils trained to enable Britain to compete successfully in the international struggle for economic competitiveness. As Michael Barber reiterated, there needed to be a 'step change' in the culture of most schools. School leaders needed to concentrate 'relentlessly' on school improvement as measured by exam results in order to achieve 'world class' standards. Target-setting and Ofsted were the major agent's to achieve this step change. The DfE and Ofsted number-crunched more remorselessly. Lip service was paid to other vital elements of schooling like creativity and ethics, but they were peripheral since their outcomes were qualitative and immeasurable. The stress on international performance was not new to Labour. When first I became a headteacher, we were found wanting in comparison with Japan, then it was Germany and later, thanks to PISA and TIMMS, with South Korea and Shanghai.

The reorganisation of the three-tier to a two-tier system in Oxford

My last years were spent working with the LEA to replace the 9–13 Middle Schools. It was a difficult exercise as some of the Middle Schools were much loved, especially the one immediately across the road that Cherwell was to absorb, and only successful because of a determined CEO, Graham Badman. Hardly anyone now doubts that it was a vital step to take in the interests of future generations, but I do wonder now, as all the Oxford secondary schools and some of the primaries are academies, how such a desirable city-wide reorganisation could ever occur.

Looking from outside 2002–2015

In 2002, I helped establish a new Prince of Wales charity, the Prince's Teaching Institute (PTI), which has given me a new perspective on recent changes in thinking at national level about curriculum design. PTI organises subject-centred Continuous Professional Development (CPD) for state school teachers. It first ran annual residentials for teachers of English literature and history, then, because of teacher demand, added maths, science, geography, art, music and MFL. We now have a project-based scheme known as the Schools Programme, annual headteachers conferences and a programme for beginning teachers, which has expanded over three years from 150 to 700 participants. Nationally, one secondary school in five now takes part in PTI activities. Research indicates that good teachers must be subject experts and subjects must be central to any secondary school curriculum. Consequently, we link our university experts to excellent experienced teachers who lead workshops on key topics. From the start our courses have been designed by teachers for teachers. Happily independent, we concentrate on what constitutes inspiring subject teaching and avoid getting embroiled in immediate concerns like how to do well at Ofsted. Our teachers tell us that we are filling a CPD vacuum, as most other CPD concentrates on generic school improvement, getting better exam grades or preparation for Ofsted.

What kept me involved in PTI activities was a growing realisation that, among university-based educationists and within the DfE of New Labour, subjects were regarded as obsolete. What really mattered were transferable skills like the 'competences' of the RSA Opening Minds project and Information Technology, which should make knowledge acquisition an individual web-based exercise. The teacher should stop being 'the sage on the stage rather the guide on the side'. I have been strongly influenced by Michael Young's *Bringing Knowledge Back In* (2009), which argues that the central function of all schools is to pass on powerful subject-based knowledge to all pupils. If only elite schools offer well-taught subjects to their pupils, and the less advantaged take the skills and competences route, a new bipartite school system will emerge with the life chances of pupils being directly affected. Powerful subject knowledge for all is essential for social justice.

Obviously, the impressions I have gained from 13 years of PTI conferences are anecdotal, stemming from conversations I have had with hundreds of teachers. The first is that a succession of Westminster initiatives has left teachers reeling. Whatever Michael Gove's virtues, his whirlwind approach to policy making without regard for teacher opinion took ministerial interference in the details of education policy to a new extreme. The second is that Ofsted has for most teachers become an ogre, distorting the activities of too many schools. Many headteachers are obsessed with the extraordinary amount of data now available to them through the statistical tool RAISEonline, which is inevitably quantitative rather than qualitative. Another obsession is how to get into the 'outstanding' category and, once there, stay there. Third an increasing number of teachers are losing confidence in the examination system, especially GCSE. So detailed are the specifications and the mark schemes that desiccated 'teaching to the test' is too often the norm. Warwick Mansell's brilliant *Education by Numbers, the Tyranny of Testing* (2007) confirms this depressing trend. A fourth is that many schools have allowed the DfE to do their curriculum thinking for them. Perhaps most serious of all, government busyness militates against teachers being able to think about what should be their priorities – for their pupils, the extent to which their school best meets the needs of their communities, and innovation. Fifth and last, for a variety of reasons, headteachers are increasingly reluctant to allow teachers time out of school for any CPD that is not directly linked to gaining better exam grades or impressing Ofsted.

As a way out of the present turmoil, the idea of a Royal College of Teaching has emerged from PTI discussions. Over the last two years, Chris Pope, Co-Director of PTI, has worked hard and skilfully to persuade the major teacher organisations that such a college, the immediate responsibilities of which should be CPD and ITT, is well worth considering seriously.

Reflections

Great improvements have occurred in these four decades. One of the most important has been the integration of young people with special needs, their greater opportunities and the greater tolerance of other pupils. The advances made by women both at school and as teachers have been remarkable. At Cherwell, only physics and technology remained male-dominated by the time I retired. In 1981 there were only a handful of female headteachers in Oxfordshire, mainly heads of girls' only schools. Now there are more women heads than men. The quality of classroom management in most schools is much better, partly because of changes in ITT but also the greater direct monitoring of individual teachers by Senior Leadership Teams. There has also been a considerable increase in the number of pupils going on to university and FE.

These changes, however, have been evolutionary rather than revolutionary. The revolution that is the subject of this book has been in the comparatively sudden takeover by central government of control of educational policy making between 1988 and 1993 and its ramifications.

There have been benefits. We needed a national curriculum and now have one, though why it is not required of all the schools in the land is a mystery to me. We needed a national system of inspection. We now have one of the strictest in Europe that, whatever its faults, provides parents with useful comparative information about all the state schools in their locality. We have fewer failing schools. Exam results have generally improved, but to what extent is a matter of fierce debate. Education is a political priority and the Secretary of State for Education a senior figure in the Cabinet. Coverage of education in the media is much more extensive. Consequently, more parents and their pupils know that education matters. Teachers' pay and working environments are better.

Harm, however, has been done. Politicians have proved both partisan and inconsistent. Inconsistency is demoralising to teachers and a waste of money. I could cover pages with examples of initiatives that have come and gone since 1988. Here are some of the most grievous. In 1988 Professor Higgenson reported on A Levels. He had achieved a professional consensus that the country needed more and leaner A Levels. Mrs Thatcher vetoed it. For her the existing A Levels were 'the gold standard' of the English system. In 2004 Mike Tomlinson, again with the backing of key professionals, recommended a radical reform of 14–19 with an overarching diploma that would cover both academic and vocational subjects. Tony Blair, anxious about a potentially hostile national media, would have none of it. We have seen how TVEI came and went and how specialist schools lasted little more than a decade. Twenty years later came the Advanced Diplomas, which Ken Boston, head of the Qualifications and Curriculum Authority (QCA) described as the most important educational reform in Western Europe since 1945. The planners were over-ambitious and out of touch with school and college realities. The initiative was already in trouble by 2008 and cancelled by the Coalition government in 2010. 'Connexions', launched with a fanfare in 2000, was intended to transform the careers advice for young people. It was flawed from the start as its designers were never clear whether it should be a universal or targeted service. I represented the Oxfordshire headteachers at fruitless meetings when Oxfordshire, Buckinghamshire and Milton Keynes attempted to get the new service going. Again, over the years, the initiative withered. The Learning and Skills Council was set up in 2001 to give the existing 16-plus system a good shake-up. New headquarters were found in Coventry. Nine years later it was disbanded.

The big issue is teacher autonomy. My main responsibility as a headteacher was to recruit the best quality teachers I could find and then give them considerable freedom. I only interfered when I thought things were going wrong. The more professional freedom teachers have, both in relation to their pupils and assisting in the direction their school is travelling, more often than not their pupils will benefit. But what limits should governments place on that freedom? In 1976 these limits were too weak. In 2015, because of the revolution in government controls described above, they are too strong, suffocating inspiration, initiative and innovation.

Since 1988, the politicians have distrusted teachers. So many mistakes could have been avoided if politicians and teachers could have achieved a workable partnership. However, neo-liberals advising Mrs Thatcher maintained that the professions were a self-serving cartel that prevented the market bringing progress. Tony Blair remained suspicious, if in a more pragmatic way. Most politicians thought that they knew enough about education from their own and their families' experience that they would be intelligent policy makers. The increasing interaction of Westminster politics and the 24/7 media (see Chapter 15) encouraged them, thinking frequently about the next election, to dream up some headline-grabbing initiative, the serious sustained viability of which was not an immediate consideration. By being told what to do for nearly two decades, teachers have been de-professionalised. They have not, however, helped their own cause. For decades four teacher unions and two separate headteacher associations have competed for membership, and their apparent readiness to prioritise their members' pay and conditions over pupil welfare has contributed to politicians' distrust.

What then is to be done?

Politicians must step back and trust teachers more.

Responsibility for curriculum and assessment should pass to a genuinely independent body in which the government should have representation and which should regularly review the NC and public examinations every ten years or so. Such a body should encourage innovation.

Ofsted should cease inspecting most schools. Rather it should concentrate on those schools clearly struggling. Other schools should self-evaluate regularly using their own criteria. Ofsted should monitor those self-evaluations.

A Royal College of Teaching should take responsibility for teaching standards and the development of both CPD and ITT. Once it has established its credibility it should also take national responsibility for monitoring performance management in schools.

The really difficult issue is how to revive local democratic involvement in education. The sustained attack by both the Conservative and Labour parties has virtually destroyed LEAs. Appointed regional commissars are no answer. With the present interest in 'localism' and the delegation of Westminster powers to cities or regions, a Committee of Enquiry should consider how to create new forms of local government of education.

References

Mansell, W., 2007, *Education by Numbers*, London: Politico's.

Tomlinson, S., 2001, *Education in a post-welfare society*, Buckingham: Open University Press.

Young, M.F.D., 2009, *Bringing Knowledge Back In*, London: Routledge.

Further reading

I found these books particularly helpful in writing this chapter and when reflecting more widely on contemporary issues in education:

Ken Jones: *Education in Britain*, Polity (2003)

Arthur Marwick: *British Society since 1945*, Penguin (2003)

Robert Phillips: *History Teaching, Nationhood and the State*, Cassell (1998)

Alison Wolf: *Does Education Matter*, Penguin (2002)

6

A VIEW FROM THE ISLAND

A very personal story

Kenny Frederick

Preparing for headship

I could never be described as a careerist as I spent the first 16 years of my working life working in two schools. I can't help but get emotionally attached to a school and have never been good at flitting from school to school. Even after 16 years I was not particularly ambitious and was enjoying my role as Head of House in a school in Haringey. However, I decided to apply for deputy headship after being told by a senior manager, during a heated argument, that I would never be a senior leader because I was too emotional. This gave me the impetus to move on. Subsequently I moved to become Deputy Head in a girl's school in Hackney in January 1990. A major part of my role was working with the business community and the work-related curriculum. One of the important initiatives at the time was Compact, which was a partnership between business and schools, and a lot of work was done to make sure students were ready for the world of work. Another responsibility was preparing the school for Investors in People (IIP) accreditation, which helped me to learn more about leading and managing people, who are our greatest resource. When I did move on to headship, I used the IIP framework to help me plan my strategy for making the most of our human resources.

About two years into my role as Deputy Head, I realised that I needed to keep my options open and, therefore, needed to learn more about leading schools. Despite my earlier reticence, I acknowledged that I did want to become a headteacher at some point in the future. Working alongside a headteacher who could be (putting it mildly) described as 'autocratic' helped me to make up my mind. I completed my Masters degree at East London University (part-time over two years) in Educational Leadership, where I discovered Tim Brighouse and lots of other education academics, who helped me develop my own vision for a school I would lead (see Chapter 12). Tim's writing was practical and real, and his appreciation for the people he worked with shone through. In addition, I also did a number of leadership courses in preparation for senior leadership, which I funded myself and often completed during the weekends and always in my own time.

I was given little or no encouragement from my headteacher at the time, who started to see me as a bit of a threat and was cross that I had the cheek to think I could put myself on to the same level as she. My life was made even more difficult from that point. After four years in post I decided that I needed to start the application process to get out before I was pushed out! I was successful in securing the headship of George Green's School on the Isle of Dogs in Tower Hamlets in April 1996. I was 43 years old with around 22 years' experience in schools. I was delighted but somewhat daunted at the prospect of becoming a headteacher.

Prior to my appointment as Principal of George Green's School I had been seconded to a boys' school in Hammersmith and Fulham for about six months. This was a school in trouble when the new headteacher had arrived and his one deputy had had a heart attack and his partner who was on the Senior Leadership Team (SLT) was also on long-term absence. An imminent Ofsted visit was expected, and most of the teachers were supply staff. This was swift learning ground for me but it meant that I had little time to do my homework in terms of schools I was applying for. If I had done so, I might have decided against applying for George Green's. Looking back now I am thankful I didn't, as ignorance is often a good thing. I had always worked in the inner city and assumed that the Isle of Dogs would be much like Hackney and Haringey. This it most certainly was not! It was unique.

Tower Hamlets – the Isle of Dogs

What I had not realised upon appointment in 1996 was that the first BNP (British National Party) counsellor to ever be elected in England was in November 1993 on the Isle of Dogs. He only lasted a couple of months before he was ousted and replaced. However, the people who had elected him were still there when I arrived in April 1996. The discontent of the white population was blamed on the housing policy of Tower Hamlets Council who placed a large number of the incoming Bangladeshi population on the Isle of Dogs. This caused resentment locally and resulted in a very divided community. This spilled into the school, where many students and their parents felt it was appropriate to express overt racist comments and attitudes. It was a difficult time and took many years to overcome and to change attitudes. Bringing the community together so that we could get on with the business of teaching and learning in a safe environment took a great deal of resilience on my part and on the part of my staff.

Therefore, the diverse ethnic background to the school was a crucial consideration in the policies that needed to be adopted and that, as the Principal, I pursued. According to the UK government's Indices of Multiple Deprivation, Tower Hamlets in 2006 ranked as the most deprived local authority in the country, with high levels of unemployment, poverty and poor health. Fifty per cent of the residents were from the black and minority ethnic communities (33 per cent Bangladeshi). Almost 100 languages were spoken locally. The school of about 1,200 boys and girls aged 11–19 reflected that ethnic and linguistic mix. About half the pupils were white (British mainly, but also Irish and other), a third Asian (mainly Bangladeshi), around 20 per cent Chinese, Afro-Caribbean, Somali and other African background. About one in sixty pupils arrived at the school with little or no spoken English. Over 50 per cent of the pupils were eligible for free school meals – more than three times the national average (14 per cent) for secondary schools.

Therefore, one of my first jobs as Principal was to work with staff, pupils and parents to develop our Equal Opportunities Policy and our motto 'All different. All equal'. Getting the community to understand that equal opportunities is not about treating everybody the same but is about meeting individual needs. This helped me counteract the accusations that I was treating different children 'differently', for instance by providing EAL pupils with additional help with their English. This policy remained firm and informed every other policy we developed over the year and it eventually became ingrained into the hearts and minds of our pupils. However, this aspect of our work took many years.

Dealing with the racial tension

The horrors of 9/11 in New York in September 2001 increased racial tensions further, and we had a particularly difficult situation in November 2001 only a few months after the tragic events unfolded. Islamophobia was rife, and *The Guardian* (20 November 2001) described one of the most difficult situations we went through when a group of parents leafleted the island to gather support on a Sunday evening following a fight at the school gates on the previous Friday afternoon. Waiting for this group to arrive was frightening but we had no option but to let them in and let them vent their anger. I was the focus of this anger but I had no opportunity to speak calmly to them or tell them what the school was doing to resolve the racial tensions. They screamed at me for about 30 minutes and left. The local newspaper described the school to be in a state of anarchy – which it certainly was not. While this was a horrible experience, it only strengthened my resolve to hang on in there and sort it out!

During this time, when racial tensions were at their highest, we were (mostly) able to keep a lid on the situation while pupils were in school, but we began to hate unstructured time and home time. My staff were having to lead different groups of pupils home at the end of the day (to avoid fighting in the street and local park). Having very narrow corridors, one minor scuffle during lesson changeover would polarise the school along racial lines and would spread out into the streets at the end of the day. Needless to say we were doing lots of work in our curriculum to address the issues at the same time. However, it was very exhausting and was not conducive to good learning. At this time one of our Bengali TAs (teaching assistants), who had by his own admission been a local 'youth' in his time, came up with the idea of taking our 'most extreme' pupils to Belfast to see what a divided community looked and felt like. After a short discussion with my senior team we decided to go with the idea. We had to do something and do it quickly!

It was agreed we would take 40 pupils and these should be those with leadership qualities and the capacity to change their views. We spent time on choosing this cohort and were so surprised that so many wanted to go. Most saw it as a free trip abroad and a week out of school! Once the group was chosen we looked at the staff who would accompany them and work with them for the week. Without a doubt I sent my most talented and experienced teachers and support staff who had good relationships with the pupils. It was a huge risk, and I had nightmares worrying about what might happen on the journey or when they were in Ireland.

The TA, whose idea it all was, sorted out the details of the trip, and they went to the 'Share Centre' in Fermanagh where they lived in 'Big Brother' style houses in mixed groups and where they had to cook for each other and get to know each other properly. My expert staff got them to confront their own racism and ingrained prejudices and to understand what had been going on. They also went to see the 'peace wall' and were shocked to see a city divided by a physical wall. However, the greatest change came after our pupils had the opportunity to meet other students, both Catholic and Protestant, and to spend time with them. Our pupils found it hard to understand what the argument was all about – they are all white and all Christian, what are they fighting about? After a number of history lessons and discussions with these youngsters, our pupils were shocked that many of those they met (not all by any means) were happy with the status quo and did not want to change. They liked things as they were.

When our pupils returned to school they formed the 'Unity Cru' and were led by my TA who went on to become a community manager in later years. They worked together as a mixed group of 40 individuals who were able to influence the whole school population. They learned to mediate and negotiate and to make presentations at assembly and elsewhere, but most of all it was the work they did with 'the youngers' in the playground that made the biggest difference in changing the culture of the school. When small incidents were in danger of exploding into bigger ones, the Unity Cru were there to intervene. We took different groups back to Northern Ireland for a number of years to reinforce the work that had been done there and, as the racial tensions ceased and gang warfare (!) blossomed to replace them, we were able to do useful work on restorative justice that helped to diffuse situations on the island.

The trip to Belfast was an extreme and expensive answer to a very difficult problem. It was just one of the many risks I took during my time as Principal. It was a risk well worth taking and taught me that procrastination is no use to anybody. I had to take a decision and take it quickly. I did not have the money to pay for the first visit but we went anyway and I raised the money from sponsorship afterwards. The trip to Belfast was used as a case study and was written about often. There was a lot of interest in our story, which is fine after the event, but not while you are in the middle of it!

Responding to government initiatives

During my 17 years as Principal, risk taking and change were constant. Much of this change was a result of government initiatives, but many of the changes were of our own making. Some were in response to what was happening to us (see above) and others were about school improvement. Schools, especially those in challenging circumstances like mine, cannot stand still and need to keep moving forward. In fact we often felt like we were frantically treading water, just to keep our heads above it. While this was exhausting it was also very exciting and created a dynamic can-do culture where there was no problem we could not find a solution to. This is the reason why I have always worked in the inner city in schools on the 'edge'. I am naturally positive and optimistic, which certainly helped me to become very resilient and allowed me to cope well with the stress that comes with the job. Furthermore, I surrounded myself with senior staff and teachers who had a similar attitude.

Changes imposed by the Labour government in their 12 years in power (1998–2010) – (see Chapter 1, p. 16) were largely positive and were not 'new' in the sense that we were not being asked to do very different or very difficult things. Many of these policies were designed to help schools share good practice and were an attempt to develop a more coherent approach to school improvement. I made sure I got involved in various advisory and focus groups and encouraged my staff to do the same. This way we felt we could inform policy change and be done 'with' rather than be done 'to'. This was and is an important fact to consider if we want schools and teachers to embrace change. Imposing changes on schools does not work.

The numerous changes to the Ofsted framework took up a lot of time and energy and have, I believe, stopped many schools taking risks and developing a curriculum to suit the needs of their students. The anxiety about the next Ofsted inspection is never far away. This was particularly true when we were judged as NTI (Needs to Improve) category in September 2008 when our results dropped unexpectedly.

When I first took over as Principal, I found myself in a financial deficit situation. I'd had very little experience of dealing with a budget as my previous head had kept that knowledge to herself. Thankfully, I had governors who had a great deal of expertise and experience in managing finances. We went immediately to asking for voluntary redundancies and found that we were able to get rid of the deficit without too much pain. However, funds were short, and I found myself along with a couple of other colleagues teaching RE (without any previous experience or expertise), as we could not afford to employ a new RE teacher.

As a new head, I discovered that the relationship between my predecessor and senior team and the rest of the staff had been a difficult one. The Ofsted inspection in 1993 (one of the first inspections in England) described 'an atmosphere of distrust between senior leadership and staff'. The situation had gotten so difficult the headteacher had refused to write personal references and instead provided a bland document saying exactly what individuals had done, without any comment about the quality of their work. I, of course, had no knowledge of this and I naïvely expected staff to follow my lead and work alongside me. Thankfully they did.

1997: changes under Labour

There was much joy when Labour won the general election in 1997 and 'Education, education, education' was the strapline. Funding increased, and there were many new initiatives. Most of my headship (12 years of it) was under a Labour government and I certainly think we benefited from this. Tower Hamlets was and still is one of the poorest boroughs in England, and, therefore, our schools received almost 60 per cent more resource per pupil than the national average, and we had higher levels of resourcing than almost all other London boroughs. This did not always go down well with heads in other boroughs and counties and I can understand their resentment. However, this high level of funding certainly contributed to the success of the borough, making it one of the most successful in the country. It allowed us to increase the number of teachers and support staff and to provide additional resources for our students.

The Excellence in Cities (EIC) initiative was introduced in March 1999 with the aim of raising standards and promoting inclusion in the inner cities (see Chapter 1, p. 15). We were delighted to embrace this initiative, especially as it was so well funded. The requirements of EIC were clear but not prescriptive, and we were able to decide exactly how we would introduce and shape the different strands into our own schools. This was a challenge we welcomed because we felt it would help us to improve the quality of our school. There were four main strands of EIC. These included:

- Learning mentors
- Learning support units (LSUs)
- Provision for gifted and talented pupils
- City Learning Centre and Education Action Zones

We had already started adding to our workforce and led the way as far as workforce reforms went. Most of these new employees were working as Learning Support Assistants (LSAs), back office staff and finally Learning Mentors. Most of these came from the local community, which really helped to bridge the gap between the school and the community. Learning Mentors proved to be valuable in helping us support some of our most vulnerable children of whom we had many.

The development of the new LSU caused much discussion in our school, and many urban myths spread across the staff, students and parents. 'Swimming with dolphins' was quoted many times and the notion that children were being rewarded for being naughty! However, as with most things, we got over that hurdle and the LSU proved to be very successful in supporting some of our most difficult and hard-to-teach students. The Behaviour Improvement strategy arrived around the same time, and I received a call one day from the private office of Stephen Twigg,

Minister for Schools (2004–2005), to see if they could visit for the day and see how we managed behaviour! Of course we agreed to this as we felt that civil servants who were developing behaviour policy ought to see what we were dealing with on a daily basis.

The focus on Gifted and Talented pupils made us think more about this group who had probably been neglected up to now. We could not live with the title Gifted and Talented as it was so difficult to come up with a clear definition of what this meant. Therefore, we settled on More Able and Talented and set about developing a support programme to develop and challenge this group. This involved tracking this group carefully, providing enrichment activities and individual mentoring. What it did not involve was a concentration on teaching. When I look back now and still see the same model in many schools I visit, I am sorry that we did not focus more specifically on strategies for raising achievement in the classroom.

Putting together a bid to become a small Education Action Zone (see Chapter 1, p. 15) with our primary feeder schools on the Isle of Dogs under the EIC banner was something that was very worthwhile. We already had strong relationships with our feeder primaries and we supported each other in any way we could. However, the small Action Zone provided the structure and funding to develop a strategic action plan to work together on improving teaching and learning. We had to go through a very vigorous process in putting our bid together, and I remember a rival group of schools (who were bidding against us) being very angry when we were chosen as the successful cluster. However, the Action Zone group are still working together in a coherent way to get to grips with the many changes that they are expected to make.

The EIC programme ran alongside the Leadership Incentive Grant, of which we were quick to take advantage. I noticed an advert asking for schools interested in taking on a Trainee Head for a year as a training opportunity and could not resist the opportunity to have a free member of SLT for a year! We were lucky to have had three trainees over three years who all went on to be headteachers. They brought three different sets of eyes and added much to our school. My senior team was always welcoming and open and we subsequently went on to host many Future Leader participants in the following years. In addition, we opened up our team to a number of Associate Assistant Heads who were middle leaders, and they also brought a great deal of expertise and ideas to the table. My aim has always been to demystify headship and to encourage others to think of themselves as leaders in the future. I had never been encouraged in this way and used to believe that senior leadership was out of my league.

The Labour government introduced *Every Child Matters* (ECM) in 2004 (see Chapter 1, p. 15), which was in my opinion the most important and relevant development that I can remember. In fact I wrote my MBA thesis on the subject. The notion and reality of different organisations working together to ensure the needs of our children were ground breaking and worked very well for us. In fact it was the way we were already working but in a very informal way, where my staff had persuaded individuals from other child-centred professions to work closely with us. ECM made these partnerships more solid and provided a framework for brokering relationships and partnerships. We became a designated Extended School, which allowed us to provide a range of services for vulnerable children and their families. For instance, it was much easier to get vulnerable families to come to school for their CAMHS (Child and Adolescent Mental Health Service) appointment rather than go to the centre that was a bus ride away. We were open from 7.30 a.m. for breakfast (provided by Morgan Stanley) and provided activities and childcare (The Place to Be) until 6 p.m. After that, the school sports facilities were used by the community until 10 p.m. at night. The community team and Sports Trust (a charity set up by governors some years before and run largely by sixth formers and ex-students of George Green's) made sure that local people could hire the facilities at a low cost while the business community paid premium prices. The Sports Trust was, and still is, self-funding and is a very efficient way of organising school lettings. ECM made perfect sense to us. It brought together all strands of the school, and we were horrified when the Coalition government decided to change the name of the DCSF (Department of Children, Schools and Families) to the DfE – families were (it seemed) no longer our problem!

Youth Services

Later on (2006) we were commissioned to deliver Youth Services on the Isle of Dogs and we readily took on this role, despite the fact that it caused so much additional work. We were keen to take this on because as a school we had spent years bringing the different communities together in school only to find they went off to different parts of the island when they left school. The youth clubs were very segregated, and white and black boys went to one club, while Bengali boys went to another. Girls did not attend any youth clubs because they (and their parents) did not think they were safe. The quality of youth services was very poor and when problems occurred in the streets, as they often did, the clubs chose to close rather than work with young people to sort them out. Staff working in the Youth Service at the time were used to working in a particular way and were not used to being led and managed. This had to change, and the process was difficult. However, the outcomes were hugely successful. Clubs were no longer segregated, girls were now participating, and the number of youngsters attending youth clubs rose dramatically, meaning youths were no longer hanging around the streets causing problems. We developed and delivered a relevant curriculum, staff were well trained and well led, and youth clubs were not closed without due notice. It was another big risk that paid off.

Vocational courses

Many new vocational courses equivalent to GCSEs started in schools in around 2002 (see Chapter 1, p. 11), but this was something we never went in for. Instead we stuck to the more traditional curriculum, including every child doing a humanities subject and a language. At the time we felt that this was the right thing for our pupils, as it gave them all the opportunity to study a wide range of subjects and would enable them to move on to the pathways they chose in the future.

This was a mistake, as the traditional curriculum did not suit lots of our children, and we should have taken more risks with the curriculum. We saw schools around us embrace GNVQs (which we did not feel were of much value), and their results soared. I believe this lift in attainment gave pupils confidence and self-belief, and these schools then went on to climb up the league tables. It was our mistake not to follow suit. However, in 2008, we did revise the curriculum so that it offered more appropriate pathways for all our young people. This development was too late to save us from plummeting results in 2008, followed by a subsequent Ofsted inspection that took us into a 'requires improvement' category. A lesson learned the hard way!

Inclusion

At some point in 2002 I was invited to a meeting at the local authority to discuss piloting the *Index to Inclusion* (produced by Tony Booth and Mel Ainscow). As a school we were already well down this road, as we were working so hard to include all members of our community, including those with special needs. The borough (like many others) was keen for schools to include youngsters with physical disabilities and learning difficulties to attend mainstream schools and we were very happy to be part of that movement. The *Index to Inclusion* was a very helpful document in helping us to audit our school and to find the gaps in provision. I often recommend it to colleagues today. Although our building was totally unsuitable (on seven floors with one unreliable lift), we were designated as the 'inclusive' school in the borough. We had the will and were able to find the way of including young people with a wide range of children with additional needs. Some years later we were able to convince the DfE to fund adaptations to make movement around the school and for the provision of more disabled toilets and other facilities. We gained a reputation for inclusion and it was a reputation we were very proud of. Though the subsequent Special Needs regulations have been strongly criticised by many, including Baroness Warnock, schools and colleges across the country have developed inclusive policy and practice, while many others, who are often those lauded as examples to us all, have rejected inclusion and those children who will use lots of resources and who may not achieve the benchmark re GCSE results. Admission policies need to be more rigorously applied so that those who want to attend a mainstream school have that opportunity. However, the new SEN Code of Practice (see Chapter 1, p. 15) and new funding arrangements are making it more difficult for schools to be fully inclusive.

Concluding comments

The change of government in 2010 was not a happy time for those of us in education. Policies introduced under the Coalition were more difficult to manage and caused great anxiety. They were seen to be punitive and targeted at schools with challenging intakes and fighting against the odds. My teachers were constantly re-writing schemes of learning and finding new ways to implement new initiatives and changes to exam syllabi. Change was imposed and not based on evidence that it (whatever *it* was) worked. The worst part was not being consulted or involved. The feeling that we were being 'done to' caused a great deal of resentment. Keeping staff morale high and keeping them positive was a great challenge but was one we managed most of the time. Teachers were blamed for all the ills of society and were constantly being told they were not doing a good job. The workload increased, although we had thought this was not possible. The autonomy of head-teachers was a piece of fiction, as we had never been so tightly controlled by central government. The Local Education Authority, who had always been so supportive, lost most of their funding and subsequently most of their personnel. The Ofsted framework continued to change, and the exams criteria changed, making it more difficult for many pupils to gain the qualifications they needed to move forward.

At this point I had reached the ripe old age of 60 and decided it was time to retire and give someone else a chance to lead the school.

PART III

Higher and further education

7

EVOLUTION OF TEACHER TRAINING AND PROFESSIONAL DEVELOPMENT

Richard Pring

Introduction

The preparation and continuing professional development of teachers have been in constant evolution ever since the 1944 Education Act, that great Act of Parliament which, in the aftermath of the war, created a 'national service locally administered'. Such a national service required of the Minister to ensure, first, there were enough school places for all school-age children, and, second, there were enough teachers trained to teach them. Not for the Minister to say what should be taught or how it should be taught. And not for the Minister to say how teachers should be trained or how their continuing professional development, if any at all, should take place.

That subsequent evolution reflected the changing understandings: of the place of teacher education within a unitary system of higher education; of the place of schools and the profession in that training; of the content of the training and professional development; and of the responsibilities of government. In this last respect, we have seen the autonomy of the profession and indeed of universities increasingly eroded by political intervention.

One might see that historical evolution in terms of positive developments, arising (through public deliberations and subsequent White Papers and Acts of Parliament) from responses to perceived difficulties regarding low standards in many schools or the ideological beliefs of the teacher trainers. The name 'blob', as such an establishment has been called by some politicians, reflects a political concern about the influence of those whose ideas permeate the training of teachers, especially the social and philosophical critiques within colleges and universities. Was John Dewey, taught in our university departments of education, mainly responsible for all the problems of our schools, as I was told by a Secretary of State and a Minister of Higher Education? Much better, it is thought, that attention should be directed more effectively and efficiently to the improvement of learning as that has come to be defined from outside the teaching profession, ever since the 1988 Education Act.

In what follows, I examine that evolution more closely, drawing upon historical record and personal experience – as teacher in training, schoolteacher, teacher of students on the new BEd degree, university lecturer on professional diploma courses, professor helping to bring about the first merger between a prestigious college of education and a university, and finally Director of the Oxford University Department of Educational Studies, when after 100 years that university finally thought the study of education was worthy of a professor.

Prelude: do teachers need to be trained?

There once prevailed the Platonic idea of the sort of education in which, 'in a place set apart', the guardian class would receive a special sort of education, partly through what was taught but partly through the initiation into a particular tradition, social ethos and network. This was accessible to relatively few (what the nineteenth-century philosopher and poet Coleridge referred to as the 'clerisy') brought up, if not on gymnastics and mathematics, then at least on the classics and games. Prep school, public school and Oxbridge would provide the right kind of educational background. Indeed, this was argued to the Bryce Commission in 1895 by Herbert Warren, President of Magdalen College Oxford, when discussion was conducted on whether the University of Oxford should be concerned with the training of teachers. The student who has read Plato's *Republic* and Aristotle's *Politics and Ethics* has whatever theory is necessary for the practice of teaching. But in addition it would be helpful:

> that a young man who has passed through an English public school, more particularly if he has been . . . a prefect has had experience in keeping order and maintaining discipline. Thus the average Oxford man, more especially the classical student, ought not to require so long an additional training, either in theory or practice, as is sometimes necessary for students elsewhere.
>
> (Bryce Report, 1895, v. 257)

Indeed, this message was reiterated by Mr Raleigh of All Souls, also to the Bryce Committee, reminiscent of John Stuart Mill's inaugural address at St Andrew's, in which he argued that the university is not a place for professional education (Mill, 1867). According to Raleigh:

> It is not the office of the University to train men for teaching, or any other profession . . . his special training must be left to those who are engaged in professional work. Almost any honours man will make a good teacher, and if he has the luck to fall into the hands of a good headteacher.
>
> (Bryce Report, 1895, v. 22)

This view may seem antiquated, but it continues to hover around the corridors of power and in many schools. Training, of whatever sort, is no longer a requirement to teach in schools released from the bonds of local authorities, as well as those that remain in the private sector. It is regarded that, with the right sort of subject knowledge from the university and with the right sort of character, training is unnecessary. Ignorance of what is referred to as the 'disciplines of education' (philosophy, sociology, psychology, history) might indeed be a bonus. One might, as with Teach First, just as well go straight into school where one will be nurtured by mature teachers. The result is that there is a rejection of those developments, especially after the Robbins Report in 1963 (to be explained below), which have shaped teacher education for 50 years and through which I have been engaged with teaching and teacher education.

The question continues to be: Do the training and development of teachers need to be made *academically respectable* through the support of universities, on the one hand, and, on the other, can the academic respectability of the universities be *practically relevant*?

Academic respectability and practical relevance: a fading example

In 1964, I quit the Ministry of Education in Curzon Street, where I had been an Assistant Principal working in my final year in the newly established Curriculum Study Group, which was the forerunner of the Schools Council and which initiated a range of papers in preparation for the new Certificate of Secondary Education. The Schools Council, established in 1964, was a shrewd combination of local education authorities, and representatives from teachers (who were the majority members), HMI, community, and employers and government. The first Joint Secretary, Derek Morrell (the civil servant who in effect created the Schools Council), argued that it aimed to support and to enhance the professional aspect of teaching:

> to democratise the processes of problem-solving as we try, as best we can, to develop an educational approach appropriate to a permanent condition of change. . . . this democracy must also be locally organised, bringing together teachers, dons, administrators and others for the study of common problems, some local and others national in their implications.
>
> (Morrell, 1966)

Later in the lecture Morrell spelled out the particular nature of this partnership between teachers (at the centre, not periphery, of these deliberations) and the research interests of the universities to which the teachers might in various ways be attached – not as neighbours knocking on the door of theory but as partners in a shared enterprise.

One influential example of such a partnership was that of the Centre for Applied Research in Education at the University of East Anglia, led by Professor Lawrence Stenhouse. Its Humanities Curriculum Project was founded on Stenhouse's scholarly research into the idea and practice of 'culture', developed in schools by teachers, rigorously evaluated by the university, and supported and promoted by the Schools Council. It gave rise to the tradition of 'action research', putting teachers at the centre of research and supported by research traditions within the universities – described by John Elliott (1991), a member of the Stenhouse team, in his book *Action Research for Educational Change*. However, there were many examples of such a partnership in the development of curriculum projects – *History 13–16*, *Geography for the Young School Leaver*, *Design and Technology*, *Nuffield Sciences*, for example.

Much inspired by the ambitions of the Schools Council, I started teaching in a London comprehensive school in 1965. Nothing in my teacher training year at a London college of education prepared me for 1x. When I asked the headteacher in July for my timetable so that I could spend my vacation in preparation, I was told to come in early on the first day of Autumn term. He asked what I had studied at the university. When I replied philosophy, he said he thought so and said I was to have the slow learners – the fifth stream of a five stream comprehensive school. I struggled. But it was the Schools Council that came to my help. The Council saw the need for professional support for teachers through the partnerships established across schools and with university-based curriculum projects. Its Teachers' Centres, throughout the country, provided that support, and it was to the Centre in Highbury and Islington that I went for support, professional engagement, and introduction to relevant thinking and research.

Unfortunately the Schools Council ceased to be granted government support in 1984 and closed. The early fears held by the teachers' unions of government desire to obtain control of curriculum proved correct. Four years later there was the 1988 Educational Reform Act.

Academic respectability

The nineteenth-century training of teachers took place in training colleges run mainly by the Church of England, though a few emerged from the Catholics and Non-conformists to support their growing number of schools. But, with the extension of secondary education to all, following the 1944 Education Act, there was a need for many more training places and for a deeper, more academic preparation. No longer were they to serve elementary schools that offered a limited education for the poor. A first step was to change the name in 1960 from 'training colleges' to 'colleges of education', and to attach them to regional universities through Area Training Organisations (created in 1955 following the proposals of the 1944 McNair Report).

The aim, following the 1963 Robbins Report, was to bring the colleges within a unitary system of Higher Education, ignoring the objections from those who, believing in a restricted pool of ability, opposed such an expansion. Indeed, the judgement of Mr Raleigh (quoted above) still prevailed in many quarters: 'it is not the office of the University to train men for teaching'. The colleges would not be granted university status. But they would be either linked to universities and thereby be able to take the newly proposed BEd degree (initially a three year Ordinary Degree, then later a four year Honours) to be awarded by their respective universities, or linked to polytechnics with degree awarding powers given to the Council for National Academic Awards (CNAA), established in 1965. The Institute of Education of London University, for example, had 30 colleges under its academic wing, from as far away as Canterbury (later to become Canterbury Christ Church University). The training of teachers would be firmly within the university sector – thereby gaining 'academic respectability'.

That, however, gave rise to the need to make the study of education academically respectable. That was not easy. The university lecturer in education was, in the words of Professor Richard Peters of the University of London Institute of Education:

> so often like the distraught Freudian ego – at one moment at the mercy of the ids in the classroom, unruly little boys and girls, insatiable in their demands and beyond the control of reason; at another moment feeling the disapproving gaze of the superego in the philosophy, psychology or sociology department, whose discipline is tough, but seemingly disconnected from the world of unreason which teachers have to inhabit.[1]

It was as a result of such doubts and criticisms that attempts were made to make educational studies respectable. At a conference of the Association of Teachers in Colleges and Departments of Education in Hull in 1964, studies for the professional development of teachers were dismissed by Peters as so much undifferentiated mush. Hence began a purposeful attempt to inject an academic rigour that respectability in the eyes of the universities demanded. There was an exponential growth of theory in what were called the 'foundation disciplines' – the philosophy, sociology, psychology and history of education, and finally comparative and curriculum studies.

This I witnessed first hand in my PGCE year. On Friday afternoons the postgraduate trainees would go from their respective colleges to hear the stimulating lectures from Richard Peters in philosophy of education, Basil Bernstein in sociology of education, W.D. Wall in psychology and A.C. Beales from Kings College London in history of education. Peters' book *The Ethics of Education* (published 1965) became deservedly a textbook on BEd courses, stimulating consideration of the aims of education and of the ethical basis of what is taught in schools. He was accompanied by Paul Hirst whose influential paper on 'the seven forms of knowledge' provided a philosophical background to the study and value of curriculum subjects (Hirst, 1965).

I joined a group of aspiring philosophers and signed up to study for a part-time PhD under the University's Philosophy Board, supervised by Professor Peters. That and similar groups in the other disciplines were most important within the development of educational studies worldwide.

First, the development of the BEd required university teachers – people who could teach philosophy, sociology, psychology and history. The newly developed diploma courses at the Institute were intended to provide these. Hence, college lecturers and schoolteachers were recruited to the courses, made into philosophers (sociologists, etc) and then dispatched to the far corners of the kingdom as missionaries. A series of books was published by Routledge and Kegan Paul (RKP), whose authors were mainly from the Institute of Education. New journals were established (for example, *The British Journal of Educational Studies* and *The Journal of the Sociology of Education*). Learned societies were set up, such as the Philosophy of Education Society of Great Britain, whose *Proceedings* published the papers given at the annual conference, which took place at the Beatrice Webb House in Surrey from 1967 and subsequently at the Froebel College.

Second, however, this became a worldwide movement. Israel Scheffler at Harvard University (whose 1958 book *Philosophy of Education* included papers from Peters and Hirst) published *The Language of Education*, which analysed in detail the use of 'definitions' in education, 'educational slogans' and 'metaphors', the meaning of 'teaching'. The prevailing Oxford tradition of analytic philosophy had entered into educational thinking, and thereby attacked mercilessly the words and assumptions of, say, the Plowden Report (1967) on primary education – for example, children's 'needs', 'creativity', 'growth'. In a visit to Melbourne University in the 1970s to give the Victor Cooke Memorial Lecture, I witnessed the impact of this literature on teacher education – the almost monopoly of reading material from the philosophers (Peters, Hirst, John and Pat White, Ray Elliott, Robert Dearden) of the London Institute of Education.

The death of the college

More was required to achieve the respectability to emerge from the Robbins' ideal of a unitary system of higher education. The 1972 *James Report: Teacher Education and Training* recommended the total abolition of monotechnic teacher training courses and the merging of them into institutions with other undergraduate studies. It recommended three cycles of continuing education, namely, a two-year Diploma in Higher Education, a two-year professional training and then professional in-service provision. It was regarded as inadequate to finish teacher preparation with no more than the successful completion of initial training. However, despite these recommendations, the 1972 White Paper, *Education: a Framework for Expansion*, dismissed the DipHE and postponed the inservice proposals and thereby the hope of much needed opportunities for continuing teachers' professional development.

By 1976, of the original 151 voluntary and municipal colleges of education, five had merged with universities, 33 were locked in with polytechnics, 63 had amalgamated into 44 newly created institutes of higher and further education, and 21 were earmarked for closure. The changes in institutional provision for teacher preparation were immense: it had become a degree-based profession; it had its own professional degree (Bachelor of Education) and it had become an intrinsic part of higher education within the 'binary system' – not the unitary system envisaged by Robbins, since, except in the case of the few that had merged with universities, colleges were not funded by the University Grants Committee. However, academic autonomy was preserved through the CNAA, which oversaw academic standards in the burgeoning public sector of higher education (including the polytechnics).

But the changes to a unitary system of higher education continued apace through more mergers and through the gradual acquisition of university status. In 1978 I was appointed to Exeter University and engaged in the merger between St Luke's College of Education and the university. The new School of Education, soon to be the largest in the country outside the Institute of Education in London, remained on the St Lukes' site. It was joined there by the staffs of the now former University of Exeter's Department and Institute of Education. Ted Wragg succeeded Michael Brock (appointed as Principal of Nuffield College Oxford) as Director. The success of the new school, in integrating within it the erstwhile separate institutions and in integrating the school within the wider university, owed much to his dynamism, reputation with schools, and combination of practical know-how in the classroom with a grasp of educational theory.

Members of the St Luke's staff had been appointed to the college first and foremost because they were excellent teachers who knew their subjects, though few had higher degrees. Their profiles did not match those of Exeter University's Department and Institute of Education. How could they fit into the academically motivated ethos of a university? There were, therefore, some nervous new members of the university. But, as I wish to develop later (and even conclude), there is a danger in the disdain for 'practical knowledge' – in not seeing the importance of the practical as the basis for the theoretical, not the other way around.

For example, on the BEd primary course, students were taught mathematics by an excellent team of mathematicians for the three or four years of their BEd, and were well prepared for the classroom once they had graduated. Compare this with the present situation, following the demise of the BEd, where only about one in ten of new primary school teachers have more than grade C in GCSE mathematics, following which they have done no mathematics during the next six years prior to their PGCE qualification. It is not surprising that many young people have been ill-prepared for their study of mathematics when they enter secondary school.

A further example would be that of teaching physical education. After the war, the Principal Smeales was determined to bring fame to St Luke's and to do so by creating the best rugby team in the country. He went to Wales to recruit for the training college the best players he could persuade to become teachers, including several internationals. One benefit that the University of Exeter saw in the merger was to have a great rugby team. I have no doubt that the new School of Education produced possibly the best-trained physical education teachers in the country, though (as we were constantly told) rivalled by Loughborough.

As educational studies were made increasingly to look like other undergraduate studies, I see the demise of the professional degree for preparing teachers as a grave mistake. Physical education gradually morphed into sports science. Drama disappeared from most teacher training places. Whereas I entered teaching (even in 1x, the lowest stream in a five-form Year 1) without any knowledge of the different kinds of learning difficulty to be encountered, those who studied for the BEd at the two universities where I was employed (Goldsmiths College and Exeter University) had clear and practical introductions to them.

Students who studied at Goldsmiths College in the late 1960s recall that the BEd degree was made *academically respectable* through the support of universities and *practically relevant* through an appropriate curriculum that provided academic knowledge and hands-on experience throughout the four-year programme. A four-year programme enabled students to be academically able and practically skilled, as there was time to address all aspects in sufficient detail. There was a balance of educational studies and specialist subject teaching that was on a par with the BA or BSc course. In addition they were taught how to identify and support children with special educational needs in mainstream schools, by attending stimulating lectures, visiting institutions that specialise in specific learning needs such as epilepsy, dyslexia, autism and Down's syndrome, and by carrying out work experience at an allocated specialist centre. This was followed up by a written assessed dissertation. For example:

> We did an intense study on dealing with children with special needs. We all visited a Centre in Kent regarding epilepsy and how to deal with it. Then we had lectures on dyslexia, autism and Down's syndrome, etc. We were required to write an in-depth study with reference to special needs and were required to include work experience. I focused on Down's syndrome, another on children with polio. I spent 2 to 3 weeks as a volunteer at a Centre for children with Down's syndrome over one summer break. This type of study is not included in courses today unless doing a special course.[2]

Such rigour, depth and breadth of preparation over a four-year period are not mirrored in teacher training programmes today. Much preparation and thought was put into the BEd degree by educationalists at that time, and as a result emerging teachers felt supported and prepared for their future careers.

Over time either all colleges merged with universities (e.g. Keswick Hall with East Anglia), or joined a polytechnic, which eventually became a university (e.g. Lady Spencer Churchill and Oxford Polytechnic becoming Oxford Brooks University and later subsuming Westminster College), or evolved slowly into universities (e.g. King Alfred's College becoming the University of Winchester), or simply went out of business. But problems remained.

Government control

It would have seemed that, in shelving teacher education firmly within the university sector, the preparation and continuing professional development of teachers would have remained safe from government interference. Universities were autonomous institutions. Though receiving money from the government, that money was channelled through the University Grants Committee, established after the recommendations of Robbins to ensure freedom from interference in academic matters. But the government believed that assurance over the quality of teacher training was as necessary as assurance over the quality of teaching in schools. Just as HMI were empowered to enter schools, so should they be empowered to enter universities for this particular set of courses.

In 1983, the government produced a paper, *Teaching Quality*, spelling out four phases of a teaching career. In 1984, it gave HMI powers of approval on teacher education courses.

Staff Inspector Pauline Perry came to Exeter University to announce the intention. But would the university allow it? It did so because otherwise the government grants would be withdrawn. There was indeed a rearguard action from the redoubtable Ted Wragg. For the first inspection he insisted that he be notified beforehand of the team of HMIs. Following his perusal of the list, he insisted that one of the team be removed because of his known insobriety on a previous occasion and because we could not allow bad influences to be imported into the high level of professional training for which Exeter was noted. The HMI was removed from the team.

In 1988, the government published *The New Teacher in School*. No doubt on the basis of the now numerous HMI inspections, it criticised the weaknesses in teacher education, especially in terms of the lack of sufficient preparation in the organisation and preparation of learning and of poor assessment and recording of pupils' progress. Had the pursuit of academic respectability diminished practical relevance?

However, 'quality' is an elastic term. It can be stretched to cover many more things than actual performance in the classroom or subject knowledge. There had long been a suspicion from the right wing of politics that educational theory was promoting a left-wing agenda, blaming poor performance, for example, on cultural and social backgrounds rather than on ineffective teaching. In 1969 the first two of the seven *Black Papers on Education*, edited by Cox and Dyson, were published: *Fight for Education* and *Crisis in Education*. These, together with other papers from the Centre for Policy Studies (CPS), identified a cause of the perceived problems in schools to arise from the prevailing theoretical assumptions that, especially following the Plowden Report on Primary Education, permeated education departments – the espousal of child-centred theories of progressive education in particular. Typical was Sheila Lawlor's *Teachers Mistaught: Training in Theories or Education in Subjects?* (1990) which argued that 'any plan designed to improve the quality of teachers should concentrate on ensuring those in the profession have a mastery of their individual subjects' rather than over the non-subject of education.

The villain of the piece was the American philosopher John Dewey. Anthony O'Hear, Professor of Philosophy at the University of Bradford and appointed by Margaret Thatcher to chair a committee on teacher training, wrote for the CPS the monograph *Father of Child-Centredness: John Dewey and the Ideology of Modern Education*, and a paper to the Applied Philosophy Society in 1980 that dismissed Dewey as subverting the central aim of education which was the initiation into the cultural richness we have inherited (O'Hear, 1987). These had considerable influence on the Conservative attitude to the 'ideologues' of university education departments. It was shortly after my arrival as Director of the Department of Educational Studies of Oxford University (1989) that I was invited to share a platform with the now retired Lord Keith Joseph at a conference at Wolfson College. Seated next to me at dinner, he ascertained that my name was Pring and then told me that I had caused all the problems in our schools. When asked what led him to that belief, he replied that it was I (or people like me) who had introduced teachers to John Dewey. At roughly the same period I was invited to be interviewed by Melanie Phillips on the radio as to whether we taught John Dewey. The *Daily Mail* sent a reporter to me to ask whether we taught John Dewey and whether we would promote child-centred education. I was cross-examined by another reporter who made the excuse that he was visiting the department to leave some books to the library. I felt chuffed that I should be seen as such an influential person, though concerned by the increasing political suspicion of teacher education. Should a university department bend to such political pressure? It would not do so in the philosophy or psychology departments – such is the value attached to academic autonomy.

The criticism, however, came also 'from within the fold'. Professor David Hargreaves upset the education academics gathered at the annual conference of the British Educational Research Association in Belfast in 1990 by attacking the value and standards of the research that, to lay claim to be educational, should be serving the training and professional development of teachers – which clearly, he argued, it was failing to do. Despite the enormous amount of money spent on research and the large number of people who claimed to be active researchers, there was not the cumulative body of relevant knowledge that would enable teaching to be (like medicine) a research-based profession; for it to be so it would be necessary to change, first, the content of that research, and, second, the control and sponsorship of it.

This criticism of theory and research in the now university-based teacher education was cumulative – harking back to that made by Lord Skidelsky to a debate in the House of Lords concerning the proposal to transfer responsibility for the funding of educational research from the Higher Education Funding Council to the Teacher Training Agency:

> Many of the fruits of that research I would describe as an uncontrolled growth of 'theory, an excessive emphasis on what is called the context in which teaching takes place, which is a code for class, gender and ethnic issues, and an extreme paucity of testable hypotheses about what works and does not work'.

> (quoted in Bassey, 1995, p. 33)

Meanwhile, in the course of my 14 years as Director of the department at Oxford, the inspection regime, as in schools, became increasingly more specific. Following the DES Circular of 1989, *Initial Teacher Training: Approval of Courses*, it set precise 'performance indicators' in preparation for the 'audits'. It became a question then of writing what we wanted to be judged on in the terms of the inspectorate without sacrificing what we believed in.

Academic respectability and professional relevance: can they be reconciled?

Despite the doubts expressed by Heads of Houses to the Bryce Committee in 1895 about the university being a suitable place for the training of teachers, there was one voice from Oxford that expressed a different opinion. Mr Haverfield of Christ Church foresaw the possible integration between theory and practice and between the academic concerns of the university and the practical purposes of the schools.

The object seems to me to be to get the future teacher thinking about teaching; then, being (on the whole) an educated and capable man, he will probably be able to take his own line.[3]

The dualism between theory and practice, condemned by the aforesaid John Dewey, is surely indefensible. Intelligent practice embodies theoretical perspectives – about aims of education, motivation of the learners, levels of understanding, logical connection of key concepts, impact of cultural backgrounds. Making such implicit perspectives explicit and enabling the teacher to subject them to informed criticism are as central as is the constant critique of theory against practical experience. The theorist needs the practice as much as the practitioner needs the theory. The development of teaching quality in both initial training and professional development requires this interrelationship and the critical attitude in their marriage. One problem with the merger of the colleges with the universities has been the danger of seeing theory (what the universities are good at) imposed upon the practice (which the teachers are good at) without recognising the experiential knowledge that is embodied in that practice.

It was in recognition of that problem that my predecessor as Director of the Department of Educational Studies, Dr Harry Judge, together with the Chief Education Officer of Oxfordshire, Sir Tim Brighouse, created the Oxford Internship Scheme to which all Oxfordshire secondary schools belonged. Eight or more trainee teachers were attached to each school, which was thereby transformed into a 'training school'. Each member of the department was attached to a school as General Course Tutor, linked to the school's Professional Course Tutor, covering the topics that concerned the trainee teachers. Each week they would jointly lead the school-based seminar. At the same time, parallel links were created between the curriculum tutors in the department and the subject teachers in the schools. In addition, subject-based seminars were held back in the department, which brought together the subject tutors from the different schools. Professional development was integrated with initial training. Theory was tested against practice. Practice was informed by theory.

How far can this now be maintained in a modern university, given the changing pressures on them? Should we not learn from Chicago? There the once prestigious School of Education, under pressure to produce world class research, found less and less time to be in schools. It joined the university's School of Social Sciences. The social scientists did not care much for the research of the erstwhile educationists. Educational studies, without friends in schools and without friends in the university, closed down.

Is not the same happening here? Every four years the Research Excellence Framework assesses the quality of research, based mainly on publications in highly cited peer reviewed journals. Each subject department's finances and prestige in the consequent league table affect not only the income for the next four years but also the readiness of the respective universities to maintain particular subjects. The intensive partnerships with schools, so necessary for the quality of teacher education in universities, are less and less reconcilable with the devotion to writing research reports in journals, many of which are rarely ever read. We are likely to see many education departments closed in the coming years, thereby reversing the evolution that has taken place over the last 60 years.

And in its place?

We are already seeing the consequences of the issues I have raised:

- suspicion of the 'ideologues' (the 'blob') in the university departments of education;
- slow death of the professional degree as a route to Qualified Teacher Status;
- by-passing of the universities by those who have already gained degrees as they enter school through Schools Direct, TeachFirst and indeed 'Troops to Teachers';
- the closing of university departments of education (already begun) and, even when they survive, the closure of particular PGCE subject courses (in Autumn 1914, 27 English, 9 history and 11 geography courses lost funding);
- the continuing suspicion that 'education' is not an appropriate subject for the university. Thus Mr Raleigh of All Souls would have been pleased that, a hundred years later, his advice to the Bryce Commission was being listened to. Is it not once again believed that 'almost any honours man will make a good teacher, and if he has the luck to fall into the hands of a good head teacher'?

And yet is there not a crisis looming in the recruitment and retention of teachers? For the third year, the government is set to miss its target figure for teacher recruitment – a shortfall of 27,000 predicted by 2017. Between 40 per cent and 50 per cent of newly qualified teachers leave the profession within five years. Two-thirds of secondary school heads had difficulty in recruiting maths teachers, according to a poll by the Association of Schools and College Leaders. Concern over teacher supply has been exacerbated by Schools Direct filling only 61 per cent of the places allocated in 2014 – places that otherwise would have been allocated to universities. The problems will be exacerbated in an expanding economy that offers other attractions for would-be teachers. Reasons given for leaving are, among others, the constant teacher bashing and the high-pressure accountability, the excessive workload and relentless pace of change (TES, 30 January 2015). Will it not be necessary to establish once again that partnership between schools and universities in initial training, continuing professional development and research?

But what about professional development – the third phase of the James Report's recommendations? We have seen the central importance of such development in the years following the Schools Council in the 1960s and 1970s. Teachers were in charge, though utilising the knowledge and research to be found in the universities. The Oxford Internship Scheme was a unique partnership between university and schools, as such professional development arose from the shared responsibility for initial training. I am sure there are many other excellent examples. But increasingly, so-called professional development is geared to courses on how 'to meet the standards' imposed by government – a far cry from the autonomous profession experienced by most contributors to this volume when they first started to teach.

However, there are interesting examples, afforded by social media, of teachers once again asserting their professional autonomy. Increasingly, teachers are systematically using the Internet for the professional interactions through which they might advance their professional knowledge and practice. Grass-roots organisations of teachers have arisen such as 'Teachmeet'.

> Teachers are doing it for themselves, using social media for professional development and advocacy. . . . In the face of increasingly centralised policy agenda, social media has created spaces for teachers to talk to each other, share . . . learn for each other.
>
> (Hardy, 2014)

Notes

1 Quoted from my inaugural lecture Academic Respectability and Practical Relevance, Oxford, Clarendon Press, 1992.
2 This quotation is from a letter sent to me by a retired teacher, a former student, who does not wish her name to be disclosed.
3 Bryce Report, 1895, v. 167 (In ref: Bryce Report, 1895, Royal Commission on Secondary Education).

References

Bassey, M., 1995, *Creating Education Through Research*. Newark: Kirklington Moor Press.
Bryce Report, 1895, *Royal Commission on Secondary Education*.
Elliott, J., 1991, *Action Research for Educational Change*. Milton Keynes: Open University Press.

Hardy, E., 2014, *Forum* 56(2).

Hirst, P.H., 1965, 'Liberal education and the nature of knowledge', in P.H. Hirst (ed.) *Knowledge and the Curriculum*. London: Routledge and Kegan Paul.

McNair Report, 1944, *Teachers and Youth Leaders*. London: HMSO.

Mill, J.S., 1867, 'Inaugural address at St. Andrews', in F.A. Cavenagh (ed.) 1931, *James and John Stuart Mill on Education*. Cambridge: Cambridge University Press.

Morrell, D., 1966, *Education and Change*. London: College of Preceptors.

O'Hear, A., 1987, 'The importance of traditional learning', in *British Journal of Educational Studies* 35 (2), 102–114.

Peters, R.S., 1965, *Ethics and Education*. London: Geo. Allen and Unwin.

Plowden Report, 1967, *Children and their Primary Schools*. London: HMSO.

Robbins Report, 1963, *Higher Education*. London: HMSO.

Scheffler, I., 1960, *The Language of Education*, Springfield, Illinois: Charles Thomas.

8

THE EVOLVING IDEA OF A UNIVERSITY

Richard Pring

Sir David Watson

It had been hoped that Sir David Watson would write this chapter. Unfortunately, he died suddenly in January. He would have been the ideal author since his own professional life (spent entirely in higher education – 'my trade for 40 years') had to cope with the evolving idea of a university and, indeed, contributed richly to that idea. Moreover, the thanks of the present author are due, not just to his many writings on this subject, but in particular to his most recent book, *The Question of Conscience*, which outlines what he referred to as the successive 'frameworks' imposed on the UK since the Robbins Report of 1963 – coinciding with the period covered in this book. As he claims at the beginning of the book, 'the system has been radically reconfigured for every third or fourth new cohort that has entered it' (Watson 2014, p. xxii).

What follows, therefore, arises very much from Sir David's 'mapping' of that 'reconfiguring of the system', reflected in his own professional life.

His senior management career in higher education began at Oxford Polytechnic before the dramatic reorganisation of higher education in 1992. That followed (finally) the Robbins Report's recommendation for a unitary system of higher education, thus getting away from the 'binary line' that had divided polytechnics and institutions of higher education from universities in terms of financial resources and degree-giving powers. Brighton University was one of the first of the polytechnics to join the university club, and that demanding process took place under the leadership of David Watson, who was Vice-Chancellor from 1990 to 2005. Here we see an instance of that changing idea of a university pioneered within a much expanded system. As Theodore Zeldin wrote in the Foreword to *The Question of Conscience*,

Sir David demonstrated in Brighton how a university could raise professional training to a higher level and become a catalyst for local community innovation. His advocacy of lifelong learning is bearing fruit.

Thereafter, David Watson became Professor of Higher Education Management at the University of London Institute of Education and then was appointed in 2010 Principal of Green Templeton College, Oxford University's newest college, reinforcing the important role which that college has in linking the academic teaching and research of a university to the professional training of medics, teachers, business leaders and other professionals. But that distinctive contribution to the idea and the practices of the university, reflected in his achievements at Brighton, continued to be developed in his publications, in particular *Managing Civic and Community Engagement* in 2007 and *The Engaged University* in 2011.

The idea of a university

As David Watson demonstrated, it could be misleading to speak of *the* idea of a university when, under that title, there are many different kinds of institution and when we have witnessed in the period covered by this book a gradual evolution and diversification of that idea within the UK. Indeed, it would be wrong to freeze the idea as defined at a particular moment of time, for universities or institutions of higher education are part of a wider network of social and educational institutions, which itself will constantly be changing in response to changing economic and social factors. But there comes a time, and surely that time is now, when the shift in meaning has been such that particular institutions of higher education should not be seen as universities, even if that title is being claimed or has been bestowed upon them.

A key reference has frequently been John Henry Newman's *Idea of a New University* where he argues for it as 'a place of teaching universal knowledge'. This is qualified by the claim that its objects are intellectual, not moral, and the 'diffusion and extension of knowledge rather than the advancement'. By 'universal knowledge' is meant those different logical forms of knowledge (defined by their distinctive concepts, modes of enquiry, procedures for verifying the truth) by which we have come to understand the physical, social and moral worlds we inhabit. There is an inheritance of knowing, reasoning, appreciating which needs to be preserved and passed on to future generations. Such an institution (the university), therefore, would need to be broad in terms of the different disciplines of thinking that it offers, and thereby a 'liberal education which viewed in itself, is simply the cultivation of the intellect, as such, and its object is nothing more or less than intellectual excellence' (Newman, 1852, p. 25).

Universities, through their teaching and scholarship, would guard the intellectual inheritance and preserve it through its transmission to the next generation – or, in the words of Michael Oakeshott (1962), introduce such a generation to 'the conversation between the generations of mankind' as they come to appreciate the 'voices' of poetry, literature, history, science. Again, as Anthony O'Hear argued in defence of traditional learning, 'the proper and effective exercise of learning must take place against the background of inherited forms of thought and experience' (1987, p. 102). It is important, in understanding this 'idea', to identify certain conditions for its practical adherence in those institutions established to promote it.

The first was autonomy, that is, freedom, particularly from the state, in deciding what such excellence was, how it might be pursued, who should be selected to engage in it. Inevitably, there are limits to such autonomy, because the pursuit of scholarship and its transmission need resources. And we have seen over 40 or so years how such dependence has shaped the idea of a university.

The second was a certain disdain for usefulness or relevance as the purpose of a university. The preservation, promotion and enrichment of the world of ideas constituted an end in itself – the maintenance of a distinctive form of human life. John Stuart Mill, at his inaugural lecture at St Andrews, agreed that universities should not be places of professional education as:

> their object is not to make skilful lawyers, or physicians, or engineers, but capable and cultivated human beings [for] what professional men should carry away with them from an university is not professional knowledge, but that which should direct the use of their professional knowledge, and bring the light of general culture to illuminate the technicalities of a special pursuit.
>
> (Mill, 1867, p. 133)

That seemed to be the idea of the university when I studied philosophy at University College London – three years of exploring ideas, engaging with key texts, interacting with such philosophers as A.J. Ayer, Stuart Hampshire, Bernard Williams, Richard Wollheim and others whose main mission seemed to be that of 'teaching universal knowledge'. Usefulness or 'professional knowledge' never came into it, but I received what Mill would have regarded as 'the general culture to illuminate the technicalities of a special pursuit'. And so I did what several in such circumstances did – I joined the Civil Service as an Assistant Principal.

Robbins Report, 1963

At the beginning of our period was published the Robbins Report, *Higher Education*, as significant for higher education as the 1944 Act had been for schools. The Committee took three years to report and it shaped the considerable expansion and pattern of higher education for the next 30 years. It questioned the assumed 'restricted pool of ability', which had limited the number of universities (and thereby access to them). The general principle for entry was that 'the courses in higher education should be available for all those who are qualified by ability and attainment to pursue them and who wish to do so' (Robbins Report, 1963).

That inevitably required a considerable expansion of universities, but also an extension of the *idea* of a university. Professional usefulness had thereby also become relevant. Thus the Report proposed bringing universities, teacher training colleges, colleges of advanced technology (CATs) and regional technical colleges into a growing 'unitary system' of higher education, with the CATs re-designated as universities. But the distinction was still there between universities and those other institutions of higher education, which were geared to professional preparation and practical usefulness – a 'binary divide' was upheld. However, the higher learning of these non-university institutions needed to be recognised, and thus the Council for National Academic Awards (CNAA) was recommended with degree-giving powers, thereby enabling regional technical colleges and training colleges to offer degree courses, albeit lacking the autonomy of universities. The CNAA was established in 1965. How this played out with the training of teachers is explained in some detail in Chapter 7.

Therefore, one might say that the Robbins Report extended the 1944 principles of publicly funded (and thereby free) secondary education for all pupils to further and higher education.

One further recommendation must not be forgotten. A characteristic of the university idea was academic autonomy. How does one reconcile the massive investment of public money in the expanded universities with the maintenance of autonomy? The University Grants Committee (UGC) was to be established with general oversight over the 60 or so universities in Britain, and it would act as the independent buffer between the government as the source of finance and the universities who were to spend it as they saw fit in the pursuit of their aims.

The binary divide and its final demise

The attainment of Robbins' 'unitary system of higher education' was slow but gradual from the establishment of the CNAA finally to the 1992 Further and Higher Education Act, when polytechnics were re-designated universities. More new universities were created. But, no doubt arising from concern over such expansion, a Quality Assurance Agency (QAA) was established, one of whose functions was to define 'graduateness'. Universities were under inspection (light though it might seem at first) for quality, thereby impinging somewhat on the autonomy criterion of the university idea. When I arrived in Oxford in 1989, I was on a CNAA panel checking the quality of Oxford Polytechnic's education degree. I also was engaged in the negotiations over the future of Westminster College of Education in the new 'unitary system' – Oxford University validated its professional degree, the BEd. Eventually there was a merger between the polytechnic and the Westminster in the new Oxford Brookes University.

However, the path to the unitary system was a thorny one. The 1972 White Paper, *A Framework for Expansion*, sought to continue the binary divide in the expanded higher education system – the pursuit of excellence in a disinterested way sat uneasily with the more practical and professional development purposes of colleges of education, colleges of technology, and business and law schools. But there should be, it was argued, a two-year professional diploma that could lead to the CNAA degree (as in the case of the new BEd). In 1981, Shirley Williams' Green Paper on Higher Education proposed three types of university for the sake of appropriate funding – R,X,T, that is, 'research universities', 'teaching universities' and 'research/teaching universities'. Again, this led to nowhere, except that the idea of research and teaching universities seems to have emerged gradually as a result of the RAE (Research Assessment Exercise), later renamed the REF (Research Excellence Framework). A differentiated idea of the university, linked to competition for certain sources of funding, was beginning to emerge.

Nonetheless, the gradual dismissal of the binary divide took different forms: the incorporation into specific universities of erstwhile independent colleges, as in the case of St Lukes College being subsumed within Exeter University (see Chapter 7 for a brief account); the slow handing over of powers to colleges that had been supported by their local university, as in the case of Canterbury Christ Church College, which, under the Collegiate Board chaired by the University of Kent, gradually developed as independent Canterbury Christ Church University. What characterised many of these new universities so developed was the promotion of professional degrees in education, social work, nursing and such like – somewhat removed in essence from the pre-Robbins idea. Finally, in this 'road to independence', the 1988 Education Reform Act enabled polytechnics to become semi-independent corporations free from the control of local education authorities.

However, in preparation for this expansion and differentiation of purpose, there inevitably emerged a gradual erosion of independence. Reference has been made to the establishment in 1992 of the Quality Assurance Agency. But also a University Grants Committee was to be replaced by the University Funding Council, with increased powers to determine the conditions under which universities were to receive funding, thereby opening up the possibility of 'contract funding' and an increase in the number of representatives from outside the university on the councils and governing bodies. Was this the end of the 'dons' dominion', as Professor Halsey called it?

The Engaged University

This title of David Watson's book, published with colleagues in 2011, points to a development of our idea of universities much influenced by the expansion referred to above, and reflected in the pioneering work at the new University of Brighton, which, under his leadership, 'developed essentially as a confederation of professional schools, created at different times by a community perceiving different needs' (Watson et al., 2011, p. 102).

Thus Coffield and Williamson (1997, p. 2) argue that 'the old elite model has run its course and needs to be replaced'. Such sentiments were reinforced by the 1997 Dearing Report, *Higher Education in the Learning Society*, which argued that 'higher education is now a significant force in regional economies, as a source of income and employment, in contributing to cultural life, and in supporting regional and local economic development' (Dearing Report, 1997, p. 228).

This was not simply an observation – a recognition of what in fact was the case – but part of Dearing's approving acknowledgement of what universities could and should become. There had been a shift in how we value the kind of knowledge that universities should both develop and teach. The Report spoke of a 'new compact involving institutions and their staff, students, government, employers and society in general'. Such a compact would involve:

- wider access, thereby transforming an erstwhile elite system into a mass system, requiring a more practical and 'useful' orientation;
- a framework of qualifications and programmes, providing for lifelong learning of people who start from different positions and have different aspirations;
- greater relevance of programmes to the social and economic needs of the local and national communities.

Dearing's 'new compact', therefore, made universities beholden to a new set of demands affecting the degree both of internal autonomy and outside accountability in shaping aims, values and indeed governance. And that coincided with 'modernising government'.

Modernising government – the growth of bureaucracy

The gradual incursion of government into the conduct of universities coincided with a shift in the control and management of public services generally (e.g. regarding schools, in the creation of a National Curriculum and National Assessment), and with the 'language of management' through which those services were to be controlled – the language of targets, performance indicators, audits and delivery. All this was explained in a series of Government White Papers from HM Treasury and the Cabinet Office: *Modern Public Services in Britain: Investing in Reform* (1988, Cm. 4011); *Public Services for the Future: Modernisation, Reform, Accountability* (1998, Cm. 4181); *The Government's Measures of Success: Outputs and Performance Analyses* (1999, Cm. 4200); *Modernising Government* (1999, Cm. 4310).

As an illustration of this shift in the underlying understanding of public institutions, one might refer to the change in language and practices in universities, following the 'efficiency review' of the Jarratt Commission, established by the Committee of Vice-Chancellors in 1984.

> The crucial issue is how a university achieves the maximum value for money consistent with its objectives (2.12). Each department should maintain a profile of 'indicators of performance' to include standing costs of space, utilities (telephones, etc), market share of applications, class sizes, staff workloads, graduation rates and classes of degrees (3.33). A range of performance indicators should be developed, covering both inputs and outputs and designed for use both within individual universities and for making comparisons between institutions (5.4). The headships of departments . . . ideally should be both a manager and an academic leader (4.27).[3]

This is clearly a very different language from that which is met in the writings of Newman or Oakeshott. Indeed, it would seem incompatible with them, namely, that open engagement with key texts, the pursuit of excellence, the fostering of critical enquiry, the struggle with difficult ideas, the entry into the conversation between the generations. The more recently developed professional studies departments were the first to suffer as the government laid down multiple and detailed 'standards' (meaning 'targets') for the newly established Ofsted Inspectorate to check and tick off. My period as Director of the Department of Educational Studies at Oxford coincided with this transition. During the soon-to-pass time of Her Majesty's Inspectorate, I was asked, over lunch in the Rose and Crown, of the 'management system' in the department. Struggling to answer, I finally referred to the regular Friday evening open meetings in the Rose and Crown. Their final report expressed appreciation of 'the light management touch'. Once Ofsted assumed the inspectorial job, there was a change, and time was spent translating the language of education into the language-speak required of the new regime.

The management language has in many ways taken over our understanding of the conduct, governance and understanding of universities. Having a Masters in Business Management is seen as a useful qualification for being a Vice-Chancellor. The newly appointed Vice-Chancellor of the Aston Business School, Professor George Feiger, speaks of universities having to adapt to the marketisation of education with fee income following student. They operate as businesses, though not having shareholders. Therefore, there is the swelling of bureaucracy and thereby a change in the now corporate governance of universities. At the time of my arrival at Oxford in 1989, the proportion of central administrators to established academics was 1:2. That has now been reversed. And there are many tales of the salaries that top administrators receive compared with those of top academics, although Freedom of Information was recently refused at one university on the grounds that such information was 'commercially confidential'.

The impact of research exercises

When I was an undergraduate in the 1960s, the university was principally (in Newman's words) 'a place of teaching universal knowledge'. Of course, those who were teaching were engaged in scholarship, and they published significant articles and books. But none had to meet targets or publish in journals that rated high on, for example, the Social Science Research Index. The UGC annual grant was given to each university for purposes of both teaching and research, irrespective of the nature and depth of that research. Research or scholarship was seen, in the main, as supporting the main function, namely, that of teaching.

However, the 1990s changed all that. A substantial amount was withdrawn from the central grant only to be returned on the basis of the quantity and quality of research.

Indeed, some are referred to as 'research universities', meaning that research is a major activity within them, supported by external grants for so doing. It is the case that most universities in the UK would now see research to be an important element in the duties of academic appointments.

Such an emphasis was intensified internationally as a result of world league tables of 'top universities' based mainly on the quality of research. In the UK the RAE (now the REF), which takes place every four years, has reshaped the idea of the university and the nature of academic life. Until the 1980s, universities were funded to teach and to devote time to the research and scholarship that would support that teaching. An academic was not pressurised to produce research of 'international standard'. He or she would not be penalised for concentrating upon teaching. The RAE changed that. The third of government funding supposedly to support research and scholarship was withdrawn and then redistributed on the basis of the quality of research – subject by subject. That sum of money is increasingly distributed to fewer and fewer universities, with considerable financial consequences.

The effects of this are several, changing the idea of the university and of the role of academics within them.

First, there is a growing hierarchy within the university sector – at the top of which are the 'research universities' – on the basis of international and national reputation and, therefore, of the greater income from research and from the attraction to overseas students. Further down the scale are 'teaching universities', where scholarship is pursued but much within the context of their teaching responsibilities. What Shirley Williams' White Paper proposed has become real.

Second, within the respective universities, there is an increasing division, between those who do research and those who just teach, on different contracts and different rates of pay. Only those are submitted for the REF whose published work is judged to be of national standard. It is a brave academic who, harking back to the nature of the university only a few decades ago, feels able to focus on the quality of teaching, and not to be intimidated by the need to produce four publications preferably in the reputable journals. Such is the pressure that more and more teaching is handed over to part-time teachers or to post-graduate students, raising doubts as to whether the university is seeing teaching (as with Newman) as its prime purpose.

Third, the competition between universities for league table rankings inhibits the collaboration between disciplines within a university and between universities, a point clearly made by Sir David Watson. A good-quality research paper, arising out of collaboration between more than one department or university, cannot be attributed to more than one person for the purposes of the REF. Better, therefore, to keep the research 'within house'.

Funding

The quite massive and rapid expansion of universities clearly had an effect on their funding. According to the Dearing Report, the decline in the unit of resource had been 40 per cent in the period of 20 years. According to the Taylor Report (2000),

New Directions for Higher Education Funding: Final Report of the Funding Options Group, that decline had continued, but more slowly. No longer could funding depend purely on government grants (as through the UGC, which had been replaced in 1988) and, given the extra public funding, no longer could the management expenditure be handed over exclusively to the decisions of the university. The Report, therefore, spelled out four options: (i) increased public funding; (ii) deregulation of fees so that each university could charge whatever the market could bear; (iii) income-contingent student loans; and (iv) institutional endowments.

The government opted for (iii) income-contingent student contributions through payment of government fixed fees and through a system of loans. This radical development in funding was extended further as a result of the Browne Review into Higher Education in 2010, which recommended undergraduate fees up to £9,000, instead of any government block grants, together with student contributions up to £9,000 to be repaid, once the student earned over a certain amount, over a 30-year period. Furthermore, there would be targeted funding of specific initiatives that, in the view of the government, would support its economic and social agenda.

In other words, there were now 'funding levers', used with considerable impact within research through, for example, the demand from Research Councils for evidence of economic and social relevance and through the search for investment as, for example, from the Science Research Investment Fund or the Joint Research Equipment Initiative. This new dependence both on research and on 'funding levers' (both public and private) inevitably affects the idea of the university as in terms of accountability, autonomy and the disinterested pursuit of excellence. The words 'stakeholders' and 'client satisfaction' enter into the language of universities.

Online and distance learning

It would have been difficult, before the Robbins Report, to foresee how radical the changed conception of a university could be. The 'idea' of a university once included the notion of a community, interacting through debate and questioning. 'Conversation' would have been seen as an essential element in the development of knowledge and critical enquiry. But such communities became increasingly difficult to maintain as universities expanded to the sizes that prevail today. The pressure for widening access, the rising costs, the employment and family demands on those who sought access, wider conception of its purposes, and the development of communications technology have all led to the most radical solution of all.

Why should courses leading to degrees require congregation in one place and community over a restricted time?

Britain's Open University was founded in 1968, whereby part-time students, scattered far and wide, matriculated to take their degrees in a range of academic disciplines. The Open University pioneered the distance learning mode of higher education. This required a different pedagogy in order to maintain the standards of learning expected of an institution calling itself a university. In the 1970s I was invited by the Open University to write material for one of its courses, with relevant exercises and stringently assessed by panels of academic experts. Weekly sessions were backed up by radio and television recordings; personal supervision was organised through correspondence.

The Internet has transformed that. In 2013–2014, of the students studying for both undergraduate and post-graduate degrees in the UK, 150,000 were with the Open University. Students and teachers meet in 'virtual' theatres and laboratories. Discussions and tutorials take place online and in forums. MOOCSs (Massive Open Online Communication Systems), provided by world-standard universities such as Stanford, Harvard and Michigan, cater for many thousands of students.

Furthermore, the Credit Accumulation and Transfer System (CATS), following the 1998 government paper, *The Learning Age*, should have been fully functioning by 2003, though it raised problems over the autonomy for the specific institutions taking part and a shift to a more modular system. However, 'transferable credits' may well be the way forward in a changing and more global world.

Private and for-profit universities

Universities obviously need funding in order to pay for staff and resources. Traditionally, this has come mainly from governments, charitable donors, though increasingly from research grants and student fees. Government support was adequate at a time when only 5 per cent or 6 per cent of the relevant cohort of young people went to university, as in the UK in the 1960s. But now the aspiration is for 50 per cent to attend university. There is, therefore, an increase in fees, to be paid by the students, financed principally from loans that have to be paid back over a period of 30 years.

But such an expansion has given rise to the private and for-profit organisations to offer university education.

The year 1983 saw the foundation of the first private university in Britain, namely, the University of Buckingham, now well established and universally recognised. The university is a not-for-profit institution with charitable status. Its teaching income depends entirely on student fees. It is aligned to the Quality Assurance Agency, which gives assurance on the quality of its teaching at university level.

However, there is now a growth of institutions, some accredited by universities abroad (such as Richmond, the American International University in London, or BPP University, whose parent company is the US Apollo Group). Others are single subject professional training institutions, such as Ashridge Business School and the College of Estate Management. The quality of some of the new arrivals has been severely questioned. As a result, a group of eight for-profit institutions with award bearing powers (including the ones just mentioned and referred to as the 'Russell Group of the private sector') has been set up to disassociate its members from the 'dodgy for-profit' colleges now attracting students, many from abroad.

This raises the question, which remains constant in the face of the changing idea of the university, concerning the compatibility of the pursuit of profit with the idea of a community of learners, teaching universal knowledge and exercising academic freedom.

Looking to the future

This chapter has outlined the many ways in which universities have changed from some ideal type of 'teaching universal knowledge' in response to changing social and economic circumstances.

First, we saw the widening of purpose and the relevance of university education to community engagement, enhancing the quality of local economic and cultural life – as pioneered by Sir David Watson's University of Brighton.

Second, greater importance came to be attached to research in terms of funding and prestige, leading to a hierarchy of universities (Russell Group research universities, on the one hand, and teaching universities, on the other – and often leading, too, to demarcation within the academic community).

Third, the gradual encroachment on the early, carefully protected autonomy of universities through funding and governance has led to a burgeoning cost of administration.

Fourth, the funding has become increasingly dependent (especially through research grants and 'impact') on relevance to economic and social needs, and to employment.

Fifth, we are witnessing the growth of private and for-profit institutions.

Finally, there is massive development of part-time, online and virtual learning, together with credit accumulation and transfer of qualifications.

It is necessary to ask how far these changes can develop before the title of 'university' is used purely equivocally, bearing few of the qualities and virtues normally associated with that name. For example:

- Is a university still a university when it loses its academic autonomy?
- Is a single-faculty university (e.g. a business school) really a university?
- Should an institution be classed as a university when it has no faculty of humanities or social studies?
- How can independent quality assurance be assured in all these developments, especially where universities are globally spread or when they are in the hands of for-profit corporations?

In an age of credit transfer on a global scale, universities and employers will need to be assured of the standards of those 'universities' from whom they are receiving their students and employees.

References

Coffield, F. and Williamson, B., 1997, *The Repositioning of Higher Education,* Buckingham: Open University Press.

Dearing Report, 1997, *Higher Education in a Learning Society,* London: HMSO.

Jarratt Report, 1985, *Higher Education,* London: HMSO.

Mill, J.S., 1867, 'Inaugural address at St. Andrews', in F.A. Cavenagh (ed.), 1931, *James and John Stuart Mill on Education,* Cambridge: Cambridge University Press.

Newman, J.H., 1852, *The Idea of a New University,* London: Longmans Green (1919 edn).

Oakeshott, M., 1962, 'The voice of poetry in the conversation of Mankind', in M. Oakeshott (ed.) *Rationalism in Politics,* London: Methuen.

O'Hear, A., 1987, 'The importance of traditional learning', *British Journal of Educational Studies,* 35(2), 102–14.

Robbins Report, 1963, *Higher Education,* London: HMSO.

Taylor Report, 2000, *New Directions for Higher Education Funding,* London: HMSO.

Watson, D., 2007, *Managing Civic and Community Engagement,* London: Open University Press.

Watson, D., 2014, *A Question of Conscience,* London: Institute of Education Press.

Watson, D., Stroud, S., Hollister, R. and Babcock, E. 2011, *The Engaged University,* London: Routledge.

Zeldin, T., 2014, 'Foreword', in Watson D, 2014, *A Question of Conscience,* London: Institute of Education Press.

9

FURTHER EDUCATION AND THE CASE FOR VOCATIONAL PREPARATION

Geoff Stanton

Further education – the unknown sector

This chapter cannot trace all the changes that have occurred in the English FE system during the last generation. They are too many, and too complicated to explain briefly to those not already versed in the system. At least with regard to schools and universities most people understand roughly what they do and for whom. But the same cannot be assumed for FE colleges, despite their catering for over 3.1 million people annually.

When attempting to answer well-meant queries about FE I find myself in 'Yes, but . . .' mode. Are most FE students over 19 and part-time? *Yes, but more 16–19 year olds attend colleges full-time than attend school sixth forms.* Are most FE courses vocational? *Yes, but one-third of all 16–18 A-Level students attend colleges.* Are most FE courses below degree level? *Yes, but 64 per cent of colleges teach foundation degrees.* Do colleges prepare people for work? *Yes, but colleges also provide 30 per cent of 19+ entrants to higher education.*

There are also powerful myths. For instance, some argue that colleges cannot offer the pastoral care available in secondary schools. In fact, colleges are more socially inclusive than school sixth forms. Of those who were receiving free school meals when they were 15, nearly twice as many go on to colleges than are admitted to their own sixth forms, and colleges also have a higher proportion of learners from ethnic minorities. Furthermore, and as I shall describe, integrated courses managed by course teams can offer close support.

Also, many current politicians seem to believe that, for those young people who do not go on to take A Levels, apprenticeships are the primary alternative. The best apprenticeships are excellent, but they vary in quality, and participants have to be employed; they can only be offered by employers, not government. So if a given class of employers is missing in a locality then training in that sector is not available via the apprenticeship route. Most crucially, the number available to young people (as opposed to those over 19) has not increased for a decade. So, despite being massively oversubscribed, apprenticeships still cater for merely 6 per cent of 16–18 year olds. On the other hand, something like 40 per cent of the cohort attend colleges on full-time vocational or pre-vocational courses.

Diversity of provision in the student body is one of the constants for FE. This has attracted criticism, on the grounds that it can result in a lack of focus and is one of the things that hinders public understanding of what colleges do. The Foster Review (2005) of FE concluded that 'FE lacks a clearly recognised and shared core purpose' and argued that this should be 'supplying economically valuable skills'. However, the very next paragraph of the report compromised this clarity by adding that 'the primary focus on skills does not exclude other significant purposes such as promoting social cohesion and facilitating progression'. As if to prove this point, FE was later given a major role in promoting Adult Basic Skills, following the Moser Report (1999). At the time of writing and following the Wolf Report (2011) into 14–19 vocational education, colleges are being asked to ensure 16 year olds who have not attained at least Grade C in GCSE English and maths do so within their first college year. Some colleges are finding this a struggle, but it needs to be remembered that the individuals concerned have often left school *because* they were not welcome in the sixth form without these grades.

Perhaps colleges have been too responsive and flexible in meeting new demands and target groups, but the irony is that it is the willingness of colleges to do this that has enabled sixth forms and universities to keep relatively stable roles and purposes, and to benefit from greater public recognition as a result.

Lack of recognition is one thing. Invisibility is another. Consider this quote from a speech by Prime Minister Tony Blair talking about plans to raise the participation age:

> No dropping out at 16, every young person either staying on in the sixth form or on a modern apprenticeship or job-related training leading to a good career. . . . So substantially more academies, specialist schools, better post-16 provision in 6th forms and 6th form colleges.
>
> (Labour Spring Conference, 2004)

No mention of FE colleges, where most of the new learners were likely to be.

This phenomenon was not new. In 1997 Helena Kennedy wrote in a report for the newly formed Further Education Funding Council (FEFC), 'There is an appalling ignorance among decision makers and opinion formers about what goes on in further education. It is so alien to their experience' (Kennedy Report, 1997). And as recently as 2014, a minister claimed that he was advised by civil servants that he should respond to austerity by 'killing off FE since nobody will really notice' (Vince Cable, as reported on the BBC, 6 October 2014).[1]

So, lack of understanding and invisibility create a problem in writing about changes that FE has undergone in my working lifetime. Therefore, what I shall do is focus on a relatively short period when the ability of FE staff to take professional responsibility for what they taught was probably greater than in a secondary school, and to trace some of the factors that resulted in this being reversed, and centrally sponsored turbulence becoming, if anything, greater than for schools and certainly universities.

In doing so I shall be mostly talking about just one of FE's many client groups. This group shares the invisibility of FE itself. I was recently pleasantly surprised to see them mentioned in an Ofsted Review published in 2015. One of its section headings read 'Where can young people, who do not have five GCSEs or are undecided about their career pathways, go?'. The report continued:

> Inspectors . . . found that this issue was exacerbated by school sixth forms, academies, colleges and providers who set high entry requirements . . . This could prevent many young people, often the most vulnerable, from following career pathways that may well be within their grasp with a little more time and effective learning support.
>
> (Ofsted, 2013/2014, para. 66)

What Ofsted does not mention is the fact that since 2014 full-time education has been fully funded only until the age of 18. After that, the rate of funding reduces, reportedly on the assumption that it is mainly used for those repeating A Levels. However, many more learners need the extra year because their school attainments mean that they need three years rather than two to reach level three, and more teaching time rather than less.

All this highlights an issue that I have, over the years, spent some time investigating, namely the process of selection that takes place at 16, even within institutions that are non-selective at 11. Of course, performance indicators and inspection grades are likely to be more favourable if the recruitment of challenging learners can be avoided. There are other ways in which the development of policy has damaged their interests. The shift towards central control and top-down qualifications-led development has brought with it a set of assumptions about what counts as good and rigorous programmes. It is thought that they should be made up of free-standing and recognised academic subjects and assessed in writing at the end. However, during a period when practitioners were able to develop their own approaches, they found that alternative curriculum designs were more effective – for instance, integrated programmes focused on a work-based theme, assessed though the ongoing observation of performance.

In what follows, I concentrate on *pre-vocational education*, with which I have been closely associated through the Further Education Unit in the 1970s and 1980s.

Teacher training: a biographical diversion

My first teaching experience was that of teaching physics in secondary schools, at a time when a teaching qualification was not required. However, I learned that knowledge of a subject was not enough to make me a fully effective teacher of it. More than that, while teaching in a large inner London comprehensive I discovered that there were things to be understood about the design and content of learning programmes, as well as pedagogy. Like, I suspect, most grammar school products, I had no concept of the range of attainment and motivations in the population as a whole. When my 15-year-old average attainers asked me why I was teaching them about specific gravity in the way I was, I realised that I had no answer. Or rather I had an answer that was very uncomfortable. Although the structure of secondary education had changed, the curriculum design had not kept up. We were offering a diluted grammar school curriculum – one that was not designed to develop a delight in science, but rather to enable pupils to gain access to the next level up and thence to university. But there would be places there for fewer than 10 per cent of the age group, and my students knew full well that this did not include them. There were things that could have been done about this, but not – as I naïvely imagined – by just being more competent and accessible than some of my own teachers had been.

As a result of this experience, I became more interested in learning about the needs of different kinds of learner, rather than the intricacies of teaching different subjects. Arrogantly, I even wrote to some well-known teacher-training colleges asking to explore this, but was always told that I first had to decide on a subject, then an age group. Then I heard about the teaching of general studies in technical colleges, where it was possible to design at least part of the curriculum in light of the personal needs of the learners, who were otherwise following a course leading to a specific occupation. I obtained a place at Garnett College, which just taught potential FE teachers. I enjoyed this course, not least because I already had a list of issues I wished to explore – another important lesson. The following five years I spent at a technical college in Cheltenham – by far the largest college in the town, but by no means the most well known. This was my first lesson in the relative invisibility of FE.

Later I returned to Garnett College, as a member of staff. All those learning to be teachers there either had a degree or had substantial experience of the working world, or both. This made for groups that were fascinating to teach. I would pick out two features that have implications for current educational issues.

First, since not all students on the course were graduates, they could not be awarded a Post-Graduate Certificate of Education (PGCE) on successful completion, but instead gained the lower-status Certificate in Education. So, people such as experienced chefs or retired merchant navy captains, who had not been to university but had managed very complex situations in the real world, were treated as if they had entered teacher training as school leavers. This was not because they had learned different things or were assessed in a different way from PGCE students. The distinction was made on the basis of the academic qualifications they arrived with. This gave me the first inkling that the hierarchy of levels that feature so strongly in English education might be problematic. There was clearly a prejudice in favour of some kinds of achievement, and some definitions of progression.

Second, while all students had to learn what was called 'general method' (that is, the techniques of questioning, structuring and differentiating relevant to all kinds of teaching), the 'special method' for vocational teachers included a whole raft of other requirements, such as understanding how practical skills could be developed and how industry-standard workshops or kitchens could be designed and used for teaching purposes. Garnett College had such teaching facilities, but my fear is that these days most vocational teacher training is generic, with special methods left to be acquired on their college placement, under the guidance of staff, some of whom do not have the time or resources of their equivalents at Garnett. Inspectors and research confirm that this is the most variable component of FE teacher training (see, for example, Gatsby Foundation, 2015).

The main content of vocational courses was clearly laid down and accepted, and was derived from qualifications produced by awarding bodies such as City and Guilds of London Institute (CGLI) or the Royal Society of Arts (RSA) who had well-established mechanisms for consulting employers and teachers in deciding on a syllabus. In the case of general studies, however, the curriculum had to be designed by the teachers, and varied with the needs of the learners, which were in turn influenced by their age, previous attainment and the occupational areas they were preparing to enter. It also had to be negotiated with the learners themselves, who frequently had to be persuaded of its value. It was no coincidence that, when in later years colleges had to cater for learners with no clear vocational or academic pathway ahead of them – many of whom were unemployed – it was often former general studies teachers who took a central role.

The negotiated curriculum

I saw this in operation in a later job, as head of the 45-strong Communications and Liberal Studies Department at a large London College. Youth unemployment was escalating. Initially, the college had no fewer than three engineering departments (production, mechanical and electrical). But the economy was changing, and four years later there was only one. Sadly, many otherwise excellent staff found it difficult to adapt. They were used to being able to select students on the basis of their previous achievement and motivation, and were apprehensive about their ability to cope with new groups, many of whom had poor basic skills and were only there because they would lose their unemployment benefit if they did not attend. On the other hand, staff in the communications section of the department had developed, partly through innovative methods promoted by the Local Authority Inspectorate, such devices as learning workshops that were based on activities rather than formal lessons. All teachers of a given group were part of a course team that met as often as weekly. It could monitor how different parts of the course related and make changes if required. The agenda for the meetings was usually a cross-subject review of individual student progress and problems. This differed from my experience of secondary school where staff were grouped together on the basis of shared subjects in a way that made such learner-centred planning impossible.

Rise and fall of UVP schemes – a case study

In 1976 the government announced the intention to test out approaches to what it called Unified Vocational Preparation (UVP) – 'unified' because the schemes were to be jointly planned and provided by education and training services. The rationale for the programme was that about half of those entering the labour market at 16 received no structured education or training. So UVP was aimed at these employees, rather than the unemployed.

In the same report (*Unified Vocational Preparation: A Pilot Approach*) the government announced the creation of a unit to undertake the development and review of further education curricula. It was argued that the FE system was 'largely responsive to perceived vocational needs', but that it was 'not well designed to respond to the curricular needs of those who enter further education as full-time students without a specific vocational commitment'. This unit became the Further Education Unit (FEU), which I joined as one of its first two development officers.

The issues that both FEU and UVP were asked to address have not gone away. But what has changed is that now the aim suggested by policy makers would be 'qualifications reform', rather than responding to 'curricular needs'. In developing guidance for UVP schemes my brief was to visit a range of locally developed schemes and to identify factors that led to success in very different contexts. This also contrasts with current approaches, in which change comes from the top down, rather than bottom up.

The UVP pilots were immensely varied, but they all focused on the needs of young people who had entered work at 16, but, because of a lacklustre school career, did not have qualifications necessary to enter a formal training programme, such as an apprenticeship. Because of this they also tended to miss out on the personal support that might come from having a tutor.

I can best illustrate some of the issues with an anecdote about a scheme involving production line operatives. It was run by the training manager, who was – significantly – also a volunteer youth worker. He ran informal group sessions on one afternoon a week, usually focused on how they were finding the adult and working world. One afternoon he noticed a youngster looking particularly glum, and gentle probing revealed that he planned to resign, 'because his supervisor had taken against him'. The previous week the young man had been unwell, and was unable to get to work. But when he did return, far from being sympathetic, his supervisor had been irritated. 'But I had really been ill, and took in a note from my mother to prove it.' When this situation was unpicked, with the help of the rest of the group, it became obvious that the problem was that the young man had not telephoned to report his absence on the first morning. As a result, the start of the production line was delayed. Perversely, if the young man had been an apprentice, his absence might have had less impact, but as an operative who only needed a day's training, he was important from day two. At school and as a reluctant learner, his absence might well have had little impact, and he naïvely adopted the school practice of a subsequent note from his mum.

This was talked through, and the young man was encouraged both to see the point of view of the supervisor, and to think about how bridges might now be mended. But should not correct protocol have been explained earlier? It turned out that it had been, along with what must have seemed a thousand other things on that first confused day. The group leader's youth worker training had enabled him to realise that it was often 'ineffective to offer solutions to problems that the young people had not yet got'. We now talk of teaching 'employability skills', which hardly covers the issue.

Similarly, a tutor on another UVP scheme introduced herself disarmingly as the 'sums lady'. Her analysis of conventional maths lessons was that learners were sitting untroubled in class when someone like her came in and gave them problems they otherwise would not have had. She attempted instead to offer maths as a series of solutions. She therefore ran a drop-in centre, to which young people on the scheme could come whenever they hit a problem in the workshop, or when they were attempting to work out how many more instalments they owed on a motor bike.

It became clear that a common factor on many successful schemes was a process of accompanying people through new experiences, helping them to reflect on them, and only then offering the learning that was demonstrably required. This 'experience–reflection–learning' process was the reverse of the pattern most participants had found in secondary school, where there was a well-intentioned attempt to offer the learning up-front, so as to pre-emptively improve the experience. But this required a degree of compliance and tolerance of boredom that many people do not have – quite understandably. I came to see it as the 'You'll wish you'd listened to me' syndrome. It also means that it is often a serious mistake to require young people to succeed at a broad-based academic programme before allowing them to engage with the adult and working world. Once confidence has been gained through success, even on a narrow front, ambitions widen.

Of course, tutors were not passive when it came to ensuring that learners had experiences that would be fruitful. Many UVP schemes included a brief residential course, often run by organisations such as the YMCA, which ensured that participants were taken out of their comfort zone. This had a powerful effect on apparently streetwise young people. It became apparent that much aggressive or dismissive behaviour was a means of avoiding the unknown.

Using qualifications as a trigger for funding

Although UVP was never a large-scale scheme, many of the lessons learned were applied to programmes for the young unemployed. But a major problem was that they were approved and funded individually. As schemes grew in number because of the recession, an administratively simpler approach to funding was needed. It was decided that the newly arrived National Vocational Qualifications (NVQs) could be used to define the required outcomes, and funding would be triggered by their achievement. At the same time there was (justifiable) pressure to increase efficiency in colleges. The net results were that only what NVQs measured was funded.

Traditionally, education and training programmes were defined in syllabus terms, as a series of topics, and taught over a specified period of time. It required an analysis of past papers to determine the kind of performance required, and only by following a prescribed course was it possible to gain the qualification. NVQs, on the other hand, based their approach on an analysis of what counted as effective performance in an occupational role. If assessment showed that this performance had been achieved, then it mattered not how this had happened.

This enfranchised many experienced workers who had acquired their skills 'on the job' and who did not have the time or resources to enrol on a formal course in order to gain the qualification their skills deserved. But the use of NVQs for courses for the young unemployed provided what has been called 'thin gruel'. In all too many cases the list of competences was treated as a learning programme. This did not allow for issues of transition from school to work, nor facilitate progression. The use of NVQs as triggers for funding and as performance indicators for providers – purposes for which they were not designed – only made things worse. For instance, it resulted in the demise of the short residential courses that contributed so much to social and team development. I cannot help comparing this cheeseparing to the importance we still attach to undergraduates going away to university, despite what this costs.

Central funding and TVEI as a model for development

Another feature of these initiatives that cast a long shadow was the source of funding, the Manpower Services Commission (MSC). One reason for using this mechanism was that it enabled central government to direct resources to its destinations of choice, and to monitor their use. At that time the Education Department could only make a contribution to the rate support grant received by local authorities, with the request that they use it appropriately. Local politics determined where it actually went, which was often not towards disadvantaged or low-status groups. The MSC, on the other hand, could issue specific contracts and refuse to pay up if their requirements were not met.

I saw some advantages of this approach later when working as the vice-principal of Richmond tertiary college, which provided both academic and vocational education for all local residents over the age of 16. The Technical and Vocational Education Initiative (TVEI) of 1983 was aimed at providing a new element to the curriculum of all 14–18-year-olds, which in our case meant working with our 11–16 secondary schools, and I acted as the TVEI co-ordinator for the area. The officials working at a national level for TVEI were clear about the aims we should work towards, but did not attempt to prescribe the best way to achieve these in our local circumstances. Instead we were asked to submit our own proposals. We did this in a hurry, and when interviewed about them were tactfully but firmly told that they did not pass muster, as we ourselves came to realise. We were, however, given the chance to re-submit, which we did successfully, largely by drawing on the ideas of the more lively of our teaching staff. Six months or so after the start of our scheme we were visited again by TVEI officials, who checked that we were still on track against our own plan, before signing the next cheque – though we were allowed to modify the plan by agreement and in the light of experience.

It has to be admitted that a lot of the most energetic development activity took place immediately before a visitation, at which time it became possible for the relatively junior staff, who had the ideas, to break though institutional inertia. TVEI has had a mixed press, often because of its diversity being perceived as a problem, but I still think that the balance it struck between the setting of national priorities and allowing for local initiatives and adaptation is something from which we could learn.

The rise of pre-vocational education

In the late 1970s many colleges began to respond to a demand from young people for whom A Levels were not appropriate, and did not as yet have a firm vocational commitment, but who wished to stay on as full-time students in order to improve their basic education and to explore vocational options. A survey commissioned by the FEU from Garnett College identified over 30 different responses to this demand, and argued for some rationalisation. The one form of response that was seen to be inadequate was the one-year course that repeated school examinations, since this had a high failure and drop-out rate. An alternative approach that seemed to be more promising was what HMI called 'the creation of task-oriented (though not necessarily job-specific) learning situations'.

These were integrated courses, focused on a general occupational area. They were different from the school curriculum in not being subject-based, though they could be designed to achieve similar learning outcomes. In a sense they followed a primary school approach of teaching through topics, but whereas 'the Romans' might be a suitable topic at that stage, for 16–18-year-olds, something that helped with the transition to adult working life was much more appropriate. They became known as 'pre-vocational' courses or as 'vocational preparation'.

The FEU set up a study group, and its report, *A Basis for Choice* (ABC), recommended a flexible programme that could become more vocationally focused and job-specific as the year progressed, but that would share a core curriculum with similar provision. This core was a result of 'curriculum development by interview', in that its content and methods were culled from a variety of schemes already in operation. The core curriculum was not the same as what subsequently came to be known as 'key skills'. Instead it was expressed in the form of a checklist of:

- those experiences from which students should have the opportunity to learn; and
- the nature and level of performance students should be expected to achieve.

The aims of the core curriculum included literacy and numeracy 'adequate to meet the demands of contemporary society', but also 11 other areas including careers education, physical and manipulative skills, study skills and problem-solving, the acquisition of relevant moral values, and economic and political literacy. Taken as a whole this was perhaps over-ambitious, particularly as different occupational skills had to be added depending on the focus of the course, but at the time something similar was supported by a spectrum of opinion ranging from teacher unions to the CBI, and all the individual elements were being done successfully by somebody somewhere. Also, the term 'checklist' was intended to allow flexibility. For instance, careers education could take the form of job sampling, and not just visiting lecturers.

Currently, our ambitions for a continuation of general education post-16 have been reduced to requiring English and maths in the form of the GCSEs designed for 15-year-olds. The argument for this is that only GCSEs have currency with employers, but the problem is, of course, that the currency derives from the fact that not everyone gets them. They can therefore be used as a selection device, to reduce an impossibly long shortlist. It is not always that the content is what employers want for the jobs they have in mind.

What was recommended in ABC was a course design, rather than a qualification, though reporting by the use of a learner profile was suggested. Attempts subsequently to convert it into a Certificate of Pre-vocational Education (CPVE) were not entirely successful, but it remains an interesting example for a number of reasons:

- It was curriculum- and practitioner-led, rather than driven by a centrally designed qualification.
- It specified learning experiences, and not just outcomes.
- It proposed continuing general education via a vocational interest, rather than setting up general and vocational in opposition to one another.
- It emphasised the value of an integrated programme in which utility of one area of learning (e.g. mathematics) could be demonstrated by its application to another topic.

My view is that an approach that could have benefited many young people has been hindered by the power of an academic paradigm that means that integrated vocational courses are converted into isolated vocational subjects, assessed by methods that privilege certain forms of excellence. Also, the use of a vocational interest as a vehicle for continuing general education, and as a means of providing active careers guidance and smoothing the transition to adult working life, has been confused with the important but different need for more strongly vocational courses that meet specific employer needs. An unfortunate example of this is the Wolf Report of 2011 about 14–19 vocational courses that, while making pertinent criticisms about false equivalences and the malign results of funding individual qualifications rather than whole programmes, also judged pre-vocational courses as if they were intended to be a substitute for apprenticeships.

The role of advisory bodies and the move to central control

When I first worked at FEU, and then returned there as CEO, the Board of Management was in the form of a representative body. The Chair was appointed by the Secretary of State, but other members were nominated by other organisations. There were members chosen by an employers' organisation (CBI) and by the TUC. Two education officers were proposed, respectively, by the Metropolitan Authorities (assumed to be left-leaning) and the County Councils (assumed to be Conservative). A college principal was balanced by someone from the teaching union. The inspectorate and the Education Department were each represented, but, despite all funding coming from the Department, it was accepted that approval for the programme of work and publications was a matter for the Board as a whole. The assumption at the time was that the curriculum had to be kept a non-political matter, and that, while a central agency might spread good practice and give guidance, the development process – and as we have seen the funding priorities – should be devolved. My sense was that there were still powerful if unspoken memories about the damage to civil liberties that could be done by totalitarian regimes, of the Left or the Right, if they could control what people learned.

The advantage of a representative system was that members usually arrived well briefed on agenda items by officers from their organisations, and could advise and challenge FEU staff on the basis of evidence. A disadvantage was that there was always a chance of members being there just because it was their turn.

The first sign of a changed climate came during the Thatcher government, when the Secretary of State objected to the appointment to the FEU Board of the nominee from the Metropolitan Authorities. The fact that there should be a nominee was still accepted, but the individual concerned was thought to have 'unhelpful' views. The next step was to decree that a new board should all be appointed in an individual capacity by the Minister, so – it was said – as to avoid the 'buggins turn' syndrome. Then, after the FEU began to be funded by the newly formed FE Funding Council (FEFC), I received a call asking about their procedure for approving FEU research reports. I had to explain that despite the source of our funding it was our Board that authorised publications, as well as agreeing which areas should be prioritised for R&D.

The basis for this prioritisation was extensive canvassing of views, via advisory groups and a network of regionally based officers. Also much of FEU's human and limited financial resources went into collaborative work involving college staff, which provided a good deal of useful intelligence. But FEFC thought that these co-workers should be seen as customers, and that FEU's independence was in fact a 'licence for the FEU to choose for itself what to become involved in and whether or not to be helpful'. The answer to the question 'helpful to whom?' turned out to be the National Council for Vocational Qualifications (NCVQ), whose roll-out of the new qualifications were going more slowly than planned. Although FEU had published a number of guides on the curriculum implications of NVQ-type competence-based qualifications, the colleges also needed help on other things that were not part of NCVQ's agenda.

The assumption was that customer requirements would be demonstrated by the workings of the market, rather than through consultation. However, when the time came, FEFC did not create such a market by providing funding to colleges themselves to commission R&D. Instead, FEU's successor organisations have been funded by direct grants from a central agency plus individual government contracts for specific activities. In effect this made government itself the customer, and this is now the current pattern, so that an agency can be closed by a simple withdrawal of contracts.

Another mechanism by which power over educational development has been drawn to the centre is the constant reorganisation of bodies that might otherwise develop a will or a culture of their own. The FEU existed for 15 years, a remarkably long period by modern standards. Five successor organisations have been, and four of them gone again, in the succeeding 20 years.

Since its creation, the FEU as an advisory body had been joined in the educational firmament by other much more powerful organisations. The NCVQ had been set up in 1986 to regulate vocational qualifications. In 1988, the National Curriculum Council (NCC) was set up with the authority to specify the content of school curricula, alongside the Schools Examinations and Assessment Council (SEAC), which oversaw the qualifications system. Personally, I valued the lack of a legislative role for the FEU. It meant that the Unit's influence on practitioners could only be based on analysis and evidence. For government, the Unit could usefully go fly kites. If an idea proved valuable, government could adopt it as its own. If not, it could be disowned.

Balancing curriculum and qualifications development: the case of core skills

There was a brief but interesting period during which all four organisations mentioned above worked together to formulate a 'core skills' policy for 16–19-year-olds in the areas of communication, problem-solving, personal skills, numeracy, information technology and a modern foreign language. Note that this list is closer to the FEU's suggestions for a 'core curriculum' than the current narrower definition, which concentrates on the subjects of English and maths.

In 1989, government (namely, John Mcgregor, Secretary of State for Education) asked NCC to lead the work. My observation of the process was that sometimes the FEU and NCVQ formed an alliance to emphasise the special features and needs of vocational students, and sometimes FEU and NCC formed an alliance to emphasise the need for curriculum-led as well as assessment-led development. Structuring the learning for pedagogic purposes led to different patterns from when content was structured for assessment purposes. Not all that could be assessed could be equally easily taught. Conversely, there were learning experiences that were known to develop some important qualities that could not easily be assessed for qualification purposes. This core-skills initiative eventually ran into the immovable barrier of A Levels. I attended many meetings where it became clear that it was felt that studying A Levels, particularly in the humanities, was itself a guarantee of a broad education. Once again the academic paradigm was at work. Core skills were needed for vocational students 'because they were only studying one subject'. In fact they were following one vocational course, which might cover, among other things, the social and economic impact of the vocational sector in question, the underpinning science, the numeracy and literacy skills required to succeed as an employee, and the history of the sector's development – a broader programme than some A-Level combinations.

The development process itself, where a useful tension existed between things being curriculum and assessment-led, has since become almost entirely replaced by a focus on qualifications reform. More than this, qualifications design has become centralised, not only with little initial involvement of teachers, but even without a feedback loop that would allow them to modify the design subsequently, in light of their knowledge of learners and their needs.

This has resulted in a series of what I call, by analogy with the motor industry, a series of 'product recalls'. The pattern is remarkably consistent. A product is issued without piloting and without the involvement of those with experience of curriculum design and delivery, often because they are defined as being 'part of the problem'. More recently, even examining bodies have been denied initial involvement, because employers or universities must be 'in the driving seat'. The development process is seen as being linear, and not iterative, as it would be in any other field of development.

Within a very few years the product is discovered to be over-complex, too expensive and failing to achieve its original purpose. Then there is a fundamental review, usually conducted by one of the great and the good from outside the responsible organisation. But this was not planned into the process, and comes after many students have been used as guinea pigs.

The National Curriculum itself was reviewed in this way by Dearing, NCVQs by Beaumont, A-Level reform (misnamed 'Curriculum 2000') by Tomlinson, GNVQs by Capey, and Modern Apprenticeships by Cassells. Sometimes, a product launched with great fanfare is simply discontinued. This has happened recently to 14–19 Diplomas and to the Qualifications and Credit Framework. The more considered and collaborative development processes of other countries are sometimes criticised on the grounds of greater delay and expense, but this is to ignore the cost and damage caused by the need to review our programmes so soon after launch.

The example of 14–19 Diplomas also illustrates the ignorance of FE and its provision mentioned earlier. They were developed after Prime Minister Blair had announced that the recommendations of the Tomlinson Committee about the creation of a single 14–19 framework were not to be implemented, because of a perceived threat to A Levels. In evidence before a select committee, the then Secretary of State was briefed to say this about the proposed new qualifications:

> It is the bit that is missing from our education system. We have had, on the one side, theoretical study and, on the other side, workplace training, job training, and there has been nothing that mixed the theoretical with the applied to any great degree.
>
> (Hansard, 2006–2007)

Similarly, in an article published soon afterwards, the official responsible for overseeing our qualifications system claimed that, without the Diplomas, 'the alternative to GCSEs was training courses' (Boston, 2007), and in his select committee evidence the responsible civil servant even claimed that some 14–16-years-olds were 'spending perhaps half or two thirds of their timetable' on 'things that are clearly narrowly focused vocational training' (John Coles, Hansard, ibid.).

All of this was, of course, plain wrong, and ignored the previous government's own GNVQ initiative, let alone the long-established BTEC courses that preceded and then outlived both of the centrally designed schemes.

Summary and conclusions

I have identified a number of factors that have remained relatively constant over my working lifetime: invisibility of FE and its courses; neglect of half the 14–19 cohort; the diversity of FE; and putting the blame on colleges themselves for this, despite the fact that diversity has protected the traditional role of universities and sixth forms.

Among the things that have changed are: a reduction in representative decision making bodies, and their replacement by individuals appointed by ministers; a shift from curriculum-led change to qualifications-driven 'reform', where qualifications are used both as performance measures and triggers for funding; and an increase in top-down developments and the influence of central government on content.

I am all too aware that I have illustrated these things by reference to a very small part of FE's activities: the area of pre-vocational education. For a broader perspective, see the 2011 Report of the Commission on Adult Vocational Teaching and Learning. But my work as a consultant in other areas of FE over the past 20 years confirms that they do have broader and current application. There are ways of addressing these issues. Development work should be iterative not linear, and both successful and abortive initiatives should be independently evaluated and lessons identified. 'Reform' should not be solely qualifications-driven but should be balanced by the need to identify suitable learning processes. Vocational qualifications should both embody national standards and allow some room for locally designed options to meet specifically local needs and opportunities.

Above all, the domination of the academic paradigm in definitions of excellence, curriculum structures and assessment methods should be recognised and reduced. The value to many of our citizens of continuing general education through a broadly defined pre-vocational programme as well as academic subjects should be recognised. At the same time, appropriately different definitions of excellence should be used for the more strongly vocational programmes being followed by those already committed to a defined career. This should include access to industry standard equipment and staff who are both skilled teachers and credible practitioners in their occupational area. Both will require regular updating. This will, of course, not come cheaply.

Note

1   Vince Cable, quoted in Brian Wheeler, 'Officials wanted to axe FE colleges – Vince Cable', BBC, www.bbc.co.uk/news/uk-politics-29496475

References

Boston, K., TES, 30 March 2007.

Foster Review, 2005, *Realising the Potential: A Review of the Future Role of FE Colleges*. London: DfES.

Gatsby Foundation, 2015, *Mentoring and Coaching for Teachers in the FE and Skills Sector in England*. London: Gatsby Foundation.

Hansard, 2006–2007, House of Commons Education and Skills Committee. Fifth report of session 2006–2007.

Kennedy Report, 1997, *Learning Works: Widening Participation in Further Education*. Coventry: FEFC.

Moser Report, 1999, *A Fresh Start: Improving Literacy and Numeracy*. London: DfEE.

Ofsted Annual Report, 2013/2014. London: Further Education and Skills.

Wolf Report, 2011, *Review of Vocational Education*. London: DfE.

PART IV

Accountability, examinations, qualifications

10

ASSESSMENT

The need to 'do nothing'

Tim Oates

Introduction: constant change

This chapter explores the role that assessment and qualifications reform has assumed in overall reform policy in England, focusing particularly on the period 1980 to the present day. The analysis will suggest that its role – already assumed to be substantial by analysts and educationalists (for example, Mansell, 2007) – has been more dominant than presumed.

To make this chapter into a listing of the myriad changes to qualifications and qualifications policy would be both to render it into a boring catalogue, but also to reproduce a historical record that is more meticulously produced by other sources (see Cambridge Assessment, 2014, *Register of Change*).

A brief look will be sufficient to indicate the constant change that has occurred. The year 1985 saw the end of the CEE (Certificate of Extended Education); 1988 the full introduction of GCSEs; 1994 A★ grade introduced; in 1996 GNVQs were introduced, a heavily outcomes-oriented qualification influenced by NVQ developments, and then withdrawn in 2007; Advanced Extension Awards were introduced in 2002 and then withdrawn in 2009; key skills at Levels 1 and 2 were introduced in general education in 2000 and withdrawn in 2013; Diplomas were first taught in 2008 and all Diplomas withdrawn in 2013. A Levels were fully modularised in 2000, and then made linear from 2015. Merely some highlights.

And . . . tiering has been reconfigured at various times in GCSEs; calculators have been allowed and then removed from GCSEs on a number of occasions; coursework serially has been relaxed, tightened and transformed; modularisation has been adopted universally in A Level and GCSE and then abandoned. January sessions for general qualifications became widely used and were withdrawn in 2014. In 2015 there came the removal of controlled assessment; and also in this year, discussion by Labour of 'ditching GCSEs within ten years' (*The Guardian*, 22 April 2015).

Journalist Peter Wilby's broadside on New Labour thinking targets exactly the tendency upon which I want to focus in this chapter – educational reform policy and accountability arrangements that have undue emphasis on assessment and qualifications. According to Peter Wilby (*The Guardian*, 14 June 2011), it was Michael Barber who helped to write prime minister-to-be Tony Blair's first speech on education during the 1994 leadership contest and, in 1996, published *The Learning Game*, which was virtually a handbook for Labour education ministers. The phrase 'standards, not structures' was his, as was the focus on failure: failing councils, failing schools, failing pupils. 'Serious debate about failure', he said in 1995, 'is . . . a precondition of success.'

Michael Barber was right to home in on the huge disparities in attainment – for example in GCSEs – across the education system. In 1989 only 30 per cent of 16–17-year-olds were attaining 5+ GCSE grades A–C (Payne, 2001), with significant variation by school type, ethnic group and social background (Gillborn and Mirza, 2000). But a rightful focus on equity and attainment, using qualification outcomes as an *indication* of educational quality, became an exaggerated focus on assessment and qualifications as instruments of improvement and reform.

Complexity of form and function

The use of qualifications and assessment as major instruments of government education policy is not new (see Sahlgren, 2014). Such use intensified in the 1950s, with the introduction of A Levels and O Levels, following the Education Act of the mid-1940s. Although major examinations at 16 and 18 have continued to be produced and owned by independent assessment bodies, successive governments have increased levels of state regulation of the form and content of the examinations, principally through the specification of codes and criteria, and development of increasingly elaborate national regulatory organisations.

But, despite this escalation of central control, it would be quite wrong to cast assessment and public examinations simply as a crude tool of government policy and, particularly, accountability policy. The reality is far more complex. Much of the complexity derives from the multiple functions that are carried by assessment. Other elements of complexity derive from who owns and drives the form and content of qualifications. Newton outlines 20 functions of national assessment (Newton, 2007), while Oates and Coles trace 40 functions of general and vocational qualifications (CEDEFOP, 2010). Some of these functions relate to curriculum intent – that assessment embodies and conveys certain curriculum intentions (e.g. to focus on specific knowledge, skills and understanding). Others relate to standards – assessment conveying 'improvement' targets, being used to monitor 'national standards' and so on.

I am not arguing for complete removal of this complexity. It is likely that the assessments will, in England as in many other nations, continue to carry multiple functions. Rather, I am arguing for recognition of the over-dependence in improvement and reform policy, on assessment and qualifications, and the relative neglect of other factors.

Qualifications and assessment have carried an enormous policy burden from 1988 to the present day. They have been principal instruments of the accountability agenda. Indeed, assessment has been far more dominant in accountability than has generally been recognised. Using public examinations in target-setting and for measuring teacher, school and national performance is an obvious example of assessment-led instruments of control. The role of national assessment at KS1, 2 and 3 in target-setting and performance measurement also was clear. Less obvious was the form of the National Curriculum itself. It is misleadingly titled – the term 'curriculum' is technically a misnomer – and this is no trivial matter. Used correctly, the term 'curriculum' actually refers to the totality of the experience of learning – it encompasses aims, content, methods, assessment, evaluation. Curriculum theory further explains the distinctions between intended curriculum, enacted curriculum and actual learning outcomes. It encompasses 'taught curriculum' and 'untaught curriculum' as elements of the experience of schooling. This is not an over-elaborated view of curriculum. Understanding these elements and the interaction between them is a vital part of understanding the performance of schools and of national arrangements. The National Curriculum obviously states content – the things that should be taught – and it does determine, *to a degree, and in certain areas*, the pedagogical approach. For example, requiring experimentation in science and development of phonological awareness in English *does* carry strong implications for pedagogy.

But the National Curriculum is not a curriculum. It is a framework of standards – of desired outcomes. Other countries use a far more accurate term, describing frameworks of outcomes as 'standards'. The moment this term is used, and the current arrangements for national assessment at KS1 and KS2 are added to the 'national standards', it can be seen that the National Curriculum is far more assessment-oriented than curriculum-oriented. It is a framework of standards and assessment that determines aspects of curriculum. It is not a curriculum, it is certainly not the 'School Curriculum' (Oates, 2010). Seen through this more accurate lens, Michael Barber's drive towards standards can be seen as policy pressure on schools that is fundamentally about assessment.

Only with the Literacy and Numeracy Strategies did government action around the National Curriculum begin substantial direct intervention in the form of pedagogy in schools. The Numeracy Strategy appears responsible for a minor elevation and peaking of mathematics attainment in TIMSS, but remains controversial in respect of curriculum control. John Bangs, the then NUT head of education, regarded the strategies as invaluable professional development support to teachers, while other educationalists regard it as inappropriate subversion of schools' autonomy (Whitty, 2006). As a non-statutory part of government policy, the Strategies do not detract from the fact that the main legislative instrument of government – the National Curriculum and its allied national testing – remains an assessment-oriented instrument; a framework of *standards*, accompanied by testing arrangements.

Research on the many advantages of having a National Curriculum (for example, Hopkins, 2001) shows many who cite a 'general culture of high expectations' as being an important part of the post-1988 era, with 'high expectations' intensified as a result of the New Labour focus on 'standards'. But while a general culture of high expectations also characterises other high-performing jurisdictions (OECD, 2006), the impact of a general concern for high standards in England has been moderated by the specific impact of detailed accountability measures and the focus on examination standards as the key metric for judging whether 'high expectations' are being met. In other words, the international evidence suggests that a general concern for high expectations is vital and can lead to a general elevation of attainment for all learners. This, however, can be distorted by an intense emphasis on specific measures, leading to a dysfunctional focus on specific learners and/or a very instrumental focus on a restricted set of outcomes (Mansell, 2007; Select Committee, 2008). This combination of assessment and accountability requirements has pushed the English system into a highly outcomes-focused educational culture – in other words, heavily assessment-biased.

During the late 1990s and first decade after 2000, the 'grade C/D borderline problem' emerged widely in the system: the focus on GCSE C/D borderline candidates (capable, with highly targeted support, of just getting into 5 A*–C territory) led to relative neglect of those well above the threshold and well below it (Mansell, op cit). At one time, the then Department for Education and Skills was advocating this focus on C/D borderline candidates as a key improvement strategy despite its known adverse impact on equity (Gillborn and Youdell, 2000). Government failed, for over a decade, to refine the measures into a more equitable form, despite the obvious nature of the emerging problems (Oates, 2014).

The second strong moderation of a general culture of high expectations was the distorting effect of highly instrumental teaching to the test (both in national assessment and public examinations). Again well documented (for example, in evidence to the Select Committee for Education, 2012), the impact has been wide ranging: general narrowing of the curriculum; dramatic rise in strategic retakes in both GCSE and A Levels; narrow assessment-driven instruction; and deleterious impact on both the relation between learning resources and qualifications and the quality of those resources.

'Curriculum narrowing' has manifested itself in a number of ways. 'Teaching to the specification' has increased dramatically through a combination of teacher imperatives to focus on outcomes in accountability *and* pupils' demands. The latter usually is expressed along the lines of 'Why should I do this?' – 'Because it's in the examination' and combines with a recognition that high grades are of increasing importance in entry to HE and in the labour market. And this narrowing of focus is taking place despite evidence that teaching beyond the syllabus enhances the chances of higher grades. The collapse of 'curriculum thinking' to 'qualifications thinking' within institutions has affected student demand (during the 2010 review of the National Curriculum, evidence cited the dominant lack of student motivation for uncertificated components of the 14–16 curriculum) as well as introducing undue narrowness into overall curriculum development in the 16–19 phase.

Objective base to pedagogic approaches

In developing this thesis, I will need to spend a short time on the issue of an objective base to pedagogic approaches. Put simply, is there a means of establishing 'effective education', and what is the role of assessment in this? The argument frequently deployed in education is that it is complex, and thus forms of enquiry that seek to establish the superiority of one approach to teaching and learning over another are not possible (Stringer, 2007). It is clear that the complexity argument is correct (Oates, 2010) – education is affected by an interaction of natural phenomena (brain development, limits posed by working memory, etc) and social phenomena (dispositions to learn, parental support to learning, organisation of learning, etc). An issue such as class size is trammelled with this interaction and complexity (Blatchford *et al.*, 2003). But it does not follow that there is no means of discriminating the impact, in specific settings, of specific approaches to teaching and learning, of identifying vital educational imperatives such as the early acquisition of complex language, and of identifying specific facets of educational provision, such as the subject expertise of teachers, as being associated with 'desirable outcomes' (Bell and Cordingly, undated). This is heavily contested territory. The conflict over the role of RCTs (Randomised Controlled Trials) has highlighted the failure of our educational establishment to tackle effectively the question of 'what kind of system are we dealing with when we attempt to understand and manage education?'. This chapter is not designed to work through forensically the details of the debate; I am intending to extract matters associated with assessment, and with change in education. I am building an argument that asserts 'we need dependable assessment to determine the impact of what we do in education'.

Lapsing into 'nothing can be certain; all is relative' (an extreme version of postmodern sentiment) is not unheard-of in the education establishment – both from teachers and from academics. This, however, denies even the possibility of rational action and meaningful communication. A further, more moderated version is that the complexity of education renders systematic enquiry and discrimination between approaches impossible, or so heavily compromised that the endeavour is fruitless. Nowhere is this sentiment more evident than in the area of comparative education, when examining the features of different national systems in the context of PISA. But – although ruling out discrimination merely on contingent complexity rather than a matter of principle – this position denies the power of underlying method and of work that has shown us, for example, the importance of early language learning and high facility in reading (Sylva *et al.*, 2003). If crude empiricism is inadequate, the pessimism of post-modernism is irrational, and the relativist leanings of much contemporary educational theory is less confident than it should be. What body of theory helps us with careful convergence on 'what works', and deliberate management of change in education, rather than a lapse into being passive victims of events?

A 'critical realist' perspective

In my own work on review of policy development in England, and on comparison of national systems, critical realism has provided some important anchor points. It enables us to understand that, in natural systems, laws apply independently of human thought and action, while in social systems, our theories are part of those social systems, and affect the processes that arise (Bhaskhar, 1998). In natural systems, apprehended by our thought but independent of them, *laws* apply – Boyle's Law, the Beer-Lambert Law. In social systems, *tendencies* apply, not laws, and things will persist when all other things are equal – the *ceteris paribus* provision.

A simple but powerful example is the history of the education of women. Start with an assumption that women are not deserving of education and, as a result of being denied access to formal education, they will demonstrably not know as much of the standard canon as men – they are 'less intelligent'. This appears clearly to justify that they are not deserving of education, since they are apparently of 'lesser intelligence'. The theory about women's abilities actually significantly *determines* their abilities. But this is not a natural law, it is simply a tendency – one that can be utterly disrupted by adoption of another theory – for example, that women are equally deserving of high-quality education. The 'all other things being equal' principle is important for analysis of change in education. Women will appear less intelligent for the time that the idea of inferiority is dominant. Shift that view, and a lot of things change. What we think and do seriously affects the way in which the education system behaves – and education is affected by a diverse set of ideas and practices, determining the shape of its many features.

Now, a further illustration of *ceteris paribus*: all other things being equal or held constant. It is true that a specific system of schooling with a late age of starting does not need to be fraught with discussion about practices of how children acquire complex language, if the family culture has a strong tradition of literacy and ensures the majority of children acquire complex language before they start school. But if culture and practices in the family shift, for example because parents feel they need to work extended hours to maintain their standard of living, then schooling can make no assumptions, and had better respond, and fast. Responding to such shifts in complex systems is absolutely the stuff of effective domestic policy (Sylva, op cit).

'All other things being equal' is nowhere more evident than in vocational education and training, where attempts to increase volumes in employer-based training for young people constantly have been adversely affected by shifts in incentives and drivers, emanating from changes in the nature of production, the labour market, profitability and a raft of other economic factors. Vocational education and training also illustrate how 'all other things being equal' can highlight contradictions *within* the different arms of education and training policy: the drive to very high levels of participation in higher education sends strong messages that the vocational route from 16 is of lower status, and that it is more important to gain a higher education degree of any kind rather than to attend to alignment of learning with the labour market – thus undermining the drive to high-quality, long-duration, employer-based initial vocational education and training.

Because of the way in which our ideas about social systems actually are part of those systems, education is indeed bewilderingly complex. It is not only continually buffeted by external factors (social change, economic issues, demographics), it is also constantly disrupted by internal shifts in ideas and assumptions, theory and practice, where these ideas profoundly affect both the way education operates and the outcomes it achieves.

Critical realist perspectives help us to understand that some things are not arbitrary – the physiology of early and adolescent development, the importance of complex language in cognition – and that other things will only hold true while certain other things are held constant – *ceteris paribus*: all other things being held constant.

So . . . rather than lapsing into 'well . . . it's all so complex that we can't really know anything or predict anything, then . . .' or the assumption that we are condemned to endless conflict about ideas and to pendulum swings in practice, I want to place assessment in a special position. I believe that it can be and should be held more constant, and that this is an asset for policy makers, not withdrawal of a policy tool.

Making control easier

Assessment IS easier to control than many elements of education systems. This makes it a very attractive target of reform policy – the first thing to which politicians and reformers turn when they wish to effect change in education and training arrangements. This ease of control stems from many aspects of assessment, but not least from the fact that when it is done, and how it is done are subject to greater regulatory control and social consensus than many other aspects of education. Pupils, parents, educationalists and employers have long agreed that exams should be administered in a highly consistent manner. The fairness and accuracy, that are at the heart of formal 'qualification', are predicated on such consistency. Dependability in recognition of achievement and in signalling attainment is essential to the very notion of 'qualification'. It can be controlled by policy makers since it is a tightly managed set of arrangements in which the participants 'follow the rules' and the controlling agencies have a commitment to and interest in ensuring that those rules are followed. The obvious temptation of policy makers is to use this established, highly proceduralised apparatus as a tool of transformation. With the (quite rational) notion that the washback from assessment is prompt and powerful, policy makers can impose relatively cheap and simple reform on arrangements. The Coalition government's use of the English Baccalaureate requirement (*The Guardian*, 17 October 2013) was entirely consistent with this approach to reform. Incredibly cheap – nothing more than a statement delivered from the centre regarding the set of GCSE results by which schools would be judged, with a re-casting of data already collected from schools – and with no legislative change required, the government effected a massive and overnight shift in the curriculum preoccupations of secondary schools (*The Guardian*, 11 January 2011). Timetables and option choices were re-cast, teachers were told that their subjects were no longer a priority. Entry patterns to GCSE underwent a seismic shift. Ministers were themselves shocked at the speed and extent of the re-alignment of arrangements. It appeared to be a strong confirmation of the power of assessment-led system transformation.

Diversity of educational arrangements – the attraction of assessment

Let us now take a brief diversion into the peculiar diversity of education arrangements in England. It provides another element of the rationale for leaving assessment alone, and keeping it constant. The system in England is large – an annual cohort of over 600,000, compared with 70,000 in Finland and 40,000 in Singapore. But the diversity of arrangements is a feature of England that seldom is commented upon in analyses of reform and development. England has retained the 11-plus in some counties (Lincolnshire, Buckinghamshire, Kent and other minor areas) while others have varying forms of comprehensive education. Some areas deliberately have retained small rural primary schools (Cambridgeshire) while others have embarked on a programme of closures (Worcestershire, Wiltshire). Some areas have retained and are committed to middle schools, some have seen growth in school sixth forms, while others have ensured the growth of sixth form colleges. The age of institutional transfer thus varies considerably across England. UTCs have introduced 14–19 as a new 'phase'. FE colleges are the location of around 30 per cent of A-Level provision and 10 per cent of HE provision (AoC, 2014). The academy and free school developments have increased variation in structural form. Preschool provision is highly diverse, with an increase in nursery provision in primary schools in a number of areas. Local 'economies' of education vary widely, depending on local 'market' composition (for example, in a given area, the existence of dominant independent schools with day school provision can strongly affect local institutional form and policy). The size of institutions varies greatly, as do governance and management forms (federated schools, academy chains, and so on).

The DfE website gives the following description of variants of state schools. The most common ones are (www.gov.uk/national-curriculum):

- community schools, controlled by the local council and not influenced by business or religious groups;
- foundation schools, with more freedom to change the way they do things than community schools;
- academies, run by a governing body, independent from the local council – they can follow a different curriculum; and

- grammar schools, run by the council, a foundation body or a trust – they select all or most of their pupils based on academic ability, and there is often an entrance exam.

And this does not include the many variants of independent schools or reflect the variation among the group of schools that includes Montessori, Steiner, Buddhist and others. And a careful look at the descriptions shows that important dimensions of variation are present in each of the categories – governance, form, curriculum restriction, etc.

Structural variations are joined by variations in curriculum requirement. Unlike Finland, English law does not stipulate the number of hours that should be devoted to specific subjects. The National Curriculum does not apply to independent schools, academies and free schools. But there is more. The 2010 curriculum review detected further dimensions of variation – profound variation running deeply into beliefs regarding the aims of education, models of and assumptions about ability, models of progression, use of teaching assistants, vocational versus academic provision, and other fundamentals.

It is thus hardly surprising that, for any given central innovation (Reading Recovery, Assessing Pupils Progress, the Literacy and Numeracy Strategies, Diploma qualifications), impact is highly variable (Ofsted, 2002). Unlike teaching practice – action distributed across thousands of classrooms – the machinery and implementation strategy for qualifications reform are highly proximal to government – qualifications specifications can readily be reviewed and changed, and then fed into an established, highly structured implementation apparatus run by examination boards. In contrast, the means of directly affecting a system factor such as teacher quality in the existing teacher workforce requires sophisticated policy formation and a highly elaborate implementation strategy.

Such a high level of diversity is not present in smaller, high-performing systems such as Singapore, Hong Kong, Finland. Crucially, my own research in Singapore and Finland shows less diversity in *ideas about education and children*, particularly regarding ability and models of progression.

It is difficult to exaggerate the challenge that this many-layered diversity poses to policy makers – it ranges across the structure of schooling, the forms of schooling, organisation of learning and ideas about education. As Andy Green (2013) has pointed out, this variation is an enduring feature of the system in England deriving from the way in which modern schooling emerged in the country, and contrasts significantly with the form of emergence of education arrangements in France, USA and Germany. The acute and chronic diversity in arrangements is not going to go away, either overnight or in the near future – the pedigree of the diversity means that it is entrenched, and yet heavily contested (Aston *et al.*, 2013). It poses a genuine challenge to centrally derived measures aimed at innovation and improvement. The effectiveness of improvement strategies tends to be heavily dependent on context. And context in England varies dramatically. Initiatives that reach deeply down into practice are expensive, complex to manage, and recently have been perceived, by both teachers and politicians, as intrusive – prime examples being the Literacy and Numeracy Strategies (Whitty, 2006). In the face of all of these factors, using assessment and qualifications and major instruments of reform looks, to policy makers, like a very attractive option – apparently cheap, and relatively easy.

Change in assessment: a deceptively seductive option

So . . . cheap and easy, but I believe that change in assessment and qualifications is a deceptively seductive option for effecting change in key aspects of the system such as quality of learning, reduction of within-school and between-school variation and so on.

The first reason has already been outlined: the impact is variable and unpredictable, partly as a result of naïve dependence on a 'trickle down' effect – erroneous assumptions that educationalists always will respond in an optimum way to the challenges of new assessments, and partly as a result of the diversity of the settings into which the new assessment falls.

The second reason is of considerable importance. Assessment is one of the ways in which evidence of the impact of teaching and learning is created. Investigation of and experimentation on human cognition require measurement, as does investigation and development in education (see Mellanby and Theobald, 2014). It is no accident that, in the USA, it is the American Psychological Association that publishes *The Standards for Educational and Psychological Testing* (APA, 2014). We need to know the impact of educational development and improvement strategies – and measurement is a key element of this. I am NOT arguing that public examinations and related assessments measure all the outcomes in which we should be interested when investigating and enhancing learning. What I AM arguing is that, for the outcomes that are legitimately assessed by public examinations and assessments, consistency of measurement is vital.

For investigation of whether a change in approach to learning yields benefit, valid and consistent measurement of outcomes is an essential part of method. This is a tenet of psychological research, and is a methodological aspect of many experimental and evaluative studies in education (Mellanby, op cit; Sylva 1999). I believe that the same discipline should enter our thinking about routine educational assessment – public examinations and national tests. These are the means by which we can measure desirable improvements in our system, as well as producing dependable descriptions of what pupils know, understand and can do. This supports an evaluative function, and a communication or signalling function – the latter to be used in admission to programme decisions (e.g. for higher education), and labour market selection. If the measures constantly are changing, we limit our ability to make rational decisions about what works in our teaching and learning, and compromise the dependability of the information that is used in admission and selection.

Although it is far more difficult to reach deeply down into our system with sympathetic and effective innovation targeted directly at practice – innovation that will enhance children's reading, scientific understanding, creative thinking, and so on – it is possible to measure with precision the impact of such innovation if valid and consistent measures are used to detect improvement in outcomes. And this kind of consistent measurement needs to be available over an extended period of time, since educational transformation typically occurs over years, not months, and the improvement often is something that society wishes to sustain. This sustained consistency of measurement is an essential basis of PISA, TIMSS and PIRLS. In public examinations, Finland provides a fascinating foil to the relentless change in post-16 qualifications in England. Finland's high-stakes leaving examination at 18/19, the Finnish *Abitur*, has at its core four external examinations in subject disciplines, with one of these being in native language. These exams resemble A Levels extremely closely, in being highly discipline-focused. But the salient feature of the *Abitur* is that it has not changed in function or form, in any significant way, for over 100 years. Through the periods of relatively slow improvement and through periods of deliberate transformation of all other aspects of the education system, this key measure of outcome was kept stable. During the 1980s, throughout the move from highly selective education to wholesale, committed adoption of a form of Asian comprehensive education, the *Abitur* remained a consistent reference point in the system. Other aspects of the system – teaching approaches, educational resources, school form, etc – all were attended to directly, not assumed to be transformed through radical change in qualifications. This provides an extreme contrast with England, where assessment-led change has assumed such dominance, and difficult confounding has occurred as a result of assessment reform being used as the main stimulant of change while the assessments simultaneously are depended upon as the prime means of measuring outcomes.

Problems of change

It is important to recognise that this does not condemn assessment and public qualifications to moribund ossification. Measurement through assessment can be introduced in new areas of disciplines and of human learning, existing measures can be updated, and new measures equated with old ones. But there are limits on this equating, as demonstrated profoundly by the controversial contemporary challenge of linking standards in the new suite of post-2015 1–9 GCSEs with the previous suite of pre-2015 A*-G GCSEs. The tendency in England is to change the entire suite of A Levels and/or GCSEs at the same time, rather than changing specific subjects according to their own necessary timeframe – for example, when new knowledge is introduced to a specific discipline (Oates, 2010). Equating and maintaining standards become highly problematic when wholesale reform of examinations is effected (Bramley, 2013). And the system has been subjected to repeated waves of this wholesale, general reform. Two key elements of 'national standards' – standards over time, and standards between awarding bodies – are threatened by wholesale change in qualifications – adversely affecting confidence in qualifications, the signalling function of qualifications, and the ability to measure the impact of reform measures outside assessment. The recent controversy over the sample assessment materials for reformed maths GCSE – with two of the three national bodies expressing concern that the 'race to the bottom' was opened up by the Regulator's chosen approval process for the new qualifications (*The Times Educational Supplement*, 6 March 2015) – demonstrates the serious risks posed by all-embracing, ambitious reform processes.

A conclusion?

There is a strong philosophical, historical and practical rationale for stating this: that changing all things all the time, in a highly diverse education system, will result in chaotic, incoherent development. Of course specific assessments have to be designed well, operate effectively and be refined through evaluation. But endless arbitrary change seriously disrupts system coherence. The very ease with which assessment can be changed from the centre is actually a rationale for it being the one thing that is kept as stable as possible. Stability in assessment should be seen as an asset by policy makers. It should be viewed as an anchor point in a constantly shifting sea – an anchor point that enables us to understand and respond to all the other shifts that occur. The importance of this cannot be overstated. Without consistent measurement, policy makers will not have dependable intelligence on the system. Given the complexity and diversity of English arrangements, enhancing the quality of learning requires sophisticated transformation policies, sensitive to context. After three decades, assessment-led transformation policy has not yet delivered the step-change in system performance that preoccupies policy makers (see *The Telegraph*, 8 July 2013). Changing assessment has at the same time been ineffective in raising underlying quality and diminished the key quality essential to assessment – the ability to measure key educational outcomes with consistency and precision. Assessment change rips educational capacity from the system, as textbooks, teaching notes, 'polished' lessons all are discarded. As each transformation through assessment has failed to deliver, policy makers have not undertaken radical re-thinking of assessment-led change, they have lapsed into Soviet-style 'one more push'. It is time to realise that stability in assessment and qualifications is a crucial element of a balanced programme of system improvement.

References

AoC, 2014, College key facts 2014/2015. London: Association of Colleges.

APA, 2014, *The Standards for Educational and Psychological Testing*. Washington, DC: American Psychological Association.

Aston, H., Easton, C. and Sims, D., 2013, *What Works in Enabling School Improvement? The Role of the Middle Tier*. Slough: National Foundation for Educational Research.

Bell, M. and Cordingly, P., undated, 'Characteristics of high performing schools'. Coventry: CUREE.

Bhaskhar, R., 1998, *The Possibility of Naturalism: A Philosophical Critique of the Contemporary Human Sciences*, 3rd edn. London: Routledge.

Blatchford, P., Basset, P., Goldstein, H. and Martin, C., 2003, 'Are class size differences related to pupils' educational progress and classroom practices?' *British Educational Research Journal*, 29 (5) pp. 709–30.

Bramley, T., 2013, *Maintaining Standards in Public Examinations: Why it Is Impossible to Please Everyone*. Cambridge: Cambridge Assessment.

Cambridge Assessment, 2014, Register of Change Report, Cambridge Assessment.

CEDEFOP, 2010, 'Changing qualifications – a review of qualification policies and practices', Report, European Centre for the Development of Vocational Training, Luxembourg.

Gillborne, D. and Mirza, H., 2000, *Education Inequality: mapping race, class gender and inequality*. London: Ofsted.

Gillborne, D. and Youdell, D., 2000, *Rationing Education: policy, practice, reform, and equity*. Buckingham: Open University Press.

Green, A., 2013, *Education and State Formation*, 2nd edn. Basingstoke: Palgrave Macmillan.

Hopkins, D., 2001, *School Improvement for Real*. London: Routledge.

Mansell, W., 2007, *Education by Numbers: The Tyranny of Testing*. New York: Politico's.

Mellanby, J. and Theobald, K., 2014, *Education and Learning: An Evidence-based Approach*. Chichester: Wiley Blackwell.

Newton, P., 2007, 'Clarifying the purposes of educational assessment', *Assessment in Education*, 14 (2) pp. 149–70.

Oates, T., 2010, 'Could do better': Using international comparisons to refine the National Curriculum in England, Report, Cambridge Assessment.

Oates, T., 2014, 'The qualifications sledgehammer: Why assessment-led reform has dominated the education landscape', in Sahlgren, G.H. (ed.) *Tests Worth Teaching To*. London: Centre for Market Reform in Education.

OECD, 2006, *Education at a Glance*. Paris: Organisation for Economic Co-operation and Development.

Ofsted, 2002, *The National Literacy Strategy: The First Four Years 1998–2002*.

Payne, J., 2001, Patterns of Participation in Full-time Education after 16: An Analysis of the England and Wales Youth Cohort Study. Policy Study Institute.

Sahlgren, G.H. (ed.), 2014, *Tests Worth Teaching To*. London: Centre for Market Reform in Education.

Select Committee for Children, Schools and Families, 2008, Testing and assessment: Third report of session 2007–2008 Vol 1, GB, Parliament House of Commons.

Stringer, E.T., 2007, *Action Research*. London: Sage.

Sylva, K., 1999, *An Introduction to the EPPE Project*. Institute of Education.

Sylva, K., Melhuish, E., Sammons, P., Siraj-Blatchford, I. and Taggart, B., 2003, The effective provision of pre-school education (EPPE) project – findings from the pre-school period, Research Brief RBX-15–03. Department for Education and Skills.

Whitty, G., 2006, 'Teacher professionalism in a new era', Paper presented at the first General Teaching Council for Northern Ireland Annual Lecture, Belfast.

11

ACCOUNTABILITY AND INSPECTION

Pat O'Shea

Starting off as an English teacher

In schools in the early 1970s, accountability was not a word that often troubled us. I began teaching English in 1973 in what was then the only comprehensive school in Kent, a very large school whose families belonged to what was disparagingly referred to as 'London overspill'. As young teachers, our three major concerns were the impact of RoSLA (Raising of the School Leaving Age), the teacher recruitment crisis, and the Houghton pay award. The first meant that many 16-year-olds had to stay in school a year longer than they had expected and, even more alarming, be persuaded to take a public examination. The second meant that we started the school year four teachers short in the English department alone, and of those of us actually there, several were in our Probationary Year (NQTs). The third, Houghton, provided some succour, as in my second year of teaching our pay went up nearly 30 per cent at a stroke. (As a dampener to the excitement of this, inflation in 1975 was 24 per cent.)

As a young and inexperienced teacher I do not recall my teaching ever being observed. There were no appraisals, nor even any kind of review of my work. The avuncular head of department and his deputy supported as best they could with ideas and materials, but never watched us teach. The head of department was in any case somewhat distracted throughout 1974, as he stood as the Labour candidate in both the general elections that year. When I applied for this and later teaching posts, the selection procedure consisted solely of an interview with the headteacher. No governors were involved, but I did spend some time with the head of department and perusing the stock cupboard (the usual class sets of *An Inspector Calls, Of Mice and Men*, and *Animal Farm* – just as now, despite Michael Gove's aversion to English literature not from England). There was certainly no question of teaching a sample lesson or of meeting any students.

Teachers did not seem to regard examination results as a measure of accountability. At age 14, students were divided into three groups: those who would take no qualifications, CSE candidates, and those on track for the more prestigious O Level. The latter had been designed for the 20 per cent of young people in grammar schools, and could lead on to A Level and thence to higher education. CSE was aimed at the 'next' 40 per cent, so qualifications were deemed inappropriate for the remaining 40 per cent. (It was reading John Newsom's report *Half Our Future*, while I was supposed to be revising for finals, that made me go into teaching.) The syllabi for O Level and CSE did not overlap. After RoSLA in 1972, all students, more or less, had to take one or the other. This meant that a system of public examinations at 16 designed for the few became a universal point of assessment. This changed its nature, and made possible the later development of the whole apparatus of accountability through performance tables and examination outcomes at 16. It led the way to examination boards becoming businesses vying for custom, examination entry fees featuring heavily in schools' budgets, and the huge change in pace and focus that comes over secondary schools from May to July.

One version of the public exam at 16 was very attractive to ambitious and creative young teachers: the CSE Mode 3. Any teacher could design and propose a syllabus which would be marked and assessed by the teachers in the school through 100 per cent coursework. The course could reflect the enthusiasms and, indeed, political predilections of the proposer. The course and its assessment followed the teaching and its objectives, rather than the other way round. This put teachers in control of every stage of the process of the CSE public examination. We were participants in the Examination Board subject committees, setting syllabi, defining grade boundaries, and devising and developing the curriculum. We were driven by the need to make sure that the exams would suit our students' needs. It almost felt as though we were holding the Examination Board to account.

Although there was some external moderation, we were effectively taking in one another's washing, since we reciprocally moderated courses from other schools. I designed and taught a Mode 3 English syllabus. It included an independent art house film I liked and thought would appeal, some Bob Dylan, and *Romeo and Juliet*. It was not, to say the least, very coherent or rigorous. I am not proud of the fact that, for several of those who took it in the mid-1970s, it probably remains the only formal qualification in English they have. Complete freedom over the curriculum was no better for learners than excessive prescription.

Deputy Head at Peers

My years as Deputy at Peers (1985–1992) saw the biggest changes to education and the organisation of schools affecting teachers and students until the current wave. Bob Moon, the inventive head who had come from the ground-breaking Stantonbury Campus in Milton Keynes, had introduced an innovative curriculum based on modular accreditation, similar to that now offered by many universities. Peers had a national profile. We regularly ran Saturday conferences for visiting teachers and heads who wanted to hear about the modular curriculum, and were often invited to conferences around the country to speak about it. We were proud of the work we were doing and its impact on the motivation and achievement of some very disadvantaged and hitherto underachieving young people. Students gained CSEs and O Levels and, from 1988, the new GCSEs, all of them continuously assessed by coursework and module tests. I sold off 300 examination desks, convinced that never again would a cohort of students sit down together to take a public examination. I was wrong.

While I was on maternity leave in 1987, Bob Moon came for tea, to inspect my son and to tell me two things: first, that he was leaving Peers for a chair at the Open University, and second, that when I returned in the autumn and before he left, we would have a full HMI inspection of the school. I received the first item of news with alarm and apprehension, but the second with complete equanimity, because I had no idea what it meant or that it was a serious business. It is said that at that time HMI inspections came round about once every 250 years, in any case at sufficient intervals for most teachers and headteachers to escape inspection throughout their careers. Bob, however, did know that our innovations were on the line, and that much was at stake. Now, those in schools are constantly aware of Ofsted's imminence; it presides implicitly or explicitly over much planning and evaluation; then, the notion of inspection was novel. For the first time I recognised that we were accountable for what we were doing, that we would be externally judged. (My infant son was judged Good with Outstanding features.)

The HMI inspection

HMI were a cadre of highly experienced and mostly well-respected senior professionals. They were responsible for inspecting and evaluating a few individual schools, but the main part of their work was to provide information on education to the Secretary of State by carrying out and publishing national surveys, thematic studies, and evaluations of the teaching of particular subjects and aspects of school life across the country. About 12 HMI were in the school for most of the week. We took all this in our stride; we thought of the inspection as a kind of support-ive professional review. We thought the HMI were interested in our modular curriculum and early use of records of achievement of our own devising (see also OCEA, discussed by Tim Brighouse), as was much of the rest of the secondary education world. On day three of the inspection one HMI was overheard saying to another: 'I have a little list – modular curriculum plus and modular curriculum minus. So far minus is ahead'. This sort of score-card tallying, rather than a more measured evaluative and reflective approach, seemed to us rather shocking.

The report was made available to the school and governors, but was not published until about a year after the inspection, by which time we had a new head and everybody had forgotten about it (HMI school inspection reports had only been published at all since 1983). Despite their misgivings about our unorthodox curriculum, we were relieved when the report was broadly very positive, on the teaching and on the curriculum offer. A significant concern was that the library was thought to be inadequate – this proved useful later when we were able to negotiate the creation of a substantial joint public library on the campus.

All of our curricular freedom was changed by the Education Reform Act of 1988. This legislation introduced parental choice, local management of schools, the National Curriculum, and Key Stages, with objectives for each. There was also provision for City Technology Colleges, which were maintained schools taken out of local authorities, the predecessors of academies. I remember a meeting of heads, deputies, and chairs of governors, at which Tim Brighouse, then Chief Education Officer for Oxfordshire, explained how the combination of these elements of legislation would exercise a vice-like grip on schools and local authorities, to the clear detriment especially of those in disadvantaged and economically deprived areas where educational achievement was low. (The introduction of grant-maintained schools posed a further threat to local authorities and their illusory 'control' of schools.) We were required to publish examination results to parents, although league tables did not begin until 1992, introduced by John Major's government after his surprise election victory. The stated aim then was to give parents the consumer information they needed, to create a free market in school choice. That 'choice' has only ever been patchy at best, varying wildly between rural and urban settings, by class, by faith, and by parents' willingness to undertake informed perusal of all the data. Performance tables, as instruments of accountability, also provide a lever whereby government can directly influence the school system and the curriculum: the later double-weighting of English and mathematics, the introduction of value-added to tackle high-attaining but 'coasting' schools, the down-valuing of vocational qualifications and ignoring any but the first shot at a subject examination, the invention of the EBacc: all provide examples of this.

Warden of a Cambridgeshire village college

By the early 1990s I was in my first headship at a village college in Cambridgeshire. Because of the rich community dimension to these wonderful schools, headteachers were known as Wardens, an idea of the visionary bureaucrat who founded the village colleges, Henry Morris, CEO in Cambridgeshire in the 1930s. I greatly valued that title, carrying as it does the notion of guardianship of the whole learning community as well as of its young people. By now, the National Curriculum had settled down a bit: the 17 attainment targets and the 17 ring-binders that specified the science curriculum alone had been reduced to a more manageable number. SATs were firmly in place, and, for the first time, we knew how well the youngsters joining us in Y7 had performed against a national benchmark, however flawed.

We were subject to a new-style Ofsted Section 10 inspection in 1994. In contrast to the current approach, the focus was very clearly on the curriculum and its subjects. The inspection team comprised 25 mostly subject specialists from the school improvement service in a neighbouring local authority. Like every inspection team, there was also a lay inspector, a kindly, interested person with no professional experience in education. They were usually deployed to consider matters considered more peripheral than the curriculum, such as attendance, assemblies, and extra-curricular activities.

We had six weeks' notice of the inspection dates. During this time the deputy head spent many of his waking hours gathering data, information, evidence, and documents of every kind. His rather cramped office was stacked from floor to ceiling with dozens of green box files in which these were obsessively filed. Teachers, too, had six weeks to prepare the lessons they would teach during the inspection, and to become anxious about them. During the inspection every teacher knew they would be seen teaching at least once. By Friday afternoon an RE teacher who taught nearly 20 different classes in the school had still not been seen, and was in tears at Friday lunchtime knowing that her fate was closing in on her.

In contrast to the HMI approach at Peers, reports were now written to a common framework, and published within a month. For the first time, we were all clear what the criteria were, and the handbook included descriptions of what each of the seven grades looked like, from Excellent to Very Poor. This clarity was welcome. Inspection was almost wholly subject-based, with inspectors only coming together for large team meetings at the end of the day, in which findings were pooled. Several never met the head, nor understood how the school worked beyond the department they were inspecting. On Thursday the head of PE approached me with a concern about the PE specialist adviser who had made a number of comments revealing these limitations, including asking the head of PE, 'Who is this Warden person, anyway?'.

We had been reassured there would be no surprises in the report, and that proved to be the case. We had to draw up and submit an action plan within six weeks, but that was already there in our school development plan. Lesson observation by heads was not routine or formalised, but the deputies and I were confident we knew our teachers' strengths pretty accurately, from MBWA (management by walking about), and from having active antennae. I had begun at Peers to look at a teacher's results and manually compare what the same students had achieved in other subjects. I later learned to call the resulting measure a residual, when computers made this sort of analysis much easier, and school leaders acquired new skills in data and statistics. We were devising our own systems of data analysis before Raiseonline and FFT came along.

In my second headship, appraisal of teachers and school leaders became part of the annual gardening calendar of a school's work. The processes were some-what cumbersome, but we tried to make them supportive of teachers' work and complementary to the planning of CPD. The unions were influential in this, and acted as guardians of teachers' interests, so that appraisal was developmental, and not linked to pay in any way. This was to change step by step in later years, with the introduction of pay thresholds, the need for clear evidence against published standards, moves away from a national pay scale, and the stealthy approach of performance-related pay – anathema in the 1990s.

Examination results days began to affect my family life and that of all heads, as holidays in Provence or Tuscany were curtailed so we could be in school on the third and fourth Thursdays of August, to celebrate A-Level and GCSE results with students, but also to issue carefully crafted press statements and begin to calculate what our value-added might be and where we might stand in the league tables. KS2 and KS3 SATs were also externally marked, but the tests were erratic in standard, and their marking was sometimes plainly inaccurate. I may have been one of the few heads who appealed against the KS3 SATs English results on the grounds that they were too high. I knew that if they stood, our GCSE value-added results two years later would look poorer than they should, and I would be held accountable.

LEA adviser and SIP

After the turn of the century, I was working for a local authority. Oxfordshire LA, like many, had set up and run its own team of Ofsted inspectors, comprising the wide range of subject and phase advisers and inspectors working for the service. We had been inspected by just such an LA team in Cambridgeshire. LA services of this kind were beginning to have identity crises, reflected in the frequent changes of name. They were also grappling with cuts, as central government endeavoured to reduce the influence of local democracy and to introduce market practices. During my time, there were at least five reorganisations (restructuring, remodelling, re-alignment . . .) and at least five different names in as many years. Were we about advice, inspection, improvement, school development, raising achievement, effectiveness? All these words figured in the names of the service.

A further string was added to the accountability bow in 2004: the School Improvement Partner (SIP) scheme was introduced, as part of a so-called New Relationship with Schools. Experienced school leaders and local authority advisers like me could, through training and assessment, become accredited as SIPs. All schools had an SIP with whom they would have a 'single conversation'. The scheme was nationally funded and ran from 2004 to 2010. It was cut as a consequence of a change of government in 2010, despite evidence that it was effective, though not consistently so. As an SIP, I developed a working relationship with schools in a way impossible for an Ofsted inspector, so there was a perspective of evaluation and change over time. We provided external challenge as well as support; schools were accountable, as SIPs reported to their LAs, but could also deploy their SIP to support school initiatives. Discussions about target setting were informed by both comparative data and a knowledge of the context; they could be tough, and many heads valued a robust exchange with a supportive but external fellow professional. Many schools have chosen to continue to seek external support and challenge from former SIPs, but the free market in school improvement services has left schools able to choose not to seek and pay for external advice.

Becoming an inspector for Ofsted

As I arrived at the LA, the Ofsted teams lost their remit, and six national companies ran inspections in England. (Later, only three companies – Tribal, Serco, and CfBT – won a competitive bidding process for contracts to run inspections across the country. Costs were cut.) In 2005 I trained as an inspector for Ofsted. The training was extensive and expensive. At the end, I spent a whole day sitting examinations in a large area of a posh hotel in Park Lane. It was an extraordinary experience to be sitting at an examination desk, one of a hundred candidates arranged in rows, doing written exams all day, complete with prowling HMI invigilators. Mysteriously, we were only allowed to use a pencil. The experience felt like a throwback: nervousness waiting for the results, relief at passing. We were tested on data analysis, evaluating evidence, applying criteria, writing clearly. It felt adequately rigorous.

As I began inspecting in 2005, the framework and the process were slimmed down enormously. Average-sized secondary schools now had nine or ten inspector days – a team of four or five for two days – and two days' notice of inspections. The emphasis on subjects and the curriculum disappeared, and with it the inspection of subject teaching by specialists in that subject. This was a major step in the decline of the place of the curriculum in the inspection framework. Apart from the growing emphasis on English and mathematics, subjects have been sidelined, and the quality of the whole curriculum, once graded separately, now merits one paragraph in the long list of aspects of leadership and management to which inspectors must attend. With my roots in curriculum development and subject expertise, this seems a significant loss.

Also in 2005, schools' self-evaluation became hugely important. Never compulsory, but always expected, the exercise of completing an SEF was onerous but arguably did much to improve the skills of school leaders, to gather evidence, to interrogate data, to plan improvements, and to evaluate impact. Heads and senior leaders began routinely to observe lessons and grade them, something rarely done before this. Comparative information about schools transformed beyond measure during this time. As deputy at Peers School in the 1980s, on open evenings for prospective parents, each year I scanned the results from the previous year with the aim of finding three things that had improved. I then designed graphs with extended vertical axes to give a visual impression of rapid and impressive improvement. In the 2000s, the accountability measures were plain to all and common across schools. Data dominated our preparation for inspection. Performance tables had been introduced in 1992 in the public domain, but gave only broad-brush data. In the 2000s, Raiseonline provided sophisticated information for school leaders, and for inspectors. For the first time it was easy to compare a school's outcomes with national figures.

Many schools and local authorities subscribed to the Fischer Family Trust. This gave a new perspective on data about progress and achievement in schools, using a complex formula including social and economic make-up, gender, incidence of special needs, deprivation factors, and ethnicity, so that there was more chance of comparing like with like. This provided a very helpful set of comparators but was never made routinely available to Ofsted inspectors. Schools offered it to the inspection team if they chose. Doubts crept in that the weighting of deprivation factors, for example, to give 'contextual value-added', might be seen as an excuse for low expectations, and the contextual part of value-added was removed from later versions of Raiseonline. The effect for us as inspectors was to remove the capacity to give due consideration to the enormous social and economic problems some schools were addressing. Social deprivation was not to be seen as an excuse, rightly so, but nor was it accorded any explanatory power. Schools were expected to compensate for the growing inequalities in society.

During this period, however, I felt that Ofsted provided a broadly accepted national standard of what good practice meant, and I used it as such when providing INSET. The evaluation schedule provided lists of the aspects of the school's work that inspectors must and should consider, in each section. There were also detailed grade descriptions of what constituted outstanding, good, satisfactory, and inadequate practice and outcomes. Ofsted was and is unpopular in schools; the process is often damaging. However, it was possible to argue that the evaluation schedule was a powerful handbook of good practice, and could be used for professional development and to help school leaders improve their schools. The descriptions of what constitute good teaching, good leadership and management, good governance, and what additional factors make them outstanding: all those in schools could draw upon these.

Despite this, there has always been some lack of clarity and evidence about whether Ofsted was an instrument of school improvement or merely its chronicler. Certainly, the motivation of many inspectors, mine included, was to help schools improve by providing an external focused view of what would make the school even better. 'Improvement through inspection' was Ofsted's strapline, though there was no mention of improvement in the Education Act 1992 that created it. Improvement could perhaps come through the action plan that schools (governors, in fact) had to produce and circulate to parents. The idea was that the governors would ensure that the school followed up the inspection, and that parents would hold the governing body accountable. The LA also had a role in ensuring action plans were fit for purpose and, for a while yet, in supporting schools to implement them. This closing of the loop has ceased, however, and the function of Ofsted in helping schools to improve has withered. Local authorities no longer have the capacity to provide practical school improvement support; many schools are not part of an LA or even an academy chain, and so schools seem to be left with judgements and only their own resources to work out how to respond to them. Gerald Haigh quotes American management consultant William Deming: 'You can't inspect quality into a process'. The separation of powers – of inspection from support for improvement – seems part of what has been called the 'decentralisation of blame'. In a climate of much-vaunted autonomy and freedom for schools and their heads, who is responsible if things go wrong, or into decline? Over time,

Ofsted's expectations of governing bodies and the extent of their accountability have increased hugely, seemingly to compensate for the diminution of the LA's role as the middle tier. My increasing awareness of the gulf between inspection and school improvement led me to withdraw from inspecting at all. It has also become ever clearer that Ofsted creates unacceptable stress, fear, and pressure for teachers, and several of us could no longer be part of that.

Political imperatives surfaced from time to time in iterations of the Ofsted schedule, under both Labour and Coalition governments. *Every Child Matters* followed in the wake of the Victoria Climbié case, bringing together national and local leadership of education and the social care of children. Working in education in an LA, it often felt as though direction was lacking, as aspects of the education service were led by people with no background in education. The five priorities of this framework each had a paragraph in an Ofsted report. Inspections at this time became something of a scramble, as each individual inspector had to chase down evidence of our allotted ECM aspects, and also the four aspects of social, moral, spiritual, and cultural (SMSC) development. Inspecting school dinners became routine in order to have something to say about how well a school enabled children to Be Healthy. The five priorities had been developed through discussion with young people, and the aim was laudable, but the implementation became unwieldy.

Safeguarding too came to the fore after the Bichard report on the Soham case. Again, the cause was right, but the mechanism faulty, at least initially. Some schools failed their Ofsted inspection if there were minor administrative errors in the single central record. On one inspection it required several frantic phone calls to head office confirming that errors had been corrected within the hour to ensure that a strong and successful school did not go into special measures because of a typographical failing.

Community cohesion entered the lexicon in 2007 and became an inspection focus, in light of the fears about the rise of the far right and increase in racism. Nobody really knew what community cohesion meant, and the descriptors for it overlapped significantly with other elements of the Ofsted framework, especially SMSC, which had its own judgement grade in an Ofsted report. The new coalition government decided in 2010 that it was no longer important and abolished it, but later introduced a requirement to inspect the promotion of British values instead, in response to developments in some Birmingham schools.

These fluctuations in what schools were being judged on, and the consequent flurry of activity to produce evidence for the newest priority, have intensified under the Coalition. Increasingly, carrying out an Ofsted inspection is about checking for compliance, and chasing down evidence for aspects of school management that had never been subject to inspection before. The clarity of focus on learning and progress, on the quality of teaching and leadership, has been muddied by additions favoured by the Secretary of State. We are now required for the first time to inspect the use of one particular funding stream (Pupil Premium), examination entry policy (because 'early' entry might limit the highest grades), and salary progression and its link to appraisal (to embed performance-related pay).

Changes to the accountability framework impose pressure on schools to offer a curriculum that will look well in tables, whether or not it motivates and meets the needs of students.

Increasingly, inspecting no longer felt like the exercise of professional judgement or the opportunity to work with schools to provide a helpful, informed external view. Rather, it felt like operating someone else's instruction manual. After the three national contractors took over, the day rate for Ofsted inspector was reduced by nearly 25 per cent. This major cut in the pay of additional inspectors opened up the gulf between salaried HMI and freelance additional inspectors. It appeared to me that quality also became more variable. HMI Lead Inspectors were almost all exceptionally skilled professionals for whom I had great respect. Increasingly, they were deployed to monitoring inspections, subject surveys, and work with schools in a category, and now lead almost no Section 5 inspections. I had only ever inspected infrequently, but now job satisfaction, never high, plummeted. Inspection provided none of the colleagueship and camaraderie that have been so rewarding through all my working life in schools. The pay cut was less important than the two experiences in 2014 that clinched my decision to stop.

First, additional inspectors received a memo from the Ofsted contract holders to emphasise that Ofsted had no preferred teaching style. It clarified the language it was permissible to use to describe teaching:

> Please consider the use of the phrase 'independent learning' or similar phrases as banned with immediate effect . . . inspectors should focus more upon aspects of teaching which will be more readily understood by lay readers and parents such as:
>
> - whether homework is purposeful and regularly set and marked
> - whether lessons begin promptly
> - whether classrooms are tidy and have stimulating wall displays.

The gulf between this instruction, and the model of a professional, rigorous, fair and consistent approach to helping schools develop seemed unbridgeable.

The second made even more plain the divorce of inspection from school improvement. I attended my final Ofsted training in September 2014. By careful questioning, a participant obliged the HMI leading the training to make explicit that Section 5 inspections had nothing to do with school improvement – this was a matter for monitoring visits and Section 8 inspections. We were to give only judgements, with no advice to teachers in lesson feedback, nor discussion of possible strategies to improve the school further with school leaders. I had already become disaffected with the work of undertaking Ofsted inspection. The territory held by the political agenda was increasing. We caused stress and distress to teachers and heads, who were under huge pressure. Fear does not improve schools for young people. My inspection life is over.

Reflections

Writing this in the approach to the 2015 election, there is a broad consensus that Ofsted must change, or be replaced. The cost in teacher stress is too high, and the gains are not demonstrable. Ofsted is increasingly driven by political imperatives, is insufficiently rooted in the context of the school, and is intrusive in the demands the process makes. It labels schools, accurately or not, but makes little contribution to helping them move forward. A publicly funded system should, of course, be accountable to those who fund it, and a future model for monitoring and evaluating schools should have at least these features:

- local democratic accountability, through LAs or some other regional forum;
- self-evaluation rigorously tested by triangulation with other local schools;
- a focus on support for improvement, from a range of sources including local expertise;
- a developmental perspective, not a snapshot in time;
- high quality and consistency across the country, assured by a renewed HM Inspectorate or its equivalent.

PART V

Reflection on policy matters

12

FROM 'OPTIMISM AND TRUST' TO 'MARKETS AND MANAGERIALISM'

Sir Tim Brighouse

It is arguable that are three definably different periods in education policy making in England since Butler's 1944 Education Act. The first lasted for nearly 30 years, the second for 15 between the late 1960s and early 1980s, and the third for another 30 almost to the present, when there are signs that it will give way to a fourth. Each is characterised by values and attitudes that reflect the wider social and economic context of the different periods. I shall argue that the first could be dubbed an age of 'optimism and trust'; the second, one of 'doubt, disillusion and uncertainty' and the third, one of 'markets and managerialism', which is even now giving way to another period of transition. As with all 'ages' of history, activity characteristic of one period spills over to the next, but in the context of a different and less accommodating climate as new values catch hold. I shall end by speculating about the next age into which we are now entering, as the limitations of 'markets and managerialism' are being exposed.

My involvement over those 70 years has been as pupil, student, teacher, academic and administrator, progressively observing, writing, and commenting on and seeking to influence policy and practice.

The age of optimism and trust

The first period, which caught the post-war spirit of optimism (and a determination not to return to the habits of the 1930s), lasted until the late 1960s and early 1970s. It was an age of 'optimism and trust', characterised by partners in education knowing their respective roles and exercising them energetically, as all were agreed that education was a public good and we needed more of it. They behaved interdependently confident that each would play their part.

The Secretary of State had but a handful of powers, the most important of which was the duty of securing a sufficient supply of suitably qualified teachers in different parts of the country. In the process of discharging this ministerial duty, meticulous planning was involved with the Local Education Authorities (LEAs), which supplied local knowledge and ran the Teacher Training Colleges through grants from central government. Likewise too with the Secretary of State's second main responsibility, namely approving the opening and closure of schools, and rationing the size of building programmes against national minimum standards. In this latter duty the Secretary of State initiated an annual bidding process from LEAs, which were expected to ensure that the bids they were all asked to produce were consistent with the 1948 Development Plan. London 'overspill' and unanticipated housing schemes, including the creation of new towns and a birth-rate induced 'bulge' in the number of children requiring schools, soon rendered these 1948 Development Plans redundant. Direct contact between DfE and LEAs mainly focused on buildings and teacher supply. There were few 'circulars' – that is to say, papers asking LEAs to consider action on a particular matter – and no legislation followed the 1944 Act until the early 1970s. Taken together, these ministerial duties and powers were intended to ensure that all children would have a fair deal in terms of their teaching and learning environment.

There was much else to be done in this first post-war period, apart from the need to train teachers and build schools. All the many other matters requiring attention could safely be left to the LEAs. This first period was a golden age for LEAs – their responsibilities, duties and powers legion and varied. Colleges of further education had to be created and staffed to respond to the long-felt need to provide further education and training for 'vocational' students. Every LEA responded to this need, guided by Regional Advisory Councils on which Industrial Training Boards were represented and which were charged with securing a fair spread of accessible courses according to employment needs. Nor did it stop there. Using the same mechanism of 'pooling' of resources, local authorities established advanced further education opportunities through Colleges of Technology and Arts whose degrees were accredited by CNAA (a Council for National Academic Awards) and were later to become polytechnics and universities in the wake of the Robbins report, which also saw the establishment of a wave of new universities in the 1960s. As I have noted, Teacher Training Colleges – later Colleges of Education – were run by LEAs and their work planned through Area Training Organisations (ATOs), and a dozen or so rural LEAs used a similar pooling mechanism to establish Colleges of Agriculture.

Local Education Authorities were busy in this age of post-war reconstruction and expansion. All established a Youth Service and a Youth Employment Service – later called a careers service – and many bought old country mansions and set up adult education residential centres where they ran courses for their local citizens, as well as outdoor pursuit centres for their schools to use. Local advisory or inspection services were established to give advice to schools, whose control of the curriculum and how it was taught was regarded as sacrosanct. Recruited from schools, LEA advisers attempted to persuade school colleagues of the advantages of different approaches to subject teaching and primary school practice, but adoption of the ideas was down to schools. Teachers' Centres, financed by LEAs, ran twilight and weekend courses for teachers whose conditions of service were general and limited solely by convention and tradition.

This brief description captures some of the features of this first period – the age of 'optimism and trust'. Despite a huge national debt, public services were established for all: indeed, a career in the public service, together with what might be called public service values, were regarded as an uncontroversial 'good thing'. This regard for the public service, which seems so odd to modern eyes, was doubtless bolstered by the twilight of Empire, which was run by copious supplies of people from public schools, but perhaps also by the nationalisation of so many services – water, electricity, steel, coal, buses, railways – and by the establishment of the new National Health Service. All classes – upper, middle and working – had careers within public service. It was the main home of professions – architects, planners, lawyers and accountants.

In education, it was for the Secretary of State and national government to set out general policy and for the LEAs to flesh it out in a way appropriate to local circumstances and then implement it. In setting out and formulating policy, the Secretaries of State were advised by civil servants and HMI; they would also consult in depth with William Alexander, the Secretary of the Association of Education Committees (AEC), the representative body of the LEAs, each of which sat within a broader democratically elected set of local authorities. They would also consult with the teacher unions, then dominated by the National Union of Teachers (NUT) and its General Secretary Ronald Gould. In practice, for many of the post-war years, Alexander and Gould could heavily influence most policy. Secretaries of State and local councillors came and went. Continuity was provided by Alexander, Gould and the senior civil servants. They were, of course, direct protagonists in terms of Burnham Committee negotiations over teachers' pay but that did not prevent them co-operating to further their common interests. School budgets were determined locally by local authorities through the rates supplemented by the Rate Support Grant, and since the early part of this period was one of low inflation – pay deals were for two-year periods for example – the issue of money was not contentious.

Within most local authorities in this first period, education was seen as the 'cuckoo in the nest' of local government, greedy of resources, consuming 60 per cent or more of most local spending, and a 'law unto itself'. There were no Chief Executives and, in all but the cities, no real party politics: many councillors were Independent. The position of the Chief Education Officer was seen as important. Many of them had distinguished war careers and some of them used their position in very creative and influential ways. For example, Newsom in Hertfordshire, Clegg in the West Riding, Morris in Cambridgeshire and Mason in Leicestershire were all in different ways innovators and extended our ideas of what education could do. The impact of their achievements is still with us, not just in education, but in our wider lives. It is arguable, for instance, that Clegg's influence on the arts has a direct link to that thriving sector today. Locally, every education officer saw it as his – and they were all men – duty to ensure that schools were well staffed, resourced and supported, and they competed with each other in extending what an LEA could and should do to discharge its limited 1944 Act duties.

My experiences in those years lie in five years after VE day in a three teacher primary school in Leicestershire, a brief six week school-phobic inducing spell in a direct grant grammar school and then seven blissful years in a relaxed 'county secondary school' where the prizes were given out by the Education Officer of the Excepted District of Lowestoft in the East Suffolk LEA, whose Chief Education Officer, Leslie Missen, preferred directing his creativity to writing books on 'after dinner speeches' rather than administration. On a full grant, I received the modern-day equivalent of £100,000 for tuition and my living expenses at university. After training to be a teacher and jobs in grammar and secondary modern schools, I became an assistant in Trevor Morgan's Monmouthshire LEA office in charge of sites and buildings. My first week's task, clearly an induction test of my powers of analysis and initiative, was to give a 'school by school' description of what would need to be done if Monmouthshire were to raise the age of transfer to 12, as both a response to the Gittins Report – the Welsh equivalent of Plowden – and the need to go comprehensive suggested in Tony Crosland's circular 10/65. My exercise was academic. Trevor Morgan had no intention of raising the age of transfer to 12 and needed quite a bit of persuasion, as did all in South Wales, that going comprehensive was a good idea. My main responsibility, both there and in my next job, in Roy Harding's Buckinghamshire, was to persuade the DfE to give us large loan consents for school building in the annual bidding round and then brief architects with the resulting work in what were called 'major' and 'minor' building programmes. In Buckinghamshire, there was a new city to be planned, as well as raising the age of transfer to 12. This change enabled selective Buckinghamshire to provide more grammar school places and accommodate the raising of the school leaving age to 16 while still living within the ban on building more places in grammar schools, which central government had imposed in an attempt to pressurise LEAs to end selection. Almost all were primary building projects to accommodate the extra age group at 11 rather than 15. At that time, Buckinghamshire faced an expansion of schools places to respond to house building in south Buckinghamshire, Aylesbury and the creation of Milton Keynes, where the County Council made an exception to its selective stance and, to the astonished dismay of the headteacher of Bletchley Grammar School, approved comprehensive reorganisation. Fortunately, the most influential Conservative County Councillor for that area, Lady Markham, approved of comprehensive schooling. It is hard to see how Buckinghamshire would have received approval for new secondary schooling for the new population within the new city, had they not held their noses and done in one small area what they would never contemplate in the other more affluent areas of their County. Their pragmatism enabled me to help plan Stantonbury Campus, an 'educational village' in Milton Keynes that excited the DfE Architects and Buildings Branch which throughout this first period issued Building Bulletins in an attempt to influence, rather than prescribe, the design of new school buildings. Their favourite secondary examples stemmed from the designs of Countesthorpe in Leicestershire, Sutton Centre in Nottinghamshire and the Abraham Moss in Manchester. In that pre-national curriculum age there was room for innovation and experimentation. At Stantonbury, Roy Harding, Buckinghamshire's CEO, took a calculated risk and appointed Geoff Cooksey, Assistant Secretary from the Schools Council, to run it. It was immense fun, and Cooksey, who might be called a 'progressive', attracted and appointed a remarkable staff, whose deeds have reverberated for decades as teachers from those pioneering years have taken up posts elsewhere.

As a teacher I had experienced the absolute freedom schools enjoyed over the curriculum and how it should be taught. It was a freedom not uniformly exercised. Stantonbury was the exception rather than the rule. For example, the curricula in many grammar schools, and their timetables too, were much the same from year to year. There was more use of the freedom in secondary modern schools, either created for new populations or arising out of the national decision to discontinue all-age schools. Primary practice varied much more, as the teachers were influenced by strong advisory services in a few LEAs: so the West Riding, Leicestershire, Hertfordshire and Oxfordshire became synonymous with progressive primary practice.

The freedom teachers were encouraged to exercise in this period is best illustrated by the Foreword written by the minister to 'Story of a School', first issued in 1949 and re-issued in the 1950s as the sole central advice to primary schools about what they should do. In effect, schools were 'encouraged to experiment as the head who had written the pamphlet had done'.

Perhaps the last national expression of this period's optimism was Margaret Thatcher's White Paper 'A Framework for Expansion' of 1971. It outlined the most ambitious plans for nursery and pre-five education ever contemplated. It was still-born, cut down first by economic crisis and then a change in beliefs on economic policies.

The age of doubt and disillusion

By the time I left Buckinghamshire at local government reorganisation in 1974, the first age of optimism and trust was giving way to one of doubt and disillusion. The causes were many and varied. The year 1968 witnessed student unrest; 1969 the publication of the Black Papers casting doubt on the progressive methods of teachers and schools and Leila Berg's 'Death of a Comprehensive School', the story of the rise and fall of 'progressive' Risinghill Secondary School in Islington, where later there was a parallel primary school failure – 'William Tyndale' – which led to the Auld Inquiry. And of course there was the oil crisis, which contributed to cutbacks in public services amid massive inflation.

The settled educational world of a 'national service locally administered' was disturbed on other fronts too.

William Alexander and his beloved AEC were sidelined by the creation of the Council of Local Education Authorities (CLEA), a body representing two of the local authority associations, the Association of Metropolitan Authorities (AMA) and the Association of County Councils (ACC). In effect they were the usurpers of the AEC. Newly created Chief Executives and their political leaders in councils where political allegiance to one party or another was the rule, were determined to put over-mighty Education Officers and their committees in their place. I had left Buckinghamshire to join the ACC as Under-Secretary for Education and my tasks included making a fist of CLEA and proving that education, even in the new world of reorganised local government, would still be a force to be reckoned with. At first there were fraught meetings with the AEC and its beleaguered secretary, whose supply lines had been cut off by all the newly created authorities paying their dues to the AMA or the ACC rather than a subscription to the AEC.

Of course, as a young administrator I had known of Alexander's influence. He wrote a 'weekly' column for the journal *Education*, edited by Stuart Maclure. This was compulsory reading, as was *The Times Educational Supplement*'s leader when Maclure moved to be editor in 1969. Both these characters were wont to have lunch at their club, the Athenaeum, with ministers and senior civil servants on a regular basis. I could tell from Trevor Morgan and then Roy Harding that they each rated Alexander highly and were pleased to be advisers to meetings of the AEC. So Alexander's demise left them and most of their Chief Education Officer colleagues with mixed emotions. The old and trusted lines of influence were broken.

New ones would have to be forged through the AMA and ACC. For me it was an opportunity to see how policy was made at close quarters, albeit at a time of retrenchment and decline. School rolls were falling, and money was in short supply as a result of the oil crisis and hyperinflation. My life was spent in reading and commenting on drafts sent by the DfE to the AMA and ACC prior to public announcement; in writing reports for the ACC education committee, both on these issues and on those raised by members' authorities; and in sitting on various bodies such as the 'Pooling Committee' or the 'Inter-Authority Payments Committee'. These two had arcane rules and procedures intended to ensure a level playing-field for all authorities. If the rules of the first of these were understood there was room for individual officers to have huge influence on policy, practice and the speed of expansion of services. It was through 'Pooling' that advanced further education in the Colleges of Advanced Technology and the polytechnics expanded to form a base for the expansion of higher education over the remainder of the century. It was also to provide me with insights that were to come to my rescue in my first Chief Education Officer's post in Oxfordshire. But that is to anticipate.

Some of my time at the ACC was also taken up in negotiations with the teacher unions, on behalf of the employers, about conditions of service, and in sitting at the Burnham Committee to witness increasingly influential government observers advised what was affordable.

Of course, at this time of inflation, falling school rolls and diminished resources, expenditure was a contested issue. The work of the Expenditure Steering Group for Education (ESGE) was key to budget settlements. In my role at the ACC I attended, along with half a dozen CEO advisers, Treasurer advisers from local government and Treasury and DfE officials who acted as hosts. Key to decision making at this time was the annual report of Her Majesty's Chief Inspector Sheila Browne. She was almost Robespierrean in her sea-green incorruptibility: she certainly had integrity and a nerveless capacity to tell the unvarnished truth as she and her inspectorate saw it. It was policy making in a world where the old certainties had evaporated and everything was open to question. Policy was forged no longer through a comfortable debate among a powerful few, as civil servants tried to work out where the power lay in reorganised local government, which still was a vital engine of translating broad policies into practice. I suspect it was then that civil servants began to form a mistrust of local government, which has grown with the years.

In both the first and second ages, the influence of HMI on policy and practice was enormous if unobtrusive, both at the ministerial table and in the classroom. One has only to look at their publication record of national surveys during the late 1970s and early 1980s to see how they were attempting to influence the direction of the education debate.

Of the whole of my career, this period at the ACC was the least enjoyable, although formative and valuable, as I could see at close quarters how policy was made nationally. Within two years I had secured the exciting position of one of three deputies to Peter Newsam, who had become the Education Officer of the Inner London Education Authority, having been deputy to the legendary Alec Clegg in the West Riding, which had been abolished in 1974. I was back at the local scene and closer to the schools where I have always gained my energy and enthusiasm for what might be possible. But by then nationally 'Doubt and Disillusion' were in full flood.

For me, two incidents epitomised that doubt and disillusion. Both were speeches, one by Sir Ashley Bramall, the leader of the ILEA, when he charged his Education Officer, Peter Newsam and his team (of which I was by then a member) to make budget cuts with the words that it was 'time to get rid of some of the expensive horses in the ILEA's many stables, as not all of them are winners'. This was in the same year (1976) as Jim Callaghan's Ruskin speech, the impact of which was to be long lasting and the tone of which signalled the end of the unqualified trust and hope afforded to educational professionals for so long. The curriculum once dubbed a 'secret garden' by a Minister of Education was soon to lose its professional mysteries.

Both these speeches made me realise only too clearly that the post-war consensus was well and truly over. It hadn't yet given way to a third age, as it would in the mid-1980s, of 'markets and managerialism'. But doubt and disillusion were pervasive.

When I took up post in Oxfordshire in 1978, LEAs received another circular enquiring forensically into their curricular oversight. It was clearly a precursor to other action. I set out from a local position to try to influence the direction of national policy. At first it was as a result of an apparent crisis, which we were able to turn into an advantage.

On arrival from the ILEA – an unlikely source for such an appointment by a Conservative-dominated council – the chairman of Oxfordshire's Education Committee, Brigadier Streatfeild, charged with making large cuts, informed me that in his view the best way of doing this was to dismiss 200 teachers. This was where my knowledge of what was called the 'uncapped pool' came in handy. I knew there was no limit on the number of teachers who could be seconded for a term or a year at approved courses at the polytechnics or universities. To the superficially informed, an impenetrable barrier seemed to be that the sending LEA had to pay for a quarter of the salary costs of the seconded teacher. It was possible on closer examination to see that, if an LEA seconded a senior teacher, the costs of a quarter of her salary plus a temporary allowance for the person replacing her, together with the salary costs of Newly Qualified Teachers (NQTs) – or Probationers as we called them – were less than leaving the teacher where she was. With natural turnover from retirements and teachers moving on, it was easy to see that seconding senior teachers to such courses would solve our financial problems, provided that we could ensure that teachers could continue to live at home. Brigadier Streatfeild, once convinced of the arithmetic, needed no further persuading. Discussions quickly followed with the Oxford University Department of Educational Studies where Harry Judge was Director and with Brian Tongue, the Deputy at Oxford Polytechnic (now Oxford Brookes University). Each was willing and inventive in creating new courses that might be suitable for curriculum thinkers among the teaching profession.

It was all very well to solve a local financial crisis, but I wanted to use it to change national policies in directions that would benefit children's experience of school. In one sense it would do so, in that nobody previously had tried to breathe reality into the recommendations of the James Committee (of which Harry Judge had been a member) that the Continuous Professional Development of teachers should be taken seriously and that, among the measures to achieve this, teachers should have an entitlement to 'sabbaticals'. In effect that's what our solution to a budget cut would ensure, but we wanted more. A couple of years earlier, Michael Rutter had published '15,000 hours: secondary schools and their effects on children', which was the first substantial piece of research that showed that schools and how they are organised make a difference to children's achievement. Oxfordshire secondary heads at the time were very interested in finding ways to improve what was going on. Feeding the intellectual curiosity of teachers through engaging them in self-chosen study in groups and on topics relevant to practice would help. Notwithstanding the cuts and falling rolls, causing the LEA to close some schools, heads and teachers in Oxfordshire recall this period as a golden one, probably as a result both of the secondments and of the sometimes orchestrated purposes for which the teachers took part. Take two examples. Keith Joseph, when Secretary of State, upset local government by announcing that he would top slice up to one half of 1 per cent to fund nationally determined initiatives. He would start with two schemes: one the Technical, Vocational, Educational, Initiative (TVEI) and what was called the Low Attainment Pupil Project (LAPP). Oxfordshire succeeded in a joint bid with Somerset for the latter, and, with Barry Taylor, their

CEO, we focused in part on Feuerstein's work in what we called the 'Thinking Skills' project. Taylor was intrigued by our capacity to add to the scheme by supporting seconded teachers who engaged in action research while carrying out their courses at the polytechnic or the university department.

Once the finances of the pooling device were shared with Taylor and his counterparts, Andrew Fairbairn and Bob Aitken, in Leicestershire and Coventry, respectively, we discussed an ambitious attempt to revolutionise what we saw as a divisive and limiting secondary exam system of GCEs and CSEs. What if such a system could be seen within the context of a broader assessment of pupils' achievements in what we would call the Oxford Certificate of Educational Achievement (OCEA), which would be accredited by Oxford University through its Delegacy of Local Examinations – then a GCE board, on which I sat as a delegate by virtue of holding my post? It would have three parts, one a 'G' part focusing on graded assessments of skills that could be assessed; another, an 'E' part containing records of exam success; and a third, a 'P' section attempting to record personal development. We could second teachers to Harry Judge's department and have them working with the Delegacy in devising the detail.

I simultaneously worked with two colleagues, Gordon Hainsworth (CEO of Gateshead and then of Manchester) and Bill Stubbs, a former colleague in ILEA and Peter Newsam's successor as its Education Officer: they too were promoting, with the Northern and London GCE boards, respectively, developments similar to OCEA. We thought it would be irresistible as it appeared simultaneously in different parts of the country. In practice it was taken over by DfE and ruined by imposition as a National Record of Achievement (NRA). In the process of universal prescription it lost the energy of its teaching progenitors.

Harry Judge was effectively my mentor in those years; a better or wiser one it would be hard to find. He had other plans for affecting policy through local innovation. He had long been doubtful about the effectiveness of the university model for PGCE. Impressed by medical analogy and some models elsewhere, he launched the Internship scheme, which effectively turned the PGCE into a partnership with schools, all of whom through their participation were inclined to focus anew on teaching and learning and staff development. In the years that were to follow, the Oxford Internship scheme shifted the balance of theory and practice and of university and school.

All these exciting ventures were happening at a time of cuts in the age of national 'Doubt and Disillusion'. In short, some of us were behaving as though the virtues of the previous age – strong LEAs and partnerships with heads and teachers in exciting development of the curriculum – still existed. Of course we could read the runes of a new age, but we enjoyed ourselves as we searched for the characteristics of the age that would emerge.

The age of markets and managerialism

Margaret Thatcher's election in 1979 ushered in an economic policy that set the defining features of this age, which was taken on by New Labour when they were elected in 1997. All the White Papers contained mantra words – 'choice', 'autonomy', 'diversity'; much mention too of 'accountability', with some exhortation towards 'equity' and of course 'excellence'. If the state was going to unleash market forces, it realised it had to regulate.

Just prior to my arrival in Oxfordshire, the council formally resolved 'to publish exam results so that parents could make a better choice of school' – 15 years before publication became a national requirement, and 3 years before parental preference became a required feature of admission to schools arrangements. Encouraged by Brigadier Streatfeild, I had supper with John Redwood, formerly a councillor and shortly to be head of Mrs Thatcher's Policy Unit. His views – to privatise everything and create a quasi-market in education – seemed bizarre at the time and certainly eccentric to the Brigadier, whose background was steeped in public service. The Brigadier encouraged me to think of ways to head off the worst possibilities of accountability. I rejected the idea of local inspectors, because it seemed unlikely that LEA advisers would walk the tightrope of being a 'critical friend' by avoiding the Scylla of 'hostile witness' or the Charybdis of 'uncritical lover'. Instead, we set up a four-year cycle of 'School Self-Evaluation' backed by a stimulating set of questions, 'Starting Points in Self-Evaluation', with the schools involving their staff and a selected outside professional. The outcome was their presenting to a small group of councillors, including the member local to the school.

Finally, I encouraged teachers, parents and governors to respond to Kenneth Baker's 1987 consultation on the 1987 Reform Bill. Local Management of Schools (LMS) seemed long overdue, as the practice of stipulating what a school should spend in great detail seemed antiquated. Removing from schools power over what is taught seemed to me entirely wrong. I wrote a 600-word piece, 'First Steps on a Downward Path', for *The Observer*, comparing the government with the 'authoritarian church states of the 16th century' and, conjuring 'images of brown and black', I worried 'for my grandchildren'. It provoked a strong reaction, including my having to sit through a Conservative censure motion in the council chamber that was lost, because the council was by then 'hung'. I could not continue to lead a community when all I had fought for seemed lost. I was no longer credible as a leader who could make sense of the external world to the teachers.

I accepted a job at Keele University as Professor and Head of Education Department to start in 1989. So it was from this academic vantage point that I saw LEAs lose their Colleges of FE, Polytechnics and the Colleges of Education. GCSE results were published as league tables, as would be Key Stage 2 SAT results for primary schools in due course. Ofsted was created, and the outcomes of regular inspections of schools were published, as was the name of the first 'failing' school. Meanwhile at Keele, I introduced the Oxford model of the PGCE, taught in schools and the university, supervised Masters and Doctorate students, founded a Centre for Successful Schooling, read voraciously, wrote about school improvement that was fascinating me, and campaigned for a movement called 'Towards a New Education Act' (TANEA). However, if one wanted to influence national policy, being in a university wasn't a good place to be effective.

In 1993 I started a ten-year period as Chief Education Officer in Birmingham. With no responsibility for further and higher education as a result of government action, and with responsibilities for the youth service, adult education and the libraries given to other chief officers, I focused on pre-school and schools, which were my first loves in any case. Armed with a set of recommendations for improvement from an independent enquiry and report chaired by Ted Wragg, and with excellent data, we set about transforming expectations and outcomes in the city. This was not something confined to the professionals: the whole city was caught up in our determination each year 'to improve on previous best'. We harnessed the considerable 'common wealth' of the city – art galleries, music, universities and other performances and the like – to establish a set of experiences or entitlements that we asserted all children should have. Schools were the guardians who would make sure they had them. Simultaneously with teachers and heads we shared a common language and map of school improvement and set targets for improvement from the 'bottom-up' rather than, as the government later imposed, the 'top-down'. We were determined to change the culture of a city, at least so far as education was concerned. After a couple of years, the data (which we collected meticulously and used imaginatively to encourage 'school-to-school' learning) suggested we were succeeding, although, in our efforts to improve, we were hampered by the DfE's inability or unwillingness to give us comparative data by ethnic and socio-economic groups. Instead, we used anecdote to help us search out what might be better practice in other LEAs. Schools enthusiastically embraced the agenda and co-operated one with another in a quest for ever-better practice and outcomes. Between 1993 and 1997, we did this largely unnoticed beyond the city, but one of the local MPs, Estelle Morris, invited David Blunkett frequently for discussions, and I was part of a small group that helped him and Tony Blair prepare their education priorities for government. Indeed, after their election, Blunkett had wanted me to work full-time in a post eventually given to Michael Barber. I had refused, partly because I knew the work with Birmingham was not yet fully rooted, partly because I loved the city and its people and partly because I knew I would fall out with David Blunkett over method. He was inclined to national prescription and imposition, which seemed unlikely to work in somewhere as vast as England. My experience suggested it would breed professional resentment and a loss of teacher energy, which is so vital to school success. In the years after 1997, both David Blunkett and Estelle Morris would tell me when I complained of their agenda that all they were doing was what they had learned worked in Birmingham. In vain did I explain that the agenda – well, most of it – might be fine, but the language (always emphasising failure and 'zero-tolerance') and the method of introducing it were counter-productive.

It is hard to overestimate the excitement of having a government that put education at the top of its agenda. I was offered the Chair of the Standards Task Force by David Blunkett, who withdrew the offer on the grounds that, for it to make a difference, he needed to chair it, but I could be vice-chair. He then made a big request that I should be joint vice-chair with Chris Woodhead, HMCI and head of Ofsted, which, as I thought then and have done ever since, needed total reform. He and I did not get on, as any glance at newspaper coverage of our fairly public disagreements at that time will testify. But I accepted to help in what I saw as a huge opportunity for education to make the difference it could when put centre stage of public policy. I soon saw, however, that the Task Force had little influence and wasn't sorry to resign when Woodhead's 'pilot' inspection of LEAs was taking place in Birmingham and was going to demand all my time to handle, if damage was to be avoided.

I had anticipated, wrongly as it turned out, that New Labour would re-establish 'planning' as a watchword to accompany and limit 'choice', 'diversity', 'autonomy' and 'accountability' in the mantra lexicon of the new government's policy and practice. Certainly they emphasised 'equity' and took many measures designed to make the schooling system less unequal and unfair, especially in the early years where they introduced and exceeded all the measures contained in Mrs Thatcher's stillborn Framework for Expansion White Paper of 1971. Nevertheless, we were still in an age of 'markets and managerialism': indeed, New Labour consolidated their influence. The first 15 failing schools were named and shamed, and 'literacy' and 'numeracy' hours introduced. Their legislation gave yet more powers to the Secretary of State who, from 1945 to 1980, had but three and, by 2015, had added another 2,000 powers, with over 3,000 schools run by direct private contracts with him.

The London challenge

By 2002, with a second LEA inspection behind me, it was time to retire. But Estelle Morris, by then Secretary of State, had other ideas. London had become synonymous with all that was wrong in education, just as Birmingham had been a decade earlier. Neither reputation was deserved and was more the result of a bad press. Would I be interested in becoming Commissioner for London School and running the London Challenge? It was an irresistible temptation. I was to be given a 'more or less free hand'.

I had written a no-holds-barred attack on markets and managerialism as the Caroline Benn–Brian Simon memorial lecture in 2002, '*Dreams and Nightmares*', speculating about two possible scenarios of ever-widening hierarchies of schools in urban areas, on the one hand, the product of market competitions, and, on the other hand, of partnerships of schools in an area, working interdependently and committed to pooling their ideas, skills and knowledge and being judged as a group. What I was witnessing was ever-harsher Ofsted regimes, a use of language that emphasised failure, challenge and 'zero tolerance' of whatever undesirable feature one was trying to eradicate. I asked all ministers to read it and only approve my appointment if they did not think it would embarrass them.

The measures put in place and expertly framed in the London Challenge prospectus and carried through by Jon Coles, the ablest civil servant of his generation, included school-to-school support, a Families of Schools database to support learning from each other, a focus on Continuous Professional Development through the Chartered London Teacher scheme and a small group of part-time expert experienced school advisers who would work with schools that elsewhere (and up to that point) DfE classified as 'failing' because of low GCSE results. We dubbed such schools 'Keys to Success' – a subtle but important change of language intended to contribute to a change in culture. After all, if these schools could transform standards, any school could. Name, blame and shame might make good headlines but it set back the chances of improvement, and I was granted some latitude in London, where my experience as deputy to Peter Newsam meant I was remembered, by teachers now leading schools, as somebody who probably understood their circumstances.

In short, in London we were allowed to try a distinctive set of practices that were tailored to London's needs but within national educational policies. What we tried to encourage was professional trust and schools learning from each other, backed by a database that enabled them to see in forensic detail what other schools in similar circumstances were doing. We talked the language of partnership and, by speculating on different solutions working in different contexts, tried to counter the belief in 'one size fits all', which was then prevalent in policy making.

There remained, however, a belief in the overall efficacy of the 'market', as expressed through creating autonomous competitive quasi-independent schools. This had first surfaced with the Grant-Maintained School, which was abandoned as a model by New Labour in 1997 but was about to make a come-back through the Academies movement.

Ten years on, as politicians celebrate the extraordinary success of London schools, and as researchers seek to explain the phenomenon, the seeds sown then are beginning to surface, and the questions crowd in. Agreement about London is by no means the only political pointer to the direction of the educational weathervane. The main parties, presumably aware of the unreasonable pressures on heads and teachers and the imminent shortage of candidates for both, are agreed that Ofsted is no longer fit for purpose and needs reform, that there should be a Royal (or National) College of Teaching, and that the autonomous independent school is an inadequate and unreliable model on which to plan a successful schooling system. Are perhaps partnerships of schools for very clearly stated purposes – including of course school improvement and teachers' continuous professional development – essential? If so, how should they be funded and held accountable? In the age of creativity, which makes new and different demands on schools, are we holding schools themselves accountable for the wrong things?

In short, there are plenty of signs that the *Age of Markets and Managerialism* may have nearly run its course and may be succeeded by one of *Partnerships and Intelligent Accountability*, where democratic influence is regional rather than national and where policies are more overtly based on research evidence tempered by an understanding of context rather than on anecdote and personal opinion.

13

SCHOOLS

A shifting landscape

Margaret Maden

Islington Green Comprehensive School

In October 1976, Prime Minister James Callaghan criticised schools, mildly but firmly, in his Ruskin Speech. I was then in my first year of headship at Islington Green Comprehensive School, part of the Inner London Education Authority (ILEA). I was already conscious of growing doubts about schools, not least through a nearby school's headteacher, Dr Rhodes Boyson, and the part he played in the 'Black Papers'. These raised questions about 'progressive' teaching methods, many of which I supported through Schools Council projects such as history, geography for the Young School Leaver, music and humanities. Through these, teachers developed learning materials and pedagogy alongside university curriculum specialists. They were properly trialled and amended in light of classroom experience. The 'progressive' nature of these appeared to be the ambition to democratise more contemporary scholarship and emphasise the modes of learning particular to each discipline. In the hands of able and motivated teachers, Schools Council projects were demonstrably raising standards of thinking and investigation on the part of pupils. Insufficient evaluation of their impact probably aided those who valued, above all else, more traditional syllabi and rote learning.

Several teachers at Islington Green welcomed the more comfortable challenge-free implications of the Black Papers, something not intended by their authors. The rhetoric at this time now seems naïve. It was, of course, in a context when the secondary school curriculum was primarily determined by examination boards. In primary schools there was no equivalent framework, and one of my main feeder schools, William Tyndale, deepened my anxiety levels about the mounting worries of many parents. I roused the wrath of NUT friends by expressing public condemnation of its teachers barring access to inspectors and 'unacceptable' school governors. None of its antics helped me at all in my determination to galvanise teachers at my school, not through idle polemics but through hard graft and appointing teachers, once the pupil roll increase permitted, who were imaginative and optimistic about their pupils' capabilities.

In 1977, I was invited to address one of the regional conferences in 'The Great Debate', the response of the Secretary of State, Shirley Williams, to her Prime Minister's expressed concerns about the nation's schools. To my best recollection, this was the first and last time I received, as a headteacher, any communication from central government. How very different now. The outcome of the 'Great Debate' was an advisory Circular in which local education authorities were to devise a 'core curriculum' for their schools and the accumulated knowledge of the Schools Council would be 'considered'. Compared with what followed in the 1980s, this was all 'business as usual' and a bit of fudge. Even at the time, it was clear that significant interest groups, including employers' organisations, were dissatisfied with many school leavers. It was quite common for a mere 20 per cent of 16-year-olds to continue in full-time education and training at the end of their time in a comprehensive school. The gap between high achievers and low achievers was not only greater than today but also seen by many as unbridgeable. Primary schools varied from creative brilliance and impressive outcomes to those characterised by an unstructured lack of challenge.

The Local Authority – London

So that many more 16–19-year-olds could voluntarily and usefully continue their studies, a changed approach was needed. In Islington, better A-Level teaching was provided through a combined approach, with its ten secondary schools working through a sixth form centre. This evolved from a loose federation to a larger college based in former London County Council Board schools. An initial student enrolment of 300, mainly part-time and still formally enrolled in one of 11 local schools, rose to over 500 in its first year, and increasingly, students were full-time as they consciously opted for the more adult ethos and better outcomes. Economies of scale plus high-level teaching skills meant that a wide range of needs could be supported. This is where the role of the local authority proved positive. It quickly located empty buildings, and its architects did wonders with unpromising conditions, making the physical provision both attractive to staff and students and appropriate in terms of specialist facilities.

The ILEA was an odd mixture of brilliance and frustration for its schools. In quickly and imaginatively responding to post-16 inadequacies in Islington, it was at its best, aided and abetted by a new head of service, Dr William Stubbs, and a new Leader, Councillor Frances Morrell, the latter being a resident of Islington. Additionally, Dr Stubbs ensured that I, as Director-designate, visited successful community colleges in the USA and sixth form colleges in England so as to raise aspirations and strengthen organisational planning. Likewise, money was found so that a core of excellent teachers could be appointed as heads of faculty, with teachers from local schools teaching on a sessional basis.

All schools and colleges benefited from the ILEA's Research and Statistics branch. This generated high-quality data about us and our performance and, equally, promoted good practice exemplars of both a qualitative and quantitative kind. With a powerful inspectorate, subject centres were a godsend, where teachers could immerse themselves in the best of their specialisms and meet each other, irrespective of their headteachers' predilections. In 1979, *15,000 hours* (Rutter *et al.*, 1979) was published, a rigorous study of how secondary schools in the ILEA with similar pupil characteristics were highly variable in outcomes and, crucially, why. 'Nowhere now to hide' as one head said. This was a project led by Professor Michael Rutter, leading a team of University of London researchers, including Peter Mortimore, who soon afterwards became Director of the ILEA's Research and Statistics Branch. This kind of expert systemic support and challenge represented the 'middle tier', between central government and individual institutions, at its best.

However, in other regards, the ILEA was cumbersome and aggravating. Limited autonomy for headteachers meant that I could not get into my school unless the school-keeper (janitor) allowed it, neither could I require the school bursar to arrange her holiday leave at a time that made sense to the school; both reported to line managers somewhere else in the ILEA firmament. I was keen, with leading governors and teachers, to develop Islington Green as a community school, combining school and adult education, 'open all hours', which I believed would improve our educational relationship with parents and neighbours. It would also enlarge our students' sense of the value and potential of education. However, I was stopped by the ILEA's Youth and Adult Education service which saw our proposal as a threat and its youth club in the school premises five evenings a week (term time only, of course) as sacrosanct. Visits to Leicestershire's community schools merely made me feel worse. When I managed to get funding from the Manpower Services Commission (MSC) for a School-Work Liaison Officer, several leading ILEA councillors complained, saying 'every school will want one if she gets one'. Only the intervention of senior officers secured this, but the time and angst wasted were absurd. The extension of our successful sixth form centre to other inner London boroughs was likewise stymied by the authority's FE lobby. That successful provision depended on the skills and knowledge of FE colleges as well as schools seemed to be lost in the struggle.

The Local Authority – Warwickshire

The reconstruction of educational systems, accountabilities and powers proceeded at breakneck speed through the 1980s and beyond. GERBIL – the Great Education Reform Bill – took up hours of angry debate among the traditional 'partners' in the education service. At the end of that decade, I was appointed to Warwickshire County Council as its County Education Officer. Councillors took a calculated risk in appointing an LEA novice, a woman at that, with London experience, but they sniffed the prevailing air and decided that headship experience was a more timely criterion. The education department wit expressed widespread surprise at my appointment, commenting that this was like 'Maradona being appointed to Port Vale'. That Warwickshire staff saw themselves as Port Vale spoke legions about this 'Middle England' local authority. Later accusations of local authority 'control' over schools were and are laughable.

My recent experience as a headteacher and Sixth Form Centre Director was certainly helpful in working constructively with headteachers and governors in this shire authority. Initially, I set up working groups of officers and headteachers to prepare a series of proposals for the council and schools as a response to GERBIL. Not all headteachers welcomed the autonomy that was offered, nor the 'freedoms' associated with devolved budgets. The role of officers and inspectors actually became stronger and more creative as school autonomy increased. From my ILEA days, the setting out of a larger vision, backed up with visiting luminaries from the education world, made many of the 380 schools feel more positive about their possible futures. Some were amused, though worried, to hear Peter Wilby, an experienced education correspondent, tell them that he felt that the new National Curriculum was, in effect, 'Mr Baker's dimly remembered prep school timetable', 'Mr Baker' being the Secretary of State responsible for the new structures being put in place.

It soon became apparent that the amiable days of government circulars were over. Schools were to be more publicly scrutinised and reported on. Quantification and grading were soon the main means of 'quality control'. In most shire counties all this was unheard of, as was any kind of local authority inspection. Advisers were important in encouraging the adoption of newer curricular and pedagogic approaches, but the kind of Quinquennial Review, a local school system inspection that I had experienced in London, was unheard of. The Warwickshire advisory team of 11 was developed as a local inspectorate with a brief to help schools work through and, hopefully, thrive in a quite new world. Some of the traditional advisory work persisted: the art adviser arranged visits for teachers to great galleries, home and abroad, and the music adviser ensured that the County Youth Orchestra was open to all, irrespective of family income, and arranged teacher excursions to major Birmingham concerts. In-service training was increased with a new Professional Centre in Leamington Spa. Helping headteachers and classroom teachers confront a rapidly changing context was our main objective, but not at the cost of some traditional customs and practices. Subject Associations were important and the nearest equivalent, for secondary teachers, to the well-resourced subject centres in London. Before budgets were almost entirely devolved to schools, we paid teachers' subscription costs to these vital national associations.

Nonetheless, the early 1990s were an unsettled period of fear and uncertainty in Shakespeare's leafy county, as a raft of central government reforms were absorbed. The appointment of a rather brilliant hands-on deputy, Eric Wood, settled initial rumblings from the teacher unions, both within and beyond the council. Five further education colleges were largely 'autonomous', irrespective of legislation, although it was clear that an expert County Treasurer's department was still needed for both capital and revenue oversight. There was no evidence that a new government quango, the Further Education Council, improved this situation. The profound changes arising from government reforms were made manageable and largely positive as much by informal exchanges and chat across and between officers, county councillors, governors, union reps and teachers as by hundreds of hours of scrutiny of central government documents and more formal council meetings. These less formal exchanges and insights strengthen the real, rather than posited, 'checks and balances' required in the proper management of public bodies . . . and money. Whitehall doesn't always know best.

School re-organisation

My final four years in Warwickshire were not easy, certainly in terms of my popularity, but hugely important for the county's 244 primary schools and 37 secondary schools. After witnessing a series of failed attempts to close individual under-subscribed schools and the negative reaction to Labour councillors' proposals to 'comprehensivise' the county's five grammar schools, I increasingly worried about the lack of overall strategy with regard to 'surplus places'. Over 20 per cent of our school capacity was surplus to needs, and this meant that we were asking more fully subscribed schools to pay for empty school desks elsewhere. We could gain more than an additional £2 million annually for schools with a more rational system and this, in turn, would trigger capital spending on improving a rather lacklustre set of buildings to the tune of £29 million. Additionally, as the National Curriculum unfolded with its key stage assessments at ages 7, 11, 14 and 16, it was increasingly apparent that our first, middle and upper school system, which applied overall – except in the south of the county – was inappropriate. This system had transfer ages that cut across the new key stages, and it would be clearer to everyone – parents and governors, as well as teachers – if key stage assessments were aligned, for accountability purposes, to one school for each child's educational phase: primary, then secondary.

A massive planning exercise, based on accurate birth data from the Area Health Authority, housing development information from District and Borough Councils and cost analyses from our own County Treasurer, was further supported by work from Price Waterhouse Coopers, our external auditors. We first consulted on basic principles and objectives, then trialled a range of formative proposals in one of our local divisions, North Warwickshire. Over 30 consultative meetings were held, all with predictable results. 'Go away' was the general message. The local Labour MP wanted me sacked. A former NUM member who was the Education committee's Deputy Chair voted for the proposals, even though two of 'his schools' were lined up for closure. He lost his seat at the next local elections because of doing what he believed was right for children. There were threats to 'opt out', as schools sought an escape route through grant-maintained status in order to evade the 'County Plan'. Secondary schools supported the proposals, as they would acquire an extra year group of pupils from the middle schools, as well as new buildings to support these. Over the following three years, as the whole county was involved, some 400 consultative meetings were held. Highly effective officers led these and took a whole load of stick. Senior officers, myself included, alongside leading councillors, attended many meetings under a vow of silence, concentrating on listening to the arguments as they raged on. At one such meeting, the Permanent Secretary from the DES sat silently at the back of the village hall, commenting later, 'I was surprised at the intensity of feelings expressed'. Indeed. On another occasion, when leaving a particularly heated consultative meeting, I saw that the tyres of my car had been cut. On a welcome Saturday break in Stratford-upon-Avon's Jaeger shop, I was concluding a purchase of clothes when the assistant looked at my VISA card and shrieked, 'Oh you're that awful woman who's trying to close all our schools'.

Final approval had to be secured from the Secretary of State for Education. A delegation of leading councillors and myself were able to present our case to the then Minister of Schools, Robin Squire, and sitting there was the Secretary of State, Gillian Shephard. We were courteously treated and on leaving, Gillian Shephard said to me, 'My husband sends you his warmest regards'. Thank goodness her husband was a former headteacher and knew me through that oddly masonic clan. We were fortunate that she was in office and not her predecessor, John Patten. As she had warned me, 'I'll have to let a few go GM you know', and indeed, of the 197 schools for whom legal notices had to be issued for restructuring purposes, five were allowed to 'opt out' and become grant maintained, outside the Local Authority. Actual site closures amounted to 30. These were hotly disputed and they were primarily very small rural schools. We learned that an inverse ratio operates: smallness and rurality of school equal largeness and fury of objections. The Deputy Secretary at the Department of Education and Science later told me that the Warwickshire school re-organisation scheme was the largest the Department or former Ministry of Education had received since the 1944 Act first established the ground rules.

The local passions roused and expressed are now avoided in that local authorities no longer close or open schools. The presumption is that new schools will either be Academies or Free Schools with sponsors, not needing to survey the intricate needs of localities or regions. Whitehall has assumed for itself the boring-sounding but vital business of ensuring that there are sufficient school places for children, ideally, in locations helpful to parents, but all this is done without deep local knowledge. The escalation of performance tables and Ofsted reports means that many parents 'shop around' much more, and so it is that a 'rational' approach to the location, size and type of school is impossible. School closures are assumed to result from market forces, which also encourage the promotion of 'Free Schools', which parents and particular local interest groups set up, irrespective of 'basic need' or the connections to, or impact on, other schools. The growth of multiple faith schools is also evident; that our Warwickshire proposals were underwritten by both the Church of England and the Roman Catholic Authorities was important. I was immensely gratified when the Bishop of Coventry came with me to persuade the Conservative MP in Stratford-upon-Avon to support our plan. We failed totally.

Neither in-depth consultation rooted in locality nor value for money is now considered. By value for money, I mean securing whatever funds are available for classroom work and the finest buildings possible for schools and colleges. Warwickshire's early 1990s re-organisation provided much better buildings across the county and increased spending per pupil, much more equitably spread. Warwickshire's administrative costs as a local education authority remained modest at 73 per cent of the English county average. Hard though the consultation exercise was, it represented public debate at its best, with significant modifications to the officers' original proposals emerging from those long, tortuous exchanges.

National Commission on Education

In 1991, following Sir Claus Moser's British Association for the Advancement of Science presidential speech, the National Commission on Education was established. A two-year investigation, equivalent to earlier government-sponsored enquiries, was funded by the Paul Hamlyn Foundation. I was one of the Commission's 16 members, and we were asked to investigate and take stock of the rapid changes, which had been set in train during the 1980s in particular. However, the main task was to look ahead some 25 years and think about educational goals and training needs in a way that responded creatively to both economic and social circumstances and 'the needs and aspirations of people throughout their lives'. Our Chair was Lord Walton of Detchant, with much medical educational experience, and other members represented all sectors and phases of education as well as industry and commerce.

The final report, 'Learning to Succeed' (National Commission on Education, 1993), was well received, primarily because our analysis and recommendations were powerfully argued and substantiated with evidence. High-quality research was commissioned, so that the report was rooted in empirical findings, not just from within England and Wales, but also from international studies.

That large-scale, well-resourced and researched commissions of enquiry are now consigned to history is depressing. The current pace of change and rapid reform are not inevitable and are often damaging to those who provide and receive education. Frequent initiatives and shifts of policy require an evidential base as well as every effort to involve and win over the support of teachers, in particular. Germany bucked this trend when it investigated and took action on its low ranking in the OECD Programme for International Student Assessment (PISA) tables, and this was a ten-year exercise (2002–2012). It stressed that 'a much improved research establishment has now fed into teacher training so that teachers are enabled to analyse and diagnose their students' specific problems' (OECD, 2011). In all high-performing systems, there is a similar emphasis on a strong relationship between universities and schools and colleges. In England, Free Schools are allowed, perhaps encouraged, to employ unqualified teachers. However, in Scotland, headteachers are to be required to continue their understanding and knowledge through Masters' courses, and the Scottish government's review of teacher training in 2011 stressed that, for teachers, 'the values and intellectual challenges which underpin academic study should extend their own scholarship and practice, equally' (Scottish Parliament, 2011).

The Centre for Successful Schools

From the National Commission on Education (1996) came 'Success Against the Odds', a series of case studies of 11 UK schools where pupils demonstrating significant disadvantage had succeeded 'against the odds'.

In this project, well-respected researchers forensically examined the factors that seemed to explain the schools' successes. Published in 1996, it coincided with my move to Keele University as the Director of the Centre for Successful Schools, originally set up by Tim Brighouse. As I read more, visited scores of schools and was asked to speak about the 11 schools in the National Commission's study, it occurred to me that a follow-up study was needed. Five years later, the original team returned to the schools to check on their further progress and found a range of significant changes, with one school having effectively collapsed. Lessons from this school were as instructive as the others who had continued their upward progress, but in markedly different ways. *Success Against the Odds: Five Years On* (Maden, 2001) is still being widely read, mainly by practitioners in and around schools. This contrasted with increasing amounts of educational research, as I rapidly learned.

I worked at Keele on a half-time contract, but was there at least three days each week. It was an odd experience, after working in schools and a local authority. In the latter, there was a daily sense of collegiality, not always smooth or consensual, but nonetheless materially evident. Meeting and greeting from 8 a.m. or earlier, planned or chance encounters throughout the day all featured as 'work'. Gradual development, in Warwickshire, of 'working from home' was piloted as computers became more important. It was necessary in trialling this to define where and when face-to-face exchanges were needed and preferable. This emerged as an effective and welcome practice.

At Keele, there was not any tradition of day-to-day, hour-by-hour, 'social' working. The 8–9 morning start didn't exist. Many meetings with lecturers were arranged by students through an appointments system rather than through chance encounters. Staff didn't seem to work as a collegium, rather odd given the origin of that term. Increasingly, email exchanges predominated (now text messaging, no doubt). Starting in the late 1990s, more research was needed for the maintenance and improvement of the university's income and reputation. The Research Assessment Exercise (RAE), followed by the Research Excellence Framework (REF), increasingly dominates the work and ethos of university departments. However, when the bulk of 'output' is teachers and other education practitioners, this can sometimes lead to conflicts of interest. In some cases, an older practitioner-learning tradition has left some staff stranded, trying, as required, to produce more esoteric research and publications.

Ofsted now inspects university education departments, so that the vocational preparation of teachers is judged and ranked. With the rise of school-based teacher training through the newer First and Schools Direct schemes, these departments are thus under the additional strain of competition. This, combined with the pressures of the REF, has led some universities to question the continuing role and existence of their education departments' vocational training work. To date, Warwick, Bath and Sheffield have closed their Post Graduate Certificate of Education programmes rather than invest in their improvement along Ofsted lines, especially if the education research output is not helping to raise the university's REF ranking and income.

A welcome change to REF in 2014 was the requirement placed on universities to demonstrate the impact of research on practice, not simply in education. It is certainly in the interests of schools that practice and innovation should be rooted in research, often of an empirical kind. The opposing of practice and theory is extremely damaging. Medical education is rooted in research as well as in practitioner advances and reflection. The same should apply to teacher training and continuous professional development.

Reflecting on the 'middle tier'

In 2003, the post of Chief Education Officer was abolished when the recommendations of the White Paper 'Every Child Matters' were put in place through Parliament. The reaction to the Victoria Climbié case in Haringey had led to understandable consternation about the public protection of such children, and subsequent events have confirmed this anxiety. Whether the removal of local educational leadership and co-ordination should have been wrapped up in this is a separate matter. I followed up my Warwickshire experiences by writing about 'the middle tier' in education and finding out how these matters were handled elsewhere.

Through my involvement in OECD reviews – Russia and Hesse, Germany – and a special study of Midi-Pyrénées in France (Maden, 2000), as well as attending Council of Europe and OECD seminars on school improvement, I tried to define why and how some kind of middle tier was necessary and helpful in the continuous development of schools and colleges. It was clear that greater 'school autonomy' was being thought about elsewhere, but it was seen as a high-risk strategy if taken too far, especially if a school's improvement halted or stuttered. Experience and expertise should be available locally, both to identify emerging problems and to advise and know where relevant support is to be found. Whether this person is in a local authority as currently organised is arguable, but there certainly needs to be a statutory body employing such advisers.

Related to this is the role of a local or sub-regional authority in tasks that even the best schools cannot carry out, but that affect how well children and young people thrive. Examples include high-level special needs assessment and provision, specialist arts and sporting facilities and instruction administering school admissions, and planning school places. I would argue that local democratic accountability is intrinsic to most of these for the qualitative reasons I have tried to describe in the Warwickshire planning exercise. Answerability to electors – and even to non-voting parents, if such exist – is a civic good and curbs, if necessary, the over-reaching power of headteachers, local-level officers or government civil servants. While I recognise that international visits and knowledge do not offer ready-made models to emulate, I continue to be impressed by the quality and citizen appreciation of local and regional government in, say, France, Germany and Italy. Our lack of a basic law protecting a middle tier of government from central government forays is damaging to the quality of our civic life.

Irrespective of the civic polity, monitoring school performance and encouraging schools to 'do even better' cannot depend solely on published performance data ('league tables') and popularity with parents on school choice. These indicators do not identify further potential or weaknesses soon enough. Neither will the vital institutional health of a well-motivated and skilled staff be assured through such data.

As a former headteacher, I increasingly question the Hollywood star model of headship – 'l'école c'est moi' now appears to be the underlying precept. The way successful orchestras work interests me, especially following my chairing of the Royal Opera House's Education and Access committee. The idea of supremely skilled, proficient instrumental players, often a bit stroppy, working at ever-higher levels of excellence under the right conductor fascinates me. The von Karajan 'dictator' model is recognisable but limited. The Claudio Abbado model is better: he's described as 'a catalyst', his most frequent urging in rehearsal is 'Listen, listen' (to other sections of the orchestra), and we're told that his work with his players is 'a tectonic generative approach to musical architecture, in which Abbado knows how each part relates to the other, how shifting weights and densities in one part of the score will affect and shape the whole landscape of the symphony' (Service, 2012).

This is a more appropriate model of headship than most others proposed by business leadership consultants. The important role of the audience is also greater than most of us imagine, a 'circle of listening' with orchestra members being clear that this dynamic affects their performance. The pupils and their parents in schools likewise affect outcomes and strategies. The sensitive 'ear' is needed, and we should be cautious about charismatic omnipotence as a worthwhile quality. Potentially excellent headteachers are lost to the profession because of this tendency to promulgate a *Dragon's Den* model of leadership and obtrusive dynamism.

In recent years I have been a school governor and have observed the intense pressures on headteachers as they worry about an unfavourable Ofsted inspection and the slightest downward shift in published performance tables. Public scrutiny is a good thing, even if occasionally uncomfortable, but when scrutiny overload occurs – as I believe is now happening – the development of teaching and of children's learning is adversely affected. The almost total lack of professional space for any kind of innovation is depressing. It is also self-defeating. The high-stakes model of intensive instruction in Shanghai or Singapore schools has been promulgated by recent Secretaries of State, and yet, more critical appraisals of these are side-stepped (Ravitch, 2014). Meanwhile, the steady teacher-centred Finnish model is ignored, even though its development over three decades has resulted in consistently high outcomes. In Finland, teaching is an enviable profession, with high levels of entry qualification, and turnover is very low, unlike in England. The potential of the teachers I see working now is great but unrealised. Headteachers watch their backs; so do teachers; so do governors. The following of laid-down rules from the centre is paramount. Yet measured outcomes are better than those two or three decades ago. Thus, a move towards more local innovation at classroom level and encouragement of the non-measurable in education should proceed, without losing the positive improvements of recent years. Without such a move, we will lose our best teachers.

Postscript: the educational undergrowth

From my first job as a geography teacher in Brixton in the 1960s through to a professorial chair at Keele University in the early years of the twenty-first century, I have been conscious of informal networking influences on my professional journey. From early NUT days to The All Souls Group, based in Oxford, making contacts from beyond the particular workplace setting has been enlightening. Around the time of the James Commission, investigating teacher training in the early 1970s, some of us set up SPERTTT, the Society for the Promotion of Educational Reform through Teacher Training, and produced a Penguin Education Special for the good Lord James to savour (Burgess, 1971). Later, while at Islington Green School, the Deputy Chair of governors, Professor Maurice Kogan, asked me to join him in establishing The Ginger Group where, again, rambling discussions in a local restaurant led to publications across and between educational sectors and phases. In The All Souls Group, invited members from senior levels of the civil service, higher and further education, as well as local authorities and schools meet three times a year to listen to and discuss with leading practitioners and theorists. By straddling issues from early years to higher education and demonstrating the connections across and between apparently separate components, we enlarge our sense of what we should be trying to achieve. This is a powerful form of continuing education. Writing also helps to distil and analyse our thoughts and experience. What I am now concerned about is the increased separation of educational professionals into their specialist 'silos'. Quality and innovation are thus diminished.

Finally, over my professional lifetime, the position of women has been a marked characteristic of change, mainly improvement. Being rejected for a deputy headship at age 30 on the basis that a 'strong man' was needed was strange. This was followed by a much better post in an Oxfordshire comprehensive where, on this front, the main problem was my membership of the 'Oxfordshire Senior Mistresses Association', its title denoting the lack, until then, of any female deputy heads in Oxfordshire secondary schools. Inner London was used to doughty women, both elected to the authority and professionally, but my 1988 interview in Warwickshire was marked by elected members not being able to decide whether my student days' membership of the British Communist Party was a worse problem than my gender. In 1993, Jenny Ozga included me in her collection of case studies on women in educational management (Ozga, 1993). She interviewed me, then ruefully observed that my progression through the educational world appeared to have been founded on 'male patronage'. At least, this dubious phenomenon is far less likely to occur today for all those able and talented women who run the education world.

References

Burgess, T. (ed.) 1971, *Dear Lord James: A Critique of Teacher Education*. Harmondsworth: Penguin.

Maden, M. 2000, *Shifting Gear: Changing Patterns of Governance in Europe*. Stoke-on-Trent: Trentham Books.

Maden, M. 2001, *Success Against the Odds: Five Years On*. London: Routledge-Falmer.

National Commission on Education, 1993, *Learning to Succeed*. London: Heinemann.

National Commission on Education, 1996, *Success Against the Odds: Effective Schools in Disadvantaged Areas*. London: Routledge.

OECD, 2011, Education at a Glance, Country Note – Germany. Paris: OECD.

Ozga, J. (ed.) 1993, *Women in Educational Management*. Buckingham: Open University Press.

Ravitch, D. 2014, *The Myth of Chinese Super Schools*. New York: New York Review of Books, November.

Rutter, M., Maughan, B., Mortimore, P. and Ouston, J. 1979, *15,000 Hours*. Open Books, London.

Scottish Parliament, 2011, *Teaching Scotland's Future*. Edinburgh.

Service, T. 2012, *Music as Alchemy*. London: Faber and Faber.

14

1944–2015

Towards the nationalisation of education in England

Sir Peter Newsam

Teacher and administrator

As a teacher for seven years, my main interest was with what happened inside schools: with the curriculum and in learning how to teach better. Since 1963, as a local education authority administrator in four different education authorities, three of them Conservative led, I was necessarily mostly concerned with what the local authority provided or managed outside the schools and colleges they maintained. Earlier, as a teacher in a grammar school immediately adjoining a secondary modern school, I had become directly aware of, as I saw it, the adverse consequences of the 11+ examination. It was the wrong examination at the wrong age, with damaging consequences for far too many children. It was in 1970, in the West Riding of Yorkshire, as Deputy to Sir Alec Clegg, that I became directly involved in discussions on ending selection in Harrogate; this was managed by a Conservative local authority with the widespread agreement of the parents, teachers and governing bodies concerned. As Deputy, from 1973, and then as Education Officer to the Labour-led Inner London Education Authority, ending selection at 45 grammar schools by 1977 proved rather more difficult. But the system of schools then created has provided the secure platform on which London's parents, teachers and governing bodies have since been able to build so successfully.

The 1944 Education Act: a national system locally managed

Educationally, the Britain of 2014 is a very different place from when I left school in 1947.

In 1947, victory in two wars had recently been enthusiastically celebrated. Britain was close to bankruptcy, with large parts of its major cities and industrial areas in ruins. India's independence had just been achieved, and it was already evident that the further dissolution of the Empire, over which Britain had ruled and from which it had benefited for many years, could not long be delayed.

In the immediate post-war years, Britain was led by people who had lived through a war against totalitarian government. Many had experienced the war at first hand. They did not intend their hopes for the future to be crushed by apparently insurmountable debt. Britain's successful staging of the 1948 Olympic Games was an early statement of that intent, followed by the Festival of Britain in 1951.

At school, we learned of the proposal for a national health service and for an education system that would provide opportunities for all, of the kind that we had taken for granted. There was a widespread feeling among many of my educated-in-war-time contemporaries that we had a duty to play an active part in our country's future.

So much for 1947. Seventy years later, England, though not the rest of Britain, has moved a long way towards nationalising its education system, without its electorate ever having been invited to say whether it wants that to happen. Any account of how this has come about begins with the Education Act of 1944.

The 1944 Education Act was a continuation of earlier thinking. The terms of the Act were devised by an able group of civil servants, working with a small number of politicians of outstanding competence. In its final form, the Act was warmly welcomed by all the parties involved: Parliament, local authorities, teacher unions, the churches, the general public and even the press.

The first of the 1944 Act's two main achievements was structural. It established a, subsequently abandoned, division between primary and secondary education. Primary schools would cater for children up to the age of 11. Thereafter, all children would attend secondary schools up to the school leaving age, soon to be raised from 14 to 15, and beyond. As part of that restructuring, the Act created a secondary school system out of two very different types of existing school. The publicly funded elementary schools, which since 1870 had provided education for most of the population up to the school leaving age of 14, were combined with a group of mostly fee-charging secondary schools, provided by a whole range of denominational and charitable individuals or agencies, that educated children up to the age of 18.

Restructuring led to many long-established and independently managed secondary schools, some denominational but many not, joining the national system as voluntary aided (VA) schools. As they brought their land, their school buildings and their teachers into the national system, these VA schools were allowed to retain important elements of their independent status. VA school trustees formed the majority on the governing body, retained the right to appoint their own staff, to develop their own curriculum and to decide which children to admit to their school. The incorporation of many of these essentially independent schools into the national system for England and Wales was a great achievement. It made possible a stated aim of the Act: secondary education for all.

The 1944 Act's second main achievement was to establish a school system that reflected the values of a democratic society. The Act had been drafted during a war against totalitarian governments in which institutions like schools, and what was taught inside them, were directly controlled by the government. The civil servants and politicians who developed the Act and the Parliament that approved it were unitedly determined to create a structure that would make such a development in England impossible. To that end, the Act ensured that responsibility for the management of education in England and Wales would be shared between the government, elected by the national electorate, and local education authorities, elected by a local electorate. Accordingly, no publicly funded school could become wholly dependent for its wellbeing or its existence on either local or national government acting alone. Neither could open, close or change the character of any publicly funded school without the agreement of the other. Proposals for a new or significantly enlarged school had to be published locally, either by the local authority or by a group of proposers. Any such proposals were then subject to consultation locally. Proposals, with any objections to them, were then sent by the local authority to the Secretary of State. His role was to approve, amend or reject these proposals. For his part, the Secretary of State could not open, close or change the character of any school. He had to await a proposal to do that from the local authority that either already was or would be maintaining it. The 1944 Education Act made it impossible for any school in England or Wales to be directly controlled by an individual government minister or by any individual local authority, because neither could act without the agreement of the other.

The 1944 Act placed a general duty on local education authorities to provide secondary education in schools, 'offering such variety of instruction and training as may be desirable in view of their different ages, abilities and aptitudes'. The Act did not stipulate how this was to be done. It was left for local education authorities to submit their plans on how they intended to meet these requirements. The terms 'grammar school', 'secondary modern school' or 'technical school' do not appear in the Act, but the government had made known its preference for a secondary school system consisting of these three types of secondary school. At a time of acute financial difficulty, this preference for what became known as the 'tri-partite' system was understandable. It broadly fitted the structure of schools already in use and was widely adopted. Existing secondary schools became grammar schools that selected their pupils as they left their primary schools; elementary schools, once primary-aged children were provided for elsewhere, were adapted to become secondary modern schools. Technical schools were provided wherever that proved possible.

The preference of a government for a tri-partite system had no statutory force. Accordingly, several local education authorities, including the London County Council and the West Riding of Yorkshire, decided to meet the age, ability and aptitude criteria by combining in one school what the tri-partite system took to be three different types of pupil requiring three different types of education in three different types of school. Schools designed to meet the full range of the 'aptitudes and abilities' of pupils within one secondary school, rather than between three, became known as 'comprehensive' schools. The London School Plan of 1947 set out the London County Council's reasons for providing schools of that nature.

A second example of shared responsibilities between central and local government was the way in which school places were provided during the post-war years of sharply rising school numbers. Under the Act, the duty to secure sufficient and suitable school places was the responsibility of local government. Central government's role was to control the total amount of expenditure involved and to approve or reject major building schemes proposed by individual local authorities. Governments had to ensure that their own national priorities were met. The most important of these was ensuring that sufficient funds were available to provide 'roofs over heads', schools needed to cater for rising school numbers. Between 1947 and the mid 1960s, local education authorities and successive governments worked together to provide over five million school places within tightly controlled cost limits. The efficiency with which the Department for Education's Buildings Branch helped to make this possible was widely recognised within local government and nationwide.

A third aim of the Act had been to extend the amount and to improve the quality of technical and vocational education. In this, it failed. The cost of the school places needed to raise the school leaving age to 15 meant there was little money left to spend on creating the technical schools required or on the system of national part-time day release the Act had designed to provide continued training for those entering employment on leaving school. These constraints meant that the need to provide systematically for such training, first identified in the latter part of the nineteenth century and only partially developed following the 1918 Education Act, was still not dealt with successfully by the 1944 Act. Despite sporadic efforts to remedy this problem, notably by Kenneth Baker in 1988, it remains largely unresolved in 2014.

The school curriculum

The 1944 Act deliberately did not deal with the school curriculum. It was not seen as the role of local or central government in a democratic society to require schools to teach pupils particular things in any particular way. Until the late nineteenth century, publicly funded schools in England had been required to work within a nationally prescribed curriculum. Teachers were paid on a set of measurable results achieved by their pupils. After some 20 years, there was general agreement that 'payment by results' had failed.

Under the 1902 Education Act, education became the responsibility of all-purpose local councils, as opposed to single-purpose school boards. In 1904, the Board of Education issued a Prefatory Memorandum, setting out the general aim of the elementary school. The Memorandum contained the following paragraph:

> The only uniformity of practice that the Board of Education desire to see in the teaching of Public Elementary Schools is that each teacher shall think for himself, and work out for himself, such methods of teaching as may use his powers to the best advantage and be best suited to the particular needs and conditions of the school.

Subsequently, the Board provided a handbook of *Suggestions for Teachers in Elementary Schools*. These suggestions covered all aspects of the curriculum and reflected an unchanged approach of successive governments to the role of teachers that lasted until the late 1970s.

Suggestions for teachers in secondary schools were not considered necessary. It was left for a variety of examination boards, working with universities and schools, to cause teachers to adapt their teaching, so far as they thought this necessary, to the questions posed by the examinations themselves.

The 1944 Act did not change the government's attitude towards the primary school curriculum. In 1949, the foreword to the Ministry of Education's publication, *Story of a School*, simply reproduced the words of the 1931 Consultative Committee's Report on the Primary School:

> Instead of the junior schools performing their proper and highly important function of fostering the potentialities of children at an age when their minds are nimble and receptive, their curiosity strong, their imagination fertile and their spirits high, the curriculum is too often cramped and distorted by over-emphasis on examinations subjects and on ways and means of defeating the examiners. The blame for this lies not with the teachers but with the system.

1960s: a period of major reports

In 1966, the Plowden Report on the Primary School broadly endorsed this approach to the primary school curriculum. Commentators with an insecure grasp of the history of English education interpreted what had been endorsed by successive governments since 1904 as an example of the supposedly collapsing standards of the 1960s. The evidence, contained in an appendix to the Plowden Report, of the marked improvement in reading standards over the previous 20 years was ignored.

The Department's circular Number 10 in 1965 is an often quoted, but evidently seldom read, example of the relationship between central and local government under the 1944 Act. The circular took the form of a request to local authorities to submit plans for developing comprehensive schools. Requests by circular lacked the force of statute; so local authorities could not be required to respond to the circular. Most did, but others did not. Those that did could not be required to carry out any proposals they had decided to submit.

The 30 years between the 1944 Act and the early 1970s saw little substantial educational legislation, but a succession of well-researched reports on primary, secondary and higher education were published. These included the Crowther (1959), Newsom (1963), Robbins (1963) and Plowden (1967) Reports. The research appendices of these reports ensured that administrators and politicians alike did not lack facts, as well as opinions, on which they could base their decisions.

The 1944 Education Act had staying power. It was based on widely shared principles of the place of education in a democratic society. Its provisions underpinned the expansion and improvement of the education service in England and Wales for some 25 years and created, in the words of Sir William Alexander, a national system locally administered. It was not until early in the 1970s, at which point Part 1 of this autobiography ends, that this balance of responsibilities between local and central government showed the first signs of developing into a national system nationally administered.

1972 to 1982: the decline of local authorities

It was during these years that the educational role of local authorities in England, either by accident or design, began to decline.

In 1966, the government had established a Royal Commission on Local Government outside London. In June 1969, the Commission's Report was presented to Parliament. So far as education was concerned, the Report made two crucial proposals and issued a warning. The first proposal was that, to be able to act as a full partner with central government, local education authorities needed to be much larger than many existing ones. The evidence from HMI, the Ministry of Housing and Local Government, local authorities and the Department for Education all indicated that large education services performed better than small ones, some of which were doing poorly. The Commission therefore proposed the creation of 78 education authorities, outside London, with a preferred population of 500,000 and a minimum size of 250,000. These 78 would replace 124 existing education authorities and the 156 other local government bodies with some responsibilities for education.

A second proposal was that, even with larger local authorities, some elements of education, such as further education, would need to be dealt with at a provincial level. The Commission suggested that the newly formed local authorities should, to deal with these issues, appoint some of their members to form eight provincial councils. The Commission did not recommend that a provincial council should be an independently elected body.

In 1970, the government set aside the Commission's recommendations, notably on the need for some provincial local authority presence. Eventually, under the 1972 Local Government Act, 97 local education authorities were created instead of the 78 proposed. In Yorkshire, 13 local authorities, some of which have, predictably, since functioned poorly, were created in place of the five much larger ones proposed by the Royal Commission.

The Commission's powerfully stated prediction that, if local government was not reformed in the way it proposed, 'local government will be increasingly discredited and will be gradually replaced by agencies of central government' has since proved correct.

A second development that substantially reduced the capacity, even the will, of some local authorities to carry out a full range of educational functions was initiated by local government itself. The Bains Report of 1972 was produced by a group of local authority chief clerks. Historically, functional legislation was administered by functional government departments. So educational legislation was devised and administered by a national education department. Similarly, health, police, housing and so on were administered by separate government departments, each responsible for the legislation relating to their function. Until the 1970s, local government committees were organised in much the same way. Senior education officials in local government, working with their education committees, dealt directly with their opposite numbers in the national Department for Education. Similarly, political leaders of education in a local authority dealt directly with education ministers. Both had detailed knowledge of the legislation they were dealing with. Nationally, until the mid-1970s, leaders of local authority education committees and their senior officials formed the highly influential Association of Education Committees. For many of these years, Sir William Alexander, as its Secretary, was able to represent the views of local education authorities directly to senior officials in the Department and to its ministers.

From 1974, most local authorities outside London became corporately managed. Once received by local government, money provided or expenditure authorised by central government departments was, to a varying extent, distributed in accordance with local government priorities rather than those of the government department that was its source. The managerial logic of corporate local government is indisputable; its practical and political consequences for the education service were disastrous, culminating in 2010 in the government removing the word 'education' from the term 'local education authority'. Under the 1944 Act, the local management of schools was the responsibility of education-specific local authorities, with their own chief officer holding the statutorily required office of chief education officer. All that was set aside, and the management of education was no longer seen by politicians, few with any experience of either, as a specific function.

While local government became corporate, government departments stayed functional and could no longer rely on corporate local education authorities deciding to spend money on the department's national priorities. Having won money from the Treasury for one purpose, ministers and their officials were not content to see it used for some other purpose. As the Royal Commission had predicted, central government's reaction was to create organisations outside local government to perform educational functions that had hitherto been exercised locally. Combined with the failure to create local authorities of an appropriate size and in the absence of the Commission's proposed provincial arrangements, this led to the creation of government agencies such as the Manpower Services Commission, the Learning and Skills Council and, later, Connexions and a series of funding and other such agencies created to do what had earlier been done by local government.

Within local government, newly appointed and corporately minded chief executives saw no reason for particular departments, of which education was by far the largest, to retain direct access to any functional government department. Many actively prevented it. From being a central element of the local authority system, education officers, almost all with teaching as well as administrative experience, found themselves spending much of their time dealing with issues that had little to do with their area of expertise. It was during the 1970s that the role of local authority education officer became less attractive as a career. With the decline of that career structure went much of the expertise and understanding needed to manage even a diminished set of educational responsibilities. In 1977, the authoritative voice for local government's education service ceased with the demise of the Association of Education Committees.

My own direct participation in educational administration ends in 1982. By the end of the 1980s, the role of local authorities in education and, in some of them, even their commitment to the education service itself had been further weakened. In a few urban local authorities, irresponsible behaviour had strengthened the government's general distrust of local government.

Nationalisation of the curriculum and schools

Between 1988 and 2014, two of the main changes to education in England have been the nationalisation of the school curriculum and, at an increasing rate since 2010, the nationalisation of its publicly funded schools. Nationalisation is here defined as a system under which all important decisions are exercised by a single government minister, accompanied by an actual or potential transfer of assets to the state. This process necessarily requires the elimination of local government and other independent institutions from anything more than a peripheral influence on decisions about the form and content of education, either locally or nationally.

The curriculum of schools in England was nationalised in 1988. This replaced the system whereby, since 1904, governments had provided advice on the curriculum, which schools were encouraged but not required to follow. From 1963, under arrangements originating with the Department for Education, a wider range of advice than in the past had been provided by the Schools Council. The Council's members included representatives of teachers, local authorities, universities, officials from the Department for Education and members of HM Inspectorate. The documents the Council produced, its advice, the research it undertook and the experimental work it supported were designed to encourage good practice. Most of what it produced was of high quality.

In 1976, a speech at Ruskin College by the Prime Minister pointed out that the government had a legitimate interest in the curriculum of schools, and that the balance between the role of local government and central government in dealing with this might well require adjustment. His carefully worded statement left open the question of how and to what extent this adjustment would be made. In the years following the Prime Minister's speech, elements in the Department for Education had come to believe themselves better qualified to deal with the curriculum than the Schools Council. They openly expressed dissatisfaction with the Council's work and commissioned a report on its effectiveness. When the report recommended that the Council should continue, in April 1982 the Secretary of State's response was to stop financing it. That left the way open for the nationalisation of the curriculum in 1988.

During the creation of a statutorily enforceable national curriculum, advice from all quarters on its scope and content was, with rare exceptions, ignored. A complex set of curricular requirements, with an accompanying apparatus for ensuring schools were accountable for meeting these effectively, was given the force of statute. The National Curriculum was poorly constructed and imposed in haste. It has since had to be regularly and expensively revised, with teachers having to be retrained to meet new requirements as these have arisen. In 2014, some schools are still required to comply with it while others are not. Its collapse has been gradual, in recent years punctuated by personal and often ill-considered interventions from government ministers.

The nationalisation of schools in England began, on a small scale, in 1988. Twenty-five years later, that process is well advanced. Nationalisation has gone through three stages, best identified by the ministers most closely associated with them. Each stage began with a good idea. The idea behind the City Technology Colleges (CTCs), promoted by Kenneth Baker, was admirable. New and forward-looking sponsors, with a strong commitment to technical and vocationally relevant education, were invited to create and lead a series of enterprising and self-managed secondary schools. The sponsors of these schools would control the governing bodies, appoint their own staff, develop their own curriculum, decide on which children to admit, and be responsible for the financial management of their school.

In creating these schools, Kenneth Baker was either unaware of or deliberately chose to ignore the fact that schools with almost exactly the same degree of self-governance as CTCs already existed as Voluntary Aided (VA) schools. Many of these had been developed as independent schools during the nineteenth century by city companies, the churches and by individuals such as Miss Beale and Miss Buss. To develop more of such schools with appropriate sponsors would not have been difficult. Two things had to be done. First, the 1944 Act requirement that proposers/sponsors of a new school of the kind required had to provide both site and buildings had to be replaced by the need to make only a token or even no contribution to the cost of the new school. Second, local authorities, in submitting their proposals for a new school in their area, as they had done since the 1944 Act, would have had to be required by the Secretary of State to include any proposal they received for a CTC. The Secretary of State would then have had to consider all such proposals on their merits and to decide which to accept, modify or reject. If he decided to approve a proposal for a CTC, it would then have been for the local authority to find the site and, as in the case of VA schools, convey it to the trustees. Within agreed cost limits, the trustees would then manage the construction of their school.

Kenneth Baker's decision to develop CTCs, in itself a good idea, as government schools instead of VA ones, maintained but not controlled by a local authority, was the first move towards replacing local government's role in education with control of individual schools in England by a government minister.

No prime minister since 1997 has been educated in a publicly funded school in England or later had any personal association with the management of any such school. This lack of understanding has made it possible for unelected and inexperienced policy advisers to play an increasingly important role in formulating educational policy. One such adviser, Andrew Adonis, later ennobled as Minister for Schools, had an excellent idea. This was to encourage enterprising groups of sponsors to run independently managed and newly built schools in areas of poor performance. Like Kenneth Baker, he was apparently unaware that the VA model could provide the legally established independent trustees and status that he believed to be necessary. That is presumably why the existence of VA schools is not mentioned in the account Lord Adonis has given of his struggle to develop, against fierce resistance, a type of school that already existed.

The academy programme

In developing academies in the form of Kenneth Baker's CTC model of school governance, the Secretary of State was authorised, under section 65 of the Education Act 2002, to enter into a contract with 'any person' to 'establish and maintain' a school, at public expense. Contracts formed in this way are at the heart of the academy programme. As the governance structure of VA schools makes clear, academy 'freedoms' can be secured without any such contract. Although, in themselves, contracts serve no useful educational or administrative purpose, what academy funding contracts successfully do – as they are clearly intended to do – is place the minister concerned in ultimate control of the schools or groups of schools contracted to him. Contracts leave it to an individual government minister, the Secretary of State, to determine exactly how much money each school contracted to him receives to run itself each year. If the governing body of any school dependent on a single politician in this way believes itself to be 'independent', it runs a severe risk of deluding itself.

Labour's enthusiasm for contracts in the form of funding agreements has caused a clause to be inserted that reads: 'the Academy Trust cannot assign this agreement'. But the Secretary of State can, and some future one may well decide to assign many hundreds of his contracts to other agencies to manage.

Academies, as essentially government schools, paved the way for Michael Gove. His declared intention has been that all schools in England, willingly or otherwise, should have rolling 7-year contracts with him, terminable by either party after due notice. In giving a Secretary of State what amounts to direct control of an increasing number of England's schools, contracts potentially involve a huge transfer of assets to the state. On becoming contracted to the Secretary of State as an academy, the trustees acquire the site and buildings of any school built and paid for by a local authority. If the Secretary of State's funding contract with those trustees is terminated, that property reverts to the Secretary of State and not to the local authority that originally paid for it. The academy programme is a nationalisation of local assets process in waiting.

As an extension of its legislative approval of the Secretary of State's move to nationalise England's schools, Parliament has further legislated to allow nearly all important decisions about education in England to be made by or on behalf of the Secretary of State, without reference to anyone else, including Parliament itself. Parliament is not a party to the contracts that it has allowed the Secretary of State to make with any set of trustees he finds acceptable. His only evident criterion for establishing the suitability of trustees to run a school at public expense appears to be that they have not been elected by anyone.

The Secretary of State's uninhibited control of education now extends to the examination system, the training or lack of it of teachers, the structure of the governing bodies of academies, including the right to decide whether any of which he disapproves are to be allowed to remain in office, where, whether and at what cost new schools are to be built, and so on.

What next?

Two consequences of this legislatively authorised control of education by an individual government minister have become evident. The first is that it is very obviously inefficient. Even the straightforward task of relating the number of school places provided to the number of school places required has been mismanaged. Public money is routinely spent on children and students who do not exist. Financial control of academies is defective. Schools are developed where new schools are not needed. This practice of creating extra school places where there are already spare places, apart from wasting money, almost always adversely affects what local schools with spare places can still afford to offer their pupils. Sixth forms are encouraged to proliferate at a time when sufficient teachers of high quality, available to teach a full range of subjects in many existing sixth forms, are lacking. Narrowly defined systems of accountability are created that give teachers perverse incentives for teaching badly. Bad practices are routinely imported from foreign countries. Over the past few years, the list of poorly structured 'initiatives' and ministerial incompetencies has become long and is lengthening.

Control of education by an individual government minister is also leading to increasingly totalitarian behaviour. As Lord Acton put it in 1887, power that verges on the absolute corrupts. The symptoms are unmistakeable. Ministerial hostility to all forms of real or imagined sources of opposition is loudly proclaimed. Enemies of 'reform', a term used to describe any ministerial initiative, however ill-considered, are said to be lurking everywhere. Local government, the universities, the judiciary, the churches, the BBC, non-conforming elements of the press and any form of independent thinking or action from teachers or their unions are all perceived as inherently pernicious. All are treated with contempt. Disciplined conformity, within schools and by everyone connected with them, is to be the order of the day.

The arbitrary and sometimes irrational behaviour of individual government ministers is just one instance of England's general retreat from its democratic past. Now that Parliament, with the notable exception of some of its select committees, has legislated away its ability to exercise effective control of the Executive,

Parliament itself is widely perceived as little more than a noisy and largely irrelevant adjunct to the Executive. This has damaging consequences for England as a functioning democracy. It is becoming difficult for England's electorate to find good reasons to vote at parliamentary elections for individual Members of Parliament. Voters correctly perceive that few of the people they vote for have any influence on what the government of the day, once safely elected, then decides to do.

Within narrowing limits, resistance to the government is still permitted, but the form democracy has taken in England is increasingly reminiscent of the 'democratic centralism' proposed by Lenin in 1917. Under such a system, further developed in parts of Europe during the 1930s, people are still allowed to discuss issues and to march about with banners, provided they behave themselves. The deployment of second-hand water cannons would, in the opinion of at least one mayor, help to remind marchers of their duties in this respect. But there is little room left for alternative sources of decision making, even on important local issues. All important decisions in England are now taken by the small group in charge of the government. Intervention from subordinate bodies such as local government, professional bodies, independent researchers or even, other than grudgingly, from Parliament itself is rarely found acceptable. In the wings, another small group of much the same composition awaits its opportunity to replace the existing one.

Education in England has been particularly badly damaged by this nationwide retreat from the widely shared beliefs in what constitutes a democratic society that underpinned the Education Act of 1944. As Friedrich Hayek put it in that same year, 'Nowhere has democracy ever worked well without a great measure of self-government'. That measure of self-government is what the 1944 Education Act secured and has since largely been legislated away.

In 2015, one simple question about education needs to be asked: is England content to place a single individual, the Secretary of State of the day, in what is close to absolute control of all elements of this country's education system? If it is, no action is needed; that is what England's schools and other educational institutions are being frog-marched towards. If it does not, a second question arises: is any political party prepared to put that question to the electorate? That is the question that hangs in the air, awaiting an answer.

PART VI

Role of the media

15

MEDIA AND EDUCATION IN THE UK

Peter Wilby

Today, nearly every British national newspaper has an education correspondent, covering schools, colleges and universities. If the numbers are fewer than they were 20 years ago – when some papers employed as many as three such specialists – that is more a reflection of newspapers' increasing financial difficulties and journalists' higher workloads than of any diminution in education coverage. Some newspapers publish weekly sections devoted to education, though these, too, are much reduced from what they were even 10 years ago. For example, *The Guardian*'s section, published on Tuesdays and branded Education Guardian, was once a separate supplement of 12 pages or more; now the section has gone, replaced by barely half as many pages within the main paper.

Yet education remains a far more high-profile subject than it was half a century ago. Before the 1960s, it was scarcely regarded as a news subject at all. Though the annual teachers' union conferences attracted attention even in the immediate post-Second World War years – mainly because they were (and are) held at Easter, when other news is in short supply – the 'popular' press particularly focused almost exclusively on teachers' pay, often linking it to difficulties in recruitment (Cunningham, 1992). More detailed coverage, particularly in the 'quality' press, tended to focus on universities (especially Oxford and Cambridge), then attended by less than 6 per cent of young Britons, and on fee-charging schools (such as Eton, Harrow and Rugby), rather than on the taxpayer-funded schools attended by the majority of the population.

According to one estimate, there were only three full-time education journalists at the beginning of the 1960s, excluding those working for specialist publications. An education correspondents group – formed to co-ordinate the reporters' access to ministers and other key sources of information – was not formed until 1962, whereas a labour and industrial correspondents group was formed in 1937, and a crime reporters' association in 1945 (Williams, 2009). By the early 1970s, the education correspondents group had around 50 members. In *The Times*, the number of articles on educational matters rose from 70 in 1960 to 184 in 1967 (Kogan, 1975). In 2013, a search on *The Times* website identified a total for the year of 439 articles devoted to education. Interviews with education journalists in the mid-2000s found that most of them saw education as 'one of the top specialist areas of reporting . . . comparable in importance to . . . health reporting, crime reporting and business/finance reporting'. Though few had sufficiently long memories to be certain, the general consensus was that it ranked higher than it did in the past (Hargreaves *et al.*, 2007).

The main drivers of this growth in education coverage – on radio and television, as well as in the press – were the politicisation and centralisation of education. Politicisation started in the late 1950s and 1960s, as Britain began to abolish most of its grammar schools, which selected the most academic children after a competitive examination at 11, and to introduce 'all-ability' comprehensives instead. Though the division between the major parties on selective schooling was never a rigid one – Conservative local councils were among the pioneers of comprehensives, and, to this day, the official Conservative policy is that comprehensives should continue – Labour was always more eager to hasten the demise of the grammar schools, by central diktat if necessary.

Until the late 1970s, however, it was widely accepted that what was taught in schools and how it was taught remained a matter exclusively for teachers. The curriculum, as an education minister observed in 1960, was the teachers' 'secret garden', and 'parliament would never attempt to dictate the curriculum'. Or, as the Lancastrian George Tomlinson, education minister during Clement Attlee's 1945–1951 government, more colloquially put it, 'minister knows nowt about curriculum'. In Westminster and Whitehall, the curriculum was not a contestable subject. An education 'parliament' for curriculum and examinations, the Schools Council, was set up in 1965, but it had no formal powers of legislation or direction and was essentially a talking shop in which, though both local and national government were represented, teachers' unions and subject associations held most of the seats. Outside the classroom, nearly all the power in education resided with local councils. Though much of their funding came from central government, they controlled the distribution of money and decided which children should go to which schools. David Eccles, education minister from 1954 to 1957, complained that, 'having succeeded in getting Cabinet support for increased funds for education, he had no real say in how those funds should be spent' (Jarvis, 2014).

Education was covered more thoroughly, and often better, in local newspapers than it was in Britain's national newspapers, radio and TV. The national press, geared to receiving most of its information from Whitehall, Westminster and assorted bodies associated with central government, found it hard to derive significant news from the subject. A row over school admissions in Newcastle, it was thought, would not interest readers in Birmingham. Similarly, a curriculum innovation in Birmingham would not interest readers in Newcastle. Only in the 1960s did the growing numbers of specialist education reporters begin to present some local developments as being of national significance. Newly opened comprehensive schools, for example, might get national coverage. So might radical developments in internal school organisation, curriculum and teaching methods that went loosely under the heading 'progressive'. But universities and the fee-charging, private boarding schools (confusingly known by the English as 'public schools') continued to get more coverage, because both drew on a national clientele that was almost entirely the well-heeled middle classes, the most sought-after audience for advertisers, even in the more downmarket papers.

In this era, nearly all education journalists favoured comprehensive schools and 'progressive' teaching styles. A columnist in the right-wing weekly magazine *The Spectator* complained in 1972 that all but one of the 48 members of the education correspondents group were 'left-wing, some extremely so'. Even on Conservative papers, they could favour the 'progressive' cause, or at least give it an easy ride, mainly because their editors had little interest in education. C.B. Cox, a Manchester University professor of English, told a conference in Australia in 1981 that newspapers had played a leading role in persuading the public of the merits of 'progressive' teaching. In the late 1960s and early 1970s, Cox and like-minded colleagues brought out a series of 'Black Papers' – written by academics and teachers who favoured 'traditional education' – that deliberately attempted, as Cox put it, to 'shift the centre' of debate. They were written in a populist, jargon-free, accessible style and were heavily promoted to the newspapers. The Black Paper editors understood that they could maximise sympathetic coverage by sending the pamphlets to newspapers on Sundays – a thin news day and one on which most specialist reporters would be off work – for publication on Monday mornings. A Labour Education Secretary foolishly assisted them by branding their first publication as 'the blackest day in English education for over a century'.

The Black Papers – alongside their offshoots such as the National Council for Educational Standards, which, again to maximise media coverage, held its conferences on Sundays – turned the tide. The 'traditionalists' had no inhibitions about wooing journalists, making their leaders accessible to the press and trying to reach a mass audience. In contrast, the 'progressives' regarded populism with distaste and the 'capitalist' press with suspicion. The Campaign for Comprehensive Education, for example, had a spokeswoman who could be reached only with the greatest difficulty, took no trouble to conceal her hostility to journalists and insisted that she should never be named.

For all the efforts of the Black Paper editors and their media supporters, the rise of comprehensives initially continued without interruption: in the 1970s, despite the Education Secretary in the first half of the decade being none other than Margaret Thatcher, more were created than in any previous decade, with grammar schools surviving only in a handful of areas ruled by true-blue Conservative councils. The media have little power in education (or indeed in politics generally), at least in the sense of 'transformative capacity' as defined by the sociologist Anthony Giddens: 'the capability to intervene in events so as to alter their course' (Giddens, 1984). But they do create an agenda and a framework – sometimes a very restrictive one – for debate. In the 1970s, the media, influenced by the Black Papers, began slowly to change the agenda. Newspapers eagerly reported research showing the weaknesses of 'progressive' teaching methods – which were nothing like as ubiquitous as journalists suggested – and highlighted the case of a London primary school that, by any standards, had gone too far in its 'progressive' methods, with its teachers apparently training pupils to become members of a revolutionary vanguard while completely neglecting the basics of reading and maths.

Public interest in education was growing, and not just because the media debate was increasingly vigorous and polarised. For most of the twentieth century, education played only a minor role in the lives of the majority of the population. Most people left school in their mid-teens and never returned to full-time education. They took no exams and had no paper qualifications. Some returned to college, a day or two a week, to learn skills for a trade, but many learned skills on the job or found unskilled factory or labouring jobs that were then in plentiful supply. Even many white-collar jobs required only minimal qualifications. Journalism itself required nothing more than a rudimentary knowledge of shorthand and law.

In the second half of the twentieth century, however, career prospects – and, as heavy industry declined, the chances of getting a job at all – depended increasingly on length of education and particularly on credentials acquired at school. Education became a distributor of life chances and a source of growing anxiety to parents of all classes. This made it a subject of interest, not only to newspapers and their readers, but also to politicians.

From the mid-1980s, Margaret Thatcher's Conservative governments introduced dramatic changes in England and Wales (Scotland and Northern Ireland have separate education systems, subject to separate regimes), which were largely accepted by Tony Blair's Labour governments from 1997 and then further elaborated by the Conservative–Liberal Democrat coalition from 2010. Parents were allowed more choice of schools and more say in how schools were run. Schools were required to publish their examination results in standardised form. Local councils were required to distribute funds according to a national formula and to delegate spending decisions to schools, leaving governors and headteachers to determine, for example, how much was spent on books and how much on repairs to buildings.

Crucially, schools were given the opportunity to opt out of local council control and to become 'independent', receiving their money direct from central government; a majority of secondary schools have now taken this route. Private companies and voluntary associations were invited to set up new schools and take over existing ones. Through a new regulatory body, the Office for Standards in Education (Ofsted), the powers of central school inspectors were greatly enhanced, and Education Ministers increasingly took it upon themselves to order a change of leadership or even closure for 'failing' schools. Most importantly, schools were required to follow a national curriculum, which different ministers determined in varying amounts of detail. Being mostly educated in the humanities, ministers were particularly anxious to specify which novels, plays and poems should be studied for English literature and which events for history. Labour dictated, not just curriculum content, but the methods used to teach reading and maths in primary schools, thus breaching what one professor of education has called 'the final frontier of professional autonomy', which, even as late as 1991, a Conservative Education Secretary declined to cross, saying that, 'questions about how to teach are not for government to determine' (Alexander, 2014).

All this led to an explosion of media interest. The secret garden was now open for everybody to trample over the flowerbeds. In the past, only teachers' pay disputes created the simple dramatic clashes of opposites on which the mass media thrive. These were only peripherally connected to educational issues; they were covered as simple employer–employee battles, similar to other labour disputes. Now, the disputes were about what was taught and how, with highly politicised debates developing about, for example, how the history of the British Empire should be taught and whether English lessons should focus on creative writing or on correct grammar and spelling.

The national media distilled such disputes into a simple opposition between mainly right-wing 'traditionalists' and mainly left-wing 'progressives'. The former favoured a strong emphasis on basic literacy and numeracy; academic subjects such as physics, chemistry, history and literature; formal instruction, with pupils sitting in rows at desks facing the front while the teacher told them what to learn; the 'phonics' method of teaching reading; selection by ability into different 'streams' within schools and, if possible, into different schools; old-fashioned written examinations, usually lasting three hours. The latter supported a more flexible curriculum that did not divide knowledge by rigid subject boundaries; informal or 'discovery' learning where pupils sat in groups and were encouraged by teachers to find things out for themselves; the 'whole word' method of teaching reading; comprehensive schools with 'mixed-ability' classes; and new-style examinations that involved continuous classroom assessment and projects completed in the pupils' own time. Most classroom teachers are pragmatists who do not fall into either camp. They prefer a balanced curriculum and a mixture of teaching and assessment methods. But the media wished to subsume almost every educational issue into the progressive–traditional framework: for example, it was thought desirable to give parents more choice of schools and the private sector more opportunities to run them, because both would bring schools 'back to basics'.

Politicians, working to their own ends, encouraged journalists and media commentators to report education in terms of this dichotomy. Indeed, politicians increasingly presented their policies in tabloid newspaper terms. When Michael Gove, Conservative Education Secretary from 2010 to 2014 and himself a former journalist, introduced a national curriculum that placed more emphasis on factual knowledge, he presented it as an attempt to wrest control of schools from what he called 'the blob': academics, teachers, school inspectors, advisers and local authority officials who were 'enemies of promise', guilty of 'valuing Marxism, revering jargon and fighting excellence'.

Unlike his predecessors, Gove was in a position to get his way. The decentralised governance of English schooling was long a source of frustration to both Westminster politicians and Whitehall civil servants. Education ministers frequently had ideas as to how to improve schools but found they had no levers to make anything happen. For example, when Sir Keith Joseph, one of the chief architects of what became known as Thatcherism, took over as Education Secretary in 1981, he wanted schools to create more pro-business, pro-free enterprise attitudes among young people. To his despair, he found himself powerless to insist on any such change. Like all previous education ministers, he was little more than a spectator, as the teachers' unions and local education authorities – among whom education journalists cultivated contacts as assiduously as they did among ministers, their advisers and civil servants – ran the system.

Largely because he had so little direct power, Joseph badly needed public support for his ideas in order to put pressure on those who were in charge. He wished, for example, to change teachers' working practices and to introduce regular assessment of their performance ('teacher appraisal', it was called at the time). But, since he did not himself employ teachers or determine what or how they were paid – though he did provide the money to fund pay increases – he needed to put pressure on the local council employers and the teachers' unions who, through a somewhat cumbersome machinery (known as the Burnham Committee), negotiated pay and working conditions. Public support and, therefore, press support would be crucial if he were to get his way.

He largely failed. The teachers' unions mounted a highly effective campaign highlighting teachers' poor pay, which required some to take second jobs, heavy workload and propensity to heart attacks and nervous breakdowns. Joseph, by contrast, was, to the despair of his department's press officers, 'unskilled and uninterested' in influencing the media. 'He was often reluctant to meet journalists, and conducted press conferences with ill-concealed distaste and indecent speed' (Wilby, 1986).

Only after Joseph left office in 1986 did the Education Reform Act, introduced by Kenneth Baker, begin to change the balance of power. Baker, like nearly all Joseph's successors (John Patten, Education Secretary from 1992 to 1994, was the only significant exception), was far more media savvy. He launched the first National Curriculum, the first legislation allowing schools to become 'free' of council control and the first experiments in persuading private sponsors to back state schooling. He also solved the problem that Joseph faced in influencing teachers' pay and working conditions by abolishing the Burnham machinery and giving himself power to determine teachers' terms of employment.

By the end of the 1980s, the media narrative was almost wholly focused on an apparent battle to the death between 'traditionalists' and 'progressives' (sometimes called 'trendies') and, after the Conservatives' centralisation of educational power, it had an increasingly political dimension. The events of 1991 showed how the narrative would now develop.

In that year, Leeds council published a report on the outcomes of a programme to transform its primary schools into exemplars of 'good primary practice', which meant – or was thought to mean – making them more 'progressive'. Normally, such a report from a provincial education authority would attract little national press attention. Nobody can be sure why this one was different. Perhaps it was just the date of publication: the end of July, when other news is thin. But some commentators suggested that the Conservative government, facing a tricky general election the following year, tipped off some of the London-based education correspondents, seeing an opportunity to discredit a Labour-controlled city council and associate their main political opponents with falling educational standards.

Whatever the explanation, the coverage of the report, written by Robin Alexander, professor of primary education at Leeds University, dealt a devastating blow to 'progressive' education, possibly the most serious in more than a decade. 'Progressive teaching in schools was £14m failure', was the *Daily Telegraph* headline. 'The education of millions of primary school children has been blighted in the name of an anarchic ideology', the paper explained. The government's reaction chimed precisely with this press coverage. John Major, who had recently succeeded Margaret Thatcher as Conservative prime minister, used the report to support 'a return to basics' and announced 'the progressive theorists have had their say and . . . they've had their day'. Later, in 1992, Alexander was invited by the government to join an official inquiry into 'the delivery of education in primary schools'. Also appointed to the inquiry were Jim Rose, the then chief inspector of primary education, and Chris Woodhead, the chief executive of the National Curriculum Council; the latter largely accepted the government and media narrative of sturdy traditionalists fighting a rearguard action against a mighty progressive juggernaut. Appointed just before Christmas, they were dubbed 'the three wise men' by the press. When they reported, newspaper headlines screamed: 'Call for return to traditional school lessons' (Alexander, 1997).

Yet, as Alexander pointed out, the Leeds report's main conclusion was that the Leeds project 'was an initiative well worth the Authority's investment', even though it found important weaknesses in some outcomes in some schools. 'A complex and carefully qualified analysis', Alexander wrote, 'was reduced to a simple pathology.' As Alexander saw it, the outcome of the 'three wise men' inquiry was similarly distorted, partly by Woodhead, who re-drafted what was supposed to be 'a discussion paper', partly by the Education Department's press release, partly by the press itself. For example, the report rejected a return to streaming by ability, a favourite demand of the traditionalists. When Alexander made public his reservations about a report that had appeared under his name, the press accused him of a U-turn and called him 'one rather unwise man' (Alexander, 1997). When, nearly 20 years later, Alexander headed an independent investigation into primary education (known as the Cambridge Review), his nuanced reports – which, as he put it, 'exposed the complexity of the data and the difficulty of making hard and fast judgements' – were simplified into headlines mostly designed to discredit an increasingly unpopular Labour government: 'Literacy drive has almost no impact', 'Primary pupils let down by Labour', and so on (Alexander, 2014).

The campaign against 'progressive' teaching was not confined to newspapers. Television played its role too. In the autumn of 1991, in the wake of the Leeds report, a prestigious BBC current affairs programme reported that 'experts with a mania for progressive education have spread a canker through Britain's classrooms'. To illustrate this thesis, the programme went to two primary schools where, according to one study, 'a small and unrepresentative sample of practice was filmed, an even smaller sample remained after editing and, stripped of much of its context, the material actually shown was employed . . . to portray progressivism in simplistic terms' (Wallace, 1993).

The narrative would change little over the next 20 years. Like the 'red menace' of the Cold War era, the 'progressives' were always lurking, never idle in their mission to subvert decent, common-sense, traditional values. The narrative was supported by the frequently repeated judgement that, while the Right won the economic wars (converting the whole world to free-market economics), the Left won the culture wars. 'Trendy' teaching methods, the narrative argued, were imposed for ideological reasons by an 'educational establishment' comprising some prominent heads and teachers, professors of education, teacher-trainers, local authority officers and advisers, and even Her Majesty's Inspectors of Schools whose pronouncements were once treated as the Holy Grail. Even the advent of a Labour government in 1997 did not significantly alter the narrative, though some of the rhetoric was toned down, and Labour ministers made greater efforts to take account of teachers' opinions. The politicisation of schooling has gone to extraordinary extremes. Even the teaching of reading, essentially a technical matter, became a struggle between the 'phonics' method, supported by the Right, and the 'word recognition' or 'look-and-say' method, supported by the Left.

Politicians, meanwhile, have become hugely more sophisticated in using the media to their advantage. When they make policy, they think, not only of how well it will work, but of how they can 'sell' it to the media. All governments aspire to keep 'control' of the media agenda, and no departmental minister will survive for long unless he or she can feed the media with policy 'initiatives'. David Blunkett, Labour Education Secretary from 1997 to 2001, employed a special adviser (separate from the department's press office) who spent at least an hour a day on the media. In the early afternoon of each day, he would ring round the education correspondents and speak to them individually (Bangs, MacBeath and Galton, 2011).

But one effect of the increasing politicisation of education is that ministers often give news of what they regard as 'major initiatives' to the Westminster-based political correspondents, not to the education specialists. Since political reporters are by definition specialists in politics, not education (or health or policing or social services), policies rarely get expert scrutiny. Moreover, the growth in the number of columnists – nearly every newspaper has two or three of them each day – who express opinions on a large range of issues, and are employed for their ability to write provocatively and entertainingly, rather than for their understanding of a particular subject, further marginalises the role of expertise and informed critical scrutiny. Professors of education and other specialist academics are almost wholly excluded both from policy making and from newspaper coverage of education.

Most social media and Internet blogs multiply the amount of poorly informed comment. True, in education as in other areas, the Internet allows a few well-informed voices to bypass the press and to address directly a wide audience in a way that would once have been impossible. The Local Schools Network, for example, defends schools that are run by elected local councils and critiques the growing number of schools run by private chains with meticulously researched comment on its website.

But that is an exception. The narrative of 'progressives' versus 'traditionalists' continues to grip education, and no education minister has made more use of it than Michael Gove, Conservative Secretary of State in the Coalition government from 2010 to 2014. Successive governments, as one account puts it, have set up 'an object of derision' that they then pledge 'to exorcise' (Wallace, ibid). This perfectly suits the media, which has the clash of opposites that it craves and can put nearly all educational issues into this simple framework.

References

Alexander, Robin (1997): *Policy and Practice in Primary Education*, 2nd edition. Routledge, London.

Alexander, Robin (2014): Evidence, Policy and the Reform of Primary Education: a cautionary tale, *Forum*, 6(3), Autumn 2014.

Bangs, John, MacBeath, John and Galton, Maurice (2011): *Reinventing Schools, Reforming Teaching: From Political Visions to Classroom Reality*. Routledge, London.

Cunningham, Peter (1992): Teachers' professional image and the press 1950–1990, *History of Education: Journal of the History of Education Society*, 21: 1, 37–56.

Giddens, Anthony (1984): *The Constitution of Society*. Polity Press, Cambridge.

Hargreaves, Linda *et al.* (2007): The Status of Teachers and the Teaching Profession in England, Department for Education and Skills, Research Report 831B.

Jarvis, Fred (2014): *You Never Know Your Luck: Reflections of a Cockney Campaigner for Education*. Grosvenor House, Guildford, Surrey.

Kogan, Maurice (1975): *Educational Policy-Making: A Study of Interest Groups and Parliament*. Allen and Unwin, London.

Wallace, Mike (1993): Discourse of Derision: the role of the mass media within the education policy process, *Journal of Education Policy*, 8: 4, 321–37.

Wilby, Peter (1986): Press and Policy: teacher appraisal, *Journal of Education Policy*, 1: 1, 63–72.

Williams, Kevin (2009): *Read All About It! A History of the British Newspaper*. Routledge, London.

This chapter is a version of a paper that was first published in *Revue internationale d'éducation*, 66, September 2014.

Conclusions

16

STORIES FROM THE FIELD – SUMMARISED

Richard Pring and Martin Roberts

Overview of contributions

The changes in the educational provision – from early years, through primary, secondary, further and vocational education, to higher education and the training of teachers – have been amply illustrated by the contributions to this book. They have shown especially the revolutionary shift from minimal central control over what goes on in schools to much greater political control, first, through a national curriculum and national assessments, second, through the decline in local authority powers and responsibilities. The recently arrived academies and free schools are contracted directly to the Secretary of State. But higher education, too, has not escaped. The autonomy once protected by a University Grants Committee has been eroded as government has exercised its powers through funding and research to ensure greater relevance to its perception of national needs.

The scene was set by Lord Baker, who, as Secretary of State, introduced the 1988 Education Reform Act, thereby creating the National Curriculum and National Assessment, as well as the local management of schools. These were revolutionary changes arising from a belief that standards were too low in many schools – an understandable belief shared by the preceding Labour government, which, as explained in the introductory chapter and referred to in other contributions, set the ball rolling with Prime Minister James Callaghan's Ruskin College speech in 1976 – a generation of 40 years ago. In particular, the endemic neglect of technical and vocational education, despite many reports on the crisis since 1851, would be challenged through the establishment of City Technology Colleges, directly funded by government and private sponsors, and in a way resurrected by the more recent University Technology Colleges.

What the contributions illustrate are the gains and losses as experienced by those with responsibilities within the system – for example, by the early years' headteacher and ILEA adviser Wendy Scott, who, not denying the need for greater accountability to ensure high standards throughout, regretted the impact of the emerging top-down, short-term interference, undermining the much needed child-focused work of good early years education.

Both she and the former primary school headteacher, Tony Eaude, pay tribute to the Plowden Report of 1967, which influenced primary schooling at the beginning of our era, encouraging the arts and creativity in different forms. However, in their experience, what was often referred to as the more child-centred approach to education was gradually undermined by rigid assessment and accountability. Even how to teach literacy and numeracy came to be directed by government in the 1980s and 1990s. The autonomy of teachers was eroded in a political distrust of their expertise.

Similar concerns were expressed by Martin Roberts, a former head of a large and successful comprehensive school in Oxford. He expressed concern, not about there being a national curriculum framework, but about its mode of implementation. During his period of headship, the National Curriculum was increasingly implemented through an outcomes-driven system of accountability and through growing dominance of the newly established inspectorate, Ofsted, which was data-driven and judgemental rather than, as in the case of the HMI (which it largely replaced in 1992), much more supportive. Kenny Frederick experienced a similar case during her experience of headship in a challenging school in Tower Hamlets. There was a need to transform the racist and islamophobic ethos of the social context that affected the school, thereby creating a very inclusive school. But she pointed to the changes that had come to make the task more difficult, especially the decline in local authority support. On the other hand, both Martin Roberts and Kenny Frederick were able to point to innovations that had made improvements possible – increase in funding, greater opportunities for women, positive approaches to pupils with special needs, and initiatives like 'Excellence in Cities'.

The changes over the half century have paradoxically reflected both mistrust in the professionalism of teachers and yet the transformation of teacher preparation into a university-based profession. Richard Pring gives an account of that transformation and at the same time its gradual erosion, first, through political criticism of the content of that university preparation and, second, through the different routes now available for aspiring teachers – while highlighting the crisis facing the next generation in recruitment and maintenance of teachers, in part resulting from changes in schooling. But higher education, too, has changed, as explained by Richard Pring in a following chapter – from a relatively small group of universities catering for a small percentage of students to a massive increase with much wider student access. It has shifted from a mainly government-funded public service to one dependent on student fees.

Further education, as explained by Geoff Stanton, is the unknown sector of education, much neglected and under-funded as a result, despite the fact that colleges of FE cater for over three million students annually. They have witnessed, too, considerable changes, partly in response to those occurring in schools, which pass on, as it were, the students unlikely to succeed along an academic route. The colleges have provided innovative responses, especially through the pre-vocational courses they developed, to the needs of such students. But there has been a failure of recognition and thus of financial support, together with a bewildering change of programmes and qualifications, known by the flow (or flash flood) of acronyms: UVP, NVQ, TVEI, CGLI365, CPVE, DoVE, GNVQ, NFVQ, QCF, OCEA (and that's just a start).

It is to this changing system of qualifications that Tim Oates turns in a dramatic contrast between the whirligig of changes in England and the stability in other countries (e.g. the post-16 qualification in Finland has not changed in form or function for 100 years). That constant change in form and range of functions that the exam system has to perform (reflected, for example, in the short lives of GNVQ, 14–19 Diplomas, modularisation of A Levels, AS Levels as part of A Level) is one of the most distinctive and frustrating features of the last 40 years – not encouraging for the longevity of yet further changes promised by the political parties. The use and role of examining have been distorted by its use as an instrument of government policy.

One such use is its employment as an instrument of accountability. Certainly, as Pat O'Shea recounts, prior to our period, accountability of schools and the system as a whole left much to be desired. But, once the regime of Ofsted and testing had been in place for some time, the earlier kind of accountability provided by HMI, which was geared to school improvement, became divorced from inspection. The scheme of School Improvement Partners provided good professional support, but, like so many innovations, it had but a short life of six years. Inspection was slimmed down to two days, making judgements with little knowledge of the social context and with a shift of emphasis from curriculum to leadership and management. This reduction in professional support coincided with the enfeeblement of local authority responsibility and support.

The following three chapters (Part V) are written by people who, as well as having taught in schools, have also been Directors of Education in local authorities, dealing with the changes imposed and the increasing centralisation of services. Peter Newsam, Education Officer for the Inner London Education Authority, points to the weakening of local authorities from their partner role in a 'national system locally managed', as had been established by the 1944 Education Act. Such weakness strengthened the power of the Westminster politicians, not only through the curriculum control and assessment regime, but also through the broader 'reforms' of local government. The new corporate model had no room for the once powerful defenders of local democracy and accountability in education, namely, the Chief Education Officers. That understanding is reinforced by Tim Brighouse, whose reign as Director in both Oxfordshire and then Birmingham enabled him to see the shift from the age of *optimism and trust* at the beginning of our period (as reflected in 'teacher-based school improvement'), through the growing *doubt and uncertainty* (as trust in teachers gave way to high-stakes testing and increased prescription), to that of *markets and managerialism* (reflected in the espousal of 'choice', the language of targets and performance indicators, and the contraction out to external bodies (some 'for-profit' companies) of these public services. Margaret Maden, whose career enabled her to witness these changes from the positions of teacher, headteacher, Chief Education Officer and university professor of education, saw the need to adapt to the changes arising from the Education Reform Act, but also the importance of preserving the role of LEAs' advisory services, county in-service training centres and the organisation of schools from the viewpoint of one who knew the local needs and context. Local education authorities may have been driven to near extinction, but the gaping hole thereby left in organisation of education demonstrates the need for a 'middle tier' of organisation.

Throughout these changes, and the professional and public perceptions of them, the role of the press cannot be ignored. Peter Wilby shows how political standpoints entered into the reporting at key stages, particularly in the early 1970s with the Black Papers railing against the prevailing 'progressive ideas' (*Teachers Mis-taught* being the title of one of those papers). Hence, with the increased politicisation of education, the media tended to subsume issues into the progressive versus traditional, especially at the time when grammar schools were being transformed into comprehensives. In order to keep control of the media, Secretaries of State have fed 'initiatives' to journalists who often were political rather than specialist education journalists.

Of course, our period follows the transformation of the system of secondary education from a tri-partite one into a largely comprehensive system, albeit with that demarcation between able and less able still enforced by the dual examination system at 16 of GCE O Level and Certificate of Secondary Education. It was only in 1988 that the two systems were merged into the one that still prevails, namely, the General Certificate of Secondary Education (GCSE) – though for how long is open to question.

17

THE WAY FORWARD FOR THE NEXT GENERATION

Richard Pring and Martin Roberts

Forty years have passed since Prime Minister Callaghan's Ruskin College speech. A generation of teachers, who commenced their careers then, are about to retire. When they commenced their careers, we had a 'national system of education locally maintained', as legislated in the 1944 Education Act. The Secretary of State had few powers, and those had nothing to do with the curriculum or how it should be taught.

One third of the time through the careers of this generation (13 years), the Education Reform Act radically changed that, giving the Secretary of State far-reaching powers over the curriculum (and its attainment targets and assessment), and over the establishment of schools no longer 'locally maintained' (namely, City Technology Colleges) but contracted to the Secretary of State.

Twelve years later, the City Academies Programme was launched, thereby opening up a system of schools (including the Free Schools) contracted directly to the Secretary of State, but maintained mainly through sponsors of various kinds.

Simultaneously, there has been an intensification of targets and performance indicators, of audits and league tables, by which schools, colleges and universities are held to account.

Therefore, these have been revolutionary times. But many aspects of that revolution are being seriously questioned, as the preceding chapters indicate. Furthermore, whatever the system, its success depends on the sufficient supply of good teachers. Yet there is a crisis looming in the recruitment and the retention of teachers. A shortfall of 27,000 is predicted by 2017, and between 40 per cent and 50 per cent of newly qualified teachers leave the profession within five years. Two-thirds of secondary schools had difficulty in recruiting maths teachers. Reasons given for leaving are constant teacher bashing, high-pressure accountability, excessive workload and relentless pace of change.

Therefore, the post-ERA education system seems now to be in much need of further reform. Although responsible for some necessary improvements, it has opened up a range of problems and is in danger, therefore, of doing more harm than good to many pupils.

Further reasons for questioning the efficacy of these years of continuous government-led reforms stem from international comparisons. One can debate the validity of the PISA tables, but they offer no evidence of England improving its position in recent years. Meanwhile, the Programme for International Assessment of Adult Competences (PIAAC) shows us performing very poorly on adult literacy measures. Uniquely within the OECD, the literacy scores of our 16–24 age group are lower than our 55–65 one. Vocational education and training is a black spot. Only 32 per cent of our upper secondary pupils are following vocational courses, compared with the OECD average of 44 per cent. As the government's own advisory group, the Social Mobility Commission, noted in 2014, there is 'a lack of a plan to prepare young people for the world of work and support them through this complex transition'. Educational experts from both the OECD and North America are critical of the inconsistencies of over-centralised political control. In its Education Policy Outlook 2015, OECD analysts noted that, in England, 'rather than build on the foundations laid by previous administrations, the temptation is always to scrap existing innovations and start afresh'. They also comment that, 'the more the government is only one partner among several, the less vulnerable programmes are to being wound up after administrative or personality changes'.

Having seen the evolution of the system of education over the last 40 years, what, in light of the considerable problems emerging, should be the direction of change for the next generation of teachers? In what follows, arising from the contributions to this book, we make the following recommendations and are confident that, if implemented and sustained over many years, they would lead to significant improvements in English education.

1 Limit the power and control by central government

Problems arise from concentration of so much power in the hands of a Secretary of State, who is not accountable even to Parliament for many of the decisions made. Those problems include:

- constant changes to examinations and qualifications that have a limited time-span or need soon to be reversed – to the frustration of employers, universities and teachers. There need to be a pause and wide deliberation before further 'reforms' are proposed and the establishment of an independent Examination and Qualifications Council to organise that deliberation and to make final decisions;
- initiative after initiative made in relation to election-driven timetables or in response to 24/7 media interests, rather than to well-researched deliberations; and

- persistent tinkering with curriculum content, which should be left to subject and pedagogical experts.

2 Create a 'middle tier' between schools, colleges and government

The pursuit of 'choice' within what has become a 'market of schools', with the drastic weakening of local education authorities throughout this generation, has led to fragmentation of schools, to competition rather than collaboration between them, and to expensively created extra places in some areas, with a lack of school places in others (while pupil numbers are rising). There is a need, therefore, for a 'middle tier' of organisation with a real democratic element to ensure:

- there are the right schools and colleges in the right places;
- schools and colleges work in partnership to ensure a fair spread of scarce resources and staff; and
- those schools receive good advisory support when needed.

3 Create a more rational and uniform system of schooling

There is now a bewildering variety of schools ('free', sponsored academies, academy chains, grammar, UTCs, local authority community, voluntary aided, voluntary controlled), each with distinctive forms of governance, funding arrangements and control over admissions. Sense needs to be restored through:

- total transparency of funding, governance and admissions;
- not allowing once again the creation of secondary modern schools through the expansion of grammar schools, either as new schools or by expanding existing ones; and the
- restoration of local accountability of all schools receiving (directly or indirectly through charitable status) public funding.

4 Ensure equal funding for pupils across schools and colleges

One result of the many different types of school, arising from different forms of sponsorship, is that the unit of resource varies from school to school, often without educational or social justification. It is important that:

- an agreed common funding formula be established for all pupils at the different age levels, irrespective of type of school;
- grounds for exception (e.g. special educational needs) should be universally agreed and applied; and

- the deficit funding currently applied to post-16, especially to FE, should be rectified.

5 Trust the teachers more

The quality of teachers is essential to good education – well educated, well trained, well supported professionally, well respected and well paid. There is now, however, a crisis in recruitment and retention, as described above. Concern over teacher supply has been exacerbated by Schools Direct filling only 61 per cent of the places allocated in 2014. And the provision of training is now increasingly fragmented, as its traditional prevalence in universities is receding. It is essential, therefore, to:

- establish an independent college of teaching (similar to the Royal College of Medicine) as an independent professional body for the regulation and support of teachers, for the provision of guidance on the training of teachers, for advice to government and for the link between teachers and the Secretary of State;
- require all teachers to have Qualified Teacher Status following an approved training course;
- ensure all teachers are required to have regular 'Continuing Professional Development'.

6 Make accountability of schools and teachers supportive rather than punitive

Characteristic of recent years has been increased accountability through examination results, testing and data-driven inspection by Ofsted. This has created a climate of fear, teaching to the test, and failure to do justice to the wider range of educational aims and achievements. It is important, therefore, to revert to a system of accountability that:

- is based on professional judgement as well as quantitative data;
- supports teachers in their efforts to improve their teaching;
- reforms Ofsted so that its members help rather than punish struggling schools; and
- encourages self-evaluation, monitored by other teachers.

There is no compelling evidence that Ofsted is contributing to the overall improvement of English education, as it concentrates excessively on individual institutions and not enough on local and regional performance.

7 Promote curriculum development, not imposition

'There is no curriculum development without teacher development.' The curriculum, within a broad national framework (but bearing in mind terminal examinations), should be developed by the teachers who know their subject and know their pupils. It should not be controlled by whichever government comes into power and at the whim of the ever-changing Secretaries of State. To assist schools in this task there is a need to:

- establish a National Council for Curriculum Development whose membership should have wide representation from teachers, professional associations (e.g. the Historical Association), universities, employers, inspectorate, government, the wider community; and
- support curriculum development by research evidence, including teacher research, which could be part of CPD.

8 Reviewing examining and qualifications

Qualifications, and the examinations leading to them, have been in constant change, often with a short life and often reversed after initial experience. This makes life exceedingly difficult for the teachers who have constantly to change their courses, and for universities and employers who depend on the qualifications for recruitment. It is important to:

- differentiate the different functions of testing and examining (formative and summative, international comparisons, national standards, school performance, personal achievement, remedial needs); and
- establish an independent Council for Examinations and Assessment with wide representation. (It could be integrated with the proposed National Council for Curriculum Development – we have been here before – several times!)

9 Promote technical education and training

The country has constantly failed to respect and to provide good-quality technical education and training, as reflected in Acts of Parliament and government papers ever since the 1851 Great Exhibition. The creation of city technology colleges and university technical colleges, together with the 14–19 Diploma in Engineering, are recent attempts to rectify this. It is important:

- to maintain this momentum and to ensure such opportunities are available for all and included in any new curriculum framework, such as a Baccalaureate.

10 Restore pre-vocational education in schools and colleges

At a time when all young people are to be in some form of education and training until the age of 18, it is important to consider ways in which, for many, general education can be continued but based on more practical and occupational interests. Hence, there is a need to:

- examine again the thinking and practices that were developed through the pre-vocational initiatives which took place within the last 40 years; and
- ensure greater partnership between schools, colleges of further education and employers, essential for success.

11 Benefit from the revolutionary developments within this generation of ICT

ICT and the electronic revolution have opened up immense possibilities for the improvement of learning. It has opened up distance learning in higher education on a massive scale (e.g. MOOCS). In schools and colleges, it has made possible online tutoring and seminars and even virtual social areas and laboratories for the house-bound and excluded (e.g. NISAI). Teacher collaboration and curriculum development have been made possible across schools and colleges. Therefore, it is essential:

- to build urgently on what has been achieved so far through teacher professional development and ready access to the necessary resources.

12 Restore 'proper' apprenticeships

Vocational education is essential, but, as the Wolf Report showed, much was of low standard and did not provide the necessary link between the hopes of students and the needs of employers. Although there are many political promises to create more apprenticeships, it is important to preserve the high standard of skill traditionally associated with apprenticeships and improve the routes through apprenticeship to employment. To that end, there is need:

- not to let quantity diminish the meaning and quality of apprenticeships; and
- to make it easier for employers to take on long-term apprenticeships.

13 Prioritise independent and professional careers guidance for all

Although this issue did not emerge in the chapters, we believe that the provision of information, advice and guidance (IAG) to students from 14 upwards is patchy and limited, and yet is essential if they are to know about the availability of apprenticeships, the many different university courses and the subject choices necessary to proceed to the right course. Therefore, it is necessary:

- to ensure every secondary school and college of FE has ready access to a professionally staffed, independent and well-informed IAG; and
- to provide courses in school about the different routes that students can take to a chosen career.

14 Reconsider the nature, shape and funding of the higher education system

It is now half a century since the Robbins Report. The higher education system has grown and changed, partly as a result of specific reports (e.g. on funding), but in particular because of much wider access and differentiation of higher education functions. Particular issues, however, have arisen through the development of open access, the greater importance attached to research, the entry of foreign and for-profit providers, and the corporate nature of current universities. Therefore:

• this would seem to be the time for another major and comprehensive report – Robbins Mark II.

So, in the interest of the future generations of schools and universities, there needs to be a new Education Reform Act encompassing many of the recommendations of this book and the insights of those who have contributed to it, ensuring a better, positive, productive educational culture.

But, learn from the past! Successful legislation has always followed a long period of deliberation, consultation, open debate and reference to relevant research. Our final recommendation is therefore:

15 Pause, think and deliberate, preferably for two years, before further 'reforms'

In the past 150 years, successful and long-standing reforms have followed major and comprehensive reports by commissions established to address problems (e.g. on the future of higher education, on examination reform, on developing a secondary school system). In the nineteenth century, these were called Royal Commissions. In the post-1944 era, they were commissioned by the Central Advisory Committee. They took time to consider every aspect, before finally making recommendations and only then legislated. Therefore:

• a crucial recommendation of this book is that, before any more reforms, a public enquiry should be established into the range of issues raised in this book, representative of the many interested parties, and should collect evidence, institute relevant research, engage in public debate, and finally (after two or three years) report to government, making recommendations for reform.

N.B. While this book was at proof stage Dr Paul Cappon, an international expert appointed by the DfE in 2014–15 to undertake a review . . . which could inform deliberations within the Department', published his findings in *Preparing English Young People for Work and Life*. Many of his recommendations are similar to the above; e.g. the government tries to do too much on its own; our accountability system needs serious realignment; we should prioritise vocational education, create a new 'middle tier', a College of Teaching and a National Council of Learning. Cappon concurs with the Wolf Review that 'in England strengths occur despite rather than because of its systems and structures'.

APPENDIX

Major education acts and reports

1976 James Callaghan's Ruskin Speech

Auld Report on William Tyndale School

Assessment of Performance Unit

1977 Further Education Unit established. Published *A Basis for Choice*

Taylor Report: *A New Partnership for our Schools*

1978 Waddell Commission Report – proposing unified system at 16+

1979 General Election: Conservative victory (Thatcher)

1980 Assisted Places Scheme

1981 Warnock Report on Special Educational Needs

A New Training Initiative: *A Programme for Action*

1982 Abolition of Schools Council, replaced by the Schools Curriculum and Development Committee (SCDC) and the Schools Examination Council (SEC)

TVEI (Technical Vocational Education Initiative)

1983 Youth Training Scheme

CPVE (Certificate of Pre-vocational Education)

1986 NCVQ (National Council for Vocational Qualifications)

City Technology Colleges

1987 Curriculum 11–16 (HMI The Red Book) unified and common curriculum

1988 Higginson Report on A Levels

1988 Education Reform Act

National Curriculum Council (NCC) and Schools Examination and Assessment Council (SEAC) established

ILEA abolished

1990 Rumbold Report (Early Years)

1992 Conservative government victory (Major)

Ofsted established

White Paper: *Choice and Diversity*

Further and Higher Education Act: ended binary line in higher education

1993 Specialist schools encouraged

Technology Schools Trust (becomes the SSAT in 2005)

SCAA (Schools Curriculum and Assessment Authority) created by merging NCC and SEAC (see above, 1988)

1994 Dearing Report on the National Curriculum

1995 FEU absorbed into the Learning and Skills Development Agency (LSDA)

Dearing Report on HE – proposes fees for full-time undergraduates

1996 White Paper: *Self-government for Schools*

(by now there were 163 grammar schools, over 100 GMS, 196 specialist schools, 15 CTCs, 30 language colleges, 151 new technology colleges, assistant places, whereby places in private schools were publicly supported)

1997 General Election: victory for New Labour

Qualifications and Curriculum Authority (QCA) formed through a merger of SCAA and NCVQ

White Paper *Excellence in Schools*: benchmarks, targets, standards, performance management, rigorous inspection

Kennedy Report, Learning Works: Widening Participation in FE

Effective Provision for Pre-School Education (EPPE)

1998 National Skills Task Force (Blair)

Graduate Teacher Programme (GTP) introduced, offering another route into teaching other than the well-established university-based PGCE

Education Action Zones (EAZs) established

National Literacy and Numeracy Strategies for primary schools introduced

Sure Start begins

1999   *Excellence in Cities* initiative

Moser Report, A Fresh Start: Improving Literacy and Numeracy

2000   Introduction of city academies

2001   Ofsted responsible for day care and childminding

Green Paper: *Schools: Building on Success*: raising standards, promoting diversity, achieving results

2002   Citizenship added to the National Curriculum

Education Act 2002 encourages the spread of academies

Birth to Three Matters

2003   The first Teach First graduates enter schools

Ouseley Report: Community Pride, Not Prejudice

2004   The Childrens' Act (*Every Child Matters*)

Tomlinson Report on 14–19 Curriculum and Qualifications Reform

Higher Education Act: variable fees, foundation degree powers to FEC

2006   Early Years Foundation Stage (EYFS) statutory standards for early years providers

Raising age for remaining in education and training to 17

2007   Ofsted responsible for FE but not universities

2008   14–19 Advanced Diplomas introduced

2010   **General Election: Coalition (Conservative and Lib Dem) victory (Cameron)**

SSAT loses government support and becomes much smaller Schools Network

Many education quangos abolished – for example, QCA, which had become the QCDA

2011   Wolf Report on the Reform of Vocational Qualifications

Rationalisation of qualifications, many scrapped (e.g. Advanced Diplomas)

Free schools and academies vigorously promoted

EBacc added as a measure of school performance

Nutbrown Review (Early Years)

2012   GTP programme replaced by Schools Direct and School Centred Initial Teacher Training (SCITT)

2014   Regional commissioners introduced

2015   Carter Report on ITT

Government refers a workload review after one-day strikes about pay and workload

Changing acronyms for the Education Department

From 1964 DES, 1992 DfE, 1995 DfEE, 2001 DfES, 2007 DCFS, 2010 DfE

Changing Curriculum and Assessment Agencies

From 1964, the Schools Council, 1983 SCDC and SEC, 1988 NCC and SEAC, 1993 SCAA, 1997 QCA, 2008 QCD(development)A and OFQUAL, 2010 QCDA abolished

SUBJECT INDEX

NAME INDEX

Crime Express

Stephen Booth
Rod Duncan
John Harvey

W F HOWES LTD

This large print edition published in 2008 by
W F Howes Ltd
Unit 4, Rearsby Business Park, Gaddesby Lane,
Rearsby, Leicester LE7 4YH

1 3 5 7 9 10 8 6 4 2

First published in the United Kingdom in 2007
by Crime Express

A CIP catalogue record for this book is available
from the British Library

ISBN 978 1 40741 491 1

Typeset by Palimpsest Book Production Limited,
Grangemouth, Stirlingshire
Printed and bound in Great Britain
by MPG Books Ltd, Bodmin, Cornwall.

Claws

Stephen Booth

CHAPTER 1

The bones were tiny. They lay in his hand like a set of pearls, translucent and fragile. When he turned them to the light, he could see their fractured ends and hollow cores. They were light as a feather, as brittle as chalk. And as easy to break as a straw.

For a moment, Detective Constable Ben Cooper stared at the narrow window and faded curtains, though they hid nothing more than a street corner in a Derbyshire mining town. He was trying to picture a shape coming out of nowhere, a shadow against the sun. He could almost feel the sudden grab, hear the sharp snap. A broken back, he guessed. Dead in an instant.

Cooper looked up. Had he spoken that last thought out loud? PC Tracy Udall had been watching him handle the bones, her expression suggesting he might do something against procedure at any moment. His secondment to the Rural Crime Squad had given him a kind of loose cannon status in Udall's eyes. He was the rogue element that no one quite controlled.

'Where did you say these were found, Tracy?' he asked.

Udall nodded at the opposite wall. 'In a Tupperware box. They were stuffed in a drawer, with his underwear and socks.'

She said it as if the socks made the presence of bones worse, somehow. A casual attitude to death was always disturbing. No one could tolerate a life tossed away like so much rubbish.

As usual, Udall was in full uniform, her duty belt loaded with equipment that rucked her yellow high-vis jacket into untidy folds over her waist. Handcuffs, baton, CS spray. And a series of leather pouches that Cooper had forgotten the use for. In fact, he didn't think there had been all those items to carry when he was in uniform. Changes happened fast in Derbyshire Constabulary, and six years in CID werea long enough to get out of touch with core policing.

'But at least they're only a handful of bones,' said Udall. 'Less than a handful.'

The only thing she'd taken off was her hat, which she laid carefully on a chair, a gesture to informality. In the enclosed space, she had to stand very close. And despite the six-inch difference in their heights, Cooper found her slightly intimidating.

This had been an unremarkable bedroom once – one of those tiny spaces that was no more than a box room. There was just enough distance between the walls to fit a bed, and a chest of drawers under the window. He'd slept in a bedroom like this himself as a child, back at Bridge End Farm. But some youngsters spent their entire lives in a space this size.

'I suppose he didn't have much interest in bones,' he said.

'No. They weren't one of his *special* trophies.'

Downstairs, officers from Serious Crime could be heard moving through the rooms, checking the kitchen, breaking open the shed in the back yard. They'd raided the house in response to intelligence that it was being used to stash the proceeds of activities by local drug dealers who were being targeted in a major police operation. It was the sort of place they might find to keep their money safe until the attention died down. The officer in charge downstairs had hopes of finding a couple of hundred grand hidden under the floorboards, or stuffed into coffee tins, the way a southern force had in a similar raid a while ago.

Cooper turned slowly and studied the room. It couldn't be called a bedroom any more. There was no bed in it, for a start – only a series of glass-fronted cabinets, a small table, and a single chair. Some of the contents of the cabinets were difficult to make out, unfamiliar shapes under a gathering layer of dust. Shoeboxes and biscuit tins had been crammed into the rest of the available space, and two suitcases lay open on the floor.

Cooper put the bones down, feeling oddly

disturbed by the way they slid and rustled in their evidence bag, like the last few crumbs in a packet of biscuits.

'Prey, I suppose,' he said.

Udall nodded. 'Aren't they all?'

She was strangely quiet this morning. Cooper wondered if some issue in her personal life had come too close to the surface. Tracy Udall had two small children at home, and he gathered that the father had been absent from the word go. Present for the conception, maybe, but missing for the birth. Udall was as professional as they came, but even police officers were human.

'A small species of some kind,' he said. 'It would have been taken by the male, then dismembered later on. You wouldn't think there'd be much flesh on it, would you? Enough to keep a few hungry mouths quiet for a while. But that's all.'

'Every scrap is important when you're a parent.'

'I see. Well . . . maybe I don't.'

'One day, Ben.'

Between them, the boxes and suitcases in this room contained a collection of several thousand eggs. Nestling between layers of cotton wool were the speckled pale greens and blues of bullfinches, redstarts and wheatears, the creamy white of a woodpecker. There were the blotched, chestnut red of the peregrine, and goshawk eggs the colour of the moon. Each item had been recorded in a notebook, with the date, time and location of the acquisition. Every egg had been labelled in precise black letters, and its insides had been blown out through a tiny hole drilled in its side. There had been a lifetime of work in these dead things.

Cooper could see other items, too – fleshless skulls, clawed feet, severed wings. Some people liked to collect the skeletons of dead birds. But avian bones were so light and fragile they soon fell apart, and all you found was a skull. A collector hoped for a fledgling to die in the nest. Only then could you retrieve a complete skeleton, if you were lucky.

'I reckon our egg thief just scooped the entire contents out of a nest,' said Udall.

'He seems to have picked up practically anything he could find.'

'Yes. You might call him a bit of a magpie.'

Relieved, Cooper felt the tension ease, without knowing what had caused it in the first place.

'He's a genuine collector, certainly. Obsessive, I'd say. Real collectors always seem slightly un-balanced to the rest of us.'

'As if the rest of us are normal, Ben?' Udall sighed. 'Yes, you're right. And that'll probably count in his favour with the courts, if we ever get him that far.'

'What do you mean?'

'Well, we can't prove he was engaged in this activity for personal gain.'

'He wasn't dealing?'

'Not so far as we can tell. By the look of this

room, he seems to have held on to everything he found, no matter how worthless and bizarre.'

Cooper picked up the file Udall had given him, and frowned at the mug shot on the first page. Kevin Hewitt, aged forty-two, an unemployed van driver.

'Single, I'd guess,' he said. 'Oh . . . no, I'm wrong. Separated from his wife.'

'That's worse than single,' said Udall, with feeling.

Leaning past her, Cooper examined the aluminium cage that stood on the table. The whole room could have done with fumigating, but the area around the cage smelled worst of all.

'And this was Mr Hewitt's most special trophy, I suppose,' he said.

'You could call it that. It makes me sick to look at it.'

The goshawk chick had been very young. How anyone had imagined they could keep it alive in an old parrot cage in a box room was beyond belief. Now it lay in a pathetic heap, its eyes glazed with death, its beak gaping to show a glimpse of red tongue. The debris around it on the soiled newspaper would be difficult to identify. It might be interesting to know what Hewitt had been trying to feed the chick with, but it made no difference in the long run.

Cooper looked at Udall. 'Definitely a goshawk? I can't tell at this age.'

'Sergeant Jackson will be here soon to confirm

it. Then we'll get the remains to the lab to do a cross-check against the DNA database.'

'But ten to one it's a wild bird, snatched from the nest?'

'Oh, a hundred to one,' said Udall. 'A thousand to one.'

The young raptor could be called beautiful, even in death. There was a kind of elegance in the angle of the head, and the way the feathers lay. Its legs were stretched out, as if reaching for its prey. Yet it would never have seen prey, except at second hand, delivered half-digested from its mother's beak. Those talons had been made to ride currents of air over Alport Castles crags in the Upper Derwent Valley, not to lie on a filthy sheet of paper in a collector's trophy room.

Cooper studied the young goshawk closely before he straightened up to his full height and faced Udall again.

'And where is Mr Hewitt now?'

'Well, that,' said Udall, 'is what we have to find out.'

Kevin Hewitt was already too high, and he was sweating badly. A hot trickle ran down his forehead, and another dripped into his shirt. He didn't have a hand free to wipe it away, so the perspiration was already in his eyes, blurring his vision and making him blink. He stopped for a rest, digging the gaffs of his irons into the bark and clutching a branch for support. He was breathing hard, and he could feel pains starting to shoot through his shoulders.

'Damn, she was right. I *am* getting too old for this.'

The only response was an angry, high-pitched cry from the bird circling above the tree. A coarse *gyak, gyak, gyak,* telling the world there was a disturbance near her nest. The bird was way up in the sky, almost too far for Hewitt to see, even if he could use the binoculars. But he knew she was watching him, her eyes so much sharper than his, observing his slightest movement.

At this time of year, the female wouldn't hesitate to attack him, if he got too close. Three pounds of angry female goshawk were quite a scary thought. The beak was fearsome enough, but you didn't want to tangle with those talons. They were designed for tearing lumps of meat off warm prey.

The male bird, the tercel, would be away hunting, soaring invisibly over the conifer plantations, or flicking among the trees, twisting and turning in pursuit of some prey on the ground. When Hewitt imagined the strike, the talons sinking into fur, he knew why people wanted these birds. Goshawks had short, powerful wings that made them manoeuvrable in dense woodland. But they were totally focused on their prey, and sometimes they collided with obstacles. He'd heard of one collector who stumbled across a stunned bird in the woods and snatched it up before it flew off again. Lucky bugger. It would never happen to him. Kevin Hewitt had to work for everything he got.

Hewitt's common sense was telling him he'd climbed too far. But he couldn't go back, not now. He coughed as a scatter of dirt fell on his face and into his mouth. That was the story of his life. Going out on a limb for people who always let him down, who'd leave him to crash and burn. When his end came, everyone would stand and watch him fall. No one would care what happened to him. Whether he ended up spending a few months in the nick, or lying down there on those rocks, with his neck broken. What was the difference?

Cautiously, Hewitt inched further along the branch, wincing as a patch of bark bit through his jeans. Even that movement shifted his balance, and he had to clutch at the rope fastened to the trunk. For a few seconds, he wobbled dangerously. His hands shook, and his palms were slippery with sweat. What he really needed was a safety harness, the kind that tree surgeons used. But there was no way he could carry a thing like that around, not without some nosey sod asking what he was up to. The climbing irons were tricky enough to hide.

Of course, if he was caught, there'd definitely be a prison sentence this time. They might even impound his old Bedford van, and then he'd really be sunk.

But it was worse than that. If he landed in jail, Janine would do what she'd threatened and file for divorce next day. She'd get to keep the kids, too. No doubt about that. Women had it all their own way in family courts. They could refuse access and ignore as many court orders as they liked – and they were never punished for it. If he blew his last chance with Janine, he'd never see Jack and Ebony again. He might as well throw himself in the reservoir if that happened.

Hewitt glanced over his shoulder. Yes, Howden was nice and handy down there. Plenty deep enough at the moment, too. He could just imagine himself taking a header off that stupid bloody dam, the one they'd built to look like a castle, with its towers and battlements.

For a moment, he thought of the male goshawk, returning to a favourite perch after a successful attack on some unsuspecting rabbit, then plucking it and pulling out the entrails before it ate the meat. That was the way he could see himself ending up. Not like the hawk, flying free over the moor. But like the poor bloody rabbit, gutted and skinned.

Hewitt sighed. 'Onward and upward, damn it.'

He began to move again, slowly and painfully, peering up into the leaves. The nest was up there somewhere, he was sure. It was almost within his grasp, if only he could see it.

'A goshawk chick all right. They can tear up their own food at about a month old, but this one is only just starting to feather.'

Sergeant Phil Jackson was approaching thirty

years' service, and no doubt counting the days to his full pension. He looked as though he'd been round the block a few times in his thirty. More than a few. Cooper had taken a liking to him immediately.

'It's a pity, but it's practically impossible to keep the breeding sites of rare species a secret,' said Jackson, as he removed the dead goshawk from its cage. 'Word gets around, and twitchers turn up in their hundreds. The only thing that works is guarding nests day and night, and no one has the resources to do that.'

Cooper was standing at the window, looking down into the street. This was an ordinary terraced house – a typical council property, identical to thousands of others on the eastern borders of Derbyshire. A cluster of spectators had gathered in the street, drawn from their houses by the sight of police activity. Actual miners might still live in some of these homes, men who were working the handful of pits left over from the closures of the 80s and 90s.

He could see that the Serious Crime team were starting to leave already. There had been no stash of money in Kevin Hewitt's house, then. No wedges of used notes under the floorboards, nothing stuffed in the coffee tins except coffee. Not even a sniff from the Springer spaniel that was now being loaded back into his van. The team would be off to raid another property somewhere, probably. Some officers enjoyed the smash and grab jobs, preferred to leave the legwork to someone else. Cooper didn't mind that.

'And birds of prey are particularly at risk, Sergeant?' he asked.

'Oh, yes – and the rarer the better, as far as collectors are concerned. At one time, the fashion was to stuff raptors and mount them on a perch in your sitting room. Then eggs became the target. As long as there's money to be made, birds of prey will be killed.'

'Supply and demand.'

'Like anything else.'

Jackson was a wildlife liaison officer working with the Peak Nestwatch project. He was also South Yorkshire Police, but county boundaries were meaningless up on the moors of the Dark Peak.

Thanks to Tracy Udall, Cooper knew the basics of Nestwatch. The Upper Derwent Valley was an area that had been associated with birds of prey for a long time. Until the 1960s, they'd been absent for more than a century, eliminated by pesticides and persecution. Then the goshawk had returned to breed, followed by peregrine falcons. For twenty or thirty years, visitors had been able to watch them displaying in the spring over the Alport Castle crags. The fastest birds in Britain, graceful and spectacular.

But alarm bells had rung in 2001, when just one goshawk chick survived from eleven nests, and adult birds vanished from the valley. It had been impossible to tell what was happening,

because most of the land was in private ownership. But something had to be done. The result
was Pak Nestwatch, a partnership between the
police and bodies like the RSPB and the national
park.

'So is the situation improving?' asked Cooper.

'Changing, anyway,' said Jackson. 'When the
powers of imprisonment came in, serial egg collectors took a step back. It wasn't a question of a
twenty-quid fine any more. Collectors knew they
could go down.'

'So—?'

'So they took one of two routes. They either gave
up altogether, or they decided it would have to
be worth the risk they were taking.'

'The stakes were raised.'

'Exactly.' Jackson looked up, assessing him with
a cool blue eye. 'Are you interested? We can always
do with some help.'

'Anything I can do, Sergeant.'

'If you've got time later, I'll show you the hide
we use.'

'I go off duty at five.'

'Fine.'

Jackson turned his attention back to the
goshawk. The bird's down was thick and woolly,
but when Jackson ran his thumb across it, Cooper
could see the first adult plumage – dark, trans-
verse bands on the flight feathers, longitudinal
markings on the wing coverts. Within a few more
days, those feathers would have been strong

enough to take the bird into the air, and even Kevin Hewitt wouldn't have caught it.

The legs had only a tinge of the bright yellow characteristic of the adult. Later, the eyes would have turned that piercing orange-yellow that gave the goshawk such an evil appearance. If it was a male bird, it would have developed the dark band behind the eyes that made it look even more fearsome. But the strength of the feet and talons was already obvious, and the sharp hook of the beak was unmistakeable.

'There's only a window of about two and a half weeks between feeding themselves, and their first flight,' said Jackson. 'Mr Hewitt took one too young. A pity the cameras didn't pick him up at the time.'

'Oh, yes, the cameras.'

Nestwatch had introduced high-tech surveillance techniques at an early stage. One year, live CCTV pictures had been transmitted direct from a goshawk nest to the Fairholmes visitor centre.

In the street, two youths looked up and saw him. Cooper let the curtain fall back. Just as in every town centre, offenders intent on raiding protected nest sites had learned to wear a hood or a hat in front of cameras to prevent identification. Nestwatch had responded by taking samples of DNA from the feathers of birds of prey and setting up a database to identify stolen specimens.

Sergeant Jackson had turned the dead bird over, lifting one of the bare yellow legs.

'See the ring?' he said.

'Yes, I noticed that.'

'A Schedule 4 bird bred in captivity has to be fitted with a ring issued by DEFRA, and stamped with a serial number. The ring is what distinguishes it from a wild bird. You have to put it on the chick soon after hatching. It passes over the foot, and becomes impossible to remove intact once the bird grows.'

'But this bird has a ring. Doesn't that mean it's captive bred?'

'No. In goshawks, there's a difference in size between the male and female birds, so there are two sizes of ring. The normal practice is to fit both rings until a chick's sex becomes apparent – and that isn't until it's fledged. Then the wrong ring is removed. This particular bird is too young for anyone to be able to judge its sex. Yet it only has one ring.'

'Can we check the serial number?'

'I've already done it. This ring was issued by DEFRA four years ago. The captive bird it was made for would be fully adult by now.' Jackson shook his head. 'You know, if this wild bird had reached adulthood, Mr Hewitt might have got away with it. Abuses can only be detected if there's a visible discrepancy between the ringed bird and its registered age. But when it's an obvious juvenile—.'

'I see. So if he got a ring on it, he must have taken the bird from the nest just after it hatched.'

'Yes.'

'Which means he managed to keep it alive for a while.'

'Three or four weeks, I'd say.'

The newly hatched goshawk would have been a sitting target for Kevin Hewitt. Cooper could picture him smiling as he peered over the edge of the nest, reaching in a hand to pick out a chick with silky white down and half-closed eyes, scarcely able to lift its head.

'So he used a fraudulent ring? But, Sergeant, you said just now these rings can't be removed.'

'Well, that wasn't quite true,' admitted Jackson. 'There is *one* way that a ring can be removed intact.'

'What way is that?'

'By cutting off the bird's leg.'

'Damn.'

Jackson stared at him grimly. 'Yes. Let's hope the captive hawk had already died a natural death.'

Janine Hewitt was just leaving her front door when Cooper and Udall arrived on the Devonshire housing estate. She had one child in a pushchair, and a boy of about four trailing behind. According to her husband's record, there was an older son, presumably at school. Janine looked a good few years younger than Kevin – not much more than thirty, but thin and gaunt-eyed, like a woman old before her time.

'Going somewhere, Mrs Hewitt?' asked Udall, subtly placing herself in the woman's path, forcing her to slow down.

'We're off to the park for an hour. Nothing wrong with that, is there?' she said.

'Giving the kids a bit of fresh air? Well, it's not a bad day for it.'

'It's for me,' said Janine. 'It drives me crazy being cooped up in the house all day. You've no idea what it's like. One of these mornings, I'm going to lose it completely and go mental. Then you lot would have reason to come round quick, I reckon.'

'We'll walk with you,' said Cooper.

'Please yourselves.'

The older child stared at the police officers as they walked across the road. He clung to his mother's hand, but showed little interest in her. Udall's uniform seemed to fascinate him instead.

'We're looking for Kevin, you know,' said Udall. 'We need to locate him urgently.'

Janine didn't answer. They entered a small recreation area – a stretch of grass grown slightly too long since the council last cut it, two lines of wooden benches facing each other, a few shrubs and flower beds, a fenced playground where children clambered on a slide.

'Did you hear me, Mrs Hewitt?'

'Yes, you're looking for Kevin. Isn't everybody?'

Cooper and Udall exchanged glances. 'Has someone else been asking about him?'

Janine settled herself on a bench. Not the first bench or the second, but the third seat along the path, with a view of the playground, near an old iron drinking fountain. She chose it as if it was routine, regardless of the fact that all the other benches were empty.

'There were some other coppers here this morning. They searched my house,' she said.

'That would be Serious Crime.'

'They said they were looking for money. Money? Do I look as though I have a secret wad of dosh? What's it all about?'

'Well, what did they tell you?'

'They didn't tell me anything. It looks like you're not going to, either. It doesn't make any sense.'

'Mrs Hewitt, where is your husband?' asked Udall.

'I don't know,' said Janine, sounding almost relieved that she was finally able to make sense of what she was being asked.

'When did you last see him?'

'He hasn't been around for weeks. Three weeks, at least. I don't know exactly. I'm not his keeper. We don't live together any more.'

'Yes, we know that. But he keeps in touch, surely? He visits the children from time to time?'

'Sometimes. But, like I said—.'

'—you haven't seen him for three weeks. Is that what you said?'

Cooper watched Janine Hewitt closely while Udall questioned her. After a few minutes, she began to get nervous.

'I don't have to answer any more questions,' she said. 'It's upsetting the kids.'

'You'll let us know if you hear from Kevin,' said Cooper, handing her his card.

At first he didn't think she was going to take it, but politeness seemed to get the better of her, and she shoved the card into her pocket.

'I'm off,' she said.

'It was a short visit to the park, Janine.'

'I didn't like the atmosphere.'

The four-year-old seemed disappointed when his mother dragged him away. Cooper felt warm, and looked at the drinking fountain. But he could see there had been no water in it for decades.

'Who else do we have on the list, Tracy?' he asked.

'A fellow egg collector, Gareth Stark. We think he was Hewitt's partner at one time.'

'So what happened? Did they fall out?'

'Stark got caught in possession and did three months. He claims to have given up egg collecting now.'

'And become a law-abiding citizen?'

'We'll see.'

They walked back to the car, which they'd been careful to leave in sight – a vital precaution on the Devonshire Estate.

'Did you believe Janine Hewitt when she said she hadn't seen Kevin for three weeks?' asked Udall.

'She didn't quite say that. Didn't you notice? She answered you obliquely – she said Kevin "hadn't been around". Evading a direct answer is a classic sign of a lie.'

Udall nodded. 'I should have pressed her on it.'

'It wouldn't have done any good. You'd just have forced her to lie directly. Then she would have resented us, and we'd lose her co-operation altogether.'

'Co-operation? Is that what you'd call it?'

'She did speak to us,' said Cooper. 'Around here, that means we're practically best friends.'

CHAPTER 2

Gareth Stark had been brought into the police station at Edendale. He was sitting in Interview Room Two with a plastic cup in a paper napkin, staring at the coffee in disgust. He had long, thin fingers and a mane of dark hair that was probably tied into a pony tail when he wanted to look trendy.

His expression changed from disgust to outrage when he heard Udall's first question.

'I wasn't just some egg collector, my dear,' he said. 'I was an oologist. For me, it was a question of scientific study.'

'Oh, of course.'

Cooper suspected that calling Tracy Udall 'my dear' was likely to earn Stark a crack on the head with her side-handled baton if he wasn't careful. But Stark seemed oblivious. He looked from one to the other, and a curl came to his lip.

'Without the early collectors, we wouldn't possess half the knowledge about bird species that we do now. And there wouldn't be specimens in the museums for future generations to study.'

'But those collectors did all the work,' suggested

Cooper. 'We don't need any more specimens now.'

'How do you know?' said Stark quickly.

'Fair enough, sir. We don't.'

The lack of argument seemed to deflate him.

'What about your partner, Kevin Hewitt?' asked Udall.

'Partner?' Stark laughed. 'Kevin was useful, that's all. He could climb trees. And he developed a sort of sly talent for avoiding getting caught. An instinctive cunning. But he never had the brains. Kevin *was* just a collector. Too obsessive, too greedy. Eventually, he was bound to make a mistake.'

'But you were the one who got caught. You received a three-month prison sentence.'

Stark's face froze. 'Not through my own mistake.'

'And yet you didn't provide information against your partner. That was very loyal.'

'Kevin wasn't—.' Stark stopped, and grimaced. 'I know what you're doing. You're trying to provoke me. Well, it won't work. I'm here voluntarily, to provide information. I can leave any time I want to.'

'Kevin is back to his old trade,' said Cooper. 'Did you know?'

'He would never have seen it as a trade. Egg collecting was always a passion for Kevin. He's never been driven by money.'

'Well, Mr Hewitt seems to have lost his principles. He's working for money now. And we'd like to know who he's working for.'

Stark gazed at the wall, and at first Cooper thought he wasn't going to respond. But then he sighed and slumped in his chair.

'He must be going after the peregrines, I suppose. Or is it goshawks?'

'How did you know that?' asked Udall.

'One of the first principles of egg collecting is "the rarer the better".'

'Who would Kevin be working with now, Mr Stark? We need names.'

'I have no idea. I lost touch with that world when I got the conviction. Suddenly, I became *persona non grata*. And don't ask me where Kevin will go. The birds he'll be looking for don't always use the same nests every year. Kevin will have found new sites. That's his skill. It's what he does.'

'Not for much longer,' said Cooper.

Back at his desk, Cooper opened Kevin Hewitt's file. Hewitt had a record of minor offences, mostly between the ages of fifteen and twenty-five. There had been spells of community service, probation and fines. Despite being a serial offender, he'd avoided prison. That was mostly because Hewitt had never been convicted of a violent offence. The prisons were too full to send away anyone except the most dangerous offenders.

Cooper put some actions in progress – an alert for the whereabouts of Hewitt's Bedford van, a request for his phone records, to see who he'd been calling in the past few days. Bank records would show if Hewitt was spending money or drawing cash out somewhere, but he'd need authorisation for those.

Jackson and Udall had provided intelligence on egg collectors and known associates of Hewitt's. Cooper felt sure he'd have more sense than to go to an address already known to the police, though. It wouldn't even take that instinctive cunning Gareth Stark had referred to.

A few minutes later, he saw Udall emerge from a meeting she'd been attending.

'Serious Crime still have Kevin Hewitt as a suspect, but he's dropped very low on their list,' she said. 'They think since the principle suspects came under scrutiny, they've been using people like Hewitt for their own purposes.'

'Like stashing the proceeds?'

Udall nodded. 'On the surface, he might not seem like the obvious choice.'

'But that's a very good reason for choosing him, right?'

'Exactly. He could have been set up as a fall guy, an expendable asset.'

'Someone is doing a bit of strategic thinking at the top, then. It doesn't sound like a bunch of unemployed steel workers making a bit of pocket money, Tracy.'

'No. I think that's why they're happy to leave Hewitt to us.'

'So we're not off the enquiry?'

'Far from it. Do you know, they even asked if the Rural Crime Squad could mount a surveillance operation in the Upper Derwent.'

'What, using CROPS?' asked Cooper.

'We have people trained in CROPS, of course. But have you seen the moors up there?'

'Yes. A bit exposed for covert rural observation points.'

'You'd need to be able to disguise yourself as a grouse to pass unnoticed.'

'From next month, a grouse would be the most dangerous thing you could look like, Tracy. They have a pretty short life span once the shooting season starts.'

Udall sighed. 'Country sports. I can't see the appeal. Give me dinner and a few glasses of wine in a nice restaurant any time.'

Cooper looked down at his desk, wondering if he'd just been given a signal. Was he supposed to respond to a cue?

'Tracy, I've been thinking about Kevin Hewitt,' he said.

'Oh, yes?'

'He's well-known to us, of course. And the funny thing is, I remember him. I even interviewed him a couple of times myself. But I never thought Hewitt was a real villain. He struck me as too much of a family man. He loved his kids, no doubt about it. I can't see him taking the risk of being put away and not seeing them for a few years.'

'Things change,' said Udall. 'Children go through phases when they become unbearable. Sometimes I feel I wouldn't mind a spell in the nick to get away from *my* two. It'd be a nice holiday.'

'I've watched my nieces grow up, but I suppose it's different when you're actually a parent.'

'There's no escape,' said Udall. 'And a lot of men can't take that responsibility.'

Cooper frowned thoughtfully. 'Hewitt must know he's likely to land a prison sentence this time.'

'Maybe he doesn't care any more, since his wife kicked him out. Some men get like that. They see themselves on the long slide downhill, and they can't face it. Then they turn reckless, as if they're inviting disaster. It's a sort of death wish.'

'Rather prison than trying to live on your own?'

'Well, at least you have a place where you belong, a status in some kind of hierarchy, even if it's right at the bottom. It's an animal instinct, the desire to be part of a pack.'

'And Kevin seems to know all about animal instincts.'

Udall pulled her hat on and adjusted her belt. 'It's true, though,' she said. 'We're not made to be solitary. Loneliness is the biggest killer there is.'

Surprised, Cooper looked up at her. But she was already leaving.

By five-thirty, it was turning into a grey, claggy day, so common in the high moorland of the Dark

Peak. Cooper had crossed the viaduct over the drowned village of Ashopton, and turned off the A57 towards the Fairholmes visitor centre. Most of the pull-ins along the eastern arm of Ladybower Reservoir were full of cars, despite the weather.

On summer weekends, the road beyond Fairholmes was closed to traffic. A shuttle bus ran visitors up the valley instead, skirting the banks of the reservoirs as far as the turnaround at King's Tree. Occasionally, the police got calls from tourists who'd missed the last bus back and were too exhausted to face a six-mile walk.

Today, though, the road was open. Cooper steered cautiously through the ducks that waddled in ragged troupes across the road and drove through a gate past the western tower of Derwent Dam. In places, these reservoirs had formed sandy beaches that were exposed when the water level dropped. On a sunny day it was a bit like the seaside. Not quite the Costa del Sol, perhaps, but you could use your imagination.

It was only from the map that the geography of the Upper Derwent became clear. The long valley was filled with reservoirs – Howden, Derwent, Ladybower. The lower slopes were covered with conifer plantations, and above them rose the heather moorland, vast acres etched by cloughs and scattered with cairns. On some of those moors, there were no signs of civilisation for miles in any direction. Well, not unless you counted grouse butts as civilisation.

Cooper met Sergeant Jackson at a gate providing access on to Lightside Moor. He had another man with him, a middle aged figure in tweed cap, green shooting vest and brown corduroy trousers – an outfit designed to blend in with the moor. An English pointer sat behind him, constantly alert. Cooper approved of that. He liked a real working dog.

'This is Harry Blakelock, who owns Lightside,' said Jackson. 'Owner – and keeper too. Eh, Harry?'

'I just have a lad who helps me part-time,' said Blakelock sourly. 'There's not enough money in grouse shooting to employ full-time keepers. Not on a moor this size.'

'Mr Blakelock says we can take my Landrover most of the way across if we want,' said Jackson. He raised an eyebrow. 'But I thought you might rather walk.'

'Suits me.'

Cooper laced his boots and fastened his leggings. With a woolly hat, he'd be indistinguishable from any walker on the moors. Blakelock watched him, his jowly cheeks sunk into the collar of his jacket. Cooper noticed a green gun slip on the ground nearby, the carrying case for Blakelock's shotgun. He'd almost missed seeing it in the heather, and he knew it wasn't approved practice to leave a gun lying around, even for a few minutes. But Mr Blakelock wouldn't have been shooting at this time of year, unless he was taking crows and pigeons. They were classed as pests, and therefore open season.

'Stay on the paths,' said Blakelock. 'Don't go disturbing my birds.'

Jackson nodded. 'Don't worry, Harry.'

Cooper gave the moor owner a smile, which wasn't returned. The birds that concerned Blakelock were red grouse. They'd be his source of income once the shooting season started next month.

At first glance, Lightside Moor seemed almost featureless, the banks of heather and whinberry blurring into the distance. As they headed up the first slope, Cooper caught a glimpse of something yellow below the crest of a ridge, but within a couple of steps it was hidden by the terrain.

Cooper looked at the map for the names of the moors. He saw Alport, Westend, Ronksley. And this one, Lightside, surrounded on all sides by more moorland, plantations to the east, and the boggy ground of Featherbed Moss to the north. Gamekeepers tended these moors all year, battling encroaching vegetation and disease-carrying ticks. And, of course, the predators – or 'vermin', as so many keepers called them.

'So where do you think the biggest risks for birds of prey come from, Sergeant?' he asked, pausing to let the older man catch up.

'Well, pigeon fanciers don't like them – particularly peregrines, because they take racing pigeons sometimes. And gamekeepers don't like any birds of prey, because they think they reduce the grouse population.'

'Well, they do. Don't they?'

Jackson's breath was getting ragged as they approached the top of the moor. 'Some do. Hen harriers.'

'Anyone else?'

'Oh, a few serial egg collectors are still out there. And raptor keepers who want to improve a captive strain.'

They came across a grouse butt that had been dug into a peat bank and shored up with sheets of corrugated iron. On the next slope, Cooper could see another butt. And beyond that a third, and a fourth.

The yellow shape he'd glimpsed turned out to be a battered fibreglass shelter. The foam insulation was peeling from the walls, and swallows had built their nest in a loose fold of foam. Two scarred wooden benches inside could probably seat about ten men with their guns and dogs when the weather turned bad during a shoot. But visitors other than shooters had engraved disrespectful graffiti in the remaining insulation.

In the valley behind him, Cooper saw Howden Reservoir, sheltering deep in its conifer plantations. The only sounds on the moor were curlew and snipe, crying at the presence of intruders.

'Nearly there now,' said Jackson. 'Thank God.'

It looked like an ordinary garden shed. A shed that someone had dropped from an aircraft on to a remote part of the moors. Okay, they'd dropped it carefully – it was perfectly intact, anchored to the ground and coated with preservative. Its weather boarding and green felt roof looked incongruous above the crags of Alport Castles, though. It was one of the most unlikely tourist attractions Cooper could imagine, even in the Peak District. This was where people came to watch birds displaying over the crags.

'We might see birds here, if we're lucky,' said Jackson.

Cooper had brought his own binoculars, an old pair of Zeiss 10 x 50s. He adjusted them as Jackson explained the excitement about eggs being laid in goshawk nests since late April. Incubation lasted for around five weeks, and that was the time when nest sites attracted the attention of predators in human shape. Egg collectors wanted freshly laid eggs, which were easier to blow, so they were out in their camouflage gear as soon as word got round that the first goshawk was laying.

'They spend all winter planning their next season, as if it's a military campaign – targets, tactics, how to avoid the enemy,' said Jackson. 'They're really getting organised.'

Alport Castles themselves towered over the valley and the farmstead way below. Tors perched precariously on the summit, and boulders were tumbled on the slopes. If the mist descended, it would be easy to look out of the corners of your eyes and mistake the thousands of gritstone boulders for the shapes of people, crowds of them standing perfectly still and ghost-like on the edge of the moor.

Cooper noticed a pair of black shapes circling over the moor, and turned his binoculars westwards. Carrion crows. This pair probablythey had their eyes on a weak lamb somewhere. Soon they'd land nearby and wait for it to weaken. Then they'd begin to work on its eyes, like delicacies that had to be eaten fresh. Once their victim was blinded, the crows could eat the rest of it at their leisure.

'And what if the goshawk's eggs survive to be hatched?'

'Then the egg collectors are replaced by people who want live chicks to sell, or to raise in captivity. It's a never-ending battle, Ben.'

Cooper tried to analyse the background noise. He couldn't see a road from here, so probably it was only the sound of the wind scything through the plantations. Close to the edge, the gusts were dangerously strong, banging angrily between the rocks. A half-grown sheep called plaintively – a strange, unnatural cry that stuck in its throat.

He lifted the binoculars again, and saw a single outline soaring over the valley. This time, it was a peregrine. The bird rose effortlessly on a thermal, then flicked a wing and swooped behind the crags, perhaps spotting the movement of prey.

'*They* don't need binoculars,' said Jackson.

Watching the bird, Cooper found the phrase 'eagle eyed' going through his mind. The only way the police could achieve that sort of surveillance in the Upper Derwent was to get Oscar Hotel 88 airborne from Ripley, and there was no way he could justify the cost of a helicopter.

'It's amazing there are still individuals plundering nests,' said Jackson. 'They obviously haven't heard about the measures we're taking to protect endangered species these days.'

'They might have done,' said Cooper. 'Publicity doesn't necessarily deter people. They always think it can't happen to them.'

'Well, the last one was caught by the cameras. He wasn't too difficult to identify, because he was a known collector.'

'I've heard you sometimes use off-duty police officers pretending to be campers,' said Cooper. 'Is that right?'

Jackson smiled. 'I believe it is.'

In fact, Cooper knew an officer who'd volunteered for the job, and had spent three days in the Upper Derwent with his tent and binoculars. A few hours of your time were worthwhile if you cared about the national park's wildlife. Maybe that was what Sergeant Jackson had in mind for him.

Cooper noticed a figure striding purposefully towards them along the edge of the moor.

'Who's this?'

'Oh, it's one of our volunteers,' said Jackson. 'A keen birdwatcher, Calvin Ryan. And when I say keen—.'

'He'd have to be really dedicated to come all the way up here.'

'Oh, he's here regularly. Cal is a bit of a crank, I suppose, but we can't discourage him. The more eyes we have, the better.'

Ryan was wearing a knitted beanie hat, pulled so low that it almost met his goatee beard. His rucksack had pockets and Velcro straps that held camera, notebook, mobile phone, and other items that Tracy Udall might have been happy to wear on her belt.

'Peregrine,' he said, gesturing excitedly.

'Yes, we've seen it.'

Ryan wiped a sheen of sweat from his forehead with the back of a hand, and looked at Cooper. 'Peregrines were almost wiped out in Derbyshire, thanks to pesticides. When they came back, Alport Castles was the first site they chose to begin breeding again.'

'This is one of my colleagues, Cal,' said Jackson. 'He's not a tourist.'

Ryan looked disappointed. 'Oh.'

But he wasn't deterred for long from expressing his enthusiasm. He followed the flight of the bird over the valley with eagerness.

'I love the goshawks and peregrines,' he said. 'They're the most fantastic of all the birds.'

'They look great when they're flying,' agreed Cooper.

'It's not just the way they look.'

Ryan laid a hand on his sleeve, gripping a bit too

tightly. 'Goshawks mate for life, you know. A bonded pair will hunt co-operatively, two of them together. Then, when the chicks are hatched, the tercel isn't allowed near the nest. He has to leave the food he catches at a distance, where the female bird can fetch it for the chicks.'

They lost sight of the bird again, and a moment of silence followed, as if they'd just been deprived of their reason for communicating with each other.

'Do they fly a long way from the nest site?' asked Cooper.

'The male hunts up to three miles away.'

'So anyone with a rifle could pick off that bird, and we'd never be any wiser.'

'That's what happened in the past, we think,' said Jackson. 'The male birds just disappeared. If they were killed, the bodies were either removed by someone, or eaten by scavengers.'

Ryan tugged angrily at his hat. 'Not this one. He'll be back. Sometimes when he catches prey, he stores it in a safe place for feeding on later.'

'I suppose a little bit of decay makes the meat tastier,' suggested Jackson. 'It's like you'd hang a joint of beef for a few days to make it sweet and tender.'

Ryan pulled a disgusted expression. 'I'd like you to know I'm a vegetarian.'

A gust of wind blew along the edge of the valley, and a shower spattered their faces.

'We need more people watching,' said Ryan. 'More eyes equals more protection.'

'So I heard.'

Yes, Cooper had heard it from Phil Jackson only a few minutes earlier, but not with so much fervour.

'Look at this place,' said Ryan, waving a dismissive hand at the grouse moor behind him. 'Birds that hunt the moorland are persecuted so much they've stopped breeding altogether in prime habitats.'

Cooper glanced at Jackson, but he was edging away, on the pretence of checking the moorings of the shed.

'So you blame the moorland owners and game-keepers, Mr Ryan?'

Ryan glared at him as if Cooper had just called his entire belief system into doubt.

'Persecution definitely exists,' he said. 'You can see that. And these grouse moors are where the conflict occurs.'

'The problem comes from a minority, though, surely? There are people who actively protect birds of prey, but also shoot.'

Ryan seemed to hold himself in with an effort. 'I don't have a problem with shooting. But I do have a problem with raptor persecution. The bottom line is that birds of prey are protected by law.'

Ryan hitched his rucksack and moved off along the edge, with the air of someone who'd won an argument through sheer righteousness. He reminded Cooper of a street preacher – one of those wild-eyed men who lurked outside shopping precincts, confident that they only had to shout at people long enough for everyone to agree with them.

Jackson smiled at Cooper when Ryan was out of earshot.

'Cal's right, though,' he said. 'At the end of the day, it was public opinion that led to a ban on fox hunting. What will be next on the public's list of things to ban if they see birds of prey being killed?'

'You think the shooters and shoot owners are worried?'

For a moment, Jackson followed the flight of the peregrine until it vanished against the background of heather.

'I think some of them will be panicking,' he said. 'There's a propaganda war going on, Ben – and they're losing right now.'

The next tree was even higher. Hewitt had to lean against the trunk for a while until he felt strong enough to carry on. He dug a bottle of water out of his pocket and took a long drink, then urinated on the grass at the base of the fir. It was supposed to bring good luck, wasn't it?

Hewitt grinned to himself, but the sweat drying on his face made smiling uncomfortable. What he really needed was a nice stream nearby. He could imagine clear, cold water tumbling over a few stones, tinged slightly brown from the peat, like a good malt whisky. Water was everywhere in the Peak District, cascading in torrents from the hills to fill up the reservoirs. But there was no stream here in the plantation. Not for half a mile or so, way back across the moor.

Then Hewitt saw the bird. It swooped over the woods, hovered for a second, then soared out again, far above his head. He caught the flicker of plumage and saw the shape of the wings against the light as it turned. A goshawk. Probably the male bird, the tercel, hunting for prey to feed its mate and the chicks in the nest.

Fumbling for his binoculars, Hewitt moved away from the tree and tried to keep the bird in sight. If it decided to pursue something on the ground, it would move too fast for him to follow. But if he could track its movements and see where it returned to, it would save him a lot of pain and effort.

He lost the goshawk for a moment, and scanned backwards and forwards over the moor anxiously, straining his eyes to pick out any movement against the background. He caught up with the bird as it skimmed low over a slope. It was swinging its head from side to side, searching for rodents in the vegetation. Hewitt admired the grace of its flight, the way it hardly seemed to move its wings to maintain height, just that flick of a pinion to change direction or catch a thermal and rise several feet in a second.

And then he heard the shot. The crack of it echoed across the moor and into the valley, bouncing of the ramparts of Alport Castles.

And suddenly the bird was gone from his field of

vision. Hewitt was left with nothing more than the impression of exploding feathers, a body that was lighter than air tossed over and over, like a rag caught in the wind. Somebody had shot the tercel.

CHAPTER 3

Next morning, Sergeant Jackson came into the CID office at Edendale. He was carrying an evidence bag that contained a dead goshawk.

'A walker picked it up, and phoned in,' he said. 'Another few hours, and the carcass would have disappeared, one way or another.'

'Shot?'

'Yes.'

Cooper watched Jackson turn the bird over in his hands, examining its wings, the talons and beak – all the hallmarks of a raptor. There was even a reason why its legs and feet were bare of feathers. It was so they didn't get covered in blood when it sank its talons into prey.

But there was blood now, and plenty of it – the whole of the bird's left side was matted.

Cooper could sense Jackson's despair at the fate of the goshawk. Almost the only action he could take was to record the incident. And even that was a recent innovation. For many years, no police force had prioritised wildlife incidents, because they weren't recordable. If you cleared up a burglary, it came off the crime figures. But catch a bird thief, and it didn't show up in any statistics. No target to be met, no performance to be measured. Now at least the public could see that offences were being dealt with.

Beyond that, Jackson's options were limited. It wasn't like a burglary, where there might be witnesses, fingerprints, a car registration to follow up. Wildlife crime happened in remote areas, on private land. Not much chance of a witness, and no forensic evidence. Even if you had a suspect, it would be someone with a legitimate reason to be at the scene. After the introduction of Right to Roam legislation, that meant pretty much everyone.

'It's very frustrating,' said Jackson. 'So many wildlife criminals are involved in other offences. Arrest one, and you collar a well-known villain.'

'But what are your chances of an arrest?'

'Zero.'

Cooper felt strangely relieved when Jackson took the goshawk away. There was always something alien about a dead bird. It was probably that third eyelid, the nictating membrane, that closed from the inside corner to protect the eye. It was so reptilian that it marked birds as survivors from an earlier age.

'Well, I think it's definitely a sadistic offence,' said Udall when she heard the news. 'These are people who take pleasure in inflicting cruelty. They're potential serial killers.'

'That's putting it a bit strong, Tracy.'

'Don't psychologists say the typical serial killer starts his careers by mistreating animals? It's part of the pattern.'

'Yes, they do say that.'

'After all, this is someone who's prepared to use violence on a casual basis. If he lacks respect for animal life, he might not respect human life, either.'

Half an hour later, Cooper's phone rang. It was Sergeant Jackson again.

'Maybe not zero after all,' he said. 'Cal Ryan says he was up at the hide when the goshawk was shot.'

'Did he see anything?'

'Yes. He saw Harry Blakelock. And Mr Blakelock was carrying a firearm.'

'I'll have to talk to him, Phil. Is that okay with you?'

'You're the detective.' Jackson sounded bitter. But a moment later, his tone changed. 'No, that's fine. I might still have to work with the man when this is over.'

'I'll get up there today. He lives at Lightside Lodge, doesn't he?'

'Yes. But he'll be out on the moor on a day like this. I can give you his mobile number so you can track him down.'

'Thanks, Phil.'

'There's another thing. A whole bunch of twitchers were down in the valley at the time. You often see them lined up near Derwent Dam with their telescopes and telephoto lenses. One or two of them have helped us in the past. And they're familiar with the major egg collectors. Word goes round the bird watching community like wildfire.'

'You mean they saw Hewitt?'

'No, Gareth Stark. Every clued-up twitcher knows about Stark. They were breaking out the champagne when he went down.'

'Don't tell me Stark was spotted in the valley when the bird was shot, too?'

'No. But his car was.'

'That complicates the picture,' said Cooper.

'Do you want me to speak to Stark?'

'Would you, Phil?'

'With pleasure.'

'I'll ask Tracy Udall if she'd like to come along. If Stark calls her "my dear" once more—.'

Jackson laughed. 'Tell her she'll be welcome. I'm getting a bit slow on my feet these days, and I might not be able to hold her back.'

Harry Blakelock was carrying a twelve-bore side-lock with a thirty-inch barrel. When Cooper got a closer look, he could see that it was a magnificent Purdey, with beautiful engravings. It must have been worth fifteen thousand pounds at least, even second hand. He knew from the firearms licensing records that Mr Blakelock had a safe somewhere at home, with at least three more shot-guns in it.

As Cooper approached, Blakelock's English pointer was creeping across a stretch of boggy ground, her body rigid from nose to tail. She'd detected the scent of grouse hiding in the heather.

'That's Molly,' said Blakelock. 'Useful dog.'

'I have a few questions to ask you, sir.'

'Go ahead, then.'

Blakelock listened in stony silence to Cooper's questions. Then he slapped the stock of his gun.

'I was up here on the moor, as you know damn well. You saw me yourself. But I was back home by six-thirty, and I went nowhere near those woods. You can check my gun over, if you want. I shot a crow a few minutes ago, and there's still a cartridge in.'

'It won't tell me anything.'

'Of course it won't.'

A covey of grouse broke cover, flapping furiously to escape. But they were in luck today. Blakelock was only checking how many birds there were, not intending to deplete their numbers. It was over a month yet before the grouse season started, and these birds would begin to plummet out of the sky. Cooper knew real shooters were scornful of the rush to be the first to kill a bird on the opening day of the season. The Glorious Twelfth was just a marketing ploy, they said, a photo opportunity for the media. But proper shooting would follow soon after, grouse being driven by beaters towards paying guns.

As the squawking birds gained speed and altitude,

Molly was already pointing out another covey in the heather. Blakelock turned to watch her.

'I know your brother, don't I?' he said over his shoulder. 'Matt Cooper? He has a farm near Hucklow.'

'That's right.'

'And I remember your grandfather – he was a grand old bloke. And wasn't your father—?'

'Yes, I'm sure you knew him, too.'

'Well, you must know the way it is – these bird groups have got to increase their membership, so they put out sensationalist reports. They quote incidents which are just plain bloody wrong. They don't know who's causing the problem, so it must be gamekeepers. But I've seen reports that disturbance by bird watchers is responsible for the loss of birds. The tercel sees a crowd of twitchers near his nest, and he says "sod this, I'm off".'

Cooper was getting irritated by the clouds of black flies dancing over the heather. They were always a problem on a warm, still day.

'There are always two sides, Mr Blakelock,' he said.

'Come off it. These bird groups, they're completely blinkered. They don't care about the wider picture. Without shoots, these moors would be abandoned to the damn dog owners, and the ramblers. There'd be no wildlife up here, that's for sure. And there's a demand for shooting, you know. Not just in this country – I have a party of

Germans who book a few days on the moor every year. Businessmen from Frankfurt.'

'You know that some people would question the morality of shooting wildlife for pleasure?'

'Pleasure?' said Blakelock. 'I get pleasure from the skill it takes to put the grouse here in the first place. I get pleasure from the surroundings I spend time in. And from the co-ordination of hand and eye, if you like. But not from the act of killing.'

'But most of the killing is done by people who pay money to do it.'

'If a hundred grouse need culling, why should I do it myself when there are people willing to pay? Anyway, we try to be selective on our shoots. If you've got a seasoned eye, you can pick out the oldest bird in a covey as they scatter. I don't allow massacres.'

'Is it always so straightforward?'

Blakelock didn't answer the question directly. He broke the shotgun open, emptied the remaining cartridge, and put the gun away in its slip.

'There's this idea some people have of putting an end to shooting and returning the moors to their original state,' he said. 'It's completely impractical, you know. The balance of nature was altered centuries ago.'

'And, as you said, the grouse bring in money.'

'A day's shooting might bring in eight thousand pounds or so. But the money gets paid straight back out to keepers and beaters. Nobody's getting rich owning a grouse moor.'

'Then why spend so much effort destroying the predators?'

Blakelock looked at him coolly. 'All your family have been shooters, Detective Constable Cooper. I bet you've even been on shoots yourself, haven't you? Local farmers and their families often get invited for a day out on the moor.'

The staccato warning call of a grouse rattled across the moors. *Go back, go back, go back.* Cooper wafted the flies from his face, trying to gain time before he answered.

'Yes, I know a bit about shooting.'

'Bagged a few grouse yourself, I dare say?'

'I stick to clays these days, Mr Blakelock.'

Blakelock called his dog to heel. 'I really don't understand it. You're shooting people, all you Coopers. You always have been. Yet here you are, harrassing people like me, just because I'm going about my legitimate business. Very odd. Give someone a uniform and a warrant card, and suddenly they forget which side they're on.'

'I'm not on anyone's side, sir. My job is to see the law doesn't get broken.'

'Sometimes, when there are bad laws, you have to choose,' said Blakelock. 'Those are the times when we all have to take sides.'

'Stark had an alibi,' said Udall, the moment Cooper returned to the office in Edendale. 'Bastard.'

'But his car was identified, wasn't it? According

47

to Phil Jackson, the twitchers even took his licence number.'

'Oh, he was in the valley all right. But he was with a woman. Can you believe it?'

Cooper laughed at her expression. 'It takes all sorts, Tracy.'

'They went to Fairholmes for a picnic, then hired a couple of bikes for a romantic ride along Derwent Reservoir. She corroborates his story in full. We've even got his signature in the book at the hire centre. Stark had the nerve to tell us that he was paying a nostalgic visit to old haunts.'

'Did you believe him?'

'No, I didn't. To be honest, I was amazed when I found it really was a woman he was with. I was pretty sure it was you he fancied in that interview room, not me.'

'For heaven's sake, Tracy—.'

'Oh, sod it. You never heard me say that.'

Cooper watched her fiddling with her belt, tugging at it as if the thing was never going to be comfortable, no matter what she did. When Udall stood close to his desk, he could smell the familiar aroma of wool and polyester. Police uniform trousers. They were notoriously ill-fitting and itchy to wear, too.

'Have you any idea how many twitchers were in the valley that day, Tracy?'

'Fifty, sixty. Why?'

'You know, some of the shooting fraternity argue that it's disturbance by bird watchers that scares the goshawks off.'

Udall sucked her teeth. 'Perhaps.'

'They've got a point, when you see the crowds of twitchers lined up with their binoculars and telephoto lenses.'

'I said "perhaps".'

Cooper picked up a file that had been left on his desk and read the first page. 'Did you know that Harry Blakelock once had his firearms certificate revoked?'

'Oh? A security breach? Or a domestic?'

'Neither,' said Cooper.

He turned the file over to the reasons for revocation. Many cases like this cropped up each year, some of them stupid and unavoidable. They mostly involved insecure storage – guns abandoned in a Landrover outside a pub, or even in a field after a shoot. Of course, people who didn't know any better shouldn't be allowed to own a gun.

But there were also an increasing number of domestic incidents. A certificate holder could be vulnerable to complaints by his partner that he'd made threats. Cooper knew of one man who'd lost his firearms certificate on a drink driving conviction. But this case wasn't any of those.

'It appears Mr Blakelock went to his GP and asked for an anti-depressant prescription,' he said. 'Grounds for revocation: a mental illness, meaning that he can't possess firearms without being a potential danger to the public'

'Damn,' said Udall. 'I bet that really pissed him off.'

'The lesson is not to be in too much of a hurry to talk to your doctor, I suppose.'

'But he must have got his certificate back?'

Cooper remembered the Purdey. 'Oh, surely.'

It was recorded in the file that Blakelock had found a solicitor in East Anglia who specialised in shooting law, and he'd lodged a successful appeal against revocation.

'I've heard the name of this solicitor before,' said Cooper. 'He handles a lot of Firearms Act appeals.'

'Part of the preventative justice system, then. Balancing the public interest against an individual's right to possess a gun.'

Cooper shrugged. 'He did a good job for Mr Blakelock.'

'Hoorah for justice.'

It was a shame to be so cynical so young, but Cooper knew he couldn't judge Udall when his life experience was so different from hers. While she was listening to a burst of chatter from her radio, he picked up another file that had been left for him.

'Now this is interesting. Tracy. Kevin Hewitt's phone records.'

'Anything of significance?'

'Mostly calls to his wife. Some long conversations – chatting to the kids, probably. A couple of calls to Gareth Stark. We'll have to ask him about those. But get this, Tracy – there have been three calls made to Lightside Lodge. That's Harry Blakelock's number.'

Udall pursed her lips. 'What's the connection between those two?'

'I don't know. But—.'

But she was listening to her radio again, and Cooper realised he'd lost her attention.

'They've found Hewitt's Bedford van,' she said. 'Parked by the Westend River bridge.'

'On the banks of Howden?'

'That's the place.'

The van didn't take long to open. In the back, they found a pair of aluminium climbing irons fitted with fibreglass shin guards and Velcro straps.

'Geckos,' said Cooper, touching a finger to the flat tips of the gaffs. 'There's a couple of hundred pounds in these irons alone. But Kevin Hewitt has been unemployed for months. He's been getting money from somewhere, all right.'

There was also a pair of climbing gloves, spare boots, a rucksack, and a set of plastic boxes like those in Hewitt's trophy room. Udall had found a rolled sleeping bag and a blanket. She turned out the contents of the rucksack, and pulled her face at the smell of dirty clothes.

'That answers the question of where he's been sleeping since we raided his council house. He couldn't go back to his wife, since she decided she didn't like living with a criminal and kicked him out. So Kevin's been living in his van.'

Cooper lifted a digital camera out of the glove compartment. 'I don't believe Janine Hewitt

51

kicked her husband out because he was a criminal. It was because she was frightened he'd get caught. She didn't want her children coming into contact with the police and Social Services.'

'I can relate to that.'

'On the other hand, I think she would certainly be reluctant to give up benefiting from the proceeds of Kevin's activities.'

'So they'd have had to get together and find a way for Kevin to pass the money on without going to the house. I can understand that, from her point of view. But why would Kevin take the risk? What was in it for him?'

'It was his only chance of staying in touch with his kids,' said Cooper. 'Whatever else Kevin Hewitt's faults are, I think he loves his children.'

Udall straightened up. 'Well, there's no hoard of cash in this van, any more than there was in his house. So where's Kevin now?'

Cooper looked at the conifer plantations surrounding the reservoirs, and the vast expanses of moorland beyond them.

'I don't know. But I'm getting a really bad feeling about Kevin Hewitt's future.'

Janine Hewitt was wearing a completely impractical pair of shoes in the park that day. They were red and strappy, with heels that wobbled when she stood up to check on the child in the pushchair.

'I bought these on eBay,' she said, when she

saw Cooper looking at them. 'They were only a fiver.'

Cooper wondered if he was supposed to compliment her on her taste. But a glance at Janine's expression told him that she didn't expect anything. No compliments, no sympathy. Not from him, not from anybody.

'How are the children?'

'They're all right,' she said listlessly. 'I'll be glad when they're all at school. But I suppose it could be worse.'

'Worse?'

'There are only two of them,' she said. 'Some women round here, they have a house full by the time they're thirty. Poor cows.'

For the first time, Cooper noticed how pale and weary she looked. He wondered if she was ill, or whether it was just exhaustion, the day to day grind of bringing up young children on her own. He knew there couldn't be much money in the household. A fiver on a pair of shoes was an extravagance, intended only to raise her spirits for a short while.

'Janine, your husband could be in danger, did you know that?'

She looked up at him. 'Could he?'

'We think so.'

She gazed across the park, tears suddenly glistening in her eyes, as if emotion had sneaked up on her unexpectedly. Cooper looked away, embarrassed. Talking to Janine Hewitt made him wonder about this whole mating for life thing. All that pairing, breeding, and caring for the young. Then watching them learn to fly and fend for themselves. And doing it all over again the next year.

'Kevin was okay until they got their claws into him,' she said suddenly.

'They? Who are "they"?'

'There were a couple of foreigners,' she said. 'Kevin said they were Germans, who came over here looking for birds.'

'Falconers?'

'I don't know what that means. They wanted birds to train for hunting. Kevin said they'd pay good money for the right bird. That's what everyone wants these days, not eggs.'

'Yes. He was talking about falconers.'

'Did he mention any names, Janine?' asked Udall. 'Or where he met them?'

'He never told me anything like that. I didn't know any details, and I didn't ask. It's best not to know. That's what Kevin always said.'

'Sometimes it's true.'

Janine found a tissue and wiped her eyes. 'You know, I told Kevin if he could get us out of this place, I'd have him back.'

'Get you out?'

'Find us a proper home, somewhere nice. Not this shit hole. I want a house of my own, a garden the kids can play in. I'm not going to stay living next door to a bunch of drug addicts who leave the yard full of syringes for Jack to pick up. I can't have my kids sleeping in rooms so damp the wall-paper won't stay on the walls. I want to get right out of the Devonshire Estate.'

'How would Kevin find enough money for that?' asked Cooper.

'There are ways,' she said. 'Everyone knows there are ways to get money. Look at some of the people round here. Do you think they live on a few quid a week in child benefit, like I do?'

'Janine – are you telling us you put pressure on Kevin to commit more and more serious crimes? You actually encouraged him to get in deeper?'

She'd begun to cry again. The child in the pushchair turned to look, stirred out of her apathy by the sound of her mother sobbing.

'No, no. I didn't do that.'

'Well, that's what happened, Janine. Isn't it?'

'I never seriously thought there was a chance he'd get enough money together. Not Kevin.'

'You underestimated him, then.'

Janine laughed through the tears. 'Hardly. I've never seen anything from him. And I don't suppose I will now.'

'You haven't seen anything? No money?'

'No. He promised me he'd do it one day. But, like I said, he never got it together. That was Kevin all over.'

Cooper and Udall looked at each other. They knew that Kevin Hewitt had found at least one source of money. So what happened to it?

★   ★   ★

55

'Germans?' said Cooper when they were back in the car. 'I can't believe she said Germans. An international connection is all we need, Tracy.'

'Our wildlife officers have contact with their counterparts in Europe,' said Udall. 'German falconers are often mentioned in their intelligence reports. They roam the whole of Europe in search of new material, even as far as Greenland to obtain gyr falcons. I'm told falconry is very popular in Germany.'

'Don't they breed their own chicks?'

'Some falconers do. But not on a large enough scale to meet the demand.'

'And, in this case, the demand is for young birds.'

'Yes. Young enough to be trained.'

'Why does everything come down to supply and demand, Tracy?'

'It's what makes the world go round.'

Cooper gazed at the Devonshire Estate as they drove down the street. Some of the addresses in this area were the homes of the most active drug dealers in town – people who certainly lived much better than Janine Hewitt.

'Harry Blakelock mentioned a party of Germans who book a few days on his grouse shoot every year,' he said. 'He said they were businessmen from Frankfurt.'

'Maybe they are.'

Cooper felt easier as the outlines of the hills became visible beyond the streets of the estate. 'You know, I bet Mr Blakelock would do anything

56

to avoid losing his shotgun licence again. He'd stand no chance of winning an appeal a second time, no matter how good a lawyer he got.'

'So if someone had a bit of information about him—? Information they might be inclined to report to the police, which could lose him his certificate.'

'Yes. Anything might do it, too – evidence of a security breach, an assault, drunk driving. Another medical problem.'

'He'd want to keep them quiet somehow.'

Cooper nodded. 'Despite his complaints, Blakelock must have plenty of money. He'd be a prime target for blackmail, wouldn't you say?'

'A sitting duck.'

Cooper sighted along the barrels, shifted his grip on the stock and breathed in the scent of gun oil as his fingers felt for the trigger. The shotgun fitted snugly into his shoulder, and the weight of the double barrels swung smoothly as he turned his body. With that movement came an eagerness to see the target in his sights, a desire for the kick and cough of the cartridge. He was ready.

'Pull!'

The launcher snapped and a clay flashed across his line of vision. The barrels swung up and to the right to follow its trajectory, and his finger squeezed. The clay shattered into fragments that curved towards the ground.

'Pull!'

The second clay flickered overhead. Cooper carefully increased the pressure on the trigger, timing the extra squeeze as the target's line steadied. The clay shattered like the first.

'Nice,' he said, breaking the shotgun open as his brother Matt walked across from the trap.

'That Remington's a well-made piece of equipment, isn't it?' said Matt.

'The best.'

It was the gun Cooper had won the Shooting Trophy with a couple of years ago, but he hardly had time for it these days, not since he'd moved out of the farm. The residents of Welbeck Street wouldn't be quite so relaxed about him carrying a shotgun around.

In addition to the trap, Matt had brought out three boxes of clay pigeons and a hundred cartridges. The small black pellets in those cartridges were enough to smash a clay. But when they caught a real bird in their lethal hail, they pierced its flesh and lodged in its muscles and internal organs, maybe in its brain. Cooper supposed it was a quick death.

'I've just bought a new gun,' said Matt. 'A Baikal Choke. I paid £400 for it.'

'A bargain.'

And probably it was. But a £400 Baikal was a bit different from Harry Blakelock's Purdey. And a clay pigeon was a different prospect from a grouse on Lightside Moor, too. Grouse were so attractive because they were uniquely difficult to shoot. It was impossible to simulate their speed, their style of flight, or the way they sprang up from the heather anywhere, even from behind you. No set of clays could match that.

Cooper knew some people saw grouse shooting as an anachronism – they pictured the tweed-clad rich blasting away at wildlife, like a scene from some nineteenth century novel. Others were uneasy about deriving pleasure from the destruction of living creatures. Killing an animal was one thing. When it had to be done, there was a satisfaction in knowing you'd done the job properly.

He turned away to put his shotgun in the Land Rover, where he locked it into a steel box. But getting pleasure from killing? Yes, he had to agree. That was a different thing altogether.

CHAPTER 4

By Friday, Kevin Hewitt lay on a stainless steel table. Entering the mortuary, Cooper could see that his egg collecting career was at an end. Janine's children were without a father.

He wondered whether Jack and Ebony would mourn their dad and remember him forever, or forget him within a few months. Maybe Janine would introduce another man into their lives and tell them he was their new dad. Unlike goshawks, people didn't necessarily mate for life.

'A heart attack?' asked Cooper. 'Or did he just lose his grip and fall?'

The pathologist, Doctor Juliana van Doon, pulled down her mask and drew off her latex gloves.

'Well, your deceased certainly fell, DC Cooper. It was the force of his impact with the ground that killed him. There are multiple internal injuries – all listed in my report, if you need them. But his heart wasn't in good condition, either. How did you know that?'

'It was just a guess, ma'am.'

Mrs van Doon smiled. 'Well, there's a lot of fatty

degeneration present, which would have been dangerous at his age – especially if he was in the habit of climbing trees. Some people never learn how to adapt their lifestyles to their physical capabilities. But Mr Hewitt didn't live long enough to experience a heart attack.'

'What do you mean?'

'I suspect *this* was what made him fall.'

Cooper realised the pathologist was holding a stainless steel bowl. At the bottom was a tiny, black metal ball that was almost invisible against the gleam of the metal, but rattled ominously when she tipped the bowl.

'An airgun pellet,' he said.

'That's what I thought. But I'm glad to hear you confirm it.'

'Where did you find it?'

Mrs van Doon pointed with her scalpel. 'I removed the pellet from a wound in the deceased's scalp, just behind the right ear. The entry wound was almost masked by a contusion from the fall – that's why it wasn't evident at the preliminary examination.'

'Could it be left over from an old injury? These things are so tiny – they can stay in the body for years without the victim being aware of them.'

'No, the wound was fresh. The track of the pellet into the flesh is still clear, and there was no sign of healing.'

'So he was shot with an air rifle while he was in the tree,' said Cooper.

'That's what it looks like.'

Cooper didn't feel convinced. Unlike a shotgun, an airgun fired a single lead pellet. It was useful for controlling pest species, provided they could be shot at short distances, thirty-five yards or less. And there had been plenty of people who'd lost an eye in a close-range accident. But an airgun pellet wouldn't normally kill a human being.

'No, the pellet wouldn't have caused a serious injury in itself,' said Mrs van Doon when he mentioned it. 'But it would have given Mr Hewitt quite a shock. There would certainly be a sharp pain. I imagine you'd instinctively put a hand up to the place you were hit.'

'And that was enough for him to lose his grip.'

'Yes, I'd say so. If you like, we could start calling him "the victim" now, instead of "the deceased".'

Cooper looked at the pellet again. 'For all Kevin Hewitt knew, he might have been stung by a wasp or something. If he never saw the shooter, he wouldn't have been able to tell the difference.'

'Yes, I'm sure you're right. The pellet would have come right out of the blue.' Mrs Van Doon shook the dish again. 'So there you have it, DC Cooper – here's a case where you could say the victim literally didn't know what hit him.'

Tracy Udall pulled up a chair in the CID room, ignoring the stares of the other detectives. Cooper had asked her to help him go over the evidence, to try to make sense of Kevin Hewitt's last few weeks of life.

'Well, let's look for a motive. Who might have had it for Kevin?'

'Gareth Stark, definitely,' said Udall. 'He has a grudge against Hewitt for his conviction. And the Germans – I bet they want the money back they paid for a goshawk.'

'Okay. And Harry Blakelock?'

'Yes, if Hewitt had something on him.'

Cooper looked up. 'Tracy, were there any photographs found in Hewitt's house?'

'No, but there was a digital camera in the van, with a spare memory stick.'

'So there was.'

'Judging by his meticulous filing, I suppose he must have taken photos to record his finds, too.'

'Have we looked what's on the camera?'

'Not yet. Well, it didn't seem important. It'll just be eggs, Ben.'

'Retrieve it from Exhibits, will you? And the memory stick, too.'

Udall returned a few minutes later with the camera, and connected it up to a PC. There were lots of photos. And Tracy was right, most of them were of eggs. There was also an entire sequence showing the acquisition of the goshawk chick – the nestling still in its nest, the young chick in its cage at Hewitt's house.

But right in the middle of the sequence, there were some shots Cooper couldn't make out at first. They had been taken from some high vantage point, possibly in the very tree Hewitt had found the nest. Shots of Harry Blakelock, and a gun left unattended on the moor. The time stamp from the camera was evidence of how long the gun was left before its owner returned.

'Blackmail material,' said Udall.

'I wonder how much Hewitt was asking for it.'

'Too much for Blakelock to stomach?'

Cooper sighed. 'So Kevin Hewitt not only upset bird enthusiasts, but his former partner, a bunch of Germans, the local drug dealers, and even Harry Blakelock. He pissed everyone off. That's quite an achievement.'

'Not forgetting his wife,' said Udall.

'Janine?'

'Possibly the most unforgiving of all.'

'You're right.' Cooper tapped his pen thoughtfully. 'Tracy, what would you have done if you'd been in Hewitt's position?'

'I'd have kept my head down. Left the area, probably. But, as Janine said, someone had their claws into him. Kevin was driven by more than a concern for his own popularity.'

Cooper thought about Hewitt's home circumstances. He still believed he'd been right in his original assessment of the man. Kevin Hewitt didn't need to have anyone's claws sunk into him, when he was already wriggling on the painful hook of family, the sharp barbs sunk into his flesh by a love for his children. He wasn't the sort of man to slip free from that responsibility.

'Anything else?' asked Udall, as if she thought he'd nodded off.

'Yes. Ballistics say the airgun pellet was a .22. Probably something like Vermin Pell.'

'Vermin Pell? What a lovely name.'

'It's self explanatory,' said Cooper. 'They're designed for taking out vermin.'

Udall looked at him as if he'd said something inappropriate.

'I'm not suggesting that Kevin Hewitt—.'

'I know, Ben.' She turned over a page of the file. 'And I see that Hewitt's clothes were marked with Smart Water. He'd found the right tree, then.'

'Yes.'

Smart Water. Another high-tech weapon in Peak Nestwatch's armoury – a chemical treatment sprayed on trees at a height where it could only be picked up by climbing. A suspect's clothes could be examined under ultra-violet light, to prove whether he'd climbed that specific tree.

Cooper stared at Udall, suddenly aware of something glaringly obvious that he'd overlooked.

'I'm being an idiot,' he said. 'It should have been the first action we took.'

'Oh?' Udall frowned. 'I'm not with you. You mean, if Hewitt's killer touched him, he might have picked up traces of Smart Water, too?'

'Well, he might,' said Cooper. 'But what about the other surveillance measures?'

Udall put down the report. 'The what?'

'Kevin Hewitt isn't the only one who's been using digital technology, is he?'

'I—.'

'The cameras, Tracy. The CCTV cameras.'

An hour later, Udall returned looking pleased with herself. She was carrying a tape which she slid into a VCR.

'You were right, Ben. Nestwatch had a camera set up on a tree that overlooks the approach to the nesting site. Sergeant Jackson retrieved the tape this morning.'

Udall pressed the play button and a grainy shot of trees and undergrowth came on to the screen.

'Did it catch Kevin Hewitt approaching the tree?'

'No, we weren't that lucky.'

'I bet he'd have known the camera was there, and come in from a different direction.'

'Yes, he was canny enough.'

Nothing happened for a few minutes. The occasional bird flickered across the screen, a branch swayed jerkily in the breeze.

'Coming up now,' said Udall. 'Watch the edge of that tree. He comes into shot there, but only briefly. And he's clearly carrying a firearm.'

Cooper could see the figure now, unnaturally bulky in a green jacket, brown corduroy trousers, a hat pulled over the ears. Most walkers on the moors dressed in bright colours, so they'd be easy to spot from a distance if they got lost or injured. But some people didn't want to be noticed. It was essential to blend in with the landscape when you went out hunting vermin.

'See him?' asked Udall.

Cooper paused the tape. 'Not only do I see him, Tracy. I know him.'

'So what do we do?'

'Call out the team.'

As soon as he got out of the car, Cooper could feel a fine rain in the air, soft as feathers on his face. Sunlight and showers passed across the hills, clouds moving so quickly across the horizon they were dizzying. For some reason, Udall was wearing her stab-proof vest. A sensible precaution on most occasions, but it looked odd when the most dangerous thing in sight was a gorse bush.

As they drove into the Upper Derwent Valley, the team had been careful not to disturb the peace with their beacons or the wail of their sirens. But now the time for discretion had passed. A Ford estate parked at the visitor centre was boxed in and surrounded. Within minutes, a suspect was sitting in the back of a police Range Rover, twisting his beanie hat in his hands.

'It's harassment. You should be going after the people who kill living animals, not me.'

'We just need to clear something up, Mr Ryan,' said Cooper. 'We're investigating the manslaughter of Mr Kevin Hewitt.'

'You're wasting your time. You've got the wrong person.'

An officer came across from the Ford, carrying two clear, plastic evidence bags that he showed to Cooper. They contained a BSA Meteor and five tins of Vermin Pell.

'I see you own an air rifle, though, Mr Ryan.'

'Well, I never said there was anything wrong with shooting in itself. I'm not one of those animal rights nutters who want to ban all country sports on principle. Is that what you took me for?'

Cooper tried never to give away what he was thinking. It didn't always work, though. You'd need a course at RADA for that, sometimes.

'So you're telling me you try to take a moderate position?'

'I think birds that have legal protection should be protected properly,' said Ryan. 'Is that a moderate position?'

'It depends.'

'And if they're going to be protected properly, that means *someone* has to enforce the law. You lot never do.'

'On the contrary, that's exactly what we're going to do now,' said Cooper. And he began to issue the caution.

Without even thinking about it, Cooper knew exactly where he'd find Janine Hewitt that afternoon. In the recreation ground on the Devonshire

Estate, he could see Jack scuffing about in the grass, as if kicking at a non-existent ball, while Ebony slumped in her pushchair, watching the trees.

Janine had chosen the same bench to sit on, close to the old drinking fountain. Perhaps she preferred it because it was on the north side of the park and caught the best of the sun.

But Janine didn't seem to have noticed the sun. Her eyes were turned downwards, gazing at her shoes. They were the same shoes that she'd bought an eBay – a real bargain, a cheap way to make a bit of a show. She didn't acknowledge Cooper's presence, even when he was standing a few feet away. He waited on the path, trying to assess her mood before he spoke. But it was Janine who finally broke the silence.

'Oh, it's you,' she said. 'I should have guessed.'

She sounded resigned, not disturbed or aggressive. Cooper moved a few steps closer, then stopped and smiled at Jack, who responded with a blank stare.

'You know Kevin won't be coming back, don't you, Janine?'

'Yes, they called me in to identify him.'

'I'm sorry.'

'Have you caught the person who did it?' she asked, without hope.

'We have a suspect in custody. And . . . well, we've got some theories on motive.'

Janine nodded wearily. 'It doesn't matter, does

it? I mean – the motive, the "why". The result is just the same.'

Cooper found he wasn't listening to Janine Hewitt any more. Instead, the voice inside his head was Calvin Ryan's. He was remembering a moment on the windswept edge of Lightside Moor, watching a black shape soar over Alport Castles. And he could hear Ryan saying something. It sounded like *Don't forget the goshawks.*

Janine's four-year-old, Jack, was playing on the grass, running round the old drinking fountain. Though it hadn't been used for years, the fountain was solidly made, and no one had gone to the trouble of digging it out and breaking it up. Cooper could see a hole at the base, where the root of a tree had pushed through the earth and left a dark cavity.

'A bonded pair will hunt co-operatively, two of them together.'

As Cooper watched, Jack bent down and peered into the hole, as if expecting to find something interesting. Perhaps he was playing some game of his own imagination. A treasure hunt, who could say? The child looked towards his mother, and for a second an expression of conspiracy passed across his face before he moved on, chuckling at the sight of a blackbird scratching in the dead leaves.

Janine had begun to gather herself together, picking up the toddler's bottle from the seat. The bench she was using was the third one from the gate on the northern side of the park. It was always the same bench that she chose, the one near the old drinking fountain. There was nothing remarkable about the bench itself, that Cooper could see. But it was always the same one.

'Then, when the chicks are hatched, the tercel isn't allowed near the nest. He has to leave the food he catches at a safe distance, where the female bird can fetch it for the chicks.'

Cooper pulled his phone out of his pocket. Then he hesitated, surprised by a stab of doubt. Instead of making the call, he left Janine and walked back to his car. For a while, he sat in the driver's seat, trying not to think about anything in particular, until he saw Janine and the children on their way home. Back to their dismal council house, the bedrooms with damp walls and the drug addicts next door. He couldn't imagine what it was like raising two small children in conditions like those.

As soon as they were out of sight, Cooper went back to the park. He followed Jack's footsteps to the drinking fountain, and examined the cavity. Something in there, definitely. It wasn't just a figment of the child's imagination. From the marks on the ground, he guessed there had been dead leaves piled over the hole at one time, but they'd been kicked aside by the blackbirds scratching for insects.

He reached in, grabbed a handful of plastic, and tugged. It was the wrapping of a package, and the plastic rustled as he drew it into the light. To Cooper, the sound seemed very loud in the suddenly silent afternoon.

The package was too big to have fallen into the hole accidentally. Too full of money. When he'd pulled it out, he saw there were hundreds of used notes, held together in bundles by rubber bands and spilling out of a rip in the plastic. It was impossible to say how much money there was. Kevin Hewitt had been gathering it from many sources, perhaps some that would never be uncovered.

Cooper turned, imagining Janine watching him. And not just her, but the children, too – the restless Jack, the lethargic toddler in her pushchair. He could picture them staring at him with those hungry eyes, helpless and desperate.

At his feet lay more money than he could count. Thousands, certainly. Right now, his duty was to call it in, make sure it was secured for evidence before he handled it any further. But what was the point, really? No one would ever come forward to claim the cash. It was a pity, because there were so many uses it could be put to.

Well, Harry Blakelock had been right about one thing. Sometimes you had to choose. There were times when everyone had to take sides.

Cooper straightened up as he looked at the notes. Yes, so many uses. For a start, he bet there was enough money here to put a deposit on a small house, somewhere a lot nicer than the Devonshire Estate. A place well away from the damp and despair, and the junkies.

Enough money, perhaps, to give one family a new start.

The Mentalist

Rod Duncan

Mentalist

One who is believed to have the
power to read other people's thoughts
and place suggestions in their minds.

A performing artist who uses
conjuring tricks to simulate
supernatural mental powers.

CHAPTER 1

In its heyday, punters might have filled the theatre and the air would have been hazy with tobacco smoke. But smoking and public access to the dress circle were both now banned, so the spotlight operator had the upper level to himself and his light left barely a trace in the air through which it passed.

Below him, he could make out the backs of the heads of the audience. Almost half the seats were occupied, which was a good turnout for this tour.

He looked along the spotlight beam to the man who stood centre stage. Harry Gysel, the showman who was described variously as a psychic, a fraud, or a meddler in the occult – depending on who was speaking. He was thirty-eight years old, according to the biography on his website. The narrowness of his face was accentuated by close-cropped sideburns sculpted to follow the line of his jaw.

Tonight he wore a long, double-breasted jacket and dark trousers, conjuring an image that fitted the theatre's Victorian past.

He had already gone through the mind reading part of the show – telling people the jobs they did or wanted to do, telling them the makes and colours of their cars. He now had four volunteers on stage and was in the process of calling up a fifth to stand in line beside them. This one, a young woman, had eyes wide with expectation. The spotlight operator shifted the beam to include her. The other stage lights dimmed, leaving Harry Gysel and the volunteers surrounded by darkness.

'You've come here to find the truth.' Gysel said to the woman. His voice sounding intimate, yet clear even from the balcony.

'Yes,' she said.

He gripped her shoulders and turned her to face him, locking eye to eye. The spotlight operator narrowed the focus of the beam. Everything else in the room seemed to disappear. The psychic and his subject. One bubble of light in the darkness.

'You've been thinking of someone,' he said.

She nodded.

'A man,' he said.

'Yes.'

'Picture his name. See it in the air in front of you. Let his name sound inside your head. You're missing him, am I right?'

'Yes.'

'Remember the sound of his voice. Keep saying his name in your mind.'

She closed her eyes. Her shoulders sagged. 'He's gone from this world.'

'His name . . .' Gysel paused, as if waiting for the inspiration to come. 'His name is Peter.'

It was as if a jolt of electricity passed through Harry Gysel's hands into her shoulders. Her head snapped up. A breath of surprise rippled through the darkness around them.

'He's gone,' she said.

'He's not gone,' Gysel replied. 'He is here.'

'Here?'

'He passed over from this world. But you can still feel him.'

There was a pause. The spotlight operator tightened the focus even further. The bubble of light contained just their upper bodies now, which seemed to hang in the darkness as if they were projections from some ghostly afterlife. The silence lengthened, becoming first uncomfortable and then mesmerising.

'Do you feel him?' Gysel asked.

Her answering whisper breathed around the room. 'Yes.'

'Do you feel him?'

'Yes.' Stronger this time. 'Yes.'

'Peter is here. He wants to tell you that he misses you too.'

She had probably been crying for some time, but it was only now that her frame began to heave with the sobs. 'Peter. Oh Peter.'

The spotlight operator had seen this moment in the show many times, but this time was the best.

Gysel stepped back so suddenly that he dipped into blackness for a moment before the beam widened enough to take him in. 'There is another in the room,' he said. 'Another spirit. His name is . . . Michael.'

'Yes!' The voice came from one of the other volunteers on the stage. A young man. 'My father. Michael.'

'Not long gone.'

'Just two years,' said the man.

'He thought more of you than you imagine.'

'I didn't get to the hospital in time . . .'

'He wants to tell you how much he admired you. He missed that chance in life so he says it now.'

The man's face dropped to his hands. He too was weeping. And the hysteria was infectious.

'You have all lost someone,' Gysel said to them.

There were nods and murmured agreement. But Gysel had shifted his focus back to the first woman. 'There is another person in your mind.'

'Yes.'

Perhaps he could have said anything and she would have gone along with it at that moment. Or perhaps he really was reading her thoughts. Either way, Gysel was going with the moment, moving away from the usual format. People in the audience were standing.

'Picture the person. See him in front of you.' Gysel paused. The held breaths of the audience electrified the silence. 'Not a man,' he said at last. 'You are thinking of a woman. Picture her name. She's still in this world. But . . .' a longer silence this time. The spotlight closed in once more. 'But she is going to die?' It was a question, said almost in surprise.

'Yes,' said the woman.

'And her name is . . . her name is Debbie.'

'Yes,' the woman said again, her whispered voice, amplified and carried to every corner of the room. 'Yes. I'm Debbie. I'm going to die.'

The energy was draining from Harry Gysel even before the curtain had fully closed. He staggered into the wings and propped himself against a wall. One of the stagehands pushed past. 'Good one,' he said.

But the last bit of the show had gone very wrong.

There were moral questions about what Harry did. When asked, he would point out that the punters left happier than they came in. But with that last volunteer he'd made a mistake. He should have got her name at the start. Alarm bells should have rung when she said it was someone about to die. He could have backed away even then. Hell, the woman was so suggestible, he could have taken her off along another track altogether. She would have agreed to anything.

'Harry, sweetheart. That was the best.'

He opened his eyes to see Davina, his agent, approaching along the narrow corridor. She bent in to kiss the air on either side of him and he saw the makeup that hid the creases of her face. For that moment the illusion of youth vanished. Then she pulled away.

'What a show! You *must* do that again.'

'It was wrong,' he said.

'Did you hear the audience react?'

'It was unethical.'

'Has she got a disease or something? How did you know, sweetie?'

'I'm psychic,' he said. And then: 'Did we make much money tonight?'

She shook her head. 'The hall was half full. After paying the theatre and your overheads there's not much left. At least you broke even.'

Harry didn't ask what was covered in the overheads category. Mainly her fee, he suspected. 'I need some cash, Davina.'

'For something exciting?'

'I need to buy a mobile.'

'You've got one already.'

'It's for someone else.'

'Sounds interesting.'

She opened her red leather handbag and fished

around inside it, the tip of her tongue running across her lips as she extracted a fifty-pound note. He reached out to take it.

She didn't let go. 'I've a friend who wants to meet you.'

'But I just need to sleep,' he pleaded.

Davina winked. 'She said the show was hot.'

For a moment he stood, dumbly, joined to his agent by the fifty-pound note. 'OK. I'll see her.'

Davina released her grip. 'Good boy. She's waiting in the lobby.'

'I'm just going to talk with her,' he said.

Davina closed her bag. 'Do you think that volunteer would do a press interview?'

'That volunteer – Debbie – you know she could sue us? For mental trauma or something.'

'Great publicity if she did.'

'I don't want that kind of publicity.'

'You want any kind.'

She didn't add that the alternative was kissing his career goodbye. She didn't need to.

'Is Debbie really going to die?' Davina asked.

He looked into his agent's eyes. 'Aren't we all?'

Harry woke with his face pressed against someone else's pillow. It was lilac, and carried a feminine scent. He tried to go back to sleep, but the light was on. Davina's friend was stepping around the bed, pulling a brush through her hair.

85

'What time is it?' he asked.

'My bus leaves in ten minutes,' she said.

'Any chance of a coffee?'

She scooped his clothes from the floor and dropped them next to his face. They were crumpled. She left the room. He heard the squeak of a tap and water splashing.

He was still buttoning his shirt as he stepped into the kitchen. He found her finishing a slice of toast.

She said, 'You'll have to find a café or something.'

He looked at her. She wasn't pretty, but there was something about her physique that carried a basic attraction.

'Last night . . .' he began.

For a moment she smiled. 'It was great.'

'Yes?'

'But, I can't leave you to lock up.'

'Of course. I'll get my shoes. Maybe tonight you could come round to my place. It's only a couple of miles.'

'I'm busy tonight.'

She was sweeping him towards the front door. Then they were outside in the chill October dawn. The road was still wet from last night's rain.

'That'll be my bus now,' she said, and ran.

Only after she'd gone did he realise that he couldn't remember her name.

⋆   ⋆   ⋆

There was a warm fug of vinegar and frying bacon in the café. The sun had risen above the slate roofs outside, turning the plate glass windows golden and lighting the steam that rose from Harry's mug. He often came here. The sound of the espresso machine and the chink of crockery were somehow comforting. He stretched, making his chair creak.

There was nothing wrong with café breakfasts. He'd got used to them since the divorce – even more so when he started touring.

The tours had been pub shows at first – a hundred and fifty quid in his pocket and no word to the social security. He could get by on that, more or less. Then Davina spotted him and he made the step up. This was the end of his second season with her, but so far no sign of the breakthrough. She wouldn't stick with him for a third.

'Egg beans and toast!' called a voice.

Harry put his hand up and a plate of food was placed on the table in front of him. He cut through the toast with his knife and pierced the runny yolk of the egg. He wasn't ready to give up the touring life just yet.

The café door opened and a man stepped inside, haloed by the low sunlight. There were people who believed in auras, to whom such a sight might have been a portent. Harry had believed in auras once. He'd believed in lots of things. He couldn't remember what that felt like any more.

The man stepped towards him. His hair was short cropped and greying. He wore an expensive suit and seemed out of place in the café. Harry raised a hand to shade his eyes.

'Mr Gysel?' the man asked.

Harry put down his fork and stood.

'Are you Harry Gysel?'

Only then Harry realised what the man was.

'You're a police officer?'

'Yes.' He flourished his ID. 'Chief Inspector Morgan. I need to ask you some questions.'

Harry felt off-balance. Chief Inspector sounded like a senior rank. 'I'm having breakfast,' Harry said.

'I'm sorry, sir. This is very serious.'

A picture came unbidden into Harry's mind – the face of the young woman whose eyes he'd stared into on stage the night before. 'Debbie?' he asked.

Morgan paused before answering. 'Yes sir,' he said. 'She's dead.'

Harry knew that the mind and personality were functions of the brain. The brain communicated with the body through nerves and through glands that sent out chemical messages,' telling the heart to beat faster, the face to flush, pores to open. Each hard-wired response had its own name – guilt, shock, anger, love.

He was sweating. If he'd been connected to a lie detector, all the needles would have been jumping.

And his awareness of what was happening was injecting even more chemical messages into his bloodstream.

Other detectives had been waiting outside the café. They'd chauffeured Morgan and Harry to the theatre then backed off respectfully, leaving them alone on the stage.

There were casual-sounding questions about his show, about how he chose his volunteers. Harry found himself staring at Morgan's black shoes, which were dulled by smears of dried mud.

'Did you hear what I said?' Morgan asked.

Harry looked up. 'I'm sorry?'

'Do you have anything else to tell me?'

'It's a shock, that's all.'

'You said you didn't know her.'

'Only last night. In the show.'

There was a metallic sound from the dress circle. They both turned to look. The house lights were up, revealing the two levels of empty seating. The spotlight operator from last night was pulling a gel plate from the front of the lens. He waved, acknowledging them, then put the plate into a carrying case and walked to the exit. The door swung closed behind him.

'Do you get fan mail?' Morgan asked, jolting Harry back to the moment.

'Some.'

'Had she written to you?'

'No.'

'You don't need to check?'

'I don't get that much.' Harry ran a hand through his hair. 'I would have remembered – if I'd seen her before.'

'Did you find her attractive?'

'What's that got to do with it?'

'I'm trying to understand. I'd assumed you'd want to help. Puzzling, don't you think? You meet this woman, Debbie, for the first time last night. You tell her she's going to die. And within a few hours . . .'

'I do want to help,' Harry said. And then: 'How did she die?'

Morgan paused before answering. 'The circumstances are suspicious. Are you really a psychic?'

'That's my job. I do shows. I . . .'

'But is it real?'

Morgan had been shifting his weight slowly from one foot to the other throughout the interview, as if in some discomfort. But now he stopped. Harry could see the man's locked-in tension. This wasn't the shallow questioning of a journalist.

A woman had died and Harry wanted to help. Really he did. But whatever information he gave would leak. The press loved psychic stories and they had their contacts among the police. Until that moment, Harry hadn't decided how much to reveal. Now he made his decision.

'I read minds,' he said.

'How?'

'I don't discuss my methods, but I could show you.'

'How am I supposed to write that one up?' Morgan asked the empty theatre after Harry Gysel had gone. Even though he was a senior officer, he was still beholden to the computer, the Home Office Large and Major Crimes System. It had to be fed with reports. Every interview ended up as signals in its electronic brain.

It occured to Morgan that there had been no one else present. If he were to skip the last bit, the psychic demonstration, no one would know. And yet it was the crux of the matter, the way to understand what had happened on stage the night before.

There were people who believed they were reading the minds of others but who were picking up on subtle hints of body language. There were also frauds and tricksters. All Morgan's training told him there was no such thing as a genuine psychic. He hated the fact that Gysel had put him in this position.

'What did I see?' he asked, speaking aloud again.

Morgan's mother had died two years before. Her obituary had appeared in the local paper. Gysel could have researched the matter if he'd known he was going to be questioned. But where did that logic lead? Gysel had been nervous. But when he started the demonstration, the man's demeanour changed. His face became calm.

'Is your mother still in this world?' he'd asked.

Morgan had shaken his head, resenting the question.

'Picture her in your mind.'

It'd felt strange staring into Gysel's face. The man's gaze didn't waver, though Morgan found himself blinking and shifting his focus from one of Gysel's eyes to the other then back. Had he given it away? Had he accidentally mouthed it?

Gysel then reached into his jacket pocket and pulled out a blank index card and a pencil, which he held behind his back so Morgan couldn't see what he was writing. He then slid the pencil back into his pocket and held the card in front of him, face down.

'What was your mother's middle name?' he asked.

'Emily.'

'And you want to know if I'm really psychic?'

'Yes.'

'What if I was? How would it change things?'

It was a question Morgan hadn't anticipated. He looked down at his hands. Did he somehow want to believe Gysel was real? 'I just need to know,' he said

'Do you want to expose me as a fraud?'

'This is a murder investigation.'

'You said it was a suspicious death a few moments ago.'

Morgan reached out and gripped Gysel's wrist, turning it to reveal the under side of the card. And there, written in a shaky hand, was the name. 'Emily.'

Davina's name card gave the address of an office in Nottingham, but in the two years Harry had known her, he'd never seen it. She conducted most of her business in pubs and on station platforms. The tools of her trade were mobile phones and rolls of cash each of which she kept in that red handbag of hers. She always seemed to know what needed to happen next, though he'd never seen her write anything down.

Today their meeting place was a coffee shop on the corner near Leicester Market. He'd drunk most of his espresso by the time she arrived. She didn't order but came directly over and sidled into the seat next to his.

'I've sent out a press release,' she said.

'Is that a good idea?'

'Of course it is darling.'

It was an optical illusion – the afternoon sun catching her forehead in that way. But with the dark interior of the shop for a background, she looked as if she was glowing like a medieval icon.

'I've called someone who works for one of the tabloids – I can't say who or which, but he owes me a favour, so he returned my call. But he'll be owing me an even bigger favour after this. Because this story is going to run big. He'll call you. He needs to know the name of the detective who interviewed you. That's a whole extra slant to the story – psychic helps police murder hunt. My God it's going to be huge. You're going to be huge.'

'Davina . . .'

'I told you – you should have done something like this before.'

'A girl died.'

'And you predicted it.'

'She was murdered.'

'It's almost like you willed it to happen.'

Davina sat looking at him for a moment, smiling. She opened her mouth and closed it again. He'd never seen her speechless before. Then she leant in and kissed him on the cheek. Real contact this time. She hadn't done that since she signed him up two years ago.

'I've done something else, Harry. And this shows how much I believe in you. I've got a filmmaker interested. Documentary. Fly-on-the-wall. You won't need to do anything different. Just be yourself. He'll follow you round. Cameras are so small these days.'

'I don't want . . .'

'Think David Blaine. Think Channel 4.'

'I'm not comfortable with that.'

'He wants to start tomorrow. Just give it a go. For me.'

She leaned in and kissed him on the cheek again. This time the corner of her mouth overlapped with his.

She winked. 'You didn't thank me for fixing you up the other night.'

'You want me to thank you?'

For a moment Davina frowned and the glow seemed to fade from her skin. 'Oh. *She* said it was good. And it's given you an alibi.'

Harry felt stung. Alibi was a word that belonged to criminals. But she was right. During the interview, Morgan had asked where he'd gone after the show. The question came out casually, as if he needed to ask it for the sake of completeness. As if it was a standard box in a standard form.

Harry had told him. He'd been with a girl, someone who'd come to see the show. No, he wouldn't have called her a groupie. He wasn't a rock star. Yes, it had happened before – one-night stands with women who'd seen him on stage. Sometimes they did get a bit obsessed with him.

He gave Morgan the address. Harry could feel the man's distaste. Or was it jealousy?

'I wish *I* was psychic,' Davina said.

Her words jolted Harry back to the present. 'I'm sorry?'

'I'd read your mind.'

'I need her number,' he said. 'Your friend, I mean.'

'So it was good. I've got other friends you could meet. You'll be a popular boy now. Your star is rising.'

'I just need to warn her,' Harry said. 'In case the police call. And . . .'

'Yes?' Davina was enjoying herself.

'. . . and I need her name. I can't remember her name.'

'You bad boy.'

She took out a mobile, tapped a couple of keys then turned it to face him. The display showed the name *Chloe* and a number. He took out his own phone and keyed the details into the address book. When he'd finished she stood up and looked down at him, and for just a moment he thought he could see pride in her eyes.

After she'd gone, Harry sat staring out through the window at the people moving past. He still had choices. He didn't need to do everything just because Davina told him to. He dialled Chloe's number and put the phone to his ear. It rang three times before the pickup.

'Hi, this is Chloe. I'm not here now so speak after the beep.'

The tone sounded. 'Uhhh . . . Hi. It's me, Harry. Listen, I . . . uhhh . . . I need to see you. Have you seen the news today? The police talked to me. I guess they might want to talk to you as well.'

The phone clicked and she was there. 'Don't bring me into this.'

'Chloe . . . they need to know where I was.'

'You can't tell them you were with me.'

'Are you married or something?'

'Don't be stupid.'

'Then what?'

'Just don't give my name to the police. I'll say you weren't with me.'

There was a click and the connection was cut.

CHAPTER 2

Morgan was standing half way up a hill-side, dressed in white scene of crime overalls, surrounded by rust-tinged bracken. Here and there, outcrops of grey rock poked through the thin soil. A hundred yards up-slope he could make out the stone folly known as Old John. A hundred yards the other way, and far below him, was a path along which a few visitors to the park wandered on this autumn morning, passing the police cars, vans and ambulance.

And at his feet, the body itself – a young woman, fully clothed, face down, one arm underneath, the other splayed to the side. Two wounds were visible. The first, on the left knee, had bled extensively before death stopped her heart. The second was on the back of the head, where angular fragments of bone protruded through a mess of caked blood and hair.

This was Morgan's second visit. The first had been at 07.30, an hour after the body had been discovered by an early morning walker. But since talking to Harry Gysel he'd felt the need to come back and see her one more time before she was removed to the morgue.

He reached down and touched the skin of her neck. There was no warmth left in her. He squeezed his fingers underneath her waist, checking again that the ground there was dry. He stood and stepped away, rubbing the small of his back to ease the joint pain.

Hearing a scuffling of loose stone, he turned to see a woman with coppery hair stepping over the cordon of incident tape that stretched between boulders and clumps of bracken, running in a wide circle around the body. She looked younger than him by a decade at least. In her mid-thirties, he thought.

'Good afternoon,' she said. 'Chief inspector Morgan?'

Morgan nodded and pointed to a box of white plastic over-shoes. She stopped to slip a pair on then picked her way through the bracken to join him.

'Dr Fields,' she announced, offering her hand. And then, when he didn't take it: 'The forensic psychologist.'

'I've been touching the body,' he explained.

'Oh.'

'She was dead before 11.30 last night,' he said. 'That's when it started to rain.'

Dr Fields tilted her head to look at the victim. 'Too young to have her head staved in.'

'There's a better age?' Morgan asked.

Dr Fields' eyes flicked to him and back to the body.

Morgan pointed towards a marker some thirty metres down the slope. 'The attack started somewhere over there. We've found blood, presumably from the leg wound. It all ended with a frenzied attack here. At least two blows to the head.'

'Frenzied,' Dr Fields said, as if trying the word out for size. 'What about the murder weapon?'

'No sign yet. Probably a rock though.'

Dr Fields pursed her lips. 'And the body was left face down?'

'We've not moved it,' Morgan said. He watched her turn a slow circle, as if trying to divine something from the autumn hues of the bracken and the distant trees. He hadn't asked for a forensic psychologist to be sent.

He cleared his throat. 'This is a chaotic killer,' he said. 'The body left where it fell. An opportunist weapon. A disorganised crime scene.'

Dr Fields was facing him again. 'I'd say he's killed before.'

For a moment, Morgan considered denying it, just to see the confidence leave her face. 'A year ago,' he said, 'there was a body found in Swithland Woods. That's a couple of miles from here. A woman in her forties. Face up that time. This one is what – nineteen? And face down.' He pulled the latex gloves from his hands. 'A year before that there was a girl in Victoria Park. That one was twenty-two and left face up. In some ways they seem different, but they were all head injuries, and all in October.'

'That shows control,' Dr Fields said. 'A highly organised pattern. The killer waiting for an entire year before killing again.'

'But the crime scene is chaotic. It doesn't fit. What made you think this wasn't his first killing?'

She started walking down the slope towards the marker. Morgan headed after her.

'You're thinking like the killer,' she said. 'Try thinking like the victim. She's slight. Vulnerable.'

They'd reached the marker now, a triangular plastic flag hanging limp from stiff wire. On the earth below it were the remains of a blood splash that must have dried before the rain started.

'Somewhere down there,' said Dr Fields, pointing, 'the killer did something to make the victim believe she was in danger. It was night. Think how scared she'd have been. Which way would she run?'

Morgan looked back up the slope towards the body. It was a steep climb. 'She'd run away from him.'

'A terrified victim tries to move as fast as possible – even when that isn't the logical thing to do. Animal panic. She'd naturally run parallel to the slope or down it. And escape lay back down there on the road where a motorist might have seen her. So you have to ask yourself what made this fragile little girl clamber up the slope, away from safety?'

Morgan watched Dr Fields, fascinated by the woman's confidence in her own conclusions – reached after such a brief examination of the scene. 'I don't know,' he said.

'He was shepherding her,' she said. 'She must have been limping with that knee injury. He could have killed her right away. But he was enjoying it too much. Ever watched a cat playing with a mouse? He had to have confidence to take his time over it. That kind of confidence means he's done it before.'

Morgan wouldn't have admitted it to her face, but he could picture it all in his head, just as she described – the woman scrambling up the uneven slope, blood running down her leg, looking black in the near dark, the killer following with a rock in his hand, easily keeping pace. He could hear the panic in her breath. Driving her up the slope, prolonging the chase.

'Mornings like this, I hate my job,' Dr Fields said. 'Don't you?'

Morgan chose not to answer. 'I've got to go,' he said.

Harry woke from a sleep so dead that he had no sense of time having passed since he lay down. He was still tired. Someone was hammering on the door of his bed-sit.

'Wait!' He slurred the word.

The hammering stopped. He pulled on yesterday's

trousers and was buttoning a new white shirt as he stepped across the room.

'Who is it?'

The answering voice was a man's. It was too muffled to make out the words. He slid the bolt and opened up.

On the landing outside stood a middle-aged man wearing blue jeans, a black t-shirt and an army surplus coat. Two boxes with handles rested on the floor, one on each side of him. They were black and battered, with scratched steel reinforcing on the corners.

Harry rubbed away a grain from the corner of his eye. 'Uhhh . . . who?'

'Davina sent me.'

Harry looked at the boxes.

'My equipment,' said the man.

'Your name?'

The man started searching through his inside coat pockets. His hair was an inch too long to be tidy and was thinning from the crown of his head. He extracted a name card, slightly dog-eared, and handed it to Harry.

Peter Pickman
Pickman Films

In the corner of the card was a small picture of a movie camera. It was the sort of thing that could have been put together on one of those vending machines in stations and airports.

'The fly on the wall man?' Harry asked.

Peter Pickman seemed uncertain about agreeing to the title, but nodded anyway. He picked up his boxes by their handles and stepped inside.

'You won't notice I'm here,' Pickman said. 'Not after the first few days.'

'Days? How long is this going to take?'

'It's hard to say. Just ignore me.'

So Harry went to the kitchenette and spooned instant coffee granules into a mug. Behind him he could hear the snap of catches as the boxes opened. He forced his mind onto the purely sensory experience of pouring boiling water and inhaling the steam. It occurred to him that Pickman could be filming already. What, Harry wondered, did it say about him that he took two sugars in his drink?

When he turned around, the camera was on him. It was smaller than he'd expected. Most of the space inside the carrying boxes was taken up with padding, spare batteries, chargers and the like. Pickman was holding the camera at waist height, looking down towards the viewfinder. 'Just act naturally,' he said. 'What are we doing today?'

'We?'

'You won't notice me.'

'I'm not doing anything.'

'That's fine.'

'Can't you start tomorrow?'

'Your manager said . . .'

'She's my agent.'

'She said we'd start today. It'll be fine. Trust me.'

Harry didn't trust him. Neither did he like the thought of ringing Davina and complaining about her plan. So, when he set out for the supermarket at 10.00am, it was with Pickman following. He found himself taking a long time over each choice, aware of the camera just behind, aware of people turning to watch. At the end of the trip his shopping bags had none of the usual comfort food and ready meals for one, but were stuffed with raw vegetables that he had only the vaguest idea of how to prepare.

He loaded up the car and closed the boot. 'I've got some business now,' he said. The camera was aimed at his face so he stepped to the side. The camera followed. 'Turn that off please.'

Pickman complied, but he was frowning. 'Please don't talk to me. It doesn't work that way.'

'I need a break from it, that's all.'

'Where are you going?'

'It's personal.'

'I should be with you.'

'No.'

'Your agent said I'd have full access.'

'She was wrong.'

Pickman looked hurt. 'She said you'd say that.'

'Right.'

'And she told me to get you to call her when you did.'

★   ★   ★

The call did not go well. Harry complained that Pickman didn't seem professional enough, that the camera looked too small, that he needed privacy. The excuses seemed lame, even to him. Davina's reply was quiet. She sounded hurt. She didn't want to lose him as a client, she said. But if their working relationship broke down completely . . .

Half an hour later, Harry was driving towards his ex-wife's house with Pickman filming from the back seat. Or not filming. The camera made no sound and there were no lights to tell him when it was on.

'Can you point that thing somewhere else, please?'

'You'll not notice it soon,' Pickman said.

But the more Harry tried to not notice it, the more he felt the back of his head itching where the lens was aimed.

As he pulled up the car, the sun came out from behind a cloud. The sun always seemed to shine on his ex-wife's house. It had a U-shaped gravel drive and a semi-circle of lawn with a striped mowing pattern.

He rang the bell and waited. Then he rang it again. At last the door opened and he saw his ex-wife standing in the hall, blouse neatly pressed as always, a small silver cross at her neck.

'Hello Angela,' he said.

'You're early.' She was looking at Pickman as

she spoke. He stood a few paces away, eyes fixed on the viewfinder.

'Twenty minutes,' Harry said. 'You're suggesting I wait in the car?'

'It's half an hour. Who's this?'

'This is . . . uh . . . Peter Pickman. He's . . .'

'Don't mention me, please,' said Pickman. 'It spoils the scene.'

'He's making a documentary.'

Angela's mouth made an 'O' shape. Somewhere behind her a girl's voice called out. 'Mum, where's my bag?'

Angela called back into the house. 'You stay there.' Then to Harry: 'This wasn't in the agreement.'

'Look,' Harry reasoned, 'it's my access time. I decide what we do. If I want to have a cameraman around, then . . .'

'No!' Angela was shouting.

'Send her out,' Harry said.

'Not with that thing on.'

'You want to take this back to court?' Harry was shouting too.

'We have an agreement. She's not to be involved with your . . . your work.'

'He's only a cameraman for Christ's sake!'

'And you're not to swear in front of her!'

'Send her out and I'll stop!'

For a moment there was silence, and then Peter lowered the camera. 'I'm not filming,' he said.

Angela wheeled and marched back into the

house. A moment later a girl emerged, a day bag in one hand. Her dark hair was short and spectacularly messed.

'Hello Tia,' said Harry.

She glared at him. 'Nice one, dad.' Then climbed into the front passenger seat and slammed the door.

'Thanks for stopping,' Harry whispered.

'The tape was full,' said Pickman.

A murder investigation is a machine for generating paperwork. Detectives have suspicions, of course. And maybe they can use those suspicions. But if they catch their killer and make it all the way to trial and if the defence barrister can suggest to the jury that they followed a hunch somewhere along the line – that's when the trouble starts. What other leads were ignored? Why did the police decide to follow a prejudice instead of the evidence?

That is why paperwork is so important. It proves to the court that all avenues were followed and that no hunches were used. Even if they were.

As lead officer, Morgan was half-buried in paper. Two of his officers were collecting all available CCTV footage of the streets through which the victim might have walked. Two were following up people who had been at the performance, tracking them down through the credit cards they used to pay for their tickets.

On top of that, the victim's mobile phone records were being gone through, her friends and housemates were being talked to, and half a dozen other lines of enquiry were proceeding at pace. In time the computer would swallow all the information. But only as fast as the data processing staff could feed it in.

Civil libertarians were always worried about the amount of information the state had at its disposal. Morgan believed that, given a deep enough pool of information, a state would drown itself.

He looked up from a pile of witness reports to see one of his sergeants at the open door.

'You won't believe this,' the man said.

'What?'

'The victim – she was on file already. She gave a witness statement for the Swithland Woods case.'

'Why didn't we know before?'

The sergeant shrugged. 'Our victim and the Swithland woman went to the same church.'

Morgan's sciatic nerve was giving him trouble again. Little jabs of pain down his left leg. It always happened when he sat for a long time or when he got too tense. He stood up and put a hand on the small of his back. 'Find the church they went to,' he said. 'Get the membership records. Cross correlate.'

'Computer told us to do that already,' said the sergeant.

'And see if you can find any connections to Harry Gysel.'

'He's got an alibi.'

'Has it been checked?'

'I'll get on to it.'

'Yes,' said Morgan. 'Do that.'

Peter Pickman didn't seem to need to eat and he somehow managed to drink while filming, balancing the camera on his knees as he sipped. He didn't even relent when Harry took him to one side, angled the lens away with one hand and begged for a few minutes alone with his daughter.

The worst thing was Tia's mood. On their days together she was usually angry with him at first. The handovers seldom went well. She'd shout, then allow herself to be bribed, then melt, then he'd get a hug. And finally she'd start to fuss and mother him, making comments about the contents of his fridge, the number of empty beer cans in his recycling bin.

It was the hugs that kept him living.

But with a camera on, she was different. She stalked around the flat, not speaking. She opened the fridge, took in the raw fruit and vegetables, closed it again and moved on without a comment. Physically there wasn't much resemblance between them, but in character she was so like him – the way he used to be – it was terrifying.

★　　★　　★

It was in the upstairs seating area of McDonalds that Pickman showed his first sign of human weakness. The cups of tea Harry had been feeding to him all afternoon were at last having the desired effect.

'I need to . . . you know,' Pickman said. He put the camera down on the table. 'Don't spill anything on it.' Then he got up and headed for the toilets.

'Dad, get rid of him,' Tia hissed.

'It's difficult, love.'

'Do something!'

And then he had an idea.

Pickman didn't ask where they were going. Presumably that would have spoiled the documentary. He followed, still filming, as they left the golden arches behind and got into the car. He didn't comment when they parked at the cinema complex, nor when Harry bought three tickets for the latest Disney feature.

'Screen three,' the attendant said. And then, as they tried to walk past him, 'You can't take that in, sir.'

'I'm making a documentary,' Pickman said.

'No recording devices allowed.'

Harry raised his hands in a gesture that he hoped would seem believably apologetic. 'I guess we'll see you out here in a couple of hours.'

★   ★   ★

The cinema was dark and all but empty. A slideshow of local adverts was showing on the screen. Harry and Tia took seats at the back. He was waiting for the rage to burst, but instead she gripped his arm and rested her head against his shoulder.

'Why do you hate Mum?' she whispered.

'Did she say that? Did she say I hate her?'

'Don't you?'

'It's not that simple,' he said.

'That's what you and Mum always say when you're wrong.'

'When your mum left me . . .'

'She said you left her.'

He stared at a slide advertising screen advertising space. The world was going mad. Sometimes he could have wished it all to Hell. All but Tia.

'When it happened, it shook me up. I felt very low. I had to go to someone to help me feel better again.'

'A shrink?' Tia asked, a new note of interest in her voice. 'Mum said you went loopy.'

'I was depressed. And it was a hypnotherapist. He helped me understand what was happening in my head. I don't hate her.'

'Do you love her then?'

'Love and hate are brain chemistry, Tia. Endorphins and Oxytocin. Understanding that helped me to be well again.' He felt her pulling away from him.

A couple with four children entered the theatre

and took seats towards the front. The man and woman sat next to each other.

'If it hadn't been for my depression, I wouldn't have got interested in hypnosis. If that hadn't happened, I wouldn't be a performer now. Every cloud has a silver lining, you see.'

Tia turned in her seat and looked straight at him. 'Mum says I shouldn't listen when you talk about what you do. She says it's devil worship.'

'That sounds more like your mum's husband.'

'She said it too.'

There was a long pause before he could speak again. 'I've got something for you.' He pulled a mobile phone out of his pocket and placed it in her hand.

'Mum won't let me,' she said.

'It's so you can talk to me if you want. And she doesn't need to know.'

Tia's hand closed around the phone. 'If love is chemistry . . . ?'

'That's what we are – machines to carry DNA. You're my daughter. I'm pre-programmed to love you.'

'But if it's *only* chemistry . . .'

'I'd die to protect you,' he said, hoping it was true.

Tia looked back to the screen. 'Don't do that Daddy.'

Ever since the phone call from Harry Gysel, Chloe had been on her guard, peering through

113

the window before letting callers in. But this time she was late for work. The bell rang just as she was picking up her handbag, ready to run for the bus. She swung the door open without thinking, took in the two suited men, then tried to slam it closed in their faces. She would have managed but the one on the doorstep was quick enough to get his foot into the gap. His strength was more than a match for hers. He eased the door back open and waved his ID in her face. Not that she needed to see it. A policeman is a policeman.

'We're looking for Chloe,' he said.

'I don't have to talk to you.'

'Don't be like that. We just need to ask a couple of questions. Did you go and see Harry Gysel's show the other night?'

'Get out of my house.'

She finally let go of the door and they stepped properly inside, their broad shoulders filling the narrow hallway. She found herself craning her neck to look up at them.

'It's nothing to do with me.'

'But did you go?'

She dropped her eyes to the floor and their polished black shoes. 'No,' she said.

'He said he came back here afterwards.'

She shook her head. 'No.'

The victim, Debbie, had lived in a shared house on Evington Road not far from Leicester

University. She'd had three housemates, all young men. Two were science students – a bearded geologist and an acne-speckled chemist. The third wore his straw-coloured hair in a ponytail and announced that he played bass guitar in a band – which sounded to Morgan like another way of saying he was unemployed.

Morgan stepped inside Debbie's room, pushed the door to behind him, then stood still, eyes closed, and inhaled. Everyone has a scent. It comes from their clothes, of course, their food, their soap, their fabric conditioner and their perfume. It comes from all the things they fill their lives with.

He opened his eyes and looked. A poster of an angel suspended in the night sky above some trees. A mosaic of cards, photographs and newspaper cuttings around the edge of the dressing table mirror and on the wall behind it. Images of rock bands, crop circles, Celtic crosses and a picture of the Buddha.

He now knew that the 'church' the other two victims had attended was an informal gathering of spiritualists and faith healers. He wondered how those beliefs compared to the beliefs implied by the pictures on the wall.

There were a couple of gaps where photographs might once have been. He peered into the narrow gap behind the dressing table to see if any had fallen. Finding nothing, he lowered himself onto a plastic chair, keeping his spine upright and his shoulders back. Even so, he felt his leg twinge. A tired man stared back at him from the mirror.

He slid a drawer open and breathed her scent again, stronger this time. Socks, pants, tights – all stuffed and jumbled together. He closed the drawer and opened another. A brush still tangled with hair, a dryer and plastic clips, a packet of auburn dye.

He sat in silence for a moment, then turned to look at the door through which he'd entered. There was a gap at the bottom. He could see a thin strip of sunlight shining through from the hall. And a shadow. The shadow moved.

'Why don't you come in,' Morgan said, keeping his voice easy.

There was a pause before the shadow shifted again. A moment of decision, perhaps. Morgan watched as the door opened and one of Debbie's housemates stepped inside. It was the musician.

'What do they call you?' Morgan asked.

'Diablo,' he said. 'I'm David, see. Di. It's a kind of joke.'

Morgan gestured to the bed. 'Sit.'

'It doesn't seem right,' Diablo said, but he sat anyway.

'Do you believe in all this – angels and stone circles?'

Diablo's eyes jumped to the poster. 'Not like Debbie. She was . . . she was really into it.'

'And you're not?'

'The band is. It's our image. We're the Witch Kings.'

Morgan felt as if he was expected to recognise the name. 'Do you have a record? An album, I mean.'

'We sell downloads.'

'You've heard of Harry Gysel?'

Diablo nodded.

'Do you think he's a genuine psychic?'

'Well he's got to be, right? After what he did.'

'I thought you didn't believe in that sort of thing.'

'Not all of it.'

'But . . . ?'

'Harry Gysel – he's different.'

'You've seen him then?'

Diablo rubbed his forehead, as if trying to ease a headache. Then Morgan's phone rang. He pulled it from his pocket, standing up as he put it to his ear.

'Sir, I checked Gysel's alibi.' It was one of the sergeants speaking. 'We went to see the woman he said he spent the night with.'

Morgan's eyes were fixed on Diablo. 'And?'

'She says she hasn't seen him.'

Sometimes you hope for a bit of news so much that when it comes, you can't trust that you've heard it right.

Morgan swallowed. 'Say again please.'

'She won't back up Gysel's story. But I think there's a reason, sir. She gave a false alibi for a boyfriend once before. She's got a conviction for perverting the course of justice. I think maybe she's scared.'

Diablo kept still. Could he hear the other side of the conversation? It didn't matter now. Morgan was sure he had his man.

'I'll be back at the station in 30 minutes,' he said. 'Have someone bring Gysel in for questioning.'

When Morgan arrived at the station he was handed another gift – news of two connections that had previously been missed in the mass of paperwork. They must have seemed irrelevant in the earlier murder investigations, but reading them now, Morgan felt the skin on the back of his neck tingle.

He was standing in the corridor outside the interview room, armed with two photographs. To make an arrest he needed 'reasonable suspicion' – something more than the growing list of circumstantial evidence connecting Gysel to the murder. A lie perhaps. Then he could sweat his suspect in a cell while they searched his flat and his car. They'd turn up something. He was sure of it.

He checked his watch. Gysel had been waiting for ten minutes. He snapped the door open, marched inside, took a seat opposite the suspect and placed the photos face down on the table.

Gysel leaned forward. 'Where's my daughter?'

'There's nowhere safer than a police station.'

'Where is she?'

'Sitting by the front desk.'

'I'd like her brought here.'

'This won't take long,' Morgan said. 'The desk sergeant will keep an eye on her. You know why you're here?'

'Should I?'

'You said you were psychic.'

'I said I read minds.'

'So you don't have supernatural powers?'

'I can leave, right, if I want to?'

'Well, let's get to the point, then. Where did you go on the night Debbie was killed?'

'I've told you already.'

'You told us you spent the night with . . .' he took a notebook out of his jacket pocket and leafed through the pages.

'Chloe,' Gysel said.

'*Chloe*. Thank you. How did you meet her?'

'Davina introduced us. They're friends.'

'Chloe says she doesn't know you.'

Gysel's mouth gaped. 'I was with her!'

Morgan turned the two photographs over. Each showed a face. 'Do you know either of these women?'

Gysel glanced down then shook his head. 'No.'

'Would you swear to that?'

He looked again, for longer this time, and Morgan wondered if lying was something that Gysel was good at from childhood, or if he had practiced in order to do the stage show convincingly.

'Well?'

'No. Never.'

'This one . . .' Morgan said, tapping the photo on his left, '. . . was a fan of yours. She went to three of your performances two years ago. Another of your groupies?'

'I . . . no . . . I can't remember every face from every audience.'

'And this one . . .' Mogan rotated the second photo for a moment so he could look at it the right way up, then twisted it back and pushed it forward till it was right in front of Gysel. 'We know she telephoned you.'

Gysel's face was screwed up with denial and apparent confusion. 'When?'

'This time last year.'

'I don't know her. A wrong number, maybe.'

'She phoned you four times on four consecutive evenings.'

'I get . . . sometimes I get crank calls.'

'Why didn't you report it?'

Gysel pushed the photograph back towards Morgan. 'I've never met her. Ask her yourself.'

'She's dead. They were both murdered.'

Harry's face went slack. He stood. 'I'm going. I need to see Tia.'

'No,' said Morgan. He didn't have enough but he couldn't let him go. 'Harry Gysel. I am arresting you on suspicion of murder . . .'

Twelve hours later, Harry had been bailed and released. Eight of those hours he'd spent looking at the wall of a cell. The other four he'd spent sitting next to a solicitor in the interview room, answering the questions of a series of detectives. The same questions each time. Where was he last October? Where was he the October before? He'd been performing in and around Leicester, he told them. No, he didn't need to check. He began and ended each year of touring here in his home city. Always in October. Yes, he did sometimes get obsessive fans. Yes, they were usually women.

When he finally emerged from the police station, Peter Pickman was waiting, camera at the ready. Strangely, Harry felt grateful.

'I need a shave,' he said.

'Was that really bad?' Pickman asked. It was the first time Harry had heard him speak other than about the documentary.

'Really bad,' Harry said. 'Did you see who came to take Tia?'

'Your ex-wife. I'm sorry.'

Harry wanted to drive across town straight away, to get his daughter back. He still had another half day of access time. But Pickman suggested a detour. Home for a shave and a fresh shirt. Time for a cup of coffee on the way.

Perhaps it was the enormity of what was happening to him, or perhaps it was Pickman's ability to be there without drawing attention to himself, but Harry caught himself not minding the camera any more.

'How did Davina find you?' he asked.

'She didn't,' Pickman said, still looking through the viewfinder. 'I approached her.'

Harry nodded. It was no surprise that his agent had been economical with the truth.

By the time they crunched to a stop on Angela's gravel drive he hardly noticed. He advanced from the car towards the front door, leaving Pickman filming through the passenger side window.

She was there, glaring at him, before his finger reached the bell. 'You've got a nerve showing up here.'

'I've still got 8 hours,' he said.

'You left her sitting in a police station!'

'There's no safer place.'

'I know about your girlfriend,' Angela said. 'You think I'd let you take Tia home to a woman like that?'

'Chloe? She isn't my girlfriend.'

'I've had detectives here. Asking questions about you. They told me what you've been doing.'

Harry tried to step into the house but Angela spread her arms to block him. He shouted over her shoulder. 'Tia!'

'She doesn't belong with you.' Angela's voice was a hiss. 'I've been trying to tell you this for years.'

'Christ!' Harry shouted. 'You should listen to yourself!'

Angela flinched. He could see the hurt whenever he swore like that.

'You've never taken my hints,' she said. 'You don't want to face the truth.'

'What do you mean?'

'Tia isn't yours.'

He understood the words his ex-wife had just spoken, but together they didn't seem to make sense. He found himself blinking rapidly.

'We're going back to court,' Angela said

'We?'

She pulled in a deep breath. 'I didn't want it to be like this. But you're ruining Tia's life. She's not your daughter, Harry. We don't want you to see her again.'

The thought of letting Dr Fields, the forensic psychologist, into his office was unsettling, so Morgan booked one of the larger interview rooms for the meeting. She was waiting for him when he opened the door.

'Good morning,' he offered his hand, which she took. Her grip was soft.

'You've had time to read my conclusions?' she asked.

'I have.'

They were sitting opposite each other. She had a copy of the report on the table in front of her. He placed his own copy to mirror hers. Her coppery hair seemed even brighter under the room's fluorescent lighting than it had on the hillside when they first met.

'I'm hoping you can clarify something,' he said. 'I'm familiar with the basic division between organised and disorganised crime scenes. When we spoke before, you told me we were looking for a killer in control of his actions.'

She folded her arms. 'The crime scene was organised.'

'Which means an intelligent, socially able killer. A sociopath rather than a psychopath. Someone with no moral inhibitions to killing. But in your report you changed your mind.'

'It's never that simple. And we didn't know then that all the victims were linked to Harry Gysel.'

'This is what I don't understand,' Morgan said. 'You haven't mentioned the possibility that Harry Gysel is the killer.'

'I do. If you read section three . . .' Dr Fields flicked through her copy of the report, then traced a finger down the margin of one page. 'Here we go . . . "Assuming Harry Gysel isn't himself guilty, I conclude that . . ."'

'Why assume?'

'". . . I conclude that the killer is fixated on him. The killer may have specific delusional fantasies of a relationship with Mr Gysel and psychic phenomena."'

She looked up from the page.

Morgan said: 'I thought delusional killers left disorganised crime scenes.'

'Not always. If Gysel was the murderer, he'd make sure the victims couldn't be connected to him. I think our killer wants Gysel to be involved – to know the deaths are related to him.'

'It could be greed,' Morgan said. 'The man is on the road to riches because of this.'

Dr Fields closed the report. 'Maybe you're right. It isn't an exact science. But I'd say you're looking for someone who came into contact with Gysel two years ago, possibly after a life-changing event of some kind.'

'Like what?'

'Accident, mental breakdown, loss of a loved one. Anything like that. When they kill again, the victim will be someone Harry Gysel knows.'

'Why not kill Gysel himself?'

'Killing Gysel would kill the fantasy. As long as the fantasy is alive, Gysel is safe.'

Morgan took a deep breath and let it out slowly. 'Is believing in psychic phenomena a mental illness?'

'Do you believe?' she asked.

'No.'

'Not in anything? Ghosts? Jesus? Love?'

'There is something I haven't mentioned,' Morgan said. 'Something Harry Gysel showed me when I interviewed him.' He began describing the way Harry Gysel had divined his mother's middle name. Dr Fields looked at him so intently that he found himself dropping his own gaze to his hands as he spoke. When he looked again, he was surprised to see her smiling. 'If he'd known I was going to interview him, he could have looked it up.'

'You must have mouthed the name,' she said.

Morgan thought back, trying to remember. 'Not the middle name.'

'Well, did you tell it to him before he showed you what was on the card?'

'Yes. But after he'd written it.'

'It's a Mentalist trick,' she said. 'Conjuring that looks like mind reading. It has to be. What you should be asking is why he thought Debbie was going to die.'

'He wouldn't tell me,' Morgan said. 'But I do have some news on that. We found out today, Debbie had liver cancer. She knew she was going to die.'

The Sorcerer's Apprentice, loud but tinny, chimed from Harry's mobile phone. He groped on the bedside table, pressing buttons at random until it stopped, then fumbled it to his ear.

'Hello?'

'Dad?'

'Tia? What time is it?'

'You said . . . you said I could call any time.'

He was more asleep than awake but the half sob in his daughter's voice was like a slap to the face. He swung his legs out of bed and blinked, trying to focus on the glowing digits of the alarm clock. 'Are you OK?'

'You were on the news, Dad.'

'I know sweetheart. Where are you?'

'It doesn't matter where I am! They said . . . they said a girl was killed. Mum turned the TV off and sent me to my bedroom. They said . . .'

'Are you there now? God, Tia, it's three in the morning.'

'Stop fussing about me! They said you were arrested.'

'They just questioned me.'

'Did you . . . did you really know? They said you predicted it all.'

'I didn't know anything. The woman, Debbie, she thought she was going to die. That's all there is.'

'But you predicted it. You should have stopped it.'

'I couldn't.'

'Mum says I'm not to see you any more. She says you're no good. She says . . .'

'I will see you.'

'. . . she says it's your fault.'

'Then she overestimates me.'

'She says you call up devils.'

'There are no devils, Tia. At least, only human ones. And I'm nothing special. All I do is conjuring tricks. Please tell me where you are.'

'Stop treating me like a baby!'

'I'm asking because I love you.'
'You said love is just chemistry.'
'Tia, I'd do anything for you.'
'I don't believe it.'
'Tell me what you want. Anything.'
'I want you to be special.'

The press conference was Harry's idea. When he told Davina about it she surprised him with an embrace so tight that he could feel her heart beating. It was as if he'd agreed to convert to her religion.

'We could book that same hotel the police used for theirs,' she said.

Davina had an instinct for the mischievous that he almost admired. Holding it there would certainly goad Morgan and that was a satisfying thought. But Morgan wasn't his target.

'The acoustics were terrible,' he said. 'Anyway, I've got a better idea.'

And so it was arranged. Back to the theatre, the exact spot where he'd stumbled on Debbie's premonition of death.

News of a serial killer had attracted reporters up from London, including correspondents from the foreign press. Harry stood on the street opposite the theatre, his face concealed under the hood of an old anorak. He watched them arriving, jostling each other as they pressed through the doors. French and Italian accents mingled with the English. When he'd heard enough, he followed them in and made his way to the wings. There he took off his coat and waited.

Davina was standing centre stage behind a bank of microphones. He listened to her addressing the audience, priming them, telling them what to expect. She would have been a good stage hypnotist.

Then, at her command the lights dimmed.

'Good luck,' whispered Pickman just behind him. Harry stepped out from his hiding place. Camera flashes strobed him as he advanced towards the microphones. He peered into the audience. There were more people here than on his last performance. Then the stage lights came up full and he couldn't see them any more.

'Mr Gysel will take your questions now,' said Davina.

There must have been a radio microphone in the audience because the voice of the first questioner issued clear from the stage speakers. 'Harry. Are you using your powers to help the police or are you a suspect?'

This one they'd expected. 'Some people see beauty and mystery in the world,' he said. 'But it's hard for the police to admit there's more between heaven and earth than the ozone layer. I predicted Debbie's death. It's natural they needed to question me.'

Out there in the audience the microphone

129

changed hands. A new voice spoke. 'Were you born with special powers or did you develop them?'

'We use only 10% of our brain capacity. We are all capable of amazing things.' It didn't matter that the statistic was made up. And it didn't matter that he hadn't answered the question. Play the mystic, Davina had said. The less you say the more they'll want.

'Mr Gysel, do you believe in God?'

'What I believe isn't the point. But there are powers in the universe that we don't understand.'

'Harry. What did you tell the police? Is the killer going to strike again?'

'All I told the police is confidential.'

'Give us a demonstration, Harry. Read my mind.'

Davina sidled between Harry and the microphones. 'Harry Gysel will be performing at venues around the country for the next month. A new tour list is on his website today. If you want demonstrations, that's your opportunity.'

Another voice from the floor. A shaky one this time, unlike the hard-bitten hacks. 'Do you . . . do you make things happen? Or is it . . . is it like everything's set?'

Harry peered into the spotlight beam but could make out no more than the silhouette of heads against the yellow haze. 'I don't understand the question.'

'Did you . . . I mean, did you make it happen? Did your powers kill Debbie?'

'What newspaper do you represent?' Davina asked.

'I'm just . . . I was Debbie's friend, that's all. She was my housemate.'

Harry could hear the movement of people out there in the audience. Camera flashes flickered, picking out a man with long hair, sitting half way back.

'What's your name?' one of the reporters shouted.

'They call me Diablo. I'm the bass player with the Witch Kings.'

If a girl hadn't died it would be almost funny – another wannabe celeb hijacking their opportunist publicity stunt. He could sense his agent stiffening as the cameramen on the front row turned to refocus on the musician.

He wondered who would watch all this tonight on the evening news? Chief Inspector Morgan, no doubt. If the man had disliked him before, he would hate him after this. Tia? Would Angela be in the room to click the TV remote?

Attention was still on the young musician, in spite of Davina's efforts.

'Diablo. What was she like as a housemate?'

'She was cool.'

'Did she believe in psychic forces?'

'She was like me and the band, we're all into it. We've got a new track out. That's about magic.'

Harry projected an image of Tia sitting in the audience in front of him. It was time.

'I can sense a presence,' he said, pitching his voice half a tone higher than before. There was a whisper of people shifting in their seats to face him again. He raised his eyes to the lights above the stage and spread his arms to stand cruciform. This was the image they'd put in the papers tomorrow. Angela would hate him for it.

Morgan had slipped into the theatre after everyone else was seated. He stood now by the wall on the left. He'd watched through the performance, taking in Gysel's agent, the hacks and then Harry Gysel himself.

As the questions came, he made himself watch the audience rather than the stage. Who were these people – all so eager to feed on stories of psychic phenomena? Then Diablo spoke drawing the camera lenses towards himself. Morgan hadn't noticed him before.

When Gysel spoke again there was something ethereal about his voice and Morgan found himself turning involuntarily.

'I can sense a presence.'

Harry Gysel, lit by the spotlight and surrounded by the blackness of the stage, had made himself into an image of the crucified Christ. As Morgan watched, the man's eyes rolled under his lids.

'I can sense . . . someone in this room . . . someone

has travelled far to be here. I can hear a name . . . It begins with L. Lucy. Or Lucia.'

A blonde woman towards the front of the audience stood up. 'I'm Lucia.'

'A republican will reward you,' he said.

'Republican?'

Gysel rocked his head from side to side. 'I don't know. Republican. Republic.'

'*La Republica?*' she asked. 'I write for *La Republica* in Italy.'

'Do you have some old photographs in your house, jumbled in a box or an envelope?'

'Yes.'

'There's a picture of an old man. It is him, he's giving you this message.'

The woman was nodding. 'Grandpa?'

'He says you have been hurt in the past. He can feel your hurt, but you are healed now and it is time to move on.'

From where Morgan watched he could see the woman stagger back a step, then slowly sit.

Harry Gysel was swaying, as if about to fall. His agent stood open mouthed next to him.

'There are forces here in this room,' he cried. 'Powerful forces . . . I sense someone watching. A killer is watching. I'm looking into the killer's heart. There is emptiness inside. Emptiness and weakness and loneliness.'

Then Harry Gysel cried out as if in pain and threw back his head. His knees buckled and he fell to the floor. There was a moment of silence, then everyone was on their feet. The photographers were the first to clamber up on stage, then everyone was following. Everyone except the boy Diablo, who turned and walked out of the back of the theatre.

Harry lay on the stage, eyes closed, listening to the uproar he'd created. He was aware of Davina's perfume. Her fingers were cool on his cheek. She fumbled his top button open.

Then other people were clambering onto the stage. The impact of their footfalls thundered into his skull through the boards. Their shadows were on him and the camera flashes were flickering. He covered his face with his hands and groaned.

'What happened?'

When he opened his eyes, they were crowding in, trying to elbow each other out of the way.

'Harry. What did the killer look like?'

'Harry, smile.'

'Harry, is it a man or a woman?'

'Harry. Harry. Over here.'

'Will you go to the police?'

'Harry. Will he be coming for you?'

He let Davina help him into a sitting position. The crush of bodies pressed closer. Cameras held over heads pointed down at him from above. He stood. 'What happened?' he asked.

Davina took his arm as if to steady him. 'Mr Gysel needs air. Please back away.'

No one did. She started leading him towards the wings. The crowd was moving with them. Cameras were in front of his face. A long lens caught him on the side of the head.

Only when Davina closed the door of the dressing room were they alone. He dropped himself into the chair and looked up at her. There was a greyness in her face that he'd never seen before.

'What was that about?' she asked.

'They're reporters. That's what they do.'

'Don't be obtuse, Harry. What did you see?'

He stared at her, suddenly unsure. It hadn't occurred to him that his agent, one of the most materialistic people he knew, would be taken in by his act. 'I'm a fake, Davina.'

There was a look on her face that he couldn't decode. Was it fear? Sadness?

'Some of what you do is fake,' she said. 'I know that. But not all of it.'

He said, 'All of it.'

'Then how did you know the girl was going to die?'

'There are signs. If you think a word in your head, your face muscles shift. It's like you're saying it out loud. Some people can't help it. That girl – she believed she was going to die. All I did was lip read.'

He'd been planning on telling her the rest – that he was going to bring this killer, who was clearly

135

fixated on him, out into the open to be caught. He'd been planning on telling her that the news story he was in the process of making would be so big that he'd finally be able to drop the pretence of psychic power and come clean and people would still flock to his shows. He wanted to tell her that she would be proud of him, that Tia would be proud of him.

But the admission he'd just made was already too much. He hadn't expected her to react in that way. Suddenly he felt too tired to move.

'I just need to sleep,' he said.

She opened her handbag, pulled out a creased tissue and dabbed it on the side of his head then showed it to him. It was stained with a drop of blood. She folded the tissue away. 'The reporters are out there,' she said. 'And they still want more.'

It was six in the morning and raining hard when Morgan heard the news. By the time he reached Harry Gysel's place, four uniformed officers were waiting. He led them up the stairs, knocked once, shouted a warning and then let them break the door down. The place was empty. Leaving the men to search, he sped across the empty city towards the house of Gysel's one-night-stand, Chloe. But that was another blank. He drove off again, peering at the empty road through sweeps of the wiper blades, running red lights, heading for the only other place he knew of where Harry Gysel might hide.

It was almost half past seven by the time he finally crashed open the door to the theatre dressing room and found Gysel apparently sleeping in a chair, covered by his coat.

'What have you done with her?' Morgan demanded.

Gysel opened his eyes, seeming confused. 'What?'

'What have you done with Tia?'

CHAPTER 3

Time does strange things when you are in shock. Harry had felt it before – the day Angela, his first love, left him for the minister in their church. He remembered walking away from her in slow motion, turning back to see her in the doorway, baby Tia held on her hip. He remembered putting together the clues of her infidelity, thinking faster than he'd ever thought before.

Stumbling ahead of Morgan, the same lucidity came to him. Even before they'd reached the end of the corridor, he knew Tia's abduction to be the result of his idiotic bravado. He'd meant the killer to confront him. He'd meant to live or die as something more than a fake, to be a hero in his daughter's eyes.

He heard his own voice saying: 'Have you searched Angela's place?'

Morgan didn't break step. 'She's the one who told us you abducted the girl.'

'Tia is my daughter.'

'Save it for the station.'

Harry fumbled his phone from his pocket. 'Her mobile number . . . it's on here. You can track her.'

Morgan took it. For a moment he seemed uncertain, then he gave Harry a shove, propelling him towards the exit.

'Don't waste your time with me! It's the killer who's got her.'

'Is that another premonition?'

Harry wheeled on the detective. 'For god's sake! Help me!' He put his hands over his face. Time compressed even further. Thoughts poured through his head. Through his fingers he saw Morgan moving towards him, about to push him again. He lashed out with his arm. The detective was falling and Harry found himself running, crashing the fire doors, spilling into the lobby then out through the front entrance and into the rain.

How many seconds did he have before Morgan raised the alarm? A car door opened on the other side of the road. His own car. Harry caught a glimpse of Pickman at the wheel and dived inside.

'Go!' he shouted.

Pickman was driving before the door was closed. The tyres screeched as they rounded the corner. Water was dripping from Harry's hair, running down his face. He looked out of the back window. No one was following.

'How did you know to be there?'

'I've been listening to the police radio,' Pickman said, steering the car into a narrow side-street.

Harry turned to look at him. 'Isn't that illegal?'

'Are you complaining?'

★   ★   ★

They parked outside a KFC, bought coffees and took them back to the car. The windows fogged as they drank.

'I've got to find Tia,' Harry said at last.

Pickman retrieved his camera from the back seat. It seemed as if he was going to continue with the documentary shoot, but this time he turned it so that the viewfinder rather than the lens was pointing towards Harry. 'You should see this,' he said. Then he pressed a button and the film started playing.

Harry saw the view from the wing of the theatre – Davina and himself standing on stage behind the bank of microphones. After a few seconds the scene cut to a view from the balcony. He saw himself taking questions. The camera swung left, picking out Morgan, who was standing next to the wall downstairs, then right again. It had that jerky, hand-held feel. Almost unusable, Harry would have thought, though that was the fashion these days. The view shifted to the spotlight operator on the balcony then down to the audience. The young man, Diablo, stood up and began speaking. Everyone turned to face him.

'What am I looking for?' Harry asked.

'Wait.'

He watched as the camera jagged back to where he stood on stage. He'd often practised in front of a mirror, but never seen himself like this. With the spotlight tight on him and his arms to either side, the illusion of being suspended in the air was compelling. He listened to his own words – his challenge to the killer. He saw himself collapse and the audience rush to surround him. The camera angle dropped. Diablo was standing in the midst of the empty seats. The boy put his hands to his forehead and stood still for a moment. Then, as he turned to go, the camera caught his face. Pickman pressed a button and the image froze.

'See?'

Harry did see. The face was full of anger. 'I spoiled his moment,' he said, almost believing it.

'His band use an old farm to practise in,' said Pickman. 'It's out of the way. If he wanted to keep someone prisoner . . .'

'You call the police,' said Harry, 'I'll drive.'

Pickman directed Harry south out of the city. They were quickly off the main road, taking turnings on smaller and smaller tracks, until there was a ridge of grass down the centre and banks high on either side. Ahead, down a gentle slope, was a cluster of dilapidated agricultural buildings. A derelict farmhouse, concrete and corrugated iron animal sheds and a large brick building that could have been some kind of barn or machinery store.

'Cut the engine,' Pickman said.

Harry did as he was told, letting the car roll the last hundred yards. 'How did you find it?' he asked.

'After the press conference, I followed him here.'

141

He pointed to the brick building. 'He went in there. Should we wait for the police?'

But Harry was getting out of the car already. He edged along the outer wall of the building with Pickman close behind. Here and there the mouldering brickwork had crusts of white crystals, as if chemicals had leached from the mortar. Overspill from a broken gutter was splattering onto the ground.

The entrance was a dark opening. He peered around the edge into a bare room with an oil-stained floor. Then he was inside, heading for the doorless entrance to what appeared to be an inner room, placing his feet, trying to make no sound.

He flattened himself against the wall. One step and he'd be able to see what was within. He made to move, but Pickman gripped his shoulder and pulled him back.

'Me first,' mouthed the cameraman.

Before Harry could think what was happening, Pickman had slipped past him and through the gap. Harry was already following when Tia screamed.

He rounded the corner and there she was, standing on the far side of a bare concrete floor, face streaked with dust and tears, cuffed by one hand to a rusting horizontal pipe above her head. Diablo was nowhere, but still she screamed. Harry started stumbling forwards but Pickman had got to her. He turned and Harry saw two things in one moment – that the man's expression had transformed from apparent concern to angry contempt and that he held a Stanley knife in his hand, the triangular blade touching the skin of his daughter's throat.

Morgan sat in the passenger seat of a patrol car, waiting. They were parked in a lay-by, listening to the stream of instructions coming through the radio. Harry Gysel's car had shown up on CCTV. They'd tracked him heading south out of the city. After that he must have turned off onto a minor road.

At first the radio messages had come fast, one after another. The trail was fresh. All available resources were being sent out to search. That had been an hour ago. Now the radio traffic was punctuated by long periods of silence.

They could have used Harry's mobile phone to track him, of course, but Morgan had it. And Tia's mobile wasn't connected to the network.

The car's side windows had misted, in spite of the air blasting from the vents. Morgan's driver turned the engine off.

'Keep it running,' Morgan said.

'What are we expecting?'

'I don't know.'

'Then what can we do?'

Morgan fixed his gaze on one raindrop from the many that were rolling down the outside of the glass. 'Do you believe in prayer?'

'I . . . I kind of do.' The man seemed uncomfortable with this admission, as if it might lose him respect. 'What about you, sir?'

Morgan thought for a long time and then shook his head.

'Do you not believe in anything?' asked the driver.

'I hope,' Morgan said. 'That's all I can do.'

With a knife held to Tia's throat, Harry had had no choice but to follow Pickman's instructions, cuffing his own wrist to the rusting pipe above them and throwing the car keys on top of a small pile of Tia's things in the middle of the room. He then watched as their captor set up a tripod and a movie camera.

While Pickman was busy, Harry edged closer to his daughter, letting the loop of the handcuff scrape along the pipe until it ran up against a bracket. He was still five paces short but could move no further. Her outstretched hand was just beyond his reach.

Pickman turned the camera to face them. Then he stepped around it, closing the distance to Harry in three long strides.

'You're nothing!' he shouted.

Harry flinched, expecting a blow, which didn't come. Tia's mobile was on the floor. He thought back to Pickman's sham phone conversation in the car. He'd been a fool to believe the man had been speaking to the police.

Tia had stopped whimpering now. He could feel her eyes on him, as if she still believed he could perform a miracle and rescue them, as if his mental powers weren't fake. But fake was all he'd ever been – as a husband, as a father, always pretending to be what he was not, even to himself.

Pickman was turning the knife in his hand, completely focussed on it. He seemed to be gathering himself, as if preparing for his grand finale. Harry looked from the knife to the camera and then to Tia.

He tried to steady his breathing, as if this was just a stage show. 'Are you really a filmmaker?' he asked.

Pickman brought his face close. 'I can be anything. Don't you remember? You're the one who told me.'

Harry made a guess. 'You came to one of my shows.'

Pickman nodded. 'I thought you were psychic. You knew about my wife. But it's me who has the power. I didn't see it then. But I'm the one who was putting the thoughts into your head.'

Harry had done so many small gigs back then, they blurred into each other. But Pickman's words were chiming in his memory. A pub in Leicester. A man whose story had been a mirror of his own. Divorce followed by breakdown followed by what? Rebuilding? 'I said you had the power to take control of your life.'

'I make things happen,' said Pickman.

'What things?'

'I think it up here . . .' He tapped his finger against the side of his head. 'I think it up here and it happens. I thought it and those women died. I thought it into your head and you knew the same would happen to Debbie.' He held the knife blade in front of Harry's face. 'I thought

145

you were like me. I wanted to show you. But now . . . now I know you're nothing.'

'Let her go and I'll show you something magical,' said Harry.

'You know she has to die. I'm the one with the power now.'

'I can . . . I can help you manifest your power.' As soon as Harry said the words, he knew he'd scored a hit. Pickman swallowed heavily.

'You could film it,' Harry said. Another hit. The man was nodding. 'You must have planned this all along.'

'Yes.'

'Undo my wrist and I'll show you.'

Pickman's slack face tightened and Harry knew he'd made a mistake. It was like seeing a curtain descending. Pickman turned and grabbed Tia's free arm. She started screaming. Then he dug the blade into her wrist and blood was trickling onto the floor.

Harry cried out.

'I'm doing you a favour,' Pickman said. 'She's not even yours.'

'Stop it!'

'Show me my power.'

Tia was pressing her wrist against her chest. The blood began to bloom into her clothes.

'Well?' Pickman said.

For a moment, Harry couldn't move. Then he put his free hand in his jacket pocket. When he pulled it out he was holding a blank index card and, stuck to his thumb, hidden from view, was a grain of pencil graphite.

He was sweating. He held the card up in front of Pickman's face, snatched a breath and said, 'You have power.'

Pickman stared at the blank card. 'What's that?'

'You have psychic power.'

Pickman screwed his eyes closed, as if trying to block out the confusion. 'She's still going to die.'

'There's a shape drawn on the other side of this card,' Harry lied. 'Use your psychic powers. Read my mind. Tell me what it is.'

Pickman opened his eyes again. 'A . . . a triangle?'

Keeping the rest of his hand still, Harry started to move his thumb, dragging the grain of graphite slowly across the card, leaving a pencil line. If Pickman really looked, he might see the movement. 'Think,' Harry said. 'What would you do if you're right?'

'Dad,' Tia called. 'I'm feeling faint.'

Pickman whipped his head towards her. 'Shut up!'

Harry moved his thumb quickly, finishing off a triangle on the card.

Pickman was facing him again. He grabbed Harry's wrist and turned it. He stared at the shape. 'I did it,' he said.

Harry paused and then said, 'Maybe.'

'Maybe?'

'It could have been chance.'

'I can do it again!'

'You can try. I don't have more cards but I did

147

send a text to Tia's phone last night. If you could read that message from my mind . . .'

'Do it,' Pickman said. 'Think it to me.'

Harry could feel his heart thumping high in his chest. Tia would play along if only she understood what he was doing.

'It's something to do with love,' Pickman said. 'Go on.'

'You said, "I love you".'

Harry pointed towards Tia's phone. 'Check for yourself.'

Pickman grabbed it from the floor, opened it and clicked it on. It chimed as it came on line. He scrolled through the menu. 'Nothing,' he said. 'No message.'

'I did send it,' Harry said.

'It would be here!' Pickman was next to him in one stride. He raised the phone and slammed it into Harry's face.

Tia shouted, 'No!'

Pickman rounded on her. 'Shut up! Shut up!'

'He did send it,' she said. 'He did! I deleted it.'

There was blood dripping from Harry's nose. He looked across the space that separated him from her. Maybe Angela was right. Maybe Tia wasn't his. That didn't matter any more. He knew he would give his life for hers.

Pickman was blinking as if trying to clear his head. 'What was the message?'

'He said he loved me.' Tia's face looked deathly white.

Harry's gaze jumped from her eyes to the knife and back. 'Why did you kill the first two women?'

Pickman took half a step towards him and stopped. He seemed stranded between his two captives. 'They were after you.'

'They were just confused.'

'They wanted your power.'

'Don't you know what it feels like to be confused?

'They . . . they were trying to use you.'

It was only then that Harry understood. 'You were saving me from being in love with another woman?'

'I thought you knew!' Pickman shouted. 'I thought you knew it was me. Until . . . until yesterday in the theatre. You said my heart was empty.'

Morgan had been shifting in the passenger seat for the last five minutes, unable to relieve the sciatic pain jabbing down his left leg into his foot. He closed his eyes and tried to focus on the sound of the rain hitting the car.

Tension always did this to him – that and sitting for too long. But the pain served a purpose today. It stopped him from focussing on a doubt that he'd been incubating since the moment Harry Gysel had handed over his mobile that morning. Morgan had been so sure of his hunch. But what if he was wrong? What if his belief in Gysel's guilt was pulling police resources away from the real killer? What if the missing girl died?

He pushed the door open and stepped out onto the roadside verge, feeling his shoes sinking into the sodden earth. Straightening his back sent a needle of pain down his leg. He took a deep breath, turned his face towards the heavens and tried to immerse himself in the sensation of the rain spotting his skin.

Then the radio crackled with a new message. Tia's phone had registered on the network. They'd triangulated it to an abandoned farmhouse just two miles from his position.

He was in the car again, slamming the door as the driver floored the accelerator. One mile straight down the 'A' road, then off onto a road with no number. The car slid as they took the turn, wheels slipping on the wet surface. Morgan braced himself. Hedges whipped past, close on both sides. The speedometer needle was touching 60. They crested a ridge and saw farm buildings below them.

The driver didn't touch the brake until they were in the yard. They were sliding but the ABS kicked in and they juddered to a stop.

Morgan was out and running before the engine had died. Into the brick barn. Through another entrance. And there they were – Harry and the girl, chained to a pipe, her clothes soaked in blood. Pickman was standing in front of them, blinking as if dazed.

Harry was speaking – that calm, performance voice. 'We're connected. We always will be. A psychic thread runs between us. You can't cut it.'

Pickman raised his hand, first towards Harry

and then towards the girl. That's when Morgan saw the knife. He made to leap forward, but Pickman's fingers were already opening. The knife dropped and clattered onto the concrete.

'Ambulance!' Harry shouted. 'Get an ambulance!'

EPILOGUE

Tia and Harry were sitting on the theatre balcony, watching the seats fill up below.

'I want to know how you did it,' she said.

'What?'

'At the press conference you told that woman she had her grandfather's photo in a box. I saw it on TV.'

'I said a box or an envelope. Everyone has *some* unsorted photos stashed away. And I said an old man. She was the one who said it was her grandfather. That's what she wanted to believe.'

'But you knew things – her name, where she worked.'

'It'll spoil it if I tell you.'

'I'll keep it secret.'

Harry weighed the decision, then said, 'She was chatting to someone before the show. I just listened in.'

'But anyone could have done that!'

'Could have,' he said, and winked. 'What you should be asking is why Pickman didn't kill us.'

Tia's hand went to her wrist. It had been four weeks now and the stitches were out but he'd noticed how she still felt for them whenever she talked about her ordeal. A lot had happened in four weeks. Harry had become a celebrity. His new tour had sold out and Davina was walking on air. But most significantly, the publicity had scared off Angela and her husband from going back to court. Maybe Tia wasn't his biological daughter. The truth was, it didn't matter to him any more. It was enough that he loved her.

'OK. Why did he release us?' Tia asked.

'Because of what I told him.'

'He was loopy,' she said. 'You could have told him anything.'

'I could only tell him what he already believed. That's the only thing anyone really hears. His wife had left him. He'd had a breakdown, just like me. For two years he'd filled his life with the fantasy that we had some kind of magical connection.'

'How did you know?'

'I guessed. And I told him what he wanted to be told.'

Tia leaned into him and placed her head on his chest. 'If people only hear what they already believe,' she whispered, 'how come they sometimes change?'

He let her rest there for a moment before lifting her off. 'I've got to go.' He kissed her on the forehead as he got up. Then he called across to the right. 'Keep half an eye on her, will you?'

'Sure thing,' said the spotlight operator. 'Break a leg.'

★　★　★

At last the house lights dropped. Harry Gysel strode onto the stage and waited for the applause and cheering to subside. 'Ladies and gentlemen,' he said. 'There is more between heaven and earth than we will ever guess. But what you see tonight will be illusion.'

Trouble in Mind

John Harvey

Kiley smoothed the page across his desk and read it again: a survey conducted by Littlewoods Pools had concluded that of all 92 Premiership and Football League soccer teams, the one most likely to cause its supporters severe stress was Notts County. Notts County! Sitting snug, the last time Kiley had looked, near the midpoint of the League Two table and in immediate danger neither of relegation nor the nail-biting possibilities of promotion via the play-offs. Whereas Charlton Athletic, in whose colours Kiley had turned out towards the end of his short and less than illustrious career, were just one place from the bottom of the Premiership, with only four wins out of a possible twenty-two. Not only that, despite having sacked two successive managers before Christmas, this Saturday just passed they had been bundled out of the FA Cup by Nottingham Forest, who had comprehensively stuffed them at the City ground, two-nil.

Stress? Stress didn't even begin to come close.

Kiley looked at the clock.

12.09.

Too late for morning coffee, too early for lunch. From his office window he could see the traffic edging in both directions, a pair of red 134 buses nuzzling up to one another as they prepared to run the gauntlet of Kentish Town Road on their way west towards the city centre, the slow progress of a council recycling lorry holding up those drivers who were heading – God help them – for the Archway roundabout and thence all points north.

His in-tray held a bill from the local processing lab, a begging letter from the Royal National Lifeboat Institution, and a polite reminder from HM Revenue & Customs that the final deadline for filing his tax return was the 31st January – for more details about charges and penalties, see the enclosed leaflet SA352.

His pending file, had he possessed such a thing, would have held details of a course in advanced DNA analysis he'd half-considered after a severe overdose of *CSI*; a letter, handwritten, from a Muswell Hill housewife – a rare, but not extinct breed – wanting to know what Kiley would charge to find out if her husband was slipping around with his office junior – as if – and a second letter, crisply typed on headed note paper, offering employment in a prestigious security firm run by two former colleagues from the Met. Attractive in its way, but Kiley couldn't see himself happily touching his peaked cap to every four-by-four driver checking out of a private estate in Totteridge and Whetstone on the way to collect Julian and

Liberty from private school or indulge in a little gentle shopping at Brent Cross.

Early or not, he thought he'd go to lunch.

The Cook Shop was on the corner of Fortess Road and Raveley Street, a godsend to someone like Kiley who appreciated good, strong coffee or a tasty soup and sandwich combo, and which, apart from term time mornings when it tended to be hysterical with young mums from the local primary school, was pretty well guaranteed to be restful and uncrowded.

'The usual?' Andrew said, turning towards the coffee machine as Kiley entered.

'Soup, I think,' Kiley said.

Eyebrow raised, Andrew glanced towards the clock. 'Suit yourself.'

Today it was mushroom and potato, helped along with a few chunks of pale rye bread. Someone had left a newspaper behind and Kiley leafed through it as he ate. Former Labour Education Minister takes her child out of the state system because his needs will be better served elsewhere. Greater transparency urged in NHS. Unseasonably warm weather along the eastern seaboard of the United States. Famous celebrity Kiley had barely heard of walks out of Big Brother house in high dudgeon.

An item on the news page caught his eye, down near the bottom of page six.

Roadside bomb kills British soldier on Basra patrol . . .

The death of the soldier, whose name was not immediately released, brought the number of British military fatalities in Iraq since the invasion of 2003 to 130.

Iraq, Afghanistan – maybe some day soon, Iran.

Kiley pushed the paper aside, used his last piece of bread to wipe around the inside of the bowl, slipped some coins onto the counter, and walked out into the street. Not sunbathing weather exactly, but mild for the time of year. The few greyish clouds moving slowly across the sky didn't seem to threaten rain. When he got back to his office, Jennie was sitting on the stairs; he didn't recognise her straight off and when he did he couldn't immediately recall her name.

'You don't remember me, do you?'

'Of course I do.'

'Really?' A smile crinkled the skin around her grey-green eyes and he knew her then.

'Jennie,' he said. 'Jennie Calder.'

Her hair, grown back to shoulder-length, was the same reddish shade as before.

Jennie's smile broadened. 'You do remember.'

The last time Kiley had seen her she had been standing, newly crop-haired, cigarette in hand, outside a massage parlour on Crouch End Hill, ready to go to work. Two years back, give or take.

'How's your little girl?'

'Alice? Not so little.'

'I suppose not.'

'She's at school. Nursery.'

Kiley nodded. Alice had been clinging to her mother, screaming, wide-eyed, when he had last seen her, watching as Kiley set about the two men who'd been sent by Jennie's former partner to terrorise them, mother and daughter both. Armed with a length of two-by-four and a sense of righteous indignation, he had struck hard first and left the questions for later. Some men, he'd learned, you could best reason with when they were on their knees.

'How did you find me?' he asked.

'Yellow pages.' Jennie grinned. 'Let my fingers do the walking.'

She was what, Kiley wondered, early thirties? No more. Careful make-up, more careful than before; slimmer, too: black trousers with a flare and a grey and white top beneath a long burgundy cardigan, left unfastened.

'You'd best come in.'

The main room of the second floor flat served as living room and office both: a wooden desk rescued from a skip pushed into service by the window; a swivel chair, second-hand, bought cheap from the office suppliers on Brecknock Road; a metal shelf unit and filing cabinet he'd ferried over from his previous quarters in Belsize Park. For comfort there was an easy chair that had long since shaped itself around him. A few books, directories; computer, fax and answer phone. A Bose Radio/CD player with an eclectic selection of music alongside:

Ronnie Lane, Martha Redbone, Mose Allison, Cannonball Adderley, the new Bob Dylan, old Rolling Stones.

One door led into a small kitchen, another into a shower room and lavatory and, beyond that, a bedroom which took, just, a four foot bed, a chest of drawers and a metal rail from which he hung his clothes.

Home, of a kind.

'You haven't been here long,' Jennie said.

'Observation or have you been asking around?'

Jennie smiled. 'I spoke to the bloke in the charity shop downstairs.'

'A couple of months,' Kiley said. 'The rent on the other place . . .' He shrugged. 'Can I get you something? Tea? Coffee? I think there's some juice.'

She shook her head. 'No, I'm fine.'

'This isn't a social call.'

'Not exactly.'

Kiley sat on one corner of his desk and waved Jennie towards the easy chair. 'Fire away.'

A heavy lorry went past outside, heading for the Great North Road, and the windows shook. The Great North Road, Kiley thought, when had he last heard someone call it that? Seven years in the Met, four in uniform, the remainder in plain clothes; two years of professional soccer and the rest spent scuffling a living as some kind of private investigator. All the while living here or here abouts. The Great North Road – maybe it was time he took it himself. He'd been in that part of London for too long.

'This woman,' Jennie said, 'Mary. Mary Anderson. Lives near me. The flats, you know. She used to look after Alice before she started nursery. Just mornings. Alice loved her. Still does. Calls her gran. She's got this son, Terry. In the Army. Queen's Royal something-or-other, I think it is.'

'Lancers,' Kiley offered.

'That's it. Queen's Royal Lancers. They were out in Iraq. Till – what? – a month ago, something like that. End of last week, he should have gone back.'

'Iraq?'

'I don't know. Yes, I think so. But not, you know, straight off.'

'Report to the barracks first.'

Jennie nodded. 'Yes.'

'And that's what he didn't do?'

She nodded again.

'AWOL.'

Jennie blinked.

'Absent without leave.'

'Yes.'

'Does she know where he is? His mum.'

'All this last week he was staying with her, her flat. Thursday morning, that's when he was due to go back. All his kit there ready in the hall, wearing the uniform she'd ironed for him the night before. He just didn't go. Stood there, not saying anything. Ages, Mary said. Hours. Then he went back into the spare room, where he'd been sleeping and just sat there, staring at the wall. Mary, she had to go out later, mid-morning, not long, just to the shops. When she got back, he'd gone.'

'She's no idea where?'

'No. There was no note, nothing. First, of course, she thought he'd changed his mind. Gone back after all. Then she saw all his stuff, his bag and that, all dumped down beside the bed. 'Cept his uniform. He'd kept his uniform. And his gun.'

Kiley looked at her sharply.

'Mary had seen it, this rifle. Seen him cleaning it. She searched through everything but it wasn't there. He must have took it with him.'

'She's phoned the barracks to make sure . . .'

'They phoned her. When he didn't show. They'd got her number, next of kin. She did her best to put them off, told them he'd been taken ill. Promised to get back in touch.' Jennie shook her head. 'She's worried sick.'

'He's what? Twenty? Twenty-one?'

Jennie shook her head. 'No, that's it. He's not some kid. Thirty-five if he's a day. Sergeant, too. The army, it's a career for him. Mary says it's the only thing he's ever wanted to do.'

'All the more reason to think he'll turn up eventually. Come to his senses.'

Jennie was twisting a silver ring, round and round on her little finger. 'She said, Mary, before this happened, he'd been acting strange.'

'In what way?'

'You'd best ask her.'

'Look, I didn't say . . .'

'Just talk to her . . .'

'What for?'

'Jack . . .'

'What?'

'Talk to her, come on. What's the harm?'

Kiley sighed and eased his chair back from the desk. The man in the charity shop below was sorting through his collection of vinyl. The strains of some group Kiley vaguely remembered from his child-hood filtered up through the board. The Easybeats? The Honeycombs? He could see why people would want to get rid of the stuff, but not why anyone would want to buy it again – not even for charity.

Jennie was still looking at him.

'How did you get here?' Kiley asked. 'Drive?'

'Walked. Suicide Bridge.'

Kiley reached for the phone. 'Let's not tempt fate twice. I'll get a cab.'

When the council named the roads on the estate after streets in New Orleans they couldn't have known about Hurricane Katrina or its aftermath. Nonetheless, following Jennie through the dog shit and debris and up onto the concrete walkway, Kiley heard inside his head, not the booming hip-hop bass or the occasional metallic shrill of electro-funk that filtered here and there through the open windows, but Dylan's parched voice singing 'The Levee's Gonna Break.'

Mary Anderson's flat was in the same block as Jennie's but two storeys higher, coping missing at irregular intervals from the balcony, the adjacent property boarded up. A rubber mat outside the front door read *Welcome*, the area immediately around swept and cleaned that morning, possibly scrubbed. A small vase of plastic flowers was visible through the kitchen window.

Mary Anderson herself was no more than five three or four and slightly built, her neat grey hair and flowered apron making her look older than she probably was.

'This is Jack Kiley,' Jennie said. 'The man I spoke to you about, remember? He's going to help find Terry.'

Kiley shot her a look which she ignored.

'Of course,' Mary said. 'Come in.' She held out her hand. 'Jennie, you know where to go, love. I'll just pop the kettle on.' Despite the cheeriness in her voice, there were tears ready at the corners of her eyes.

They sat in the lavender living room, cups of tea none of them really wanted in their hands, doing their best not to stare at the pictures of Terry Anderson that lined the walls. Terry in the park somewhere, three or four, pointing at the camera with a plastic gun; a school photograph in faded colour, tie askew; Terry and his dad on a shingle beach with bat and ball; a young teenager in cadet uniform, smart on parade. Others, older, head up and shoulders back, a different uniform, recognisable still as the little lad with the plastic gun. Bang, bang, you're dead.

On the mantelpiece, in a silver frame, was a carefully posed shot of Terry on his wedding day – in uniform again and with a tallish brunette in white hanging on his arm, her eyes bright and hopeful, confetti in her hair. Arranged at either side were pictures of two young children, boy and girl, Terry's own children presumably, Mary's grandchildren.

Jennie's cup rattled against its saucer, the small noise loud in the otherwise silent room.

'You've heard nothing from him?' Kiley said.

'Nothing.'

'Not since Thursday?'

'Not a thing.'

'And you've no idea . . . ?'

She was already shaking her head.

'His family . . .' Kiley began, a nod towards the photographs.

'They separated, split up, eighteen months ago. Just after young Keiron's fifth birthday. That's him there. And Billie. I always thought it a funny name for a girl, not quite right, but she insisted . . .'

'Could he have gone there? To see them?'

'Him and Rebecca, they've scarce spoken. Not since it happened.'

'Even so . . .'

'He's not allowed. Not allowed. It makes my blood boil. His own children and the only time he gets to see them it's an hour in some poky little room with Social Services outside the bloody door.' Her voice wobbled and Kiley thought she was going to break down and surrender to tears, but she rallied and her fingers tightened into fists, clenched in her lap.

'You've been in touch all the same?' Kiley said. 'With Rebecca, is it? To be certain.'

'I have not.'

'But . . .'

'Terry'd not have gone there. Not to her. A clean break, that's what she said. Better for the children. Easier all round.' She sniffed. 'Better for the children. Cutting them off from their own father. It's not natural.'

She looked at him sternly, as if defying him to say she was wrong.

'How about the children?' Kiley asked. 'Do you get to see them at all.'

'Just once since she moved away. This Christmas past. They were staying with her parents, Hertfordshire somewhere. Her parents, that's different. That's all right.' Anger made her voice tremble. 'We can't stop long,' she said, Rebecca, almost before I could close the door. And then she sat there where you are now, going on and on about how her parents were helping her with the rent on a new house and how they were all making a fresh start and she'd be going back to college now that she'd arranged day care. And the children sitting on the floor all the time, too scared to speak, poor lambs. Threatened with the Lord know what, I dare say, if they weren't on their best behaviour. Little Billie, she came up to me just as they were going, and whispered, 'I love you, Gran,' and I hugged her and said, 'I love you, too. Both of you.' And then she hustled them out the door.'

Kiley reached his cup from the floor. 'Terry, he knows where her parents live? Hertfordshire, you said.'

'I suppose he might.'

'You don't think Rebecca and the children might still be there?'

'I don't think so.'

'All the same, if you had an address . . .'

'I should have it somewhere.'

'Later will do.'

'No trouble, I'll get it now.'

'Let me,' Jennie said.

With a small sigh, Mary pushed herself up from the chair. 'I'm not an invalid yet, you know.'

She came back with a small diary, a number of addresses pencilled into the back in a shaky hand. 'There, that's them. Harpenden.'

Kiley nodded. 'And this,' he said, pointing, 'that's where Rebecca lives now?'

A brief nod. West Bridgford, Nottingham. He doubted if Rebecca had joined the ranks of disheartened County supporters just yet.

'Thanks,' he said, finishing copying the details into his notebook and passing back the diary.

'A waste of time, though,' Mary said, defiantly. 'That's not where he'll be.'

Kiley nodded. Why was it mothers insisted on knowing their sons better than anyone, evidence to the contrary? He remembered his own mother – 'Jack, I know you better than you know yourself.' Occasionally, she'd been right; more often than not so wide of the mark it had driven him into a frenzy.

His gaze turned to the pictures on the wall. 'Terry's father . . .'

'Cancer,' Mary said. 'Four years ago this March.' She gave a slow shake of the head. 'At least he didn't live to see this.'

After a moment, Jennie got to her feet. 'I'll make a fresh pot of tea.'

Further along the balcony a door slammed, followed by the sounds of a small dog, excited, yelping, and children's high-pitched voices; from somewhere else the whine of a drill, someone's television, voices raised in anger.

Kiley leaned forward, the movement focussing Mary's attention. 'Jennie said your son had been acting, well, a bit strangely . . .'

He waited. The older woman plaited her fingers slowly in and out, while, out of sight, Jennie busied herself in the kitchen.

'He couldn't sleep,' she said eventually. 'All the time he was here, I don't think he had one decent night's sleep. I'd get up sometimes to go to the lavatory, it didn't matter what time, and he'd be sitting there, in the dark, or standing over by the window, staring down. And then once, the one time he wasn't here, I was, well, surprised. Pleased. That he was sleeping at last. I tiptoed over and eased open the door to his room, just a crack. Wanted to see him, peaceful.' Her fingers stilled, then tightened. 'He was cross-legged on top of the bed, stark naked, staring. Staring right at me. As if, somehow he'd been waiting. And that gun of his, his rifle, he had it right there with him. Pointing. I shut the door as fast as I could. I might have screamed or shouted, I don't know. I just stood there, leaning back, my eyes shut tight. I couldn't move. And my heart, I could feel my heart, here, thumping hard against my chest.'

Slowly, she released her hands and smoothed her apron along her lap. Jennie was standing in the doorway, silent, listening.

'I don't know how long I stayed there. Ages it seemed. Then I went back to my room. I didn't know what else to do. I lay down but, of course, I couldn't sleep, just tossing and turning. And when I asked him, in the morning, what kind of a night he'd had, he just smiled and said, "All right, mum, you know. Not too bad. Not too bad at all." And drank his tea.'

Jennie stepped forward and rested her hands on the older woman's shoulders.

'You will find him, won't you?' Mary said. 'You'll try. Before he does something. Before something happens.'

What was he supposed to say?

'What do you think?' Jennie asked.

They were walking along the disused railway line

that ran east from Crouch Hill towards Finsbury Park, grassed over now to make an urban footpath, the grass itself giving way to mud and gravel, the sides a dumping ground for broken bicycles and bundles of free newspapers no one could be bothered to deliver.

'I think he's taken a lot of stress,' Kiley said. 'Seen things most of us wouldn't even like to consider. But if he stays away there's always the risk of arrest, dishonourable discharge. Even prison. My best guess, he'll get himself to a doctor before it's too late, take whatever time he needs, report back with a medical certificate and a cart load of pills. That way, with any luck he might even hang on to his pension.'

'And if none of that happens?'

A blackbird startled up from the undergrowth to their left and settled again on the branches of a bush a little further along.

'People go missing all the time.'

'People with guns?'

Kiley shortened his stride. 'I'll go out to Harpenden first, make sure they're not still there. Terry could have been in touch, doing the same thing.'

'I met her once,' Jennie said. 'Rebecca.' She made a face. 'Sour as four-day old milk.'

Kiley grinned. They walked on, saying little, just comfortable enough in each other's company without feeling really at ease, uncertain how far to keep walking, when to stop and turn back.

*   *   *

The house was to the north of the town, take a left past the golf club and keep on going; find yourself in Batford, you've gone too far. Of course, he could have done the whole thing on the phone, but in these days of so much cold calling, conversations out of the blue were less than welcome. And Kiley was attuned to sniffing around; accustomed, where possible, to seeing the whites of their eyes. How else could you hope to tell if people were lying?

The house sat back, smug, behind a few straggly poplars and a lawn with too much moss in it for its own good. A mud-splashed four-wheel drive sat off to one side, the space in front of the double garage taken up by a fair-sized boat secured to a trailer. How far in God's name, Kiley wondered, were they from the sea?

The door bell played something that sounded to Kiley as if it might be by Puccini, but if he were expecting the door itself to be opened by a Filipino maid in a starched uniform or even a grim-faced au pair, he was mistaken. The woman appraising him was clearly the lady of the house, a fit-looking fiftyish with a fine tan and her hair swept up into what Kiley thought might be called a French roll – or was that twist? She was wearing cream trousers, snug at the hips, and a grey marl sweater with a high collar. There were rings on most of her fingers.

'Mr Kiley?'

Kiley nodded.

'You're very prompt.'

If he were a dog, Kiley thought, she would be offering him a little treat for being good. Instead she held out her hand.

'Christina Hadfield.'

Beneath the smoothness of her skin, her grip was sure and firm.

'Please come in. I'm afraid my husband's not here. Some business or other.'

As he followed her through a square hallway busy with barbour jackets, green wellingtons and walking boots, the lines from one of his favourite Mose Alison songs came to mind.

> *I know her daddy got some money*
> *I can tell by the way she walks*

The room they went into sported two oversized settees and a small convention of easy chairs and you could have slotted in most of Mary Anderson's flat with space to spare. High windows looked out into the garden, where someone, out of sight, was whistling softly as he – or she – tidied away the leaves. Presumably not Mr H.

Photographs of the two grandchildren, more recent than those on Mary Anderson's wall, stood, silver-framed, on the closed lid of a small piano.

'They're adorable,' she said, following his stare. 'Perfectly sweet. And well-behaved. Which is more than you can say for the majority of children nowadays.' She pursed her lips together.

'Discipline in our society, I'm afraid, has become a dirty word.'

'How long did they stay?' Kiley asked.

'A little over a week. Long enough to help undress the tree, take down the decorations.' Christina Hadfield smiled. 'Twelfth night. Another old tradition gone begging.'

'Terry, their father, he was home on leave while they were here.'

'If you say so.'

'He didn't make any kind of contact?'

'Certainly not.'

'No phone calls, no . . .'

'He knows better than to do that after what happened.'

'What did happen?'

'When Rebecca first said she was leaving him he refused to believe her. And then when he did, he became violent.'

'He hit her?'

'He threatened to. Threatened her and the children with all manner of things. She called in the police.'

'He was back in England then, when she told him?'

'My daughter is not a coward, Mr Kiley, whatever else. Foolish, I grant you. Slow to acknowledge her mistakes.' Reaching down towards the low table beside her chair, she offered Kiley a cigarette and when he shook his head, lit one for herself, holding down the smoke before letting it drift up towards

177

the ceiling. 'What possessed her to marry that man I was always at a loss to understand, and unfortunately, circumstances proved my reservations correct. It was a mismatch from the start. And a shame it took the best part of four years in non-commissioned quarters – bad plumbing and condensation streaming down the walls – to bring her to her senses.'

'That's why she left him? For a better class of accommodation?'

Christina Hadfield's mouth tightened. 'She left him because she wanted a better life for her children. As any mother would.'

'His children, too, surely?'

'Is that what you're here for? To be his apologist? To plead his cause?'

'I explained when I called . . .'

'What you gave me to understand on the telephone was that the unfortunate man was having some kind of a breakdown. To the extent that he might do himself some harm.'

'I think it's possible. I'd like to find him before anything like that happens.'

'In this, you're acting for his mother?'

'Yes.'

'Poor woman.' Smoke drifted from the corners of her mouth. 'After speaking to you, I telephoned Rebecca. As I suspected she's heard nothing from him. Certainly not recently.'

'I see.' Kiley got to his feet. Whoever had been whistling while they worked outside had fallen silent. Christina Hadfield's gaze was unwavering. What must it be like, Kiley thought, to entertain so little doubt? He took a card from his pocket and set it on the table. 'Should Terry get in touch or should your daughter hear from him . . . Unlikely as that might be.'

No call to shake hands again at the door. She stood for a few moments, arms folded, watching him go, making good and sure he left the premises.

Was it the fact that his grandfather – his father's father – had been an engine driver that left Kiley so susceptible to trains? The old man – that was how he had always seemed to Kiley, though he could not have been a good deal older than Kiley himself was now – had worked on the old London and Midland Railway, the LMS, and, later, the LNER. Express trains to Leeds and Newcastle, smuts forever blackening his face and hair. Kiley could see him, home at the end of a lengthy shift, standing by the range in their small kitchen, sipping Camp coffee from the saucer. Rarely speaking.

Now, Kiley, who didn't own a car, and hired one from the local pay-as-you-go scheme when necessary, travelled by train whenever possible. A window seat in the quiet coach, a book to read, his CD Walkman turned low.

His relationship with Kate, a freelance journalist whom he had met when working security at an Iranian Film Festival on the South Bank and who, after some eighteen months, had cast him aside in favour of an earnest video installation artist, had left him, a sore heart and a taste for wine beyond his income aside, with a thing for reading. Some of the stuff that Kate had off-loaded on him he couldn't handle – Philip Roth, Zadie Smith, Ian McEwan – while others – Graham Greene, the Chandlers she'd given him as a half-assed joke about his profession, Annie Proulx – he'd taken to easily. Jim Harrison, he'd found on his own. The charity shop below his office, where he'd also discovered Hemingway – a dog-eared Penguin paperback of *To Have and Have Not* with the cover half torn away. Thomas McGuane.

What he was reading now was *The Man Who Liked Slow Tomatoes*, which, when he'd been scanning the shelves in Kentish Town Oxfam, he'd first taken for yet another celebrity cookery book, but which had turned out to be an odd kind of crime novel about Mario Balzic, an ageing cop trying to hold things together in a dying industrial town in Pennsylvania. So far, more than half the book was in dialogue, a lot of which Kiley didn't fully understand, but somehow that didn't seem to matter.

For a few moments, he set the book aside and gazed out of the window. They were just north of Bedford, he guessed, the train gathering speed, and most of the low mist that had earlier been clinging to the hedgerows and rolling out across the sloping fields had disappeared. Off to the east, beyond a bank of threadbare trees, the sun was slowly breaking through. Turning down the

Walkman a touch more, Mose Allison's trumpet quietly essaying *Trouble in Mind*, he reopened his book and began chapter thirteen.

Nottingham station, when they arrived, was moderately busy, anonymous and slightly scruffy. The young Asian taxi driver seemed to know where Kiley wanted to go.

Travelling along London Road, he saw the flood-lights of the County ground where he had once played. Had it been just the once? He thought it was. Then they were crossing the River Trent with the Forest pitch away to their left – the Brian Clough stand facing towards him – and, almost immediately, passing the high rows of white seats at one end of Trent Bridge, where, in a rare moment of recent glory, the English cricket team had sent the Australians packing.

It was a short street of smallish houses off the Melton Road, the number he was looking for at the far end on the left, a flat-fronted two-storey terraced house with only flaking paint work to distinguish it from those on either side.

The bell didn't seem to be working and after a couple of tries he knocked instead. A flier for the local pizza parlour was half-in half-out of the letter box and, pulling it clear, he bent down and peered through. Nothing moved. When he called, 'Hello!', his voice echoed tinnily back. Crouching there, eyes growing accustomed to the lack of light inside, he could just make out a toy dog, left stranded, splay-legged, in the middle of the narrow hall.

'I think they're away,' a woman's voice said.

She was standing at the open doorway of the house alongside. Sixties, possibly older, spectacles, yellow duster in hand. The floral apron, Kiley thought, must be making a comeback.

'Most often I can hear the kiddies of a morning.' She shook her head. 'Not today. Quiet as the grave.'

'You don't know where they might have gone?'

'No idea, duck. You here for the meter or what?'

Kiley shook his head. 'Friend of a friend. Just called round on the off chance, really.'

The woman nodded.

'She didn't say anything to you?' Kiley asked. 'About going away?'

'Not to me. Keeps herself to herself, mostly. Not unfriendly, but you know . . .'

'You didn't see her leaving? Her and the children?'

'Can't say as I did.'

'And there hasn't been anybody else hanging round? A man?'

'Look, what is this? Are you the police or what?'

Kiley tried for a reassuring smile. 'Nothing like that. Nothing to worry about.'

'Well, you could try next door the other side, they might know something. Or the fruit and veg shop back on Melton Road, I've seen her in there a time or two, chatting like.'

Kiley thanked her and rang the next door bell but there was no one home. Between serving customers, the fruit and veg man was happy enough to pass the time of day, but could provide nothing in the way of useful information.

There was a narrow alley running down behind the houses, mostly taken up with green wheelie bins; a low gate gave access to a small, square yard. The rear curtains were pulled part way across.

Through the glass Kiley could see the remains of a sliced loaf, left unwrapped beside the sink; a tub of Flora with no lid; a pot of jam; a wedge of cheese, unwrapped. A child's coat lay bunched on the floor; a chair on its side by the far wall. Signs of unseemly haste.

The back door seemed not to be sitting snug in its frame. When Kiley applied pressure with the flat of his hand it gave a few millimetres, loose on its hinges, rattled, then stuck. No key, Kiley guessed, turned in the lock, but bolted at the top. A swift kick would have it open.

He hesitated, uncertain what to do.

Dave Prentiss's number was in his mobile; Prentiss, whom he'd worked with as a young DC when he'd first made it into plain clothes, and now in line for commander.

'Dave? Hi! It's Jack. Jack Kiley . . . No, fine, thanks. Yes, grand . . . Listen, Dave, you don't happen to know anyone up in Nottingham, do you? Someone you've worked with, maybe. Might be willing to give me the time of day?'

Resnick had been up since before five, Lynn heading up some high power surveillance and needing to be in place to supervise the changeover, a major drugs supplier their target and kudos all round if they could pull it off. Resnick had made them both coffee, toast for himself, a rye loaf he'd picked up on the way home the day before, Lynn crunching her way through Dorset muesli with skimmed milk and a sliced banana.

'Why don't you go back to bed?' she'd said. 'Get another couple of hours.'

She'd kissed him at the door, the morning air cold against her cheek.

'You take care,' he'd said.

'You too.'

One of the cats wandered in from outside, sampled an early breakfast and, despite the presence of a cat flap, miaowed to be let out again.

Instead of taking Lynn's advice, Resnick readied the smaller stove top pot and made himself fresh coffee. Easing back the curtains in the living room, the outside still dark, he sat thumbing through the previous night's *Evening Post*, listening to Lester Young. Would he rather have been out there where Lynn was, the heart of the action, so called? Until recently, yes. Now, with possible retirement tapping him on the shoulder, he was less sure.

He was at his desk by eight, nevertheless, breaking the back of the paperwork before it broke him. Dave Prentiss rang a little after eleven and they passed a pleasant enough ten minutes, mostly mulling over old times. There was a lot of that these days, Resnick thought.

At a quarter to twelve, an officer called up from reception to say a Jack Kiley was there to see him. He got to his feet as Kiley entered, extending his hand.

'Jack.'

'Detective Inspector.'

'Charlie.'

'Okay, then. Charlie.'

The two men looked at one another. They were of similar height, but with Resnick a good stone and half heavier, the buttons on his blue shirt straining above his belt. Both still had a fullish head of hair, Resnick's darker and, if anything, a little thicker. Kiley, thinner-faced and a good half-a-dozen years younger, had a leaner, more athletic build. Resnick, in contrast, had the slightly weary air of a man who has spent too long sitting in the same comfortable chair. Balzic, Kiley thought for a moment, harking back to the book he'd been reading, Mario Balzic.

'Dave Prentiss said you might need a favour,' Resnick said.

'You could call it that.'

Resnick gestured towards a chair. 'Better sit.'

Kiley gave him a succinct version of events, what he knew, what he feared.

'You think they might be inside?'

'I think it's possible.'

Resnick nodded. There had been a case not too long ago, north of the city. A man who'd discovered his wife was having an affair with a colleague and was planning to leave him; he had smothered

185

two of the children with a pillow, smashed their mother's head open with a hammer and left her bleeding on the kitchen floor. The police had found a third child hiding in the airing cupboard, limbs locked in fear.

There were other instances, too.

Almost a commonplace.

'You say the back door's only bolted?'

'So it seems.'

'You didn't go in yourself?'

'I thought about it. Thought it might not be such a great idea.'

Resnick considered, then reached towards the phone. 'I'll organise a car.'

'This could be a wild goose chase,' Kiley said as they were descending the stairs.

'Let's hope, eh?'

The driver was fresh-faced, carrot-haired, barely out of training. They're not only getting younger, Kiley thought, this one can only just see over the top of the steering wheel.

In the back of the car, Resnick was studying Kiley intently. 'Charlton Athletic, wasn't it?' he said eventually.

Grinning, Kiley nodded.

'Cup game down at Meadow Lane,' Resnick said.

Another nod.

'90/91.'

'Yes.'

'A good season for us.'

'You had a good team.'

'Tommy Johnson.'

'Mark Draper.'

Resnick smiled, remembering.

'Good Cup year for you, wasn't it?'

'Through to the Sixth Round. Spurs beat us 2–1 at White Hart Lane.'

'We should've stopped you sooner.'

'You had your chances.'

Kiley looked out through the window. Off licence. Estate agent. Delicatessen. He had spent most of the game on the bench and only been sent on for the last fifteen minutes. Before he could adjust to the pace, the ball had come to him on the edge of the area and, with the centre half closing in on him, he had let fly and, leaning back too far, his shot had ballooned over the bar. Then, a goal down and with less than five minutes to spare, he had nicked the ball away from the full back, cut inside, and, with only the goalie to beat, had skewed it wide. At the final whistle he had turned away disgusted as the Notts players ran towards their fans in triumph.

'All a long time ago,' Resnick said. 'Fifteen years.'

'And the rest.'

'Think about it much?'

Kiley shook his head. 'Hardly at all.'

The car swung round into Manvers Road and they were there. Still no one was answering the door. Round at the back, Resnick hesitated only a moment before putting his shoulder to the door, once, twice, before the bolt snapped free. He stepped carefully into the kitchen, Kiley following. Nothing had been moved. The cloth dog, two shades of brown, still sat, neglected, in the hall. The front room was empty and they turned back towards the stairs. A chill spread down the backs of Resnick's legs and along his arms. The stairs creaked a little beneath his weight. A child's blue cardigan lay, discarded, on the landing. The door to the main bedroom was closed.

Drawing a slow breath, Resnick turned the handle. The bed had been hastily made; the wardrobe doors stood open and several garments had slid from their hangers to the floor. There was no one there.

They turned back towards the other room, its door ajar.

The closer of the two, Kiley looked round at Resnick enquiringly then nudged the door wide.

There were bunk beds against the right hand wall. Posters on the wall, a white melamine set of drawers. Several clear plastic boxes, stacked on top of one another, filled with toys. Stuffed animals and pieces of Lego and picture books strewn across the floor.

Kiley felt the muscles in his stomach relax. 'They're not here.'

'Thank God for that.'

Back downstairs they stood in the kitchen, Resnick taking in the evidence of hasty sandwich making, the fallen chair.

There were a dozen explanations, mostly

harmless, some more plausible than the rest. 'You think they've done a runner?' he said.

'I think they might have tried.'

'And if they didn't succeed?'

Kiley released a long, slow breath. 'Then he's taken them, that's what I'd say.'

'Against their will?'

'Odds are.'

Resnick called the station from the car; arranged for the place to be secured and scene of crime officers to attend. Jumping to conclusions they might be, but better that than to do nothing and wait for bad news.

Terry Anderson had waited, cautious, van parked just around the corner on Exchange Road, back towards the primary school. From there he could see the house, see if Rebecca had any callers, visitors in or out, make sure the coast was clear. Waiting. Watching. Alert. Ready for danger, the least sign. It was nothing to him. What he was trained for. Northern Ireland. Iraq. Afghanistan. Belfast. Basra. Sangin. Someone waiting to take your head off with a rifle or blow you to buggery with an RPG.

Little happened. The occasional couple returning home from visiting friends, an hour in the pub, an evening in town. Men taking their dogs for a last walk around the block, pausing perhaps, to light a cigarette. Television screens flickering brightly between half-closed blinds. House lights going on, going off.

He sat behind the front seats, leaning back, legs stretched in front of him, out of sight to passers by. Beside him in the van were blankets, sleeping bags, bottles of water. A few basic supplies. First aid kit. Ammunition. Tools. Tinned food. His uniform, folded neatly. Waterproofs. Rope. Prepared.

As he watched, the downstairs room of Rebecca's house went suddenly dark and he imagined, rather than heard, the sound some moments later as she turned the key in the front door lock. Careful, he liked that. Not careful enough.

Eleven thirty-five.

She'd been watching, he guessed, a re-run of some American soap or a late night film and had either got bored or found her eyes closing, unbidden. How many times had they sat together like that in the semi-dark, the change in her breathing alerting him to the fact that she had dropped off, unwillingly, to sleep? Her warm breath when he had leaned over to kiss her, her head turning away.

The upstairs light went on and, for a brief moment, he saw her in silhouette, standing there, looking out, looking down; then the curtains were pulled across, leaving a faint yellowish glow.

Automatically, he rechecked his watch.

Imagined the children, already sleeping.

The houses to either side had gone dark long since, but up and down the street there were still signs of life.

He would wait.

★   ★   ★

That night, Rebecca stirred, wondering if she had ever really been asleep and, if so, for how long? The bedside clock read 01:14. It was her bladder that had awoken her and, grudgingly, she slid her legs round from beneath the duvet and touched her feet to the carpeted floor. The house was smaller than she might have liked, and at times, even for the three of them, barely large enough – bedlam when one or more of Keiron's friends came round after school to play. But the fixtures and fittings were in better nick than in many of the other places she'd seen and the rent, with her parents' help, was reasonable enough. If it weren't for them, she didn't know what she could have done.

Careful not to flush the toilet for fear of waking Billie – a light sleeper at best – she eased back the door and slipped into their room. Keiron's thumb was in his mouth and carefully she prised it free, causing him to grunt and turn his head sharply to one side, but not to wake. Billie, pink pyjama top gathered at her neck, was clinging to edge of the blanket she had slept with since she was three months old.

Straightening, Rebecca shivered as if – what did her grandmother used to say? – as if someone had just walked over her grave.

Rubbing her arms beneath the sleeves of the long T-shirt she was wearing, she turned and went softly back to bed, this time, hopefully, to sleep through. The morning would come soon enough.

When she woke again it had just gone two. Levering herself up on to one elbow, she strained to hear. Had one of the children woken and cried out? A dream, perhaps? Or maybe Keiron had got up and gone to the toilet on his own?

No, it was nothing.

The wind, perhaps, rattling the window panes.

Her head had barely touched the pillow, when she heard it again, for certain this time, the sound that had awoken her, a footstep. Next door, it had to be next door. Quite often, late at night, she heard them moving. Early, too. Her breath caught in her throat. No. There was somebody in the house, somebody down below, a footstep on the stairs.

Rebecca froze.

If I close my eyes, will it go away?

It.

He.

Whoever . . .

For the first time she wanted a phone beside the bed, a panic button, something. With a lunge, she threw back the covers and sprang from the bed. Three, four steps and she was at the door and reaching for the light.

Oh, Christ!

The figure of a man, turning at the stop of the stairs.

Christ!

Her hand stifled a scream.

'It's all right,' the voice said. 'It's all right.' A voice she recognised, reassuring, commanding.

'Terry?'

He continued slowly towards her, his face still in shadow.

'Terry?'

'Who else?' Almost smiling. 'Who else?'

With a sob, she sank to her knees, and he reached down and touched her hair, uncertainly at first, easing her head forward until it rested against his body, one of her hands clinging to his leg, the other pressed hard against the floor.

They stood in the bedroom, Rebecca with a cotton dressing gown pulled hastily round her. She had stopped shaking, but her breathing was still unsteady. He was wearing a black roll-neck sweater, camouflage trousers, black army boots.

'What are you . . . What are you doing?'

When he smiled, nothing changed in his eyes. 'Terry, what . . .'

'Get the children.'

'What?'

'Get yourself dressed and then get the children.'

'No, you can't . . .'

When he reached towards her, she flinched.

'Just something sensible, jeans. Nothing fancy. Them the same.'

She waited until he turned away.

'Keiron and Billie, they're in back, are they?'

'Yes, but let me go first, you'll frighten them.'

'No, it's okay. You get on.'

'Terry, no . . .'

'Get on.'

'You won't . . .'

He looked at her then. 'Hurt them?'

'Yes.'

He shook his head. 'They're my kids, aren't they?'

Billie was awake when he got to the door and when he moved closer towards her she screamed. Rebecca, half-dressed, came running, brushed past him and took the three year old into her arms. 'It's all right, sweetheart, it's only daddy.'

She sobbed against Rebecca's shoulder.

On the top bunk, Keiron stirred, blinking towards the landing light. 'Dad?'

Fingers and thumbs, Rebecca helped them into their clothes, Keiron with a school sweat shirt pulled down over his Forest top, Billie snapped into her blue dungarees.

'Where we going, mum?' Keiron asked.

'I'm not sure, love.'

'An adventure,' his father said, coming through the door. 'We're going on an adventure.'

'Really?'

'You bet!' He tousled the boy's hair.

'You mean like camping?'

'Yes, a bit like that.'

'Like you in the army.'

'Yes. Like that.'

'Some of the year sixes go camping overnight.

Cook their own food and everything. Can we do that?'

'Prob'ly, we'll see.'

'And take a pack-up? Can we take a pack-up?'

'No need, son. I've got all the stuff we need.'

'But they do, carry it with them. Can't we?'

'Yes, all right, then. Why not? Becca, how about it? Like the boy says. Fix us something quick. Sandwich, anything. Go on, I'll finish up here.'

When he got down to the kitchen, a few minutes later, there were bread, a pot of jam and some cheese but no Rebecca; he found her in the front room, texting.

'The fuck!'

Before he could reach her, she'd deleted the message. Swinging her hard towards him, he snatched the phone from her hand. 'Who was that going to be to? The police? The fucking police?' He hurled the phone against the wall and, pushing her aside, crushed it with the heel of his boot. 'Now get in that kitchen and get finished. Five fucking minutes and we're leaving. Five.'

Keiron was standing, open mouthed, at the living room door and behind him somewhere Billie had started to cry.

It was early evening and they were sitting in Resnick's office, a light rain blurring the window, the intermittent snarl and hum of traffic from the street.

'Here's what we've got so far,' Resnick said. 'Two sets of adult prints in the house, one we're assuming Terry Anderson's. Looks as if he forced the lock on the back door. Not difficult. Explains why it was only bolted across. There was a mobile phone, Rebecca's, in the front room. Beneath the settee. Broken. Smashed on purpose.'

'Used recently?' Kiley asked.

'One call earlier that evening, to a friend. We've already spoken to her, nothing there.'

'No mention of going away, taking a trip?'

'Nothing.'

'And the husband? She didn't say anything about him? Being worried at all?'

Resnick shook his head. 'We've checked with the school and the nursery where she takes the little girl. Both surprised when the kids didn't turn up this morning. Nursery phoned but got no answer, assumed she'd been taken sick. School, the same.'

Kiley shifted uncomfortably on his chair.

'More luck with the neighbours,' Resnick said. 'Old lady next door, bit of a light sleeper, reckons she heard a child scream. A little after two. Either that or a fox, she couldn't be sure. Person from across the street, sleeps with the window open, thinks he might have heard a vehicle driving away, that would be later, around two thirty. There's not a lot more. A couple of people mentioned seeing a van parked in Exchange

Road, just around the corner. Not usually there. Small, white, maybe a black stripe down the side. Could have been a Citroën, according to one. We're following that up, checking CCTV. That time of night, roads shouldn't be too busy. Might spot something.' He leaned back. 'Not a lot else to go on.'

'You've sent out descriptions?' Kiley said.

'As best we can. Local airports. Birmingham.'

'They could have gone with him willingly,' Kiley said.

'Is that what you think?'

'What I'd like to think,' Kiley said. 'Not the same thing.'

Keiron helped him put up the tent. The trees in that part of the forest had mostly lost their leaves, but the undergrowth was thick enough to shield them from sight. None of the regular paths came near. Tent up, they foraged for fallen branches and dragged them to the site, arranging them over the bracken. Several times, Keiron cut himself on thorns and briars, but he just sucked at the blood and bit back the tears. Big boy, trying not to be afraid.

'How long?' Rebecca wanted to ask. 'How long are we going to be here?' Reading the look on Anderson's face, she said nothing.

The sandwiches were finished quickly. Amongst the supplies he had provided were tins of corned beef and baked beans, peach slices in syrup.

Biscuits. Bottles of water. Tea bags and a jar of instant coffee, though he didn't want the risk of lighting a fire. They had driven the van some way along the main track then gone the rest of the way on foot, making two journeys to carry everything. Still dark. Just the light of a single torch. Taking Keiron with him, Anderson had gone back to move the van.

Before leaving, he had taken Rebecca to one side. 'You'll be here when we get back, you and Billie. Right here. Okay?'

'Yes.' A whisper.

'I'm sorry?'

'I said, yes. Yes, all right.' Not able to look him in the eye.

'It better be.'

By the time they had returned, Keiron was exhausted, out on his feet, and his father had had to carry him the last half mile. Billie was asleep, stretched across her mother's lap. While he had been away, she had tried walking a little way in each direction, taking Billie with her, careful never to wander too far and lose her way back. She had seen nobody, heard nothing. She felt stupid for not doing anything more, without knowing what, safely, she could have done.

'You look knackered,' Anderson said. 'Tired out. Why don't you get your head down? Get a bit of sleep while you can.'

When she opened her eyes, not so many minutes later, he was sitting cross-legged at the far side of the tent, rifle close beside him, painstakingly cleaning his knife.

Not wanting to stand around like a spare part, waiting, Kiley had walked into the city, found a halfway decent place for breakfast and settled down to a bacon cob with brown sauce and a mug of serious tea, trying to concentrate on his book. No such luck. Jennie had rung him earlier on his mobile and he'd hesitated before giving her a truncated version of what little they knew, what they surmised.

'Don't say anything to his mother,' he'd said. 'Not yet, anyway.'

'What d'you take me for?'

'I'll call you if I know anything more definite.'

'You promise?'

Kiley had promised.

Breakfast over, he wandered around the city centre. The square in front of the council building was going through some kind of makeover; maybe they were turning it into a car park. The pavements were busy with early shoppers, people hurrying, late, to work, the occasional drinker with his can of cider clutched tight. He walked up the hill towards the Theatre Royal. Duncan Preston in *To Kill a Mockingbird*. All next week, *The Rocky Horror Show*. Big Time American Wrestling at The Royal Concert Hall. He was half way down King Street, heading back towards the square, when his mobile rang. It was Resnick. They'd found something.

There was an OS map open on the table when Kiley arrived, the blurred image of a van frozen on the computer screen. Night time. Overhead lights reflected in the road surface. There were several other officers in the room.

'Two sightings of the possible van,' Resnick said.

One of the officers, dark hair, dandruff on his shoulders, set the CCTV footage in motion.

'The first here, junction 27 of the MI, leaving the motorway and heading east towards the A608. And then here – see the time code – not so many minutes later, at the roundabout where it joins the 611. Turning south.'

'Back towards the city?' Kiley said, surprised.

'Could be,' Resnick said, 'but for my money, more likely heading here. Annesley Forest.' He was pointing at a patch of green covering almost two squares of the map.

'Why there?'

'Couple of years back, just north of here, Annesley Woodhouse, this man was found dead outside his home, ex-miner, lacerations to the head and upper body, crossbow found close by.'

'Robin bloody Hood,' someone remarked.

'According to what we heard,' Resnick continued, 'there'd been one heck of a row between the dead man and a neighbour, all harking back to the miners' strike, '84.

When we went to talk to the neighbour, of course he'd scarpered, gone to ground right there.' Resnick pointed again. 'Two and a half kilometres of woodland. Then, as if that weren't bad enough, a second man, wanted for turning a shotgun on his own daughter, went missing in the same area. Bloody nightmare. We had extra personnel drafted in from all over, round five hundred all told. Dog teams, helicopters, everything. If that's where Anderson's gone, he could stay holed up for weeks.'

'But we don't know for sure,' Kiley said

'We know next to bugger all,' one of the officers said.

Resnick silenced him with a look. 'There's forest all around,' he said, 'not just this patch here. A lot of it, though, is criss-crossed with trails, paths going right through. Sherwood Forest especially, up by the Major Oak, even at this time of the year it's pretty busy with visitors. But this is different. Quiet.'

Looking at the map, Kiley nodded. 'How sure are we about the van?' he said.

'Traced the number plate. Citroën Berlingo. Rented from a place in north London – Edgware – two days ago. Name of Terence Alderman. Alderman, Alexander, TA, close enough. Paid in cash.'

'If he's gone into the woods . . .' Kiley began.

'Then he'll have likely dumped the van. We've got people out looking now. Until that turns up, or we get reports of a sighting, it's still pretty much conjecture. And, as far as we know, nobody's been harmed.'

'I doubt if he's taken them for their own good.'

'Even so. I need a little more before I can order up a major search. Request one, at least.'

By which time, Kiley thought, what they were fearing but not yet saying, could already have happened.

'I thought I might take a ride out that way,' Resnick said. 'Want to come along?'

While Rebecca watched, Anderson had talked both children into a game of hide and seek, warning them not to stray too far. Billie giggled from the most obvious hiding places, waving her arms, as if the point of the game was to be found. Once, Keiron skinnied down inside a hollow oak and stayed there so silent that his father, fearing maybe he'd run off, had called his name in anger and the boy had only shown himself reluctantly, scared of a telling-off or worse.

They picked at the corned beef, ate biscuits and cold beans, drank the sweet syrupy peach juice straight from the cans.

'We should have done this more often,' Anderson said.

'Done what?' said Rebecca sharply.

'Gone camping,' he said and laughed.

Sitting on the ground outside the tent, he showed his son how to strip down the rifle and reassemble it again.

'Can we go after some rabbits?' Keiron asked.

'Maybe tomorrow.'

'Will we still be here tomorrow?'

He left the question unanswered.

Just out of sight, beyond some trees, Anderson had dug a latrine. Walking back, Rebecca was aware of him watching her, the movement of her body inside her clothes.

'Are you seeing anyone?' he asked.

'Seeing?'

'You know what I mean.'

'No.'

'No man then?'

'No.'

'Why not?'

'I don't know. I'm just not.'

'You should.'

She went on past him and into the tent.

The day was sealed in with grey. Low hedgerows and mudded tracks and the occasional ploughed field. Why was it, Kiley asked himself, they didn't seem to plough fields any more, ploughed and left bare? Londoner that he was, he could swear that was what he remembered, travelling north to visit relations in Bucks. Mile after mile of ploughed fields. That rackety little train that stopped every- where. What was it? Hemel Hempstead, Kings Langley, Abbots Langley, Berkhamstead, Tring? His uncle, red-faced and – now, he thought, looking back – unreal, waiting outside the station at Leighton Buzzard, to take them home in a Rover that rattled more than the carriages of the train.

Resnick had opted to drive, the two of them up front as they made a careful circuit: Newstead, Papplewick pumping station, Ravenshead, south of Mansfield and back again, the A611 straight as a die from the corner of Cauldwell Wood, across Cox Moor to Robin Hood's Hill and the supposed site of Robin Hood's Cave. Then back down towards the forest, the trees at first bordering both sides of the road and then running thickly to the left.

'Do you ever miss it?' Resnick asked, out of nowhere.

It took Kiley a moment to respond. 'Playing?'

A grunt he took to mean, yes. What answer did he want? 'Sometimes,' Kiley said. 'Once in a while.'

'Like when?'

Kiley smiled. 'Most Saturday afternoons.'

'You don't play at all?'

'Not for years. Helped a friend coach some kids for a while, that was all.'

Resnick eased down on the brake and pulled out to pass an elderly man on a bicycle, raincoat flapping in the wind, cloth cap pulled down, bottoms of his trousers tied up with string.

'Up and down this road, I shouldn't wonder,' Resnick said, 'since nineteen fifty three or thereabouts.'

Kiley smiled. 'How about you?' he said. 'County. You still go?'

'For my sins.'

'Perhaps we'll catch a game some time?'

'Perhaps.'

Resnick's phone rang and he answered, slowing to the side of the road. 'We've found the van,' he said, breaking the connection. 'Aldercar wood. No more than a mile from here. Off the main road to the left.'

It had been driven beyond the end of the track and into some trees, covered over with bracken, the inside stripped clear. The main area of forest was clearly visible across two fields, stretching north and west.

'Looks like your surmise was correct,' Kiley said.

Resnick nodded. 'Looks like.'

Anderson had gone silent, drawn back into himself. No more family games. Once, when Keiron had run over to him, excited about something he'd found, his father had just stared at him, blank, and the boy had backed nervously away, before running to his mother and burying his face against her chest.

Billie fretted and whined until Rebecca plaited her hair and told her the story of Sleeping Beauty yet again, the little girl's face lighting up at the moment when the princess is kissed awake. She'll learn, Rebecca thought, and hopefully before it's too late.

'How did the prince find her?' Billie asked, not for the first time.

'He cut his way through the undergrowth with his sword.'

'Perhaps someone will find us like that,' Billie said.

Rebecca glanced across at Anderson, but if he had heard he gave no sign.

A light rain had started to fall.

Without preamble, Anderson sprang to his feet and pulled on his cagoule. 'Just a walk,' he said. 'I'll not be long.'

A moment later, he was striding through the trees.

Keiron ran after him, calling; tripped and fell, ran and tripped again; finally turned and came limping towards the tent.

'He isn't coming back,' the boy said, crest-fallen.

Rebecca kissed him gently on his head. 'We'll see.'

An hour passed. Two. Once Rebecca thought she heard voices and called out in their direction, but there was no reply and the voices faded away till there were just the sounds of the forest. Distant cars. An aeroplane overhead.

'I told you,' Keiron said accusingly and kicked at the ground.

'Right,' Rebecca said, making up her mind. 'Put on your coats and scarves. We're going.'

'Where? To find daddy?'

'Yes,' Rebecca lied.

Billie fussed with her buttons and when Rebecca knelt to help her, the child pushed her away. 'I can do it. I can do it myself.'

'Well, get a move on.'

'I am.' Bottom lip stuck petulantly out.

Calm down, Rebecca told herself. Calm down.

Billie pushed the last button into place.

'All right?' Rebecca said. 'Come on, then. Let's go.'

They were a hundred metres away, maybe less, heading in what Rebecca thought was the direction they'd originally come, when they saw him just a short way ahead, walking purposefully towards them.

'Come to meet me? That's nice.'

As the children went into the tent, he pulled her back. 'Try that again and I'll fuckin' kill you, so help me.'

There were only a couple of hours of daylight left. By the time they had got a decent-sized search party organised there would be even less. Best to wait until first light.

'I've been talking to the Royal Military police,' Resnick said. 'Seems as though one sergeant going AWOL isn't too high on their list of priorities. Too many of them, apparently, done the same. Not keen on hurrying back to fight for someone else's democracy. More interested in tracking down a batch of illicit guns, smuggled into the UK from Iraq via Germany. Bit of a burgeoning trade in exchanging them for drugs and currency. Cocaine, especially. Still, they're sending someone up tomorrow. If we do find Anderson, they'll want to stake their claim.'

'Till then we twiddle our thumbs.'

'Do better than that, I dare say,' Resnick said.

Tony Burns was up from London, sitting in with a local band at The Five Ways. Geoff Pearson on bass, the usual crew. Last time Resnick had heard Burns, a good few years back, he'd been playing mostly baritone, a little alto. Now it was all tenor, a sound not too many miles this side of Stan Getz. Jake McMahon joined them for the last number, a tear-up through the chords of 'Cherokee'. By now the free cobs were going round, end of the evening, cheese or ham, and Kiley was having a pretty good time.

Resnick had called Lynn and asked her if she wanted to join them, but instead she had opted for an early night. She'd left him a note on the kitchen table, signed with love.

Resnick made coffee and, feeling expansive, cracked open a bottle of Highland Park. They sat listening to Ben Webster and Art Tatum and then Monk fingering his way through 'Between the Devil and the Deep Blue Sea', Kiley not without envy for what seemed, in some respects, a fuller, more comfortable life than his own.

'Well,' said Resnick, finally, levering himself up from his chair. 'Early start.'

'You bet.'

The bed was made up in the spare room, a clean towel laid out and, should he need it, a new tooth-brush in its plastic case. He thought he might manage a few more pages of *The Man Who Liked*

Slow Tomatoes before dropping off, but when he woke in the morning, the book had fallen to the floor, unread.

Wherever he'd gone in those two hours, Anderson had come back with a bottle of Vodka. Stolichnaya. Perhaps he'd had it with him all along. He sat there, close to the entrance to the tent, drinking steadily. Rebecca tried to get the children to eat something but to little avail. She forced herself to try some of the corned beef, though it was something she'd never liked. The children drank water, nibbled biscuits, and moped.

The rain outside increased until it began seeping under one corner of the tent.

Billie lay down, sucking her thumb, and, for once, Rebecca made no attempt to stop her. If Keiron, huddled into a blanket near her feet, was asleep or not she wasn't sure.

The bottle was now half empty.

Anderson stared straight ahead, seeing something she couldn't see.

'Terry?'

At the softness of her voice, he flinched.

'How long is it since you got any sleep?'

Whenever she had awoken in the early hours after they'd arrived, he had been sitting, shoulders hunched, alert and keeping guard.

'How long?'

'I don't know. A long time.'

'What's wrong?'

For an answer he lifted the bottle to his lips.

'Perhaps you should talk to someone? About what's troubling you? Perhaps . . .'

'Stop it! Just fucking stop it! Shut up!'

'Stop what?'

'Wheedling fucking round me.' He mimicked her voice. 'Perhaps you should talk to someone, Terry? As if you gave a shit.'

'I do.'

'Yeah?' He laughed. 'You don't give a shit about me and I don't give a shit about you. Not any more.'

'Then why are we here?'

'Because of them. Because they have to know.'

'Know what?'

He moved suddenly. 'Wake them. Go on, wake them up.'

'No, look, they're exhausted. Let them sleep.'

But Billie was already stirring and Keiron was awake.

Anderson took another long swallow from the bottle. His skin was sallow and beads of perspiration stood out on his forehead and his temples. When he started talking, his voice seemed distant, even in the confines of the tent.

'We were on patrol, just routine. There'd been a firefight a couple of days before, so we were more on our guard than usual. Against snipers but also for explosives. IEDs. We were passing this house and this woman came out, just her face showing, part of her face, the eyes, and she's waving her arms and wailing and pointing back towards the house as if there's something wrong, and Sean, he jumps down, even though we're telling him not to be stupid, and the next thing we know, he's followed her to the doorway, and the next after that he's been shot. One gets him in the body and knocks him back, but he's wearing his chest plate, thank Christ, so that's all right, but the next one takes him in the neck. By now we're returning fire and the woman's disappeared, nowhere to be fucking seen, Sean's leaking blood into the fucking ground, so we drag him out of there, back into the vehicle and head back to camp.'

Beside Rebecca, Keiron, wide-eyed, listened enthralled. Billie clutched her mother's hand and flinched each time her father swore.

'He died, that's the thing. Sean. The bullet'd torn an artery and the bleeding wouldn't stop. By the time we reached camp, he was dead. He was our mate, a laugh. A real laugh. Always saw the funny side. Just a young bloke. Twenty-one. And stupid. Young and stupid. He'd wanted to help.' Anderson took a quick swallow and wiped his mouth. 'Two days later, we went back. Went back at night, five of us. We'd been drinking before-hand, pretty heavily, talking about what had happened, what they'd done to Sean.'

Rebecca shivered and hugged the children close.

'We went in under cover of darkness. There was no moon, I remember, not then. Sometimes it'd be,

211

you know, huge, filling half the fucking sky, but that night there was nothing. Just a few stars. Everyone inside was sleeping. Women. Men.' He paused. 'Children. Soon as we got inside one of the men reached for his gun, he'd been sleeping with it, under the blankets, and that's when we started firing. Firing at anything that moved. One of the women, she came running at us, screaming, and Steve, he says, 'That's her. That's her, the lyin' bitch,' and, of course, dressed like she was, like they all were, he had no way of knowing, but that didn't stop him all but emptying his magazine into her.'

'That's enough,' Rebecca said. 'Enough.'

'There was a girl,' Anderson said, ignoring her, 'hiding in one of the other rooms. Twelve, maybe thirteen. I don't know. Could've been younger. Steve grabbed hold of her and threw her down on the floor and then one of the others started to tear off her clothes.'

'Stop,' Rebecca said. 'Please stop. They don't need to hear this.'

'Yes, they do! Yes, they do!'

Keiron was not looking, refusing to look, pressing his face into his mother's side.

'We all knew what was going to happen. Steve's standing over her, pulling off the last of her things, and she calls him a name and spits at him and he leans down and punches her in the face, and then he's on his knees, unzipping himself, and we're all watching, a couple cheering him on, give it to her, give it to her, clapping like it's some game, and that's when I tell him, I tell him twice to stop and he just carries on and I couldn't, I couldn't, I couldn't just stand there and watch – she was just a child! – and I shot him, through the back of the head. Blood and gunk all over the girl's face and she wriggles out from under and grabs her clothes and runs and we're left standing there. All except for Steve. He was my mate, too, they all were, and I'd killed him over some girl who, even before that happened, would've happily seen us blown to smithereens.'

He wiped away some of the sweat that was running into his eyes. Tears were running soundlessly down Rebecca's face.

'We all agreed, the rest of us, to claim he'd got caught in the crossfire. After what had happened, no one was going to want to tell the truth.'

'Except you,' Rebecca said.

'This is different.' He nodded towards the children. 'They needed to know.'

'Why?'

'So they can understand.'

And his hands reached down towards his rifle.

Not long after first light, a police helicopter, flying low over the forest, reported a woman and two children standing in a small clearing, waving a makeshift flag.

Armed officers secured the area. Rebecca and the children were escorted to the perimeter, where paramedics were waiting. Anderson was found lying inside the tent, a dark cagoule covering his face, his discharged weapon close at hand. At the hospital later, after she had rested and the medical staff had examined her, Rebecca slowly began to tell Resnick and a female liaison officer her story. The children were in another room with a nurse and their maternal grandmother.

Later still, relishing the chance to stretch his legs, Resnick walked with Kiley the short distance through the city centre to the railway station. Already, a rush edition of the *Post* was on the streets. It would be national news for a moment, a day, page one beneath the fold, then a short column on page six, a paragraph on page thirteen. Forgotten. One of those things that happen, stress of combat, balance of mind disturbed. Rebecca had told the police her husband's story, as well as she remembered, what he had seen, the attack at night, the confusion, the young Iraqi girl, the fellow soldier caught in the crossfire and killed in front of his eyes. He hadn't been able to sleep, she said, not since that happened. I don't think he could face going back to it again.

'Not what you wanted, Jack,' Resnick said, shaking his hand.

The 15.30 to London St Pancras was on time.

'None of us,' Kiley said.

'We'll catch that game some time.'

'Yes. I'd like that.'

Kiley hurried down the steps on to the platform.

He phoned Jennie Calder from the train. In a little over two hours time he would be crossing towards the flats where Mary Anderson lived and climbing the stairs, welcome on the mat, but not for him, her face when she opened the door ajar with tears.

Any Notts County supporters reading this will forgive me, I trust, for playing fast and loose with the details of the club's highly successful F.A. Cup run in 1990/91. Manchester City not Charlton Athletic. Come on, you Pies!